In Good Faith

IN GOOD FAITH

Arabic Translation
and Translators
in Early Modern Spain

Claire M. Gilbert

PENN

UNIVERSITY OF PENNSYLVANIA PRESS

PHILADELPHIA

Published by
University of Pennsylvania Press
Philadelphia, Pennsylvania 19104-4112
www.upenn.edu/pennpress

Printed in the United States of America on acid-free paper
1 3 5 7 9 10 8 6 4 2

A Cataloging-in-Publication record is available
from the Library of Congress
ISBN 978-0-8122-5246-0

*For my family, whose faith in this project
has made everything possible.*

Contents

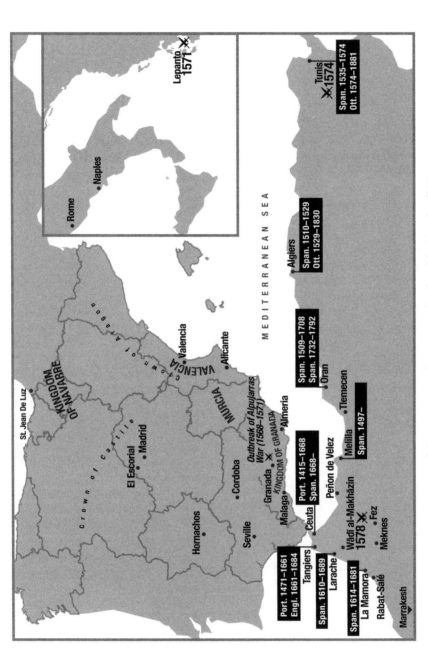

Map 1. Map of the western Mediterranean. Produced by Domhnall Hegarty.

Introduction

The Arabic Voices of Imperial Spain

Arabic translation was at the core of early modern Spanish society. So too were the translators who carried it out, though their work was and has remained "invisible," to borrow Lawrence Venuti's revealing formulation.[1] Even more so than during the twelfth- and thirteenth-century translation movement around the Toledo School, the use and translation of Arabic texts and speech shaped law, religion, and politics in Renaissance and Counter-Reformation Spain. The legacy of this latter-day translation movement of Islamic legal texts had enduring probative effects in later lawsuits that relied on those same texts and their translations. Such models for creating evidence through translation then came to affect the use of Arabic texts and testimony in the Spanish Inquisition. Arabic texts were collected and translated to support national history-writing projects and thus helped justify political decisions about who and what languages were legitimately part of Spain's history, or its future. The political usefulness of Arabic translation and translators at home and abroad mediated Spanish interests in North African and Mediterranean diplomacy, which ultimately produced a market for translations of Arabic political theory. Indeed, Arabic translation in early modern Spain was far from the faint echo of a distant medieval past; it was, rather, a connecting tissue in the fabric of Spanish culture.

In this book, I study the strategies of Arabic translators and the administrative functions of Arabic translation as part of a suite of techniques for political rule and social discipline. Translation underpinned the elaboration of Spain's administrative empire from the expansionist policies of Ferdinand and Isabella (r. 1474–1504) through the end of the Habsburg era.[2] Using state, local, and religious archives, this book presents individual actors who help adjust the analytical frame of translation history away from disembodied texts. By renewing focus on practices and networks, a social history of Arabic translation adds complexity to our understanding of religious minorities, international relations, and statecraft in early modern Spain.

Indeed, once translators and their practices become the target of inquiry, they emerge hidden in plain sight. One need look no farther than the ninth chapter of Book 1 of *Don Quixote* (1605), in which Miguel de Cervantes interrupted his narration just as Don Quixote and the Basque were about to split one another open with their swords ("como una Granada"). The authorial intervention asserted that his manuscript source had finished, leaving Cervantes with no choice but to search out the rest of the story in scholarship and local folklore. Luckily for Cervantes and his readers, he soon found himself in Toledo, where he stumbled upon Arabic papers being sold for rags. He recognized the Arabic script immediately and went searching for a Spanish-speaking *morisco*—a descendant of Spain's former Muslim population—who could serve as interpreter. He quickly found just such a person and hired him to translate the Arabic papers:

> Then the *morisco* and I went to the cloister of the church and I begged him to translate into Spanish all of the quires which had to do with don Quixote, without erasing or adding anything. I offered to pay him whatever he liked. He was satisfied with two sacks of raisins and two bushels of wheat, and he promised to translate well and faithfully (*bien, y fielmente*) and to do so quickly. However, to make it easier and so as not to let such a wonderful find slip out of my hands, I took him home with me, where in just over six weeks he had translated all of it, in the way described here.[3]

What experiences and information could Cervantes have drawn upon when writing this vignette? Whom did he imagine as the Arabic translator that provided the frame tale of Cidi Hamete Benengeli's history, and thus the authentic source for the story of Don Quixote? What was the enduring legacy of such translation episodes in Spain in the seventeenth century and after? These are the questions this book sets out to answer.

The political consequences of knowing Arabic in early modern Spain were variable but could be devastating. Before 1492, there had been no real issue with multilingualism in Iberian kingdoms, which were the product of centuries of political, cultural, and linguistic exchange among speakers of various Romance and Arabic dialects.[4] Politically, the Castilian conquest of Granada (1482–1492) initially imposed a familiar regime of mudejarism. In this system, Muslims (and, until 1492, Jews) could live legally in their own law and languages as vassals of the Spanish kings, subject to extra taxes and lower social status.[5] In the capitulation agreements by which the last Nasrid sultan, Muḥammad XII, surrendered Granada to Ferdinand and Isabella at the end of 1491, the use of Arabic was tacitly permitted in the provision by which Muslim subjects were allowed to continue using Islamic law. When these provisions were signed and promulgated in early 1492, there would have been little reason to expect a radical change in the relationship of language to subjecthood.

Nevertheless, as early as 1502, Isabella and Ferdinand began to design an official language policy that indexed language and religion to political-legal frameworks in new ways.[6] As elsewhere among European imperial and would-be imperial powers, the "ennoblement of national vernaculars" supported exclusive political systems in which language became linked to political and religious communities, effectively erasing the complexity of medieval "contact zones" at the same time that new contact zones were produced through European colonization.[7] The early manifestation of these processes in Spain also affected Iberian multilingualism, and the policies of the Catholic Kings insisted that new Christians were "to learn the fundamental prayers in Castilian and Latin, never in Arabic."[8] This policy coincided with a wave of forced conversions that began in 1499 and which would continue until 1526 and the rule of Charles V (r. 1519–1556). These events would inaugurate a century of political debate and legal proscription concerning language in Spain. The religious conversion of *mudéjares*—Muslims living under Christian rule—to *moriscos* that unfolded between 1499 and 1526 across the peninsula also brought about the conversion of what had been a regime of legal pluralism to one of religious and legal orthodoxy. This shift created new needs and institutions for Arabic translation that simultaneously reflected, subverted, and ultimately reaffirmed the normative anti-Arabic language politics that culminated in the debates over the "*morisco* question" and concluded in mass expulsion between 1609 and 1614.[9]

During this "*morisco* century" (1492–1614), the personal and political consequences for individuals who knew Arabic could be severe. For those Arabic speakers who found themselves before the Inquisition, loss of property was almost certain and loss of life was a real possibility. Nevertheless, Arabic was recognized to be a sacred language whose power derived not only from being read but by possession. Thus all kinds of people were likely to desire Arabic texts—whether Arabic speakers, Muslims, or otherwise.[10] On the collective scale, language politics could be equally devastating, and language became a primary marker of what made a good Christian and a good subject. This process was undoubtedly shaped by the effect of Reformation-era politics through which national languages were codified and indexed to the fortified tandem of state and religious identities.[11] Indeed, the 1560s proved to be a turning point for language politics across Europe in the wake of new challenges from Protestantism and the resolutions of the Catholic Church's meetings at Trent (1545–1563). In Spain, the consequences of Tridentine reform were felt throughout the population.[12] For Arabic speakers, the effect was especially drastic. By the 1580s, the twin projects of evangelization and inquisition were deemed unsuccessful, and Spanish politicians debated a third path, already tested against Iberian Jews a century before: expulsion.

In this period, some individuals benefited simultaneously from their knowledge of Arabic and anti-Arabic politics, particularly those who secured official positions or commissions as translators. Increased professionalization among Arabic translators coincided with new discourses about service throughout the imperial administration. Translators played an important role in the administration of domestic rule, imperial connections, and international relations via translation, whether they were religious minorities, foreigners, or "old Christians."

It was in this context that Cervantes developed his frame tale of fictive translation and thereby created one of the most enduring (and frequently translated) examples of world literature and a quintessential window into early modern Spanish society. For his seventeenth-century Spanish readers, however, the idea that the pseudo-chivalric adventures of a Spanish *hidalgo*—a member of the lower nobility—would be narrated in Arabic would have been perfectly intelligible. Arabic texts—real and forged, legible and unread—were prestigious sources of information and evidence about past events across Iberian institutions and Spanish society. No early reader of Cervantes would have been surprised to learn about an Arabic translator in the streets of Toledo at the turn of the seventeenth century.[13] Indeed, in 1600 Iberia remained a robust marketplace for Arabic knowledge and Arabic texts, which required Arabic experts. Nevertheless, given the decades of anti-Arabic legislation and punishments handed down by the crown and the Inquisition to those who had knowledge of Arabic or possessed Arabic texts, such experts balanced ambivalent social and political status. One legacy of this ambivalence is that the details of the work and lives of individual Arabic translators and the legacy of their practices in Spanish culture have escaped scholarly attention.

In early modern Spain as in medieval Iberia, a variety of materials and information, used by diverse groups of people on a regular basis, moved from language to language. The fragmentary evidence that remains of this quotidian multilingualism paints a vivid picture of an early modern Spanish society that ran on translation, including to and from Arabic. Ignoring these kinds of sources, and the history of the individuals and institutions who produced them, means that historians risk unintentionally reifying the categories we mean to interrogate (e.g., religious, ethnic, national, and linguistic labels, particularly those used to enforce orthodoxy). Tracing these translations and their translators permits study of the rhetorical strategies and other practices and tactics used to create or contest such labels in conjunction with social contexts. This analysis connects Spanish practices with Mediterranean and imperial contexts, moving beyond narratives that index language to monolithic religious minorities or essentialized enemies.[14] The significance of Spain's Arabic legacy in early modern politics and culture reveals itself through the analysis of the massive "paper trail" left behind by the translation of daily life: legal squabbles with one's neighbor, property assessment at tax time, the principals of literacy and numeracy, commercial transactions, and military reconnaissance and the negotiation of provisions and local security. Everyday translation would eventually come to inform the use of Arabic at the highest levels of Spanish statecraft: international diplomacy and political thought. Turning our ears toward the common and all-too-often silenced voices that emerge from multiple archives and institutional repositories allows this study to uncover the fears, hopes, tactics and habits that shaped translation practices, and, in consequence, the ideological legacies of those translations.

From this range of genres and sites, *In Good Faith: Arabic Translation and Translators in Early Modern Spain* pieces together the history of Spanish Arabic translation and the translators who performed it in the Iberian Peninsula and the western Mediterranean. The study reveals a striking ambivalence in the politics of language of the early modern western Mediterranean: as Spanish institutions of power first restricted—then eliminated—the use of the Arabic language and marginalized its speakers, officially appointed translators continued to play a crucial role in brokering minority administration, commercial exchange, diplomatic agreements, and religious conversion. In addition, despite the hardening of ideologies about Arabic and Arabic speakers in Spain, the ongoing vitality of Arabic-Spanish translation in the western Mediterranean facilitated the rise of Spanish as an inter-imperial lingua franca among northern European powers with commercial and political interests in North Africa and the Mediterranean. In addition to addressing the significance of this legacy of Arabic translation in later Spanish culture, I argue that Arabic translation was an important mechanism in the development of the domestic and international practices of the Spanish empire and its early modern encounters.

For those Arabic speakers who became translators, the greatest social and professional advantage was a reliable reputation. Signs of translator trustworthiness—articulated through claims of fidelity, expertise and experience, generations of family service, or patronage and other social connections—became a currency that could be exchanged in the so-called Iberian mercy economy ("economy of *mercedes*").[15] In the texts they produced both *in* translation and *about* their service, translators generated evidence of their expertise and service along with new authoritative sources that became inscribed in Spanish texts and institutions. Like the transimperial and colonial "brokers" of contemporaneous Ottoman and American contexts, Spanish Arabic translators relied on a set of discursive strategies and professional tactics to convert Arabic-language sources into intelligible and credible evidence in institutional and extra-institutional contexts.[16] Their strategies participated in and underpinned the state structures in which they found employment, reward, legitimacy and—in some cases—protection from anti-*morisco* and anti-Jewish policies.[17] Their tactics—to build on Michel de Certeau's conceptualization of how institutions of power can be tactically reshaped through the very language of those constrained by those same institutions—were the mechanisms by which translators found agency and benefits for themselves, for their families, and sometimes for their communities.[18] I call this multilateral set of discursive and social mechanisms "fiduciary translation."

This book argues that fiduciary translation was the dominant mechanism of Arabic translation in the Habsburg period across diverse genres and institutions. My conceptualization and use of this term builds on the work of the translators and translation historians Manuel Feria García and Juan Pablo Arias Torres, who have identified and defined the practice of "trustworthy translation" (*traducción fehaciente*) in Spanish history as an "authorized translation, whose function is to create juridical or institutional effects, generally immediate. It is characterized by being remunerated, subject to a disciplinary regime by which the translator enjoys an appointment or contract that attests his formal qualifications."[19] This trustworthy translation as conceived by Feria and Arias is performative—from a speech-act-theory perspective—and its performativity is conditioned by and conditional upon its institutional setting, analogous to the contemporary practice of "official translation" described by the translation scholar Roberto Mayoral.[20] However, to this linguistic and traductological perspective should be added Pierre Bourdieu's sociological reading of how the "conditions of felicity" (or infelicity) surrounding performative utterances are socially embedded by constant assertion, negotiation, and recognition of symbolic capital.[21] That is, speech acts are felicitous only when conjugated with the sociological conditions by which the "speaker" (or, in our case, translator) has the recognized authority to perform a "trustworthy translation." For Arabic translators in early modern Spain, this authority was derived from a constellation of ambivalent social and political conditions, and it was contingent upon many factors. Translators valued as experts in one context could nevertheless find themselves in precarious political or economic positions due to that same expertise. As experts in a language that was simultaneously prestigious and suspicious, the ways in which individual translators consolidated their own professional positions and transmitted the attendant social capital to their families or communities (or tried to) were constantly tested, negotiated, and revised. My work as an historian has been to trace the expressions and legacies of these negotiations through diverse primary sources related to translators, their work, and their social and political contexts.

Across genres, the performance of trustworthy translation, by which the translator guaranteed his translation with his signature and his official position and was then rewarded for this act, was usually achieved with some expression of the claim, "I performed the task of translation *faithfully* (*bien y fielmente*)." These were the same words used by Cervantes's *morisco* translator in Toledo to assure the reader of the legitimacy of the tale and its source. As in the case of other official translations, Cervantes's translator was paid for his work (e.g., "two sacks of raisins and two bushels of wheat"), commissioned to guarantee the accuracy of the information (e.g., "without erasing or adding anything"), and constrained in the space and time allowed for the work (e.g., "so as not to let such a wonderful find slip out of my hand, I took him home with me, where in just over six weeks he had translated all of it"). Cervantes was portraying a familiar practice and setting.

Reading transversally across archives, paratexts, and printed works allows me to show that the felicitousness of these claims and the fiduciary quality of the translation they accompanied—whether a legal instrument, a diplomatic missive, a religious text, a military report, or a political treatise— were consubstantiated by the competencies and social position of the translator, his patrons, and his readers.[22] Whether in fiction or in courts of various kinds, in order to be trustworthy, the translation had to be certified by the evidence of the translator's universally recognizable credentials and status as a trustworthy man.[23] This recognition embodied what Bourdieu referred to as "symbolic capital," which he conceived as the necessary condition for felicitousness of performative linguistic exchanges.[24] In the legal contexts of royal, local, commercial, and church courts in early modern Spain, the symbolic capital of translators and their trustworthiness became a source of legal proof that was closely associated with the credentials of the notary. As elsewhere in Europe, the universally recognized notarial capacity (Sp. *Fedatario,* to *dar fe* or notarize) became subject to stricter professional norms beginning in the sixteenth century.[25] Nevertheless, in contrast to the centuries-long development of the notarial profession in tandem with newly theorized evidentiary regimes created by commentators on the *ius commune,* notaries in Christian Granada had to conjugate two distinct legal traditions—Christian and Islamic—and this process took place through translation.[26] Many early Arabic translators (*romançeadores*) were also notarial scribes (*escribanos*), whose probative authority derived from their capacity to *dar fe.*

Arabic translators also had to prove themselves outside the context of translations. Thus, in this study, I use the concept of fiduciary translation as a way to capture a broader range of social and discursive phenomena related to the work and lives of Arabic translators in Habsburg Spain. Like *traducción fehaciente* or "official translation," fiduciary translation relied on processes by which credible and authoritative information was generated through the work of a translator. Crucially, the fiduciary work of translators was manifested in translated texts as well as across the textual economies that they helped create in multiple genres and settings. In many ways, the English word "fiduciary"—with its etymological and actual significance of trustworthiness, credit, and public confidence—exactly captures the task of the Arabic translator in early modern Spain. Though *traducción fehaciente* described by Feria and Arias underpinned the fiduciary work embodied by translators, "fiduciary" adds an important valence to the Spanish term *feha-ciente* by emphasizing the multiple positions of the translation and the trans-lator him or herself in social, political, and cultural systems.

By the later Middle Ages, Latin *fiducia* came to reflect the embodiment of *fides*—trust or confidence—rather than solely its performance.[27] This is another reason why "fiduciary" makes a good heuristic tool for doing a social history of translation, particularly one that traces the transmission of reli-ability as a social asset across family and patron networks.[28] The fiduciary quality of translator work may be added to long-running scholarly discus-sions of the discursive and social mechanisms underpinning diverse agency relations across local and global trade networks.[29] Finally, "fiduciary" is a more neutral term than "faith-making"/*fehaciente*, allowing me to study together the varied forms and sites of faith-making with which Arabic translators engaged in early modern Spain. This included notarial work, and also conducting local and international diplomacy, facilitating religious instruction or examining religious knowledge, and navigating the political uses of philology, including as a metric for loyalty.

"Fiduciary" thus encapsulates the variety of discursive and social strate-gies and cues generated by Arabic translators in early modern Spain. Fidu-ciary translation offers an amplified perspective on concepts of cultural brokerage that have been used very adroitly by other early modernist histori-ans of translation like Natalie Rothman, Simon Ditchfield, Daniel Richter, Yanna Yannakakis, Alida Metcalf, Carla Nappi, Peter Burke, Peter Russell, Fernando Bouza, and José Carlos de la Puente.[30] The anthropological and now historical use of "brokerage" as a way to classify certain groups or certain actions has struggled—often very productively—with how to define the quality of brokers as "in-between" other reified categories. Like other early modern translators, Spain's Arabic fiduciaries held their ambivalent positions within administrative structures while embedded across Spanish society (occupying varied, and sometimes multiple, positions). Eventually, in Cer-vantes's magnum opus and elsewhere, the fiduciary position of the Arabic translator was guaranteed in the Spanish imagination.[31]

In this framework, the fiduciary position of Arabic translators in Span-ish society was a precondition of their work with texts. This was a position determined by diverse political commitments and social connections among different individuals. Indeed medieval *fiducia* (from the twelfth century onward) had already become a synonym for classical *fides* and *fidelitas* as an "oath of fidelity or of allegiance."[32] That political meaning, and the social

consequences (patronage) deriving from it, is particularly observable in the
language of fidelity used by Arabic translators in early modern Spain, especially in claims made about performing translation and other service *fielmente* and the quality of oneself or one's family being *fiel* or *fidedigno* (both
terms are ways of expressing trustworthiness). The multivalent political
links comprehended by the term *fiducia* and its derivatives help me situate
translators not only "in-between" or "on the margins" but also at the very
center of political decision-making, even those decisions in which they had
no direct voice. Fiduciary status allowed translators to transmit information—often with legal or probative value—across the many overlapping
jurisdictions of the ancien régime. Their work thus produced conditions for
multivalency that were structured by their social positions (that is, to perform a translation could advance a range of interests—even interests in
competition—based on potentially divergent modes of legibility for a single
text). Thus, using "fiduciary" heuristically helps capture additional levels of
"in-between-ness" to understand how the very claims that offered access to
the royal economy of *mercedes* fueling state service would ultimately encourage
discourses and policies by which language use became tightly indexed to
political loyalty and underpinned linguistic justifications for mass expulsion.

This book joins a growing body of scholarship that aims to reposition
the history of Arabic in Spain as an integral part of Spanish and European
intellectual history and to identify how the use of and ideas about this language had an important effect on Spanish political culture. I follow the lead
of scholars like Mercedes García-Arenal and Fernando Rodríguez Mediano
who have demonstrated during decades of erudition that Spain had a robust
network of Arabic scholars and academicians in sites like Granada or the
Escorial library.[33] Daniel Hershenzon, Nina Zhiri, and Nuria Martínez de
Castilla, among others, are now showing that the Escorial Arabic collections were not simply a repository of medieval and Mediterranean texts but
also the site of regular Arabic training and study, both for the Hieronymite
librarians who were the custodians of the collections until the nineteenth
century and for visiting scholars from elsewhere in Spain and Europe.[34] The
work of these scholars engages with other debates and represents an ongoing and much needed corrective to received narratives about Spain's cultural
and political decline in the seventeenth century. I thus build on contributions in *morisco* studies to unpack more extensively the ambivalent relations between *moriscos*, Arabic experts (not necessarily one and the same),

and Spanish as well as foreign and Mediterranean (particularly Moroccan) institutions of power.

In addition, whereas the study of early European orientalism tends to associate the origins of that scholarship with biblical philology and history writing, this book shows how early Spanish orientalism yielded diverse pragmatic expertise and experiences outside libraries and universities that were acquired by Spanish scholars and politicians through translation.[35] In relation to the arguments advanced by scholars like Barbara Fuchs, Elizabeth Wright, Ryan Szpiech, and Seth Kimmel about the sources of late medieval and Golden Age literature, history, and polemic in Spain, I show how translation between Arabic and Spanish and across religious and cultural lines played an important role in constructing the social fabric and political rule in Tridentine Spain.[36] This book also takes seriously the fact that translating was a fraught *business* that many individuals used as a means of securing their survival and that of their families.

Indeed, like other Arabic speakers (and readers and writers), over the course of the sixteenth century, many translators found themselves increasingly under suspicion and marked by language as belonging to a category other than orthodox Catholic. Nevertheless, translators simultaneously embodied a precious expertise for nascent early modern orientalism through their participation in biblical studies, global missions, and imperial commerce. This early modern orientalism was distinct from that studied by Edward Said in his 1978 book describing French and English colonial intervention in the Middle East in the nineteenth century and its consequences for American intervention there in the twentieth (and now twenty-first). Nonetheless, both orientalisms exhibited a strong reliance on linguistic expertise and translation in the service of state interests abroad. For example, Nicholas Dew describes a "Baroque orientalism," or "orientalism before empire," in Louis XIV's France (1643–1715) by which "scholarly engagement with exotic learning was made possible—inevitably—by the movement of people and books around networks created by diplomacy and trade."[37] Studies of English early modern Orientalism such as G. J. Toomer's classic *Eastern Wisdome* or William Bullman's recent account of "Anglican enlightenment" in English Tangier and John Paul Ghobrial's recovery of "whispers of cities" from Istanbul to London recognize the important place of commercial interests and the Mediterranean experiences of English agents.[38] From a philological and codicological perspective, Thomas Burman explores the Islamic studies and reading practices that fueled late

medieval polemic and subsequent early modern Qur'ān editions and translations.[39] Meanwhile, polemic traditions were adapted to new Mediterranean
geopolitics in which the Ottomans and the *moriscos* were significant political
actors.[40] Likewise, Arabic and Islamic studies fueled proxy polemic among
Protestant and Catholic confessions.[41] New approaches to the study of early
modern orientalisms thus provide a more sensitive history of the Mediterranean politics that shaped European attitudes toward Arabic and Islam,
showing how even the most recondite scholarship in the libraries of Oxford
or Cambridge was in fact an outgrowth of commercial and political interests. Meanwhile, scholars of Middle Eastern Christianity are demonstrating the important role of Christian Arabic speakers as sources of "Oriental"
and "Orientalist" knowledge in Reformation Europe, including Spain.[42]

The extent to which the use of Arabic in Spain was connected to developments in "orientalism before empire" is much discussed in recent scholarship across fields. Although Said did not include Spain in his analysis,
literary scholarship about the legacy of Arabic and Islam in Spanish literature and culture engages the limits and potential of Said's 1978 thesis.[43]
Barbara Fuchs has indicated the doubled position of Spain in the history of
European orientalism, as both a source for "oriental" culture and materials,
and as an orientalized other from the perspective of much of the conti-
nent.[44] García-Arenal tackled the issue of Spanish orientalism qua "Orientalism" through her answers to the question of whether Arabic is a Spanish
language, concluding that Spanish orientalism (lowercase *o*) was distinct
from Said's Orientalism and its precursors by virtue of being "an early orientalism that has little to do with colonial enterprises."[45] Nevertheless,
Spanish orientalism was certainly connected to broader early modern European orientalism—including imperial ventures—through scholarly practices and networks.[46]

The publications produced by García-Arenal and her coauthors Fernando Rodríguez Mediano and Gerard Wiegers during the 2009–2014 com-
memoration of the *morisco* expulsion significantly advanced the turn to
"*morisco* studies" and "late Spanish Islam," which began in the middle and
end of the twentieth century, joining a renaissance in the scholarship on
Spain's Jewish and *converso* communities and their diasporas.[47] Indeed,
García-Arenal's 2014 question was a bookend to an equally important question that she posed in 2009 in the journal *Arabica*, "Is Arabic an Islamic language?" with a view to exploring how politicians, theologians, and everyday
citizens in early modern Spain would have answered such a question and

with what consequences.[48] While some *morisco* advocates sought to promote a practice of tolerant relativism by which religious belief and cultural forms were not indexed to one another, their political opponents waged an ultimately successful campaign arguing the contrary position. Thus, those Spanish Christian subjects who were designated as culturally *morisco* (through language, dress, food habits, lineage, or other exterior signs) were deported en masse beginning in Valencia in 1609 and forbidden to return.[49]

Nevertheless, even in 1614 at the conclusion of the *morisco* expulsion, debates about the status of Arabic as a *Spanish* language continued to rage. Using a linguistic-anthropological approach, Kathryn Woolard has demonstrated how those arguments—many of which were articulated around the famous affair of the forged Arabic Lead Books of Granada, which gripped late Renaissance Europe for a century beginning in the 1580s—shaped vital debates about the relationship between language and nation and fostered an incipient historical linguistics.[50] Building on the early work of James T. Monroe, Fernando Rodríguez Mediano leads the way in demonstrating how the "fragments of orientalism" that remained in seventeenth-century Spain were not only robust but among the foundation blocks of modern scholarship, including the importation and use of Spanish Arabic knowledge and experts in the scientific academies of Rome and Naples and the courts and universities in France and England.[51] My debt to and engagement with this work as well as scholarship in linguistic anthropology, translation studies, and cultural and intellectual history will be clear throughout the book. Drawing on Bourdieu, tracing translators and translations across European and Moroccan archives and libraries has also pushed me to recover the social dynamics and conditions that created institutional spaces for Arabic translation and contributed to new political attitudes by and about many different Spanish subjects, not only *moriscos*.

To trace the wide social and political implications of the business of Arabic translation in early modern Spain, my analysis is organized to feature different but interconnected scales of Spanish society and its transregional connections. Arabic translators rarely operated in a vacuum, and one of the goals of this book is to reveal the collaborative processes behind producing an Arabic translation in early modern Spain, as well as to show the different ways in which Arabic translators were fully embedded in Spanish society—whether *morisco*, *converso*, Muslim, Jew, renegade, or "old Christian." Whatever positions of liminality many of these individuals occupied, they were

never fully "outside" the Spanish system, itself a complex composite of jurisdictions, institutions, and identities.

The first three chapters recover the institutionalization and professionalization of Arabic translation in legal, military, and diplomatic contexts. Beginning with the fiduciary translation of Islamic legal texts after
1492, the professionalization of Spain's Arabic translators and the institutionalization of their office in the Spanish monarchy was consolidated early
in the *morisco* and Habsburg period. Local translators had ties to royal institutions well before the conclusion of the Granada conquest in 1492, and the
use of translation in different spheres of *morisco* government after 1499—
from collecting taxes to adjudicating property disputes—was overseen by a
range of officials with diverse ties to state institutions and patronage networks ultimately linked to the king. These precedents—and sometimes
even the personnel—were subsequently used to establish the translation
offices in Spain's North African presidio system after 1497 and again two
generations later with the development of official diplomacy between Spain
and Morocco after 1578.

In all these settings, family networks and patronage relationships were
crucial components of the translation process. The process known as the patrimonialization of offices—a well-studied phenomenon in late medieval and
early modern Spanish society that helped drive the economy of *mercedes*—
was a crucial dynamic in fiduciary translation. Indeed, this study brings to
light a little-studied paradox by which those groups traditionally associated
with multilingual mediation in Spanish society—Jews, *mudéjares*, *moriscos*,
and *conversos*—were early participants in the process of patrimonialization, at
the very same time that legal and cultural codes like the blood-purity stat-
utes shaped the rhetoric and practice of that process in Spain during the sixteenth and seventeenth centuries. Analyzing the changing role of Arabic
translation and the statuses of the translators, as it was represented in the
language of service upon which the economy of *mercedes* ran, helps shed light
on this paradox as it obtained throughout the early modern period.

Finally, the examples and analysis developed across these three chapters contribute to the debate about the relationship between professionalization and state building in the early modern period. Like other officials,
Arabic translators developed a set of practices and tactics—rhetorical and
social—through which they navigated different levels and geographies of
the administrative apparatus of the monarchy.[52] Arabic translators with
official positions in local government and other regional institutions (like

the Royal Appellate Courts, or the military, or the Royal Library) were subject to similar processes of professionalization, patronage, and service as other officials in the early Habsburg regime.[53] Ultimately, Arabic translators helped construct a complex field of knowledge about Arabic and Arabic speakers that had tremendous effects on individual lives, law, and government policies in Spain.

At the same time that fiduciary translation became a cornerstone of government in *morisco* Spain, the arrival of Charles V and his international and multilingual court in 1517 and his election as emperor in 1519 made Spain part of the multilingual political framework of the Holy Roman Empire.[54] Soon after—though Charles passed the imperial title to his brother in Vienna—the rest of the Spanish Habsburgs would rule over a diverse and multilingual political and multi-normative legal regime that spanned the American, European, African, and eventually Asian territories of Iberian empires during the period of the Union of the Crowns of Spain and Portugal (1580–1640).[55] The functional multilingualism of Habsburg politics is a fascinating story, and it is no surprise that translation played an important role. Indeed, Charles V founded the first modern state translation office at the Spanish court in 1527 to manage European diplomacy in French, Italian, Latin, and other languages, though it would not be until the beginning of the seventeenth century that this state office would develop an official branch for "eastern" languages (*lenguas orientales*) like Arabic, Persian, and Ottoman Turkish.[56] This timing reflected the new diplomatic relations of the Spaniards with the Safavid, Ottoman, and Moroccan courts and were more of a function of international relations than the domestic policies for ruling over the *morisco* minority.

The central claim of the book is that Arabic remained a vital cultural and administrative language in Spain throughout the *morisco* period (c. 1492–c. 1614) and long after, despite the legal prohibitions and cultural attitudes that made public use of Arabic dangerous for many individuals. Fiduciary translation was the mechanism that ensured this enduring integration of Arabic texts and Arabic speakers within political structures and cultural settings in which those texts and speakers had ambivalent positions. Chapters 1 through 3 explain the foundations of fiduciary translation and the sites and practices of translators who contributed in *morisco* Spain and in Spanish territories and to negotiations across the Maghreb.

Chapter 1 makes the case that, although the sixteenth century was a period of regular and repeated anti-Arabic legislation and of the development

of hostile cultural norms and policies that affected Arabic speakers, it was
also a time during which an intensive and officially sanctioned translation
movement of Arabic Islamic legal texts took place. This translation movement was disrupted when a civil war over language—the Second War of the
Alpujarras (1568–1571)—shifted the postures of the Spanish crown definitively away from linguistic toleration. Following these examinations of the
Spanish translation movement of Islamic law and the elaboration of an institutionalized system of fiduciary translation, Chapters 2 and 3 explore the
place of Spanish-Arabic translation across the early modern western Mediterranean. Departing from an analysis of how translators in the presidios
organized and channeled communication between the Spanish monarchy
and North African powers, including the Ottoman Empire and its regencies
and the Moroccan sultanate and its spheres of influence, Chapter 2 argues
that presidio translators sustained their own inter-imperial information networks to create political and social capital, while cultivating professional
standing and security for themselves and their families. Chapter 3 explores
the mechanisms by which Spanish-Arabic translation took on new importance in Mediterranean trade and politics and from that theater channeled
global imperial rivalries after the 1570s. This translation shaped political
negotiations over alliances and territories as well as the resolution of local and
international legal disputes across religious and linguistic lines.

The final two chapters build on the recovery of fiduciary translation in
broader religious and political contexts to show how technical professional
activities echoed across a range of normative texts and institutions and
affected Arabic speakers and many others. Fiduciary translation supported
two language-ideological processes—the mutual influence of linguistic
forms and language politics—that eventually transformed the position of
Arabic and Arabic speakers in Spanish society: *reducción* and domestication.
Reducción was a historical metaphor for political conquest in the fifteenth
century that by the seventeenth century came to symbolize linguistic regulation according to normative codes (reflected in philological materials like
grammars, as well as language policies that outlawed Arabic). In tandem
with these codifications, translation practices and language policies helped
define a new linguistic minority in Spain. Through political and linguistic
regulation, *reducción* left a strong mark in Late Spanish Arabic (LSA)—for
example, traditionally Islamic vocabulary came to represent Christian concepts, and loan words, or calques, related to Spanish normative institutions
were adopted into LSA. One vector for the language contact that helped

"reduce" LSA was the institutions, procedures, and personnel of fiduciary translation. These processes were particularly relevant in the mission and inquisition translation work discussed in Chapter 4.

In the context of Arabic translation in Spain, domestication was the other side of the coin of the *reducción* that came to regulate minority languages and their speakers. In translation studies, domestication refers to a translation practice that produces "natural" translations which erase the autochthonous identity of the source text. That is, domesticated translations do not *seem* like translations, for they obscure "the violence that resides in the very purpose and activity of translation: the reconstitution of the foreign text in accordance with values, beliefs, and representations [from] the translating language and culture."[57] Domestication has become the dominant mode of translation in the modern world, and translation historians and linguistic anthropologists, among others, chart a correlation between this style of translation and the politics surrounding colonization and national vernaculars that intensified over the early modern period. In the case of Spain, a growing trend to domestication began in the early seventeenth century in the aftermath of the *morisco* debates and expulsion. Chapter 5 shows how fiduciary translation was transformed by *reducción* and domestication. The fiduciary translation that had been used for over a century to create legal and historical resources in Spanish whose value was encoded in the record of their Arabic origins came to be used to "naturalize" Arabic and Islamic knowledge so that their sources were no longer immediately identifiable. That is, Arabic translations made in the seventeenth century were identified as such in the paratext—the prestige of their Arabic source material explained and guaranteed by the translator—but the translations themselves read as if they had been composed directly in Spanish by authors firmly engaged in the concepts and vocabulary of the Spanish Baroque. Such later practices yielded long-form Arabic translations that— were it not for the titles and assertions of the translators—could have been mistaken for an original Spanish text. Indeed, as in the case of Cervantes's *Don Quixote*, sometimes they *were* an original Spanish text, marketed with titles and assertions of being an Arabic translation. Thus it was that the intertwined political and linguistic processes of *reducción* and domestication transformed Spain's fiduciary translation movement of legal, commercial, and political texts into an industry of "imaginary Arabic," which reflected the enduringly ambivalent attitudes in Spanish culture about an Arabic past.

Though the main events of this book and the bulk of its documentation come from the Habsburg period, I have chosen to open this book's chronology in 1492 with the transition of power from the ruling elite of Muslim Nasrid Granada (1246–1492) to the new Trastámara government. The year 1492 was indeed a watershed in Spanish history for many reasons: the final surrender of Granada on January 2, the expulsion edict targeting Castilian and Aragonese Jews in March and April, and Columbus's departure from Spain in August and landfall on San Salvador on October 12. Beginning the story around this familiar date allows us to open the scene *in media res* to get a grasp of the source of the continuities and innovations that will derive during the sixteenth century and beyond. If anything, Arabic became even more important to the state administration than it had been during the *morisco* period. Official diplomacy opened with Morocco (1579), Persia (1601), and eventually the Ottoman Empire (1649), and all the while Arabic translation continued to be a key part of the administration of Spain's North African presidios. The Spanish state employed a range of Arabic specialists of different backgrounds in the aftermath of the *morisco* expulsion (1609–1614): renegades, Jews and *conversos*, traveling European scholars, Spaniards trained at the Escorial, personnel borrowed from the Austrian court, and eastern Christian, Ottoman subjects with connections to Rome. By the 1680s and the concluding section of this book, the position of Spanish royal translator would be secured in the hands of an eastern Christian family who were native Arabic speakers of a very different dialect from Late Spanish Arabic.

The cases studied in this book inhabit an early modern Mediterranean characterized by religious rivalries that culminated in military conflicts, the imposition (by force and otherwise) of orthodoxy and social discipline, and new legal thinking about sovereignty and subjectivity. At this time, those identities, and the boundaries between them, were being radically redefined in Spain through laws about language use and cultural practices, along with modes of enforcement influenced by debates and norms produced at the Council of Trent (1545–1563). Knowing Arabic and possessing Arabic texts were effectively criminalized during the very same years that Spain's royal Arabic collections and central translation office for "eastern" languages were established. Spain's Arabic translators walked the knife's edge of these institutional and ideological processes while at the same time helping to foster them.

Chapter 1

The Foundations of Fiduciary
Translation in *Morisco* Spain

In the aftermath of Ferdinand and Isabella's conquest of Granada in 1492, the new religious policies of the Castilian crown at the turn of the fifteenth century had striking political consequences for all Spanish subjects, especially for Arabic speakers. Formerly Muslim and Jewish Spanish vassals took on an altered legal status as Christians following programs of mass baptism, notwithstanding whether or not their baptism was compelled or desired. Conversion contracts were imposed upon Spanish *mudéjares* across Castile (including Granada), Navarre, and Aragon between 1500 and 1526. Although the surrender treaties drawn up between 1482 and 1492 had permitted Spain's new subjects to practice their religion in whatever language suited them, the new regime effected by the conversion contracts decreed that the newly Christian vassals of the Spanish Catholic Kings could *only* be indoctrinated in Castilian or Latin.[1] This edict in 1502 set the stage for a new wave of language legislation prohibiting Arabic speech and the possession of Arabic texts. Linguistic legislation issued between 1511 and 1518 enforced new cultural norms regarding language, bathing, dress, and foodways.[2] For the first time in Spain, language became one of a range of categories that defined a politico-religious status of vassalage and the relationship between subject and sovereign. Translation thus came to have tremendous legal power in Spanish politics, foreign and domestic.

In response to new language policies, during the crucial opening decades of the sixteenth century, Arabic translation in Habsburg Spain developed into a fiduciary system that ran on personal credit and relationships. This system was regulated by the recognition of skill and fidelity and

spanned a number of institutions from the appellate court to the town council. In this system, intermediaries who could provide credentials attesting to
their skill and fidelity were sought out to facilitate or perform vital functions of government, including guild and marketplace oversight, discussion
and voting in the town councils, the information services of the military
aristocracy and church elites in charge of administering their own and royal
interests, producing evidence for court cases, and tax collection. The fiduciary work of Arabic translators generated the material and mechanisms of
government: regulations, votes, evidence in lawsuits, and tax records.

The first royally appointed Arabic translators in post-conquest Granada
were drawn from elite Muslim and Jewish families with generations of experience communicating across the Castilian-Granada frontier. At the same
time, the spaces and institutions of fiduciary translation were shaped through
the work of two principal groups of experts in Islamic law: Nasrid *fuqahā'*
(Islamic legal experts who remained after conquest) and *mudéjar alfaquíes*
(Muslim community leaders and administrators who immigrated from
other parts of Christian Iberia to Granada during the conquest).[3] This dual
continuity of practices and personnel ensured that Islamic legal expertise
was valued and transmitted by Arabic speakers working within Spanish
institutions, despite the blanket legal prescriptions against Arabic use or
signs of Islamic knowledge after 1500.

Arabic-speaking *moriscos* did not have a monopoly on access to legal evidence and other information or materials generated by translation in
Granada. "Old Christians" also used Arabic texts and Islamic legal expertise
in lawsuits, ensuring that Arabic translation had meaningful legal consequences for all kinds of Spanish subjects, whether they were related to
moriscos or not. For example, in the 1550s two "old Christian" settler communities in Granada sued each other over municipal boundaries, recurring
to Nasrid Arabic documents and employing municipal translators.[4] The
church and the clergy also collected and used Arabic documents for legal
purposes. Granada's Hieronymite monastery kept translations of property
records and other transactions with the original Arabic documents, among
other papers potentially useful during legal conflicts, such as the royal foundation deeds, tax receipts, and original architectural plans.[5]

Legal thinking was rapidly changing in early modern Spain.[6] Nevertheless, the transmission of non-Christian legal practices and precedents into
Spanish law by means of translation and the endurance of those practices and

precedents is rarely explored. Across Spanish society, translation provided access to legal evidence, ensuring the adoption of Islamic precedent into Spanish institutions. This post-conquest translation movement of Islamic legal documents after 1492 facilitated the "colonial" implantation of Castilian institutions and settlers in formerly Muslim (Granada) or *mudéjar* (Valencia) areas and left a lasting mark on Spanish law.

This chapter describes the foundations of fiduciary translation in the aftermath of the conquest of Granada (1482–1492) until the Second War of the Alpujarras (1568–1571)—a civil war over language during which the precedents of fiduciary translation affected military strategy, wartime propaganda, and the memory of the conflict. To conclude, the chapter explores how the techniques of fiduciary translation shaped the representation of the Alpujarras war in the first published histories of the conflict. By tracing the professionalization and institutionalization of fiduciary translation in the first generations of *morisco* Spain, the chapter establishes key precedents and vocabulary that shaped the development of fiduciary translation in other parts of the composite monarchy—including the Crown of Aragon and Iberian presidios in North Africa—and its legacies in the culture and political thought of Habsburg Spain.

Harnessing Islamic Legal Expertise Through Fiduciary Translation: Continuity and Change in Granada from 1492 to 1567

Multilingual government in Granada after 1492 soon became distinct from medieval traditions of local mudejarism that had operated across relatively small communities in Castile, Navarre, Aragon, and Valencia for generations. Bilingual rule in *mudéjar* communities was traditionally effected by local elites who simultaneously negotiated with and represented their communities and the crown.[7] In Aragon, for example, an *alcaydus* was nominated and granted jurisdictional powers by both the king and nobles.[8] In Castile, *alcaldes mayores* were royal appointees with regional power, and their position extended the traditional *qāḍī* (judge) position in Muslim society into the context of minority rule, though with significant long-term adaptations to the exigencies of working within a Christian legal framework and political culture.[9] For example, in the fifteenth century Isabella centralized the office through the position of the *alcalde mayor de moros,* part of her general administrative reforms designed to foster more centralized power around the crown.[10]

The short-lived period of Granada mudejarism immediately presented as a hybrid of traditional approaches and innovations brought about by Isabella and Ferdinand.[11] Despite large-scale emigration of elites to North Africa, Granada's *mudéjar* population remained significant while new "old Christian" settlers arrived following the resettlement incentives of the Catholic Kings. Meanwhile, although the surrender treaties promulgated during the Granada War (1482–1492) had by and large approached Islamic law and Arabic in ways similar to the *mudéjar* contracts drawn up during the conquests of Muslim kingdoms by Christian monarchs in the thirteenth century, administration of the new kingdom quickly adapted to Castilian structures.[12]

In *mudéjar* Granada, governing institutions after 1492 mirrored those throughout Castile, including a *cabildo* (town council) and the southern branch of the Royal Appellate Court (Real Chancillería), founded in 1494 in Ciudad Real and moved to Granada in 1505.[13] The transfer insured a regular influx of officials, plaintiffs, and defendants to Granada from the entire southern half of the peninsula, many of whom were Arabic speakers.[14] This court oversaw numerous suits that concerned property in the Granada province and thus relied on documentary or testimonial evidence in Arabic. Across institutions, royal oversight was ensured by the appointment of a *corregidor* (royal representative), among the presence of other royal officials at various times, and the defense of the realm of Granada was the charge of a royally appointed military governor, the captain-general of the Alhambra. The Catholic Kings even installed a mint in Granada in 1497 to commemorate (and effect) new monetary and fiscal policies throughout their kingdoms.

Nevertheless, though *mudéjar* Granada was reformed according to Castilian administrative norms, Islamic legal documents continued to be produced within the new institutions and by the same personnel who had occupied Nasrid administrative positions as part of the governing elite. Indeed, the Castilian administration needed prestigious figures with genuine local connections to represent it and to mediate interactions with the newly subject population. This is nowhere clearer than in their organization of a central translation office in Granada, headed by their *trujamán mayor* (head translator).[15] This position was occupied in 1494 by don Alonso Venegas,

formerly 'Ali 'Umar ibn Naṣr. Don Alonso was the son of the former governor of Baza, Yaḥya al-Najjār (or al-Nayyar), who converted to Christianity
and took the name Pedro de Granada in 1500.[16] As a descendant of Nasrid
Muslim and Castilian Christian nobles, don Alonso was an ideal embodiment of the two constituencies he was supposed to mediate between: Castilian elites and their Granadan *mudéjar* subjects.[17]

Don Alonso received the title of *trujamán mayor* on February 15, 1494.
That the title was *trujamán mayor* echoed Isabella's earlier establishment of
an office of *intérprete mayor* in neighboring Murcia in 1476 and, indeed, the
way she achieved administrative reforms through the creation of professional hierarchies.[18] Thus, don Alonso's 1494 appointment as *trujamán mayor*
in Granada was representative of the assertion of royal authority not only
over the new province but also over Castilian institutions in general. As a
centralized institution, Granada's translation bureau drew on earlier models of using linguistic translation, especially across confessional boundaries, as a technique of rule. For example, Gabriel Israel, the Murcian *intérprete
mayor* appointed by Isabella in 1476, also oversaw a team of subordinates.[19]
Though Israel was the first documented translator to hold the title of *mayor*
in the vibrant southeastern commercial corridor between Castile and
Granada, he took over a defined position that had previously been held by
Ali Xarafi, a Castilian official related to an important *mudéjar* family in
Toledo with a branch working in Nasrid Granada.[20] Israel would also establish family connections with Nasrid patrons while in Castilian service.
Sometime before 1492 his daughter married Ysaque de Perdoniel, a Jewish
vecino (resident) of Granada and also an interpreter who was granted a license
for his entire family so that they might keep their movable goods, their jewels, money, and so forth, and that they be granted the right to emigrate
either by land or by sea.[21] Thus the main founders of fiduciary translation in
Granada—Venegas, Xarafi, and Israel-Sosa—were simultaneously embedded in Nasrid and Spanish royal patronage networks before the conquest
was achieved.

The office of *trujamán mayor* itself was designed in continuity with earlier Nasrid institutions. Venegas's appointment specified that he would
occupy the same position previously held by three *trujamanes mayores* who
worked for Granada's Muslim kings: "Cydy Alamin," the "*alcaide* [Ar. *al-
qā'id*, a military commander] Nayyar," and Simuel Habenatahuel.[22] In 1494
a royal decree designated these men as the "former *trujamanes mayores* who
worked for the aforementioned Muslim kings (*reyes moros*) and for us."[23]

Don Alonso's office was confirmed in 1495, with the "same rights and salary held by the previous *trujamánes mayores* who worked for the Nasrid kings."[24]

Indeed, their appointment of don Alonso in 1494, who had converted to Christianity in 1491 and thus secured the status of "old Christian" *morisco*, was a harbinger of a new strategy of governance that depended on Christians rather than Jews and Muslims and thus was a departure from centuries of mudejarism.[25] Though before 1492 Jewish translators, such as Israel and Habenatahuel, were common employees of Iberian kings, in 1492 they were expelled by royal edict along with their coreligionists.[26] It is uncertain what happened to Cydy Alamin and the al-Amīn family, who had served the Nasrids loyally as translators and diplomats for generations. They may have decided to emigrate in 1493 with the rest of the royal family and many of their officials.[27] The third Nasrid *trujamán mayor*, the *alcaide* Nayyar, was in fact don Alonso's father, Yahya, who changed his name to Pedro de Granada after his conversion in 1500. Thus, the 1494 appointment of don Alonso was emblematic of the hybrid forms that post-conquest rule took in Granada and of the ways that the institutionalization of translation was articulated on family lines. By adopting the Nasrid Translation Office and then appointing the newly converted son of its most senior official, Ferdinand and Isabella ensured continuity despite the upheaval of conquest and resettlement.

Don Alonso is one of the most visible (in the archives) members of Granada's *morisco* elite, who are sometimes characterized as "collaborators" in scholarly literature.[28] He and his father, don Pedro, became voting councilmen (*regidores*) in Granada as early as 1498, joining other key Castilian officials who held simultaneous royal appointments, like the *corregidor* Andrés Calderón; Granada's military governor, Íñigo López de Mendoza (*capitán general del reino* and *alcaide* of the Alhambra); and Hernando de Zafra, the royal secretary. In 1501, don Alonso inherited the position of bailiff (*alguacil mayor*, from the Ar. *al-wazīr*) from his father. He served as a captain in the campaign against Orán in 1509 and as Granada's delegate to the *cortes* in 1517 and 1520, among other stays at the royal court. He planned strategic alliances for his family in order to incorporate them into Castilian nobility, and by 1643 members of the Granada Venegas clan had become Marquises of Campotéjar and Knights of Santiago and Calatrava, circumventing blood-purity requirements as "old Christian *moriscos*."[29] Along with his noble kinsmen the Mendoza, don Alonso founded an important literary salon in Granada that endured over generations.[30]

Other well-known members of the converted Nasrid elite joined the council. The participation of this legal and scholarly elite in the early Castilian government institutions included the former Nasrid chief judge (referred to as *cadi mayor* in Spanish documents) Fernando Enríquez el Pequení (formerly Mahomad el Pequení), who then became the *alcalde mayor de los moros* of Granada, and the former *alfaquíes* (*fuqahā'*) Pedro López Zaybona, Francisco Jiménez Xamá (formerly Mahomá Xamá), and don Andrés de Granada el Bastí (formerly Mahomá el Bazty), to name only those appointed to the town council between 1498 and 1501.[31] Their nominal conversions and participation in Castilian government did not necessitate an assimilation into Castilian language or culture. For example, council records indicate that several of the former Muslim elites, including el Pequení and Zaybona, never mastered Castilian and required don Alonso to translate for them when casting their votes.[32] Collectively, this group of *morisco* councilmen—many of whom were Nasrid *fuqahā'* who had served as administrative elites before the conquest—represented a significant site of Islamic legal expertise at the heart of Granada's new government.[33] This legal expertise was then deployed by the Castilian state through translation.

In addition to its importance as a technique of rule, translation underpinned a system of social organization embodied and enforced by the agents who mediated information across institutions and jurisdictions. In Granada's capital, for example, six official interpreters worked under don Alonso in the Translation Office.[34] Among other bilingual officials were Diego de Écija, Lope de Castellanos, Pedro García de Castillo, Luis de Luque, and members of the Tristán family of scribes and notaries. These men, along with Diego Fernández de Jaén, a city magistrate (*procurador de la ciudad*), regularly acted as paid translators (*lenguas* and *intérpretes*) between 1497 and 1502.[35] Several other bilingual officials were employed, including at least one Arabic-speaking town crier, Mahomet Henton, and an Arabic-speaking executioner.[36] The importance of translation in criminal law was also reflected in municipal payments to Lope de Castellanos (formerly Suleyman de Valladolid) for his work in the jails as both prison magistrate (*procurador*) and translator (*trujamán de los presos de la carcel*).[37] In the port town of Almería, this magistrate was Francisco de Belvís, a member of an important Valencian *mudéjar* family who had competed with the Xarafi for positions as *alcaldes mayores de moros*.[38] In Málaga, Gabriel Israel—the former *intérprete mayor* of Murcia—became the head tax assessor (*arrendador mayor de rentas*). Israel left following the expulsion edict in 1492, and by 1493 he converted to

Christianity in Portugal under the name Fernando de Sosa. In 1494 he returned to Málaga, where he took up his former office as *arrendador de las rentas del Obispado de Málaga*.[39] Throughout the litany of lawsuits and investigations that marked his career from Murcia to Málaga, Israel-Sosa was always referred to as an *intérprete de sus Altezas*.[40] As another example, following the forced conversions of 1501, the Spanish monarchs appointed Alonso Serrano as a public scribe (*escribano público*), with the specific mandate to expedite contracts and other documents in Arabic.[41] Serrano, who held the office until 1513, before conversion was Mahomad Algazil (in Spanish documents) and a trusted intermediary of both sides during the war.[42]

Translators like Israel-Sosa and the *cabildo* interpreters worked outside of the halls of local and royal power, usually in teams. For example, interpreters assisted merchants who traveled to rural *morisco* communities to sell their wares and accompanied council officials as they oversaw the ongoing process of property assessment and land distribution (*repartimiento*), a part of the Castilian settlement project that subsequently became the process by which people and property were inventoried for taxation. Until 1522, at least four interpreters were employed by the *cabildo* to assist in assessment, inventory, and taxation.[43] In 1512, two new interpreters were hired by the town council: Hernando de Talavera and Antonio de Aguilar. These field translators also worked in teams. Aguilar was a particularly active agent, specializing in the important physical and fiscal process of *repartimiento*.[44] He received approval for his nomination directly from Alonso Venegas.[45] In 1516, Lope de Castellanos ceded his post to Juan de Baena.[46] Aside from the fees they collected for specific commissions, *cabildo* interpreters received annual salaries of two thousand *maravedíes*.[47] Through the appointment of these agents, their regular salaries, and assignments across different specialized areas (prisoners, field work with tax collectors, etc.), the *cabildo* interpreters came to form a professional corps headed by Venegas and governed by administrative norms.

These bilingual institutions and practices were hybrid. The social act of translation was an important channel for the mutual influence of Islamic and Christian institutions in post-conquest Granada. Across the cases heard in the Royal Appellate Court, *moriscos* and "old Christians" relied on different kinds of evidence or support for their suits, evidence that was often translated from Arabic by teams of different kinds of experts. The translators who were called upon to perform technical translations in these lawsuits needed deep competence in both languages and both Muslim and

Christian legal traditions, and thus they were drawn from the scribal and notarial elite already present in the city. A striking example is the appointment of the *qāḍī* of Granada, Mahomad el Pequení, to the town council in 1493. From that position, the former head of the Nasrid judicial branch helped run the new Castilian administration. As is well known, el Pequení (as he is referred to in Spanish sources) converted by 1500 along with many of the Nasrid *fuqahā'*. Indeed, two principle translator dynasties working in the Chancillería were founded by Ambrosio Xarafi and Alonso de Mora (formerly the *alfaquí* Hamete Xarafi and Yuça de Mora). During the *mudéjar* period, the Moras and the Xarafis enjoyed the support of Ferdinand and Isabella and the last Nasrids.[48] Both came originally from Muslim families with roots in Toledo, where the Xarafi in particular had a long tradition of collaborating with the crown in minority governance.[49] Members of both families worked as intermediaries during the war.[50] Alonso and Ambrosio both went to work immediately after the final conquest in administrative positions. Mora became an *alcalde mayor* of Granada's *mudéjares*, an analogous position to that of Castilian medieval minority governance, and a guild leader of the silkmakers (*alamín de la alcaicería*). Xarafi—who had held a position in the Nasrid royal household—by 1499 held the title of "Scribe of Sharī'a law in Granada, loyal servant of Their [Catholic] Majesties," which denoted his status as an expert in Islamic law in the service of the crown. Both Xarafi and Mora were appointed as *cabildo* scribes, and in the town council both served as interpreters for Mahomad/Fernando Enríquez, el Pequení, the Castilian-appointed head of the *mudéjar* community in Granada and former *qāḍī* of Nasrid Granada. Using specialized legal knowledge, both men eventually found work translating in the Real Chancillería, where Alonso de Mora became a specialist in collecting witness testimony.

Thus, although conversion cut short the public use of Islamic legal forms, it did not affect the position of the *fuqahā'* in government, where they continued to participate in the transmission of legal documents by authenticating them through translation. In short, the bilingual officials of Granada's new Castilian institutions used fiduciary translation to convert Arabic Islamic texts and practices to be legible in the Castilian legal system. Let us examine how this process worked discursively and socially across Castilian institutions.

The most important primary source for fiduciary translation in postconquest Granada are the *romanceamientos*—Spanish translations of Arabic documents—generated primarily in the *cabildo*, Real Chancillería, and

Inquisition of Granada. These texts—only a small fraction of which are extant across many kinds of Spanish archives (local, state, ecclesiastic, noble)—have occupied scholars in Granada, Málaga, Madrid, and elsewhere for over half a century. Many of them have been edited and published one by one as they have been discovered in Spanish archives. These valuable contributions often appear in local journals that are not widely accessible beyond Spain.[51] Though the *romanceamientos* are of great value and interest to those studying *mudéjar* and *morisco* Granada, there has not yet been a systematic, book-length study of the documents. Based on their readings of multiple translations used in one dispute, Manuel Feria García and Juan Pablo Arias Torres have contributed useful observations about the notarial effects of translation as *traducción fehaciente* (official translation), but they stop short of exploring the nondiscursive components of this phenomenon in relation to the politics and society of post-conquest Granada.[52] In what follows I demonstrate how *romanceamientos* must be read transversally to trace the foundations of fiduciary translation as a social rather than a purely discursive phenomenon.

One rich example of the clues *romanceamientos* give to fiduciary translation can be derived from the records of property transactions extant in the Municipal Historical Archive of Granada, which preserves a handful of original Arabic documents with their contemporaneous or near-contemporaneous translations.[53] The presence of the Arabic originals with the Spanish paperwork makes this small collection (around nine documents in total) one of the most valuable collections of *romanceamientos*, which have most often endured in archives in their Spanish versions alone.[54] The transactions were recorded between 1492 and 1499 by Muslim notaries (*muwaththiqūn*) in Arabic and according to Islamic legal norms and procedures.[55] Those legal norms included the presence of a judge (*qāḍī*) to sanction the transaction and the presence of at least two instrumentary witnesses, who had been judged by the *qāḍī* to be *'adl* ("just," or in the case of witnesses, "upstanding"). The assurance of the *qāḍī* confirming a witness's *'adāla* (probity) was a prerequisite for their testimony to be valid, and since "Muslim procedure does not recognize documentary evidence as proof but only the oral evidence of eye-witnesses, such people were preferred for the verification of legal matters whose *'adāla* had already been proved."[56] The document was recorded by a scribe (*kātib*), who was also likely a notary (*muwaththiq*).[57]

As Amalia Zomeño and her colleagues working on the Islamic Law Materialized project have shown, normal Islamic legal procedures continued after 1492 until at least 1499, the date of the last extant Arabic Islamic legal document produced in Granada by a *muwaththiq*.[58] The transactions represented by the Granada *mudéjar* documents (1492–1499) always involved at least one Muslim (buyer or, most often, seller). The transaction could take place among Muslim parties or between a Muslim and a Christian party, and so it extended the traditional forms of *mudéjar* legal pluralism from elsewhere in Iberia in which members of different religions had done business and made legal agreements together for centuries. This practice is also indicative of the Nasrid familiarity with commercial transactions with Christians from other Iberian kingdoms or from elsewhere in the Mediterranean like the Florentine factors in Málaga or the long-standing Genoese community.[59] In Granada, the transactions were registered and deposited with the municipal council and a translation was made. In some cases, additional Spanish documents were included to explain the transaction or to refer to other related Arabic documents. In this paperwork process, translation was part of a set of prescribed and recognizable procedures that converted the legal value of the Islamic documents into legal value within the Christian administration, and those officials who participated in these processes were part of the bilingual legal and notarial elite, which included translators.

One representative example from this collection is a purchase record from April 1499, which was drawn up by a scribe (*kātib*), registered at the *cabildo*, and translated that same year, before the mass conversions were sparked by rebellion in December 1499. The transaction was a sale of a plot of land between a Muslim owner, 'Abd al-Raḥmān ibn 'Alī al-Maknāsī, and a Christian purchaser, Alonso de Cáceres, resulting in a quitclaim in exchange for a price of twenty-six dinars, two and one-third silver dirhams. This contract shows that Nasrid coinage was still in use in Granada in 1499.[60] The dossier was translated again in 1514 for reasons that are not specified, though 1515 was a year from which many *romanceamientos* are extant and there may have been a drive to translate *cabildo* records around that time. Of particular interest to this analysis of the social aspects of fiduciary translation is the fact that many of the same officials worked in the *cabildo* before conversion in 1499 and after in 1514 and thus participated in both translation events.

Figure 1. Quitclaim for properties from the *mudéjar*
'Abd al-Raḥmān ibn 'Alī al-Miknāsī to the settler
Alonso de Cáceres, witnessed by the *qāḍī* of Granada.
April 8, 1499. AMGR, legajo 4471, pieza 2, doc. 4r.
© Ayuntamiento de Granada.

When an Islamic legal document was translated in Granada after 1492,
it became subject to the normative and procedural regime of Castilian civil
law. In that civil law, from at least its codification in the thirteenth century
by King Alfonso X (1221–1284), legal instruments like quitclaims or other
contracts were recorded by notaries who also served a scribal function. In

general, the legal validity of the instrument was achieved through the notarized presence of sworn instrumentary witnesses who had promised to tell
the truth based on direct and certain knowledge.[61] Unsurprisingly, official
translators were often notarial scribes, and their translation work had the
same effect as their notarial work in creating legal validity. Part of the work
of translation, thus, was converting the Islamic norms and procedures into
legible Castilian norms and procedures while retaining the legal validity
under both regimes. Elsewhere in medieval Iberia, there existed a precedent
for notarial translation between Hebrew deeds and Latin legal forms and
required the work of specialists conversant in both languages and legal systems.[62] In *mudéjar* Granada, fiduciary translation helped achieve a similar
conversion in large part because the Castilian notarial scribes who were
appointed as translators had been *kātibūn* or *muwaththiqūn* or performed
related functions as *alfaquíes*, or *fuqahā'*. As a consequence of this professional
continuity across legal, religious, and linguistic conversion, much of the
social significance of the Islamic legal system was retained as legible in the
Christian legal institutions.

Indeed, the socially constituted concept of *'adāla* and its translation was
fundamental for ensuring an enduring role for the *fuqahā'* in post-conquest
Granada.[63] Because *'adāla* relied on direct knowledge of the witnesses' character, the social bonds and knowledge of Nasrid Granada remained highly
pertinent in Castilian institutions. For this reason, in the case of the sale
between al-Maknāsī and Cáceres, a translation of the quitclaim was made
right away after the deed was drawn up in Arabic in 1499 by Alonso de Mora
(formerly Yuça). Then the deed itself was further authenticated with an Arabic certification made by a converted *faqīh* and member of the *cabildo*, don
Andrés de Granada el Basti, who is specified in Spanish sources as "antes
alfaqui Mahomad el Bazty."[64] In an undated encounter, he was asked to read
the deed and confirm its authenticity based on the work of the judge and witnesses as well as on what he knew of their identities. Don Andrés wrote his
own addendum to the deed in Arabic, explaining what he had been asked and
that it was indeed valid (*ṣaḥīḥ*) according to Muslim contracts and their regulations (*'alā ḥasab 'uqūd al-muslimīn wa-rusūmihim*). Don Andrés's intervention was effectively an additional mechanism for authenticating the document
according to Islamic legal norms, performed in Arabic by a former *alfaquí*
who was now a Christian councilman. He would later engage in the same
procedure to register his own properties with the town council, in April 1501,
when he "presented a royal order (*cédula*) granting him the right (*merced*) to

have Arabic documents (*escrituras moriscas*) translated in order to divide up his legacy."[65]

Before conversion, Mahoma el Basty was Abū 'Abd Allāh Muḥammad ibn Faḍl ibn Ibrāhīm al-Basṭī, a Nasrid *faqīh* and *muftī* who remained in Granada after the conquest and even issued a *fatwā* conceding that some Muslims would remain in *dār al-ḥarb*.[66] In the pre-1492 fatwa, al-Basṭī specified that "a Muslim community must be regulated according to Islamic law, [thus] it required the presence of individuals who possessed legal knowledge and whose testimony was considered *'ādila*."[67] Indeed, Mahoma el Basty became don Andrés de Granada after the forced conversions began in December 1499 and was named to the town council as a voting member (*regidor*) in November 1500.[68] He was well aware of the importance of legal and social knowledge for judicial matters, and through his later work in Castilian institutions and that of others like him, *'adāla* would prove to be a cornerstone of fiduciary translation in Spain.

In the case of the al-Maknāsī–Cáceres quitclaim, the social knowledge embedded in Don Andrés's Arabic-language certification of the probity of the original witnesses was also conveyed through translation. The quitclaim was translated twice in close succession, first by Alonso de Mora and then by Bernardino de Xarafi. Mora's translation is less literal than Xarafi's later version, though the deviations from the source text seem designed to help later readers understand the social factors behind the legal validations that underpinned the deed. For example, where the Arabic had simply specified the information of multiple witnesses (*ya'lamuhu shuhūduhu*), Mora provided additional details about how those witnesses arrived at the transaction, as if he had been himself an eyewitness to it: "witnesses who were presented by [the seller, al-Maknāsī] and by order of the *cadi*." Likewise, translating don Andrés's addendum, Mora included additional information revealing how the transaction was conducted on the basis of social knowledge and legal authority—the *'adāla* of witnesses that had to be certified by the *qāḍī*. In his translation Mora wrote: "On the back of the document don Andrés was asked if this document and its witnesses are reliable (*firmes*) and if he knows them, and he confirmed—in his own handwriting and with his signature—that the above mentioned [Mahamad Çayd Bona y el alfaqui Ozmin Alarrach] are notarial scribes (*escribanos públicos*) and he has met them and on that account he put his signature, don Andrés." Alonso de Mora then added his own signature. This practice of revalidating witnesses is indeed an important part of the transmission of Islamic legal documents,

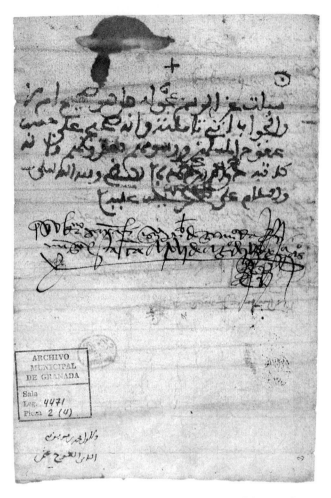

Figure 2. Certification of the legal validity of the quitclaim
in Arabic by the *nuevamente convertido (morisco)* alderman
(*regidor*) and former *alfaquí* Andrés el Basty (n.d.).
Scribal notarization below in Castilian by Bernardino
Xarafi, *romanceador* of the Granada Town Council,
August 16, 1514. AMGR, legajo 4471, pieza 2,
doc. 4v. © Ayuntamiento de Granada.

since the legitimacy of the witness derives from his *'adāla* and its legibility even in later generations, rather than from a professional credential like a scribal appointment. This is why don Andrés's certification of the *'adāla* of those particular witnesses was important for updating the legal relevance of the document in its new setting. Contemporaneous Christian translations, on the other hand, went so far as to eschew individual names in favor of legally relevant titles (*alfaquíes escrivanos públicos*).[69] In Chapter 3 we will examine a later trans-Mediterranean case in which a divergence in the translation of witness confirmations—through professional titles rather than personal names—affected the course of diplomatic translations.

Social position and professional credentials are often related, but the distinction between each as a source of legal validity is important. Analogous to the Islamic requirement for witness *'adāla*, in Roman-derived Castilian law, witnesses were required to be trustworthy (*fiel*), that is, to embody *fides*.[70] However, once their probity was established during legal proceedings, the legitimacy of a witness was permanently encoded by his signature in all subsequent copies or translations of the document. In the Christian tradition by the turn of the sixteenth century, it was the performance of a notarial office in producing a new document rather than the social position and reputation of the original witness that mattered most for ratifying the legal authority of the instrument in translation.[71] Thus, the tandem of el Basty's witness certification as a former Nasrid *qāḍī* and its accompanying translation by Castilian-appointed functionaries was a hybrid ratification of Islamic procedure as the document was incorporated into a Christian legal regime.

It should be clear that, as translators, Mora and Xarafi did more than render Arabic documents literally into Spanish. They also explained, using translation choices backed by their reputations as experts, the meaning or legitimacy of the Islamic legal norms that governed the original transaction and that were being transferred to the Christian legal record. For example, in one transaction from April 1499, the original Arabic explained that a Christian had purchased a plot of land from a Muslim by means of a quitclaim (*wa-abrā'ahu min dhālik al-barā'*) by which the buyer took "full and free and complete possession according to the *Sunna*" (*wa bi-dhālik khalaṣa li-l-mabtā' al-madhkūr tamliku al-mabī'a akmal khulūṣ wa-atammahu 'alā sunna*). To express this transaction and its validity under Islamic law, Xarafi explained in Spanish translation that, by means of the quitclaim receipt, the seller "fulfilled the purchase of the Christian buyer with the land he bought, fully and completely according to the rules of the Muslims ("entera y cumplida-mente por la regla y çinna de moros").[72]

In addition to explaining the legal procedures that produced the document in question, Xarafi used a mixture of translation and non-translation to explain whose actions made those procedures valid according to Islamic law. For example, the original Arabic deed included the information that the seller, 'Abd al-Raḥmān ibn 'Alī al-Maknāsī, sold his property on behalf of himself and on behalf of his three brothers. He had a notarized and witnessed authorization from his brothers that he presented at the time of sale, which had been issued, according to the document, "from he whose [authority] was required in Granada" (mimman wujiba bi-Gharnaṭa). Xarafi reintroduced the title and role of the Islamic judge, "on the part of the Qadi (cadi) of Granada," expecting his Spanish-speaking audience to find the loanword meaningful. Mora used similar strategies to those chosen later by Xarafi, but he also eschewed certain information that would have to be recaptured later in 1514. For example, like Xarafi, he translated man wujiba as cadi, and both translators used the loanword sinna where the Arabic text gave sunna. Both also specified the date conversions from the Hijra calendar to the Christian dates.[73]

The performative work of translation in creating a Spanish legal instrument from an Arabic source—the traducción fehaciente or official translation of Feria and Arias—is amply on display in both Mora's and Xarafi's choices and strategies. Beyond the discursive performance of translation, however, Xarafi also had to encode the professional and institutional contexts of the original procedures into the translated document. Thus he converted the Arabic references to instrumentary witnessing into the analogous Spanish institutions; for example, "it was recognized by its witnesses" (ya'lamuhu shuhūduhu) changed to: notarial scribes "giving faith" (del cual dan fee los escriuanos). What was understood as a given in Arabic—that the responsible party was a judge and that the witnesses were the correct kind, whose individual identities would be given later—had to be made clear with specialized vocabulary in Spanish in which the general professional identity replaced the need for an individual name.

On top of rendering the social signals legible in Spanish, the fiduciary translation undertaken by Xarafi was itself collaborative, requiring several people to gather and read Arabic documents and agree both on a legally authoritative translation and on the social and professional statuses of those involved in the transaction as well as the production of the documents. Xarafi and Mora often worked together in *cabildo* commissions, and with other familiar names from Granada's bilingual officials, such as Hernando de Sosa (formerly Gabriel Israel) and, of course, don Alonso Venegas himself. These men were also the primary translation staff called upon by the newly established Real Chancillería in Granada, which oversaw many kinds of lawsuits in which Arabic documentation or witness testimony was relied upon. As a royal institution, the effect of the suits heard in the Chancillería could be felt across the Iberian kingdoms. In this way, fiduciary translation and its effects were transmitted beyond Granada. For example, the lawsuit brought by the so-called Ynfantes de Granada, don Juan and don Fernando de Granada, to reclaim rights to Granada properties they asserted had been granted to them by their father the Nasrid Sultan, was fueled by the fiduciary work of the Granada translators.

In the 1980s, the details of this case were studied in revelatory detail by one of the most important figures in the historiography of *mudéjar* Granada, José López de Coca Castañer, who used the lawsuit records to fill in missing pieces of a dynastic drama that fractured the last Nasrids into civil war during the ten-year defensive war with Castile. In 1992, two of the leading *romanceamientos* scholars, Antonio Malpica Cuello and Carmen Trillo San José, published an edition of some of the translations that were used in the suit.[74] When analyzed together, these sources are another window into the intertextual and interpersonal workings of fiduciary translation.

The basic outlines of the case and its backstory are the following. Amid the dynastic factionalism that plagued the last Nasrids—and that likely facilitated the eventual Castilian conquest—Sultan Abū al-Ḥasan ʿAlī (r. 1464–1482, 1482–1485) had two sons by a Christian captive convert, the infamous Zoraya/Isabel de Solís of later chronicles and fiction. Zoraya and her sons, Saʿd and Naṣr, became part of the household of Abū al-Ḥasan's brother and rival, Muḥammad al-Zaghal, after the former's death in 1485. When al-Zaghal was defeated by the armies of Ferdinand and Isabella at Málaga in 1487, he and his retinue became Trastámara vassals. Though al-Zaghal would eventually flee to North Africa, Saʿd and Naṣr remained in Spain and were converted to Christianity in April 1492 at the Santa Fe encampment under the patronage of Queen Isabella herself. Now called don Juan and don Fernando de Granada, the two Ynfantes (princes) would remain with the Castilian court for most of their lives, marrying Christian women and seeking favors and honors through Castilian channels.

Though the story of the Ynfantes, and particularly of their mother, became the stuff of legend, it is in the grubby details of the lawsuit recovered by López de Coca Castañer and the *romanceamientos* published by Malpica Cuello and Trillo San José that the real workings of politics and society in post-conquest Granada are illuminated as a facet of fiduciary translation. The lawsuit itself derived from a constellation of inheritance disputes whose precedents dated to the Nasrid period. According to the claims of the Ynfantes, their father had granted them and their mother extensive income-producing territories across Granada. The rights to those territories and incomes were preserved after conquest, even when the Ynfantes and their mother became Christian vassals of the Spanish monarchs. However, the aftermath of conquest led to frequent rebellions, including in the territories of the Ynfantes, who were absentee landlords with little connection to their own peasant vassals. One witness testified that, following a particularly violent episode in 1493, Queen Isabella confiscated large portions of the Ynfantes' territories in exchange for a valuable bond (*juro*), a common mechanism for granting income, an exchange that would later be recounted in the *Historia de los reinos de Granada* of Luis del Mármol Carvajal (see below).[75] When the queen died in November 1504, her obligations were "discharged" (*descargo*), a process overseen by specialized judges (*jueces de descargo*) and recorded in the account books of Gonzalo de Baeza. Beginning in 1505, don Juan and don Fernando began a lawsuit to reclaim those territories left to them by their father and exchanged for Isabella's *juro* in 1493. To support their claims, they instructed their advocate (*procurador*) to question witnesses and to have the relevant Arabic property records translated into Spanish.

López de Coca Castañer's masterful study of the investigation (*probanza*) outlines the details and ramifications of the claims of the Ynfantes for late Nasrid politics and their own lives as Castilian courtiers. However, the *probanza*—which includes witness testimony records, many of which were recorded in Granada's Real Chancillería via translation—becomes a valuable window into the world of fiduciary translation when studied transversally with the *romanceamientos* of Nasrid documents that were generated as part of the same process. First, among the thirty-seven witnesses who were called in 1505 and 1506 to testify, all had been *mudéjares*, and many of them were registered as former *fuqahāʾ*. These included Hernando Enríques el Pequení, don Andrés de Granada el Basty, Micer Ambrosio Xarafi, and don Alonso Venegas. Venegas was in a particularly important position to testify since his father, Yaḥya al-Nayyar, had effectively divided territories with al-Zaghal in 1487 after the conquests of Málaga, Almería, and Baza, and don Alonso likely knew don Juan and don Fernando well from the Nasrid court context as well as from the Trastámara court, where he was a frequent visitor.

The testimony responded to a set of twenty-six standardized questions designed to establish the credibility of the witness and the plaintiffs by asserting personal knowledge of the Ynfantes, their family, and their possessions, particularly details of the properties in question and who had owned them when. Throughout the testimony, witnesses again and again recurred to sight and hearing as the source of legally valid knowledge. For example, el Pequení commented on earlier property transactions he reported seeing with his own eyes (vido), probably in his capacity as chief qāḍī, and testified to his personal acquaintances with members of the extended royal family. Based on his legal expertise, el Pequení also specified the changes that had come with the conquest and conversion of legal regimes, explaining that "in Muslim times (tiempo de moros), that kind of property could be neither bought nor sold. And after the kingdom became Christian, they decided to sell their thousands in income for around ten thousand maravedies more or less." Thus what was likely a pious endowment (waqf) was converted into saleable property. Meanwhile, Xarafi's testimony, like that of many others, derived from having lived among the royal household and thus acquiring intimate knowledge of their family life and properties. He claimed to have "lived with the alcaide Ibn Kumisha, and he saw (vido) when the aforementioned king Muley Haçen married the aforementioned queen Isabel [de Solís] and when the aforementioned princes were born and he recognized them when our Lord king [Fernando] converted them from captivity in which the princes were living."[76] Xarafi's testimony was considered particularly important because he was able to comment on the value of the lands, especially the income derived from their cultivation, likely a result of his long experience alternating between the scribal work of the notary and the field work of the assessor. In spite of the details of fiscal and legal administration in Nasrid and mudéjar Granada that are revealed in the comments of these witnesses, none of those interviewed brought documentary evidence to bear.

Nevertheless, there were documents that the Ynfantes wished to offer in support of their claims, including deeds and purchase records dating to the

1450s, and that they petitioned to have translated in July 1506. Both don Alonso and Xarafi participated in the translation, along with Fernando de Sosa and Alonso de Mora. In the fall of 1506, Alonso de Mora and Fernando de Sosa. working as one team, and don Alonso Venegas, don Miguel de León, and Ambrosio Xarafí, working as another team, translated sets of Arabic documents related to the Ynfantes' properties.

As in the witness testimony, the value of eyewitnesses was paramount, and translators made sure to indicate the presence of "testigos de vista" in the historical documents, or that those witnesses reported having personal knowledge, by sight, of the territories in question ("vieron las heredades"). Part of assuring the translation was also the claim that the original documents had been *seen* as part of the authenticating process of fiduciary translation:

> In the renowned and grand city of Granada, on the seventh day of the month of September, in the year of our Savior Jesus Christ of 1506, before Mr. Lope de Montenegro, B.A., *alcalde mayor* of this city and by order of the gentleman Mr. Alonso Enriquez, *corregidor* of this city and surrounding territory by order of their highnesses the king and queen, our Lords, in the presence of me, Diego Tristán, scribe of the royal chamber and notarial scribe of the municipality of Granada, and the two above-mentioned witnesses, Fernando de Mendoça appeared in the name and by the authority (*en nombre de y por virtud del poder que tiene*) of the *ynfantes* don Fernando and don Juan of Granada and their mother, the queen Isabel, and he presented three letters written on paper and in Arabic (*letra arauiga*). Presented thusly, Fernando de Mendoça stated, as their representative, that they wished to translate the letters into our Castilian language (*nuestra lengoa* [*sic*] *y letra castellana*) in order to present them to their Highnesses along with other items in support of their rights. Thus he asked the *alcalde mayor* to find some *alfaquíes* and experts to declare what was in the letters and translate them. Once translated, he asked that a copy be sent to him, signed by him [an *alfaquí*] and by me as notarial scribe so that they are legally valid (*en manera que haga fee*), investing it with his authority and judicial decree, so that they will be accepted everywhere just like documents drawn up

by notaries (*para doquiera que paresçiere se les de fee y credito como a cartas escritas de manos de escriuanos publicos*), and he asked for this justice.

Then the *alcalde mayor* said that the city had appointed Alonso Hernández de Mora as interpreter (*lengoa ynterprete*), who knows how to read and write in Arabic, and that he will appoint the aforementioned Alonso Fernández de Mora and Hernando de Sosa—who is someone very expert in Arabic and Castilian (*vien esperta en la dicha lengoa araviga e en nuestra lengoa castellana*). They both know Islamic law (*saben la xaara çuna de los moros*) and they both know how to declare and interpret the aforementioned Arabic documents in our Castilian language. Present as witnesses were [Diego] Tristán and Pedro Tristán and Alonso Hernández de Mora, interpreters, residents of this city (*vecinos*).

And after that, in the city of Granada, on the eighth day of the month of September of the same year, the *alcalde mayor* received the oath as the commission to the abovementioned Alonso de Mora and Hernando de Sosa, by which he commanded them to look at (*les mando viesen*) the Arabic documents that had been presented by Hernando de Mendoça, and having looked at them, determine by sight if they were made by the hands of the *fuqahā'* according to Islamic law (*e vistos, viesen sy heran fechas de mano de alfaquíes segund la costunbre de los moros*), and to declare and translate the Arabic documents into our Castilian word for word (*a la letra*) according to what is written and agreed within them and without adding or subtracting anything.[77]

Many of the strategies and discursive moves in this extensive translatory instrument occurred commonly in other translations, both in this episode and in evidence from other *romanceamientos*. As in the cases of *cabildo* translation, translators worked together to determine the genres of the documents in question (e.g., *carta de vendida*, "sale record"), explaining toponymns (e.g., "que quiere desir la Puente de bem Raxid"); to convert the hijra dates to the Christian calendar; and to explain which Islamic authorities had been present at the transaction recorded in the document (e.g., "que es juez de vnyversidad en la çibdad de Tremeçen") and what they had done to render it legally valid (e.g., "dieron fee ante el señor alfaquí").[78] When necessary, they commented that something from the original document was carried out according to Islamic law, as, for example, clarifying when a portion of a 1478 inheritance had not been transferred automatically to the king, "conforme a la constumbre de los moros y a los saneamientos de las leyes de ellos."[79] In the 1506 texts, the translators even created discursively a professional category with retroactive legal validity: the *alfaquí escriuano público*.

In all cases, the legitimacy of the translator work was underpinned by recognized expertise in Islamic law, the "xara" and "çuna." As Robert Burns has demonstrated in his studies of thirteenth-century Valencia, prerequisite familiarity with Islamic law was far from exceptional in Christian Iberia.[80] In *mudéjar* Granada, many *romanceamientos* included fully extant instruments guaranteeing the work and position of the translator and provided a comment about the legal expertise of translators as "expert[s] in the aforementioned Arabic language and our Castilian language, and both [Israel and Mora] know about Islamic law (*saben la xaara çuna de los moros*) and they know how to translate the aforementioned Arabic documents into our Castilian language and letter."[81] Both the former Jew, Israel (now Sosa), and the former Muslims Mora, Xarafí, and Venegas relied on professional reputations to guarantee their expertise with Muslim legal formulae. The recognition of their expertise and pre-conversion reputations ensured their fiduciary position in Granadan society.

Royal recognition of this kind became an intangible asset for minorities during a period of ambivalent and often dangerous cultural policies. After the conquest, and their eventual conversion from Islam to Christianity, members of families like the Venegas, Xarafi, and Mora secured stable administrative positions in the post-conquest regime translating Islamic legal documents into Spanish and assisting in the information gathering necessary for effective taxation. Indeed, it is worth noting that posts in the bilingual administration in translation became a unique avenue for minorities to secure a position (*officium*) in government administration and the corresponding salary or other benefit (*beneficium*) from the crown.[82] This development occurred at the same time that minority life became the target for conversion, assimilation, and, eventually, expulsion. Interpreters were in the ambivalent position of perpetuating the linguistic frontiers while at the same time ensuring the general social and cultural processes of forced assimilation.

The transactions discussed here would have been far from exceptional, in spite of their value to us as particularly complete examples of highly regularized and regular processes. What the chains of authentications and translations reveal is the habitually collaborative nature of translation across linguistic and religious boundaries and the way in which translation derived legitimacy both from its intertextual relationships—for example, target text and source text, additional certifications, and so forth—and the social relations and institutions that produced those intertextual relationships. Translation was guaranteed both through collaborative work and an explicit chain of transmission that reflected the social bonds and institutional settings that conditioned everyone's actions. Fiduciary translation effectively created new sources upon which to make legal arguments, and those sources were based upon the specific social connections, working habits, and colonial institutions in *mudéjar* and then *morisco* Granada. The effects of these translations then reached far beyond Andalucia.

The harnessing of Islamic legal expertise that was taking place on a daily basis in Granada was of intense interest to the crown. For example, although the Ynfantes' lawsuit dragged on for decades, it was not forgotten. Though the *probanza* and the *romanceamientos* were concluded in Granada, copies were made and sent to other court centers, including Valladolid and Toledo, at the request of don Juan as he continued to agitate for his properties throughout the 1520s and 1530s. Don Juan's service on behalf of the Crown in the *comuneros* revolt and his tenancy as the governor of the Galicia province ensured that he would be remembered as a *buen vasallo* of the Spanish kings, especially among *moriscos* themselves.[83] Despite the Ynfantes's claims to the region, Charles eventually granted the *taha* (county) of Orgibe to the "Gran Capitán" Gonzálo Fernández de Córdoba in 1527. Beyond the use of Granada properties to appease his courtiers, the crown remained vitally interested in legal precedent and historical evidence from Granada. In 1548— five years after the death of the second Ynfante—Prince Philip (the future Philip II) requested a copy of the Ynfantes' lawsuit along with the Granada capitulations from 1492.

Indeed, Granada was never far from the minds of the Spanish kings, even after the dynastic transfer to the House of Habsburg in 1517. In 1526, the now emperor Charles V traveled to Granada to celebrate his wedding to Isabel of Portugal. While in Granada he met with a council of regional leaders to receive advice about what would become known during the rule of his son Philip (r. 1556–1598) as the *morisco* problem—the extent to which the loyalty of Arabic-speaking subjects to the Crown could be guaranteed. Motivated by ecclesiastical reviews of the province (*visitas*) determining that evangelization was ineffective, Charles ordered complete assimilation in language, dress, ceremonies, and food, threatening to enforce orders given by Ferdinand and his daughter Juana (Charles's mother) repeatedly over the preceding decades.[84] When he issued his Royal Chapel Edict in 1526, however, representatives of the *morisco* community convinced him that those changes were too difficult to make immediately and negotiated for an extension in return for a sizable payment of ninety thousand *ducados* and subsequent yearly payments of twenty-one thousand *ducados*.[85] In 1526, with the memory of the *comuneros* revolt of the early 1520s still immediate for Charles, the *moriscos* were able to invoke their loyalty during that episode and protest the gap between religious identity and cultural practice to convince Charles to forestall the implementation of the edict for a generation, or forty years. The details of this agreement were the subject of debate and negotiation throughout Charles's reign, but the forty-year term was never rescinded.[86]

In this context, Arabic translators working for the town council continued to play a crucial role in the organization of Granadan society through the *repartimiento*, that is, the official assessment of people, goods, and properties upon which tax obligations were based. The *repartimiento* produced more Arabic translation than the Inquisition and Chancillería combined, but evidence of the translations that generated the means of assessment left scant evidence in the archives. It is thus necessary to read between the lines of a variety of administrative documents to understand how integral the Translation Office was to the running of the Granada government well into the 1570s. Despite the small quantity of examples of what must have been an exceptionally common type of translation, it is certain that these documents were likewise designed to provide sources for legal arguments or assertions of fiscal authority, all based on the work of the field translators.

The initial Granada *repartimientos* were produced in Castilian as part of the settlement of "old Christians" recruited from the north even during the Granada campaign. Arabic property, usufruct, and water-rights records that informed the *repartimiento* were translated as needed (as in the case of the *repartimiento* of the waters of Genil, translated by Ambrosio Xarafi in 1502).[87] In the following generations, however, the process of *repartimiento* remained a fundamentally bilingual process, and one in which the increasing tension between the place of Arabic and the place of Castilian in Spanish institutions was becoming ever more obvious. For example, in July 1545 Francisco Núñez Muley, a well-known *morisco* leader, initiated a lawsuit in his capacity as *repartidor por mayor del seruiçio que los nuevamente convertidos deste Reyno de Granada hazen a su magestad* (in other words, a top official who oversaw the collection of specific *morisco* taxes, in this case the *farda*). Núñez Muley accused the scribe Hernán García de Valera of calling him a liar, among other insults ("perro moro"), and punching him. The encounter that sparked the violence was directly related to the bilingual processes of the *repartimiento*. Sitting around after lunch while out gathering the taxes in the Parish of San Gregorio, some of the tax collectors began to discuss a case in the parish, using Arabic. García de Valera tried to forbid the group from speaking in Arabic and also disagreed with them about what should be done about the case in question. Núñez Muley defended the rights of the Arabic speakers to talk about whatever they might want in Arabic ("fablaron en aravigo cosas que les convenía fablar"). What followed was an argument about jurisdiction and authority, essentially whether García de Valera had to do what Núñez Muley told him both in terms of language and in the case of the parishioner, and the debate ended in a fistfight and both parties in jail. They received the same punishment: to be confined to the city of Granada (and thus not able to participate in the lucrative activities of *repartimiento*).[88] From this episode, we learn that many of the officials who were involved in programs like tax collection were bilingual and that it was possible for state officials (tax collectors) to carry out their business in one language and bring it to the state in another. The episode also shows that language choice was not always perceived as neutral. By 1545 this flexibility inspired strong contrary feelings among some officials, like García de Valera, who thought all state business should be done in Castilian, even when carried out between bilingual officials.

Everyday bilingualism, language contact, and casual translation in Granadan society shaped official activities at all levels, ensuring that the fiduciary position of the translator was a vital component of social organization. But evidence of how translation informed this everyday bilingualism is meager. One rare example is the *repartimiento* of 1549–1550 that took place in the territories of the Marquis of Cenete. This tax assessment resulted in two sets of registers (*libros de repartimiento*), one in Arabic and one in Castilian.[89] These records were created in parallel—first in Arabic and then translated into Castilian—by the *romançeador* (interpreter) and *escribano del rey* (royal scribe) Juan Rodríguez and his team from Granada.[90] What remains significant about this episode, like that of the *repartimiento* of San Gregorio in 1545, is that, as late as 1550, bilingual agents acted as intermediaries between an

Arabic-speaking people and a Castilian-speaking state while they carried out state business directly in Arabic.

The most emblematic state official who conducted government business in Arabic and Spanish was don Alonso Venegas, Granada's original head translator. His noble status and early conversion placed Venegas close to royal officials and other Spanish grandees, but he nonetheless worried about centralized control of the Translation Office. He retained his position as *trujamán mayor* until 1536, when he ceded the title to none other than the above-mentioned Juan Rodríguez, with the provision that once both he and Rodríguez died the position would return to the council for them to make the appointment, rather than to the king or any other institution.[91] When Alonso Venegas died is unknown, but Juan Rodríguez had passed away by the fall of 1556.[92] Not until 1582 was there another royally appointed *romançeador*: Alonso del Castillo, Rodríguez's successor to the municipal position in 1556.[93] Though he did not gain a royal appointment (which came with a much higher salary) until much later in his career, while working under his municipal appointment, Castillo decoded the Arabic inscriptions of the Alhambra, corrected the earlier legal translations made by his predecessor Rodríguez, and worked for the Inquisition.[94]

By 1567, according to Francisco Núñez Muley, only one interpreter was regularly employed by the city. This evidence has led scholars to believe that there were few official interpreters in *morisco* Granada; however, a careful look through the patchwork of extant town council, notarial, and ecclesiastic records shows that maintaining an active bilingual corps continued to be a high priority for both the local and royal administrations.[95] For example, both Xarafi and Mora brought their sons into the family business. Ambrosio Xarafi became the head of a family translation workshop, in which his sons Bernardino and Íñigo helped him with the technical legal processes of reading and witnessing as part of authentic translation. Bernardino took over his father's position in 1510. Íñigo Xarafi, also a royal scribe, was poised to take over the family business, having trained alongside his father and brother as a witness to the translation until the family practice was suspended in 1521 for unknown reasons.[96] Alonso de Mora and Íñigo de Mora collected salaries from the town council for work done as *lenguas e intérpretes* in 1555.[97] Even as late as 1566, at least two translators were employed by the *cabildo* (Alonso del Castillo and Diego Hernández el Malaquí), and many others worked regularly as notaries.[98]

In addition to their use of local and royal institutions from the *cabildo* to the Chancillería, *moriscos* continued to request help from interpreters to draft their last wills and testaments, significantly requesting assistance to perform Christian acts such as leaving bequests to a Church or receiving extreme unction.[99] These notarial registers include the names of several of the officially employed *cabildo* and *chancillería*, and even some Inquisition translators, including the Xarafi, the Mora, Morales el Fisteli, Zacarías de Mendoza, and Diego Hernández el Malaquí.[100] In short, *moriscos* were not outside Spanish law or passive subjects to its normative force. Arabic translation offered access to institutions of power for *moriscos* as well as "old Christians." Contrary to their usual depiction as passive objects of legislation or outsiders to Spanish institutions by scholars focused on *moriscos* as representatives of a crypto-Muslim minority, *moriscos* were frequent, and frequently successful, litigants in Spanish courts, confronting both *moriscos* and "old Christians," using Arabic records and Arabic translation to their advantage. *Moriscos* and non-*moriscos* brought suit against one another in property and other disputes heard in the Real Chancillería. *Morisco* peasants sued their lords for cruelty and other abuses. For example, the *morisco* vassals of Cenete brought suit in the Royal Appellate Court against their lords for wrongful taxation beginning in 1515 and again in the 1530s.[101] *Moriscos* employed (and were employed as) notaries, scribes, and other legal officials associated with the court and government.[102] Although practices like *taqiyya* (dissimulation) can explain some *morisco* approaches to living with Spanish law and doctrine, silence or subterfuge were not the only possibility for *moriscos* faced with Spanish authorities.[103] *Moriscos* were adept users of Christian legal institutions and shaped the development of those institutions, often through the social and discursive mechanisms of fiduciary translation.

Over at least two generations, a robust and multigenerational corps of Arabic translators worked within and as an official institutional body in post-conquest Granada. Both under the last Trastámara and the Habsburgs, Islamic legal expertise was incorporated as evidence into the Castilian legal system. Already in the *mudéjar* regime under Ferdinand and Isabella, Islamic law had an official place in the Castilian judicial system, as in the cases of rulings according to Islamic *sunna* found in the Castilian appellate court in Valladolid.[104] Once all Castilian subjects were nominally Christian after 1502, Arabic translation in the appellate courts and other secular governmental institutions became a viable means in Counter-Reformation Spain to maintain the validity of Islamic private law in those transactions that used Arabic documents or their translations as evidence.

A Civil War over Language:
The Second Alpujarras War, 1567–1571

Both Granada and Valencia were subject to radical new language policies beginning in the 1560s. In 1564 in Valencia and in 1566 in Granada, the use of Arabic and possession of Arabic texts were explicitly outlawed. This turning point was conditioned in large part by the political and religious outcomes of the Council of Trent (1545–1563) in Spain. In the 1560s, increasing anxiety spread among sovereigns across Europe about the uniformity and orthodoxy of their realms, an unease linked to the intensifying European wars of religion in addition to rivalry with the Ottomans and fear about a *morisco* "fifth column." Philip II of Spain was no exception. In 1566 he was beginning his second decade of rule, which coincided with the conclusion of the Council of Trent and its effects in Spain, and a stressful period in Philip's European, as well as Mediterranean, politics. As a result, he issued a new and much less permissive royal edict governing *morisco* cultural forms.

The first priority of the text of the 1566 *pragmática* was the eradication of Arabic, and four of ten articles were dedicated to this topic. They prohibited spoken or written Arabic in Granada and deprived all Arabic texts of their legitimacy, legal or otherwise:

[1] First it was ordered that, within three years of the publication of this decree, the *moriscos* must learn to speak the Castilian language and from then on no one will be able to speak, read, nor write [Arabic], neither in public nor in secret.

[2] [It was then ordered] that all there be no more contracts or writings drawn up in the Arabic language, and that they have no effective validity, and that they [the texts] not be taken as security (*fe*) in a court of law nor out of it, and neither may anyone use [those texts] to ask for or request anything, and they have no [legal] force whatsoever.

[3] [It was then ordered] that all books that may be in the Arabic language, *no matter their subject nor condition,* be brought to the president of Granada's royal court within thirty days so that he can order them to be seen and examined; and those that have nothing inappropriate may be returned for the period of three years, but no longer,

[4] As for the order that [the *moriscos*] must present themselves in order to learn the Castilian language, the president and the archbishop of Granada have promised, with the advice of persons of practical experience (*personas prácticas y de experiencia*), to provide [the funds and facilities] which seem to them to be the best for the service to God and for the good of those people (the *moriscos*).[105]

In addition, the seventh article prohibited *nombres de moros,* that is, Islamic Arabic names. Fully half of the decree was thus dedicated to the articulation and writing of Arabic and to the possession and preservation of Arabic texts.[106] The anti-Arabic edicts were specific and comprehensive, iron-clad after decades of evasion and payoff. Unlike earlier decrees, however, nowhere in the 1566 decree was Islam or religion mentioned. The letter of the law was not a reprimand for crypto-Islam or a call for conversion. It was a series of normative cultural reforms designed to make the population *seem* as Christian as possible. Though Tridentine Catholicism was highly concerned with internal sincerity and complete understanding of religious doctrine (thus the emphasis on instruction), the legal expression of religion—in this case assessed through cultural practice and observation—was just as important to the bureaucracy of state power.

The edict was drawn up in secret in Madrid on November 17, 1566. It was then sent to Granada, where it was promulgated on January 1, 1567, the eve of the politically freighted anniversary of the *toma* (taking, possession) of Granada.[107] Granada's *moriscos* could scarcely believe that such drastic measures, so often threatened, would actually be effected. They sent an experienced representative to negotiate with the president of the Royal High Court, Pedro de Deza. This was don Francisco Núñez Muley, who was present at previous negotiations when Juana and Charles's edicts against traditional Granadan language, dress, and ceremonies were staved off with extraordinary payments.[108]

The *memorial* of don Francisco is one of the most evocative documents from the *morisco* period.[109] Summed up in his frank criticisms and palpable outrage were the anxieties and hopes of the entire *morisco* population. The fundamental disagreement was over which treaty governed the *morisco* population: the original surrender treaty of 1492 (which Núñez Muley claimed took precedence) or the treaties of conversion beginning in about 1500 and subsequent edicts governing cultural practices like dress and language (the position of the Castilian administration). Núñez Muley reviewed the history of treaties, agreements, and payoffs concerning the cultural practices of the *moriscos*, rehearsing the location and legitimacy of all documentation pertaining to the events, participants, and records of those treaties and payments. He then took on the 1566 articles one by one, beginning with dress, privacy, baths, celebratory ceremonies, veils, names, and slaves, leaving for the end the language question. This item was perhaps the most important, for which reason Philip II began his edict with it and Núñez Muley ended his *memorial* with its discussion.

Countering Philip's prominent Arabic prohibitions, Núñez Muley's first point was that "the Arabic language has no direct relation whatsoever with the Muslim faith." He described the Arabic of Eastern Christians, including the inhabitants of Jerusalem who knew no Castilian, to undermine the argument that the *moriscos* needed Castilian to be good Christians. Then he turned to pragmatic arguments, noting that even if the will to forget Arabic and learn Castilian was strong, immediate linguistic conversion was impossible since it was simply too difficult for Granada's rural inhabitants to learn a new language when, Núñez Muley explained with revealing prejudice, they had not even learned their own well. According to the *memorial,* the decree's true destructive force lay in the dismantling of the archive of Arabic legal documents that underlay the legitimacy of most individual and collective claims to properties and rights, the very source of fiduciary translation. Núñez Muley warned:

> Caution! We are now beginning to see the extreme (and well
> known) damage that is caused by those who wish to see the aboli-
> tion of all documents, land titles, books, or anything else written in
> Arabic, as the natives now have an extreme and urgent need for
> their legal documents and land titles in their legal suits. . . . Let us
> say that it is possible to translate all of these materials into Castilian.

> How long would it take to do so, and how many translators would
> be needed to translate all of the kingdom's documents? Currently
> there is only one such translator, and it is thus inevitable that
> Arabic documents will be lost, and after three years these docu-
> ments would be worthless, as the decree stipulates. What will be
> lost in terms of property and records, given that there will be no
> original legal code (documents) [*ius antigua*] by which we might
> know who owns what?[110]

Taking away Arabic was intended to hobble Granada's inhabitants by effectively destroying their legal traditions, an act which, Núñez Muley went on
to show, would ultimately harm the crown. These were the same kinds of
documents and legal traditions that were subject to translation, and thus
incorporation, into Castilian institutions over the past seven decades.

In addition to the legal muddle, the edict had severe and broad-reaching
economic repercussions for sovereign and vassals. All transactions, Núñez
Muley explained—with the exception of "the records of the tax collector
and the customs agent" (in contradiction to what was indicated by his own
bilingual tax collecting activities in 1545)—were conducted in Arabic.
Without Arabic, Granada's economy would collapse. Producers, consumers,
and middlemen would be unable to carry out what was, fundamentally, an
economy of texts. Núñez Muley explained, "They [the *moriscos*] conduct
business not on the basis of any obligation or personal acquaintance; rather,
they rely on written accounts and records of who owes what to whom that
they keep in their registers."[111] Prohibiting Arabic and depriving existing
Arabic texts of their legitimacy would bring the entire system of production
to a halt. Rendered mute, dyers and merchants would be unable to carry out
any exchange, whether linguistic or commercial. The threat that went
unsaid, but that Núñez Muley certainly meant based on his experiences as a
former tax collector, was that the stagnation of the *morisco* economy would
prevent the *translation* of revenue into Castilian coffers. As a postscript to
his *memorial*, perhaps worried that the threat was too subtle, Núñez Muley
added that "the most important issue with respect to the writing of Arabic
in this kingdom are the tax assessment registers ["padrón de servicios," a synonym for *repartimientos*]." He described the bilingual system that had been in
place for eighty years. As seen above, this system functioned through the
work of bilingual teams of scribes who interviewed Castilian and Arabic
speakers and recorded inventories of their lands and properties. He concluded:

"Must the king lose his tax income and his vassals along with it? These registers and other written records are kept in order to determine and effect the aforementioned tax payments. And if this requirement of the aforementioned decree should be put into practice, His Majesty will not be paid, and the kingdom will be made blind and will lose its natives."[112] The realities of language use were far more tightly connected to financial and commercial practices than to religious ones. From the perspective of Núñez Muley, the bilingual agent was in fact the engine of the economy that supported the health of the state, using Arabic texts and their translation and exchange as fuel. Without Arabic, the engine would cease to run, and the body politic would be irredeemably crippled, left idle, blind, and mute.

Núñez Muley's protests were not a dead letter. Arabic remained a key economic language in *morisco* regions throughout the sixteenth century. Rather than a decline in Arabic use due to the royal prohibitions, there was steady use of the language across *morisco* regions, though the composition of those regions changed after the 1560s, the second Alpujarras war, and subsequent resettlement policies. The preservation of such sources—letters between family members and business partners, as well as legal documents like marriage contracts, records of sale, and so forth—was due to renewed efforts by the Spanish Inquisition post-Trent to confiscate and evaluate all Arabic texts, as will be discussed in Chapter 4.

Philip's 1566 edicts against Arabic use proved to be the harbinger of a devastating civil war over language. Núñez Muley's pleas went unheeded, and on Christmas Day 1568, after a year of failed negotiations back and forth between Granada and the court, the *moriscos* of the Albaicín in Granada rebelled. The consequences of the conflict affected the entire kingdom, as all *morisco* communities throughout the region were forcibly uprooted and resettled in small groups across Castile beginning as early as 1569.[113] The Alpujarras war of 1568–1571 was thus not only a war over language but also one in which language was deployed as a strategic and symbolic weapon, and this is seen nowhere better than in the work of Granada's Arabic translators who remained loyal to the crown. Though according to the minutes of the town council, the Mora family continued to work on *cabildo* business and Arabic interpreters were still needed for notarial transactions, the interpreter who has left the greatest impression on the documentary record was the *morisco* Alonso del Castillo.

Castillo began to work for the Real Chancillería just after Juan Rodríguez's death in 1556, when he was called upon to redo his predecessor's translations.[114] Castillo was, at least in his self-identification, first and fore-most a medical doctor, but he is best known to scholars for his well-documented career as an Arabic translator in many different domains. Castillo translated legal documents, ancient inscriptions, Inquisition testi-mony, scientific manuscripts, and diplomatic correspondence. He effectively embodied the trajectories of Arabic translation in Spain during the six-teenth century, including the transition that occurred over the course of the Alpujarras war.

As a wartime translator in the early 1570s, Castillo elaborated new tac-tics of fiduciary translation in military correspondence. This transition becomes evident in his wartime workbook, *A Summary and Compilation of Everything Translated from Arabic to Castilian by the Graduate Alonso del Cas-tillo . . .* , which was dedicated and submitted to Pedro de Deza, president of the Royal Appellate Court of Granada, in 1575.[115] In this collection Castillo vaunted his important role in the war, not only as a translator of intercepted rebel correspondence but also as the producer of strategic Arabic texts. The majority of the collection, more than thirty translations of Arabic letters preserved in manuscript in the Real Academia de la Historia and the Biblio-teca Nacional in Madrid, are Castilian versions of letters exchanged between *morisco* rebel leaders, some with Ottoman agents from Algiers, from 1569 to 1572.[116] The first five letters, however, are translations of Arabic letters writ-ten by Castillo on the order of different Castilian generals and royal officials. These Arabic letters, written in 1570 and 1571, helped circulate disinforma-tion among rebel troops and persuade them to surrender. According to Cas-tillo, the subterfuge was so effective, that "these letters were the principal motive that caused the 'moors' to surrender."[117] This military success was achieved through a set of rhetorical strategies by which Castillo disguised the letter as if it had been written by a learned Muslim leader, and he did so in order to cast doubt on the possibilities of success for the revolt and the known perfidy of the Ottoman Algerians whom the *moriscos* were counting on for aid. Castillo disguised his (apparently well-known) Arabic handwrit-ing and peppered the text with quotations from the *sunna* and Qur'ān and Muslim dates. Arabic translation became a significant site of dissimulation and intentional deception, though it was still "authenticated" by an official who was well versed in fiduciary translation techniques and whose position amid the ranks of Spain's military and political elites depended on the rec-ognition of his fiduciary role.

The role of language in the discourse of war went beyond disinformation campaigns, and Castillo demonstrated the powerful metaphor that language came to embody in Granada during the Alpujarras war. The *Sumario é recopilación* was a formal collection, presented by Castillo to his patron and primary connection to the royal administration, Pedro de Deza, later to become Cardinal Deza. As such, Castillo prefaced the collection with a dedicatory letter, "To the Illustrious and Reverend Lord don Pedro de Deça, President of the Royal Audiencia and General of this kingdom, etc. [From] the *licenciado* [Bachelor of Medicine] Alonso del Castillo, his servant. A brief prologue about the reasons for, effect, and representation of these writings." His description of the conflict, its participants, and its outcomes were laden with explicitly expressed language ideologies and linguistic metaphors. He thanked his patron, declaiming that "every Christian tongue (*lengua xpiana*) should give thanks to Your Lordship for such a good and great victory, against such terrible enemies, who spoke that evil language." Of course, Castillo aligned himself as one of those *lenguas xpianas*, that is, the loyal *moriscos* who gave voice to their praise of the king (including Castillo himself from his official position as the homonymic *lengua* or "interpreter") against "such terrible enemies," who were defined by their Arabic voices. To complete the politico-linguistic metaphor, Castillo a few sentences later described the enemy as a "horrible monster, who spoke that fierce and ugly language," defeated by the brave captains of the Castilian army. He continued, evoking the image of "the poisonous flower (*aconita*) that the demon would have disgorged, and the language in which it spoke when it thought to put an end to this kingdom."[118] For all his loyalty to the crown, Castillo most likely believed that Arabic was a part of regional rather than religious identity. Language nevertheless provided him with powerful political metaphors. As an Arabic translator and *morisco* advocate in Castilian service, he had to tread a fine path. This vivid depiction of a charging, poisonous, Arabic-speaking demon, for whose destruction the people of the realm (the *moriscos*) were grateful, played on the hostilities about Arabic while at the same time insisting that *moriscos* were part of the body to be defended by the king.

In addition to the anti-Arabic metaphors and arguments presented in the *Sumario*, a handful of examples of the original Arabic correspondence that Castillo dealt with are extant. Morisco military leaders wrote in their Granadan Arabic (part of the dialect bundle that linguists today refer to as Late Spanish Arabic) to their allies but without the benefit of a chancellery

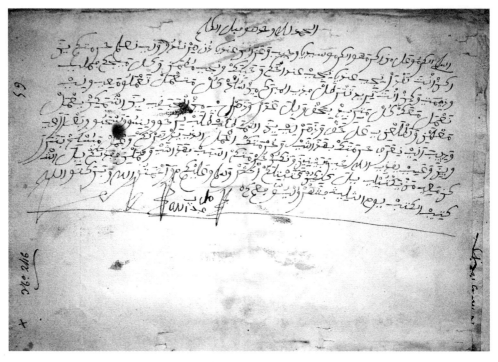

Figure 3. Original Arabic Letter from the *morisco* rebel general Muley 'Abd Allah
"Aben Aboo" requesting negotiations with the Spanish general don Juan
de Austria, via Hernando de Barradas. July 3, 1554 [*sic*]. Archivo Municipal
de Écija. Fondo Marquesado de Peñaflor, de Cortes de Graena y de Quintana
de las Torres, libro 93, número 246.

or skilled secretarial staff, as for example, in the case of the letters sent from
the Granada *moriscos* to the Ottoman Sultan in 1570 confirming the upris-
ing and asking for military support.[119] One of the most famous examples of
a *morisco* military letter written in LSA and for which the original exists is
the Letter of Abenaboo, which was sent from the later leader of the *morisco*
rebellion to an intermediary who was supposed to negotiate between the
rebel leader and the Spanish general Don Juan de Austria.

The Letter of Abenaboo was first published as a facsimile edition in
1915 and has been studied occasionally since by other specialists of Granadan Arabic.[120] Focus on the "exceptional" nature of such a text in the broader
narrative about written Classical Arabic has obscured its special testimony to
the very unexceptional process of using Arabic speech and texts to negotiate

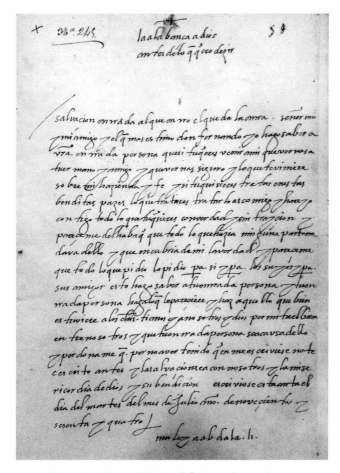

Figure 4. Alonso del Castillo's Spanish translation
of Aben Aboo's letter. July 1574 [*sic*]. Archivo Municipal
de Écija. Fondo Marquesado de Peñaflor, de Cortes de Graena
y de Quintana de las Torres, libro 93, número 245.

with Spanish institutions of power and how those institutions marked the
language itself. The letter, and its translation, show a number of interesting
marks of the language contact between Spanish and Late Spanish Arabic,
in particular Aben Aboo's use of the Castilian loanword *tratar* ("to negotiate," in this case, a peace, conjugated and transliterated as *tatraṭal*) in the
same sentence that he used an Arabic word (*taʻmalū*) to express the same
idea and action.[121]

Why use the Spanish loanword *tratar* conjugated according to Arabic morphology at all? It seems likely that the author Aben Aboo—at this time the *morisco* rebel leader—considered the prospect of negotiating with Spanish representatives, conditioning his choice of *tratar* rather than *'ml* to open the sentence. And could Aben Aboo's *tratar* have been a signal to Castillo—the most likely translator—for how to render the sense of *'ml* (a word with many possible meanings)? Using the Spanish loanword was a choice, since a non-loanword was clearly available. It was perhaps meant as a clue to the translator. This choice, intentional or not, shows how the negotiations were already marked by differences in the power of the institutions and individuals involved. Military correspondence and its translation show that even the rebel communities were irrevocably marked in their language by Spanish institutions of power and language contact. At least a full generation beyond the experience of mudejarism, conquest, and conversion, Spanish subjects who used Arabic—either in speech or text—operated within a system bounded in significant ways by the political and cultural hegemony of Spanish.

Arabic Translation Enters Spanish Print Culture After 1571

After the second Alpujarras war, Granada was no longer governed by functionally bilingual institutions. Nevertheless, the Alpujarras war did not signal the end of Arabic translation, in particular the practice of fiduciary translation. If anything, a new market for Arabic translation was created that demanded reliable Arabic historical sources in translation. Thus, in the last third of the sixteenth century, Arabic translations entered Spanish print culture, reaching an expanded potential audience and leaving a significant mark in Spain's cultural imagination. One of the main vectors for incorporating Arabic translations into Spanish printed books was their use as evidence in works of Spanish history related to recent wars in Granada.[122] This new use for Arabic translation was closely related to antecedents in legal translation and the production of authoritative sources, and manuscript transmission remained important alongside the flourishing print culture.

Initially, translation of Arabic sources was used first and foremost to make arguments about the history of the present. Since the 1567 *pragmática* had been an attack (as Núñez Muley highlighted) on the legal validity of Arabic documents (and economic activities), the turn to historical writing may have been a means of compiling and using Arabic evidence to create new kinds of legal arguments about Arabic-speaking communities.[123] Indeed, the post-Alpujarras legacy of Arabic translators working for the state and other institutions in the first two-thirds of the sixteenth century is most visible in two related subgenres of Spanish histories: the historiography of the Alpujarras war and the Barbary Chronicles (*crónicas de Berbería*), which recounted recent Spanish experiences in North Africa that began to flourish in print in the 1570s.[124] These two genres represented the present history of Arabic speakers (Spanish and otherwise) to Spanish readers. As representations of then present-day history, these narratives reported direct experience and eyewitness testimony, sometimes supported with long quotations from Arabic texts or accounts, all designed to create authenticity for the Spanish text. The evidence of such authenticity of experience as it was based upon access to or information in Arabic sources was rendered into Spanish through translation.

Both Classical and LSA texts were adopted into Spanish historiography through translation. For example, Castillo's translation of the letter of Aben Aboo became well known through its inclusion in the printed works of Luís del Mármol Carvajal.[125] Mármol Carvajal's version is very close to Castillo's translation, indicating that he may have worked from a copy of the text rather than from hearsay about its contents. However, there are slight differences that show how Mármol Carvajal performed an additional passage of translation into printed Spanish. The original Arabic letter from Aben Aboo opens with a conventional Islamic invocation of thanks to God alone: "*al-ḥamdu li-llah wiḥdahū* [sic] *qabla al-kalām.*" Castillo translated this invocation, eschewing the precision that it was God *alone*, as "*La alabanza a dios antes de lo que quiero decir.*" He was probably influenced by one of the most contentious points between Christian and Islamic theology in *morisco* Spain: persuading converts to accept the idea of the divine Trinity. Where Castillo rendered the more neutral translation "thanks be to God," perhaps in an effort to avoid calling attention to what was in fact a major theological issue, Mármol Carvajal reintroduced the precision of the Arabic: "Las alabanzas sean a Dios *sólo*, antes de lo que quiero decir," that is, insisting on divine singularity over trinity as would have been appropriate in an Islamic invocation.

This slight but significant difference indicates that Mármol Carvajal may have seen the original Arabic and corrected Castillo's translation by choosing a more literal formulation—"God and his unity"—which at the same time would have reflected the Islamic identity of its author, the *morisco* rebel Aben Aboo. Castillo's original choice could have been the result of a translation made in haste, but it was likely personally pragmatic. Mármol Carvajal's position as an "old Christian" with significant military service to the crown was less precarious than Castillo's as a *morisco*, and the latter would have had many incentives to produce a Spanish version that invited no potential criticism for anti-Trinitarian allusions.

Meanwhile, Mármol Carvajal also converted Castillo's singular second person verbs to plural (*vosotros* rather than *tu*). In this case, Castillo's translation was the more correct, since Aben Aboo also used the singular form, but Mármol Carvajal's translation converted the style to a more formal register of Spanish that was most common in letters between kings, and he also preferred the plural form of address in other Arabic translations that he published in his text (but for which there are no Arabic originals to compare).

These small changes created a literary device that domesticated the text of the rebel leader through translation.[126] These texts had already been produced in a situation of stark power difference, while they were channeled through and translated by the Spanish military and political institutions that drove back the rebels. Castillo's translation was a first means of domesticating these LSA texts into Spanish. Once he had furnished Mármol Carvajal with copies of his translation, a more enduring legacy of domestication became possible through print. Through this double transmission of the translation, Aben Aboo was made to speak using linguistic forms of subservience and respect to address the Spanish general who, as readers by that time knew, was to go on to defeat him.

In addition to primary-source quotations in translation, obtained via personal networks like the longstanding friendship between Castillo and Mármol Carvajal, the Alpujarras historiographers accessed Arabic texts and knowledge through much-mediated routes of transmission. Indeed, the well-known intertextuality of Alpujarras historiography should be understood in connection with practices of reading, transmission, and translation, including of Arabic sources and experience. For example, the information about properties and inheritance given in the testimony of the Ynfantes and the *romanceamientos* they generated as supporting evidence for their lawsuit found its way eventually into Mármol Carvajal's history of Granada. When describing the events of 1489, including the conquests of Baza and Guadix, Mármol Carvajal described how "their Majesties granted the rights (*merced*) to the regions (*taas* [*sic*]) of Órgiba and Jubelein to the *infantes* Ali and Acre [*sic*], sons of the king Abu al-Hasan and Zoraya, who became Christian and

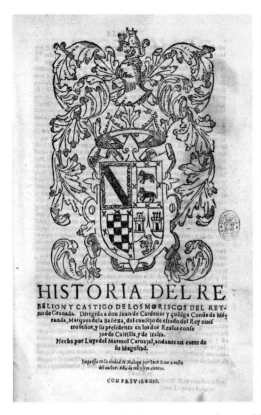

tuuiesen pena, porque el le tenia preso, y breuemente le soltaria. Muerto el Habaqui, Aben Aboo despachò a su hermano Hernando el Galipe a las sierras de Velez, y Ronda a que esforçasse la reducion, y animase a los que no se auian alçado para que se alçasen, y para dissimular mas escriuió luego a don Hernando de Barradas vna carta en letra Arabiga, que traduzida en nuestro romance Castellano dezia desta manera.

Carta de Aben Aboo a don Hernãdo de Barradas.

Las alabanças sean a Dios solo, antes de lo que quiero dezir, saluacion onrada al que onro el que da la onra, señor y amigo mio, el que yo mas estimo, don Hernando de Barradas, hago saber a vuestra honrada persona, que si quisieredes venir a veros conmigo verneys a vuestro proprio hermano y amigo muy seguramente, y lo que de mal os viniere sera sobre mi hazienda y fee, y si quisieredes tratar destas benditas pazes, lo que trataredes tratarlo eys conmigo, y hare yo todo lo que vos quisieredes con verdad, y sin traycion. Pareceme que el Habaqui de todo lo que hazia ninguna parte me daua, antes encubria de mi la verdad, porque todo lo que pidió lo aplicaua para si y para sus parientes y amigos. Esto hago saber a vuestra onrada persona, y conforme a ello podra hazer lo que le pareciere, y lo que viere que estara bien a los Christianos y a nosotros, y Dios permita este bien entre nosotros y que vuestra onrada persona sea causa dello, y perdonadme, que por no auer tenido quien me escriuiese no e es

LIBRO

crito antes de agora, la saluacion sea con nosotros, y la misericordia de Dios y su bendicion, que fue escrita día martes. A esta carta respondió luego don Hernando de Barradas que holgaria mucho de verse con el para efetuar el negocio de la reducion por la orden que dezia, y que le hiziese plazer de auisarle donde estaua el Habaqui, y lo que se auia hecho, y Aben Aboo le tornò a escriuir otra carta en Castellano del tenor siguiente.

Otra carta de Aben Aboo a don Hernãdo de Barradas.

Muy magnifico señor. La de vuestra merced recebi, y en quanto me embia a dezir por ella de la prissió del Habaqui, y si vuo causa para ella, digo que las causas que vuo para prenderle fueron estas que agora dire. La primera, que andaua engañando a vuestra merced y a mi, porque cosas que yo le dezia no las yua el a dezir alla, ni menos me daua parte delo que le hazia, ni que era lo que trataua, porque si yo le uiera dado mi sello, entendiera vuestra merced que yo lo sabia, y que passaria por lo que el hiziese, mas entendi que andaua engañando a vna parte y a otra, y halle luego tambien auia hecho vna barca para yrse con sus hijos a Berberia, y por estas razones, y otras lo tengo preso hasta que estas pazes se acaben de efetuar, y de mi parte ruego a vuestra merced las acabe, y que se apague este fuego para que le quite tanto mal, hecho esto yo lo soltare, y entienda vuestra merced que no tiene mal ninguno, porque si al presente estuuiera aqui cerca el escriuiera a vuestra merced de su mano. Vua

Figure 5. Manuscript translations like Alonso del Castillo's were used as historical documents in the earliest works of Alpujarras historiography. Mármol Carvajal, *Historia del rebelión*, libro 9, capítulo 10, f. 228v. © Biblioteca Nacional de España, R/51.

were called don Juan and don Hernando; and they possessed them until their Majesties took them away after the Alpujarras rebellion of 1493, awarding them in exchange an account with four-hundred thousand in bond income (*juro*) per year, the tenancy of the castle at Monleón, and the governorship of Galicia."[127] The rest of Mármol Carvajal's chapter is devoted to describing the parallel fortunes of this family and that of the Venegas.

Finally, the lasting marks of fiduciary translation as embodied by the *trujamán mayor*, don Alonso Venegas, can be seen clearly in the ur-text of Alpujarras historiography, Diego Hurtado de Mendoza's *Granada War, which King Philip II waged against the moriscos of that kingdom, its rebels* (1627).[128]

Though Hurtado de Mendoza's work was the last of the "eyewitness" histories to be printed, it was the first to be completed and it circulated widely in manuscript. Other Alpujarras authors, such as Juan Rufo, Mármol Carvajal, and Pérez de Hita, borrowed directly from the manuscript.[129] Like Mármol Carvajal, Hurtado Mendoza's history began with the history of Muslim Granada. He specified from the outset of his history that he had used Arabic sources from Granada ("los libros Arábigos de Granada") as well as those captured from the library of Muley Hacen of Tunez, probably during the campaign of 1535 in which his relative, Luis Hurtado de Mendoza, had participated.[130] Mármol Carvajal also claimed to have used *libros árabes*, in particular the work of one Aben Raxid. Pérez de Hita, meanwhile, in addition to the Arabic letters he reported, paid special attention to the Arabic inscriptions on objects that circulated through wartime capture, like a small tablet embossed with a short romantic verse and a tapestry inscribed with a verse referring to its depiction of a chained lion.[131] Pérez de Hita's eye for material detail gives another glimpse into the variety of media subject to Arabic translation in Granada, especially during the Alpujarras war, while also offering an example of incipient Arabic antiquarianism that would come to dominate Spanish history writing well into the seventeenth century. Underpinning the authenticity and narrative of all these works was the industry of fiduciary translation that had developed in Granada over the first part of the century.

Indeed, the collective and social aspect of Arabic translation as practiced in the first part of the "*morisco* century" left a strong mark on Alpujarras historiography. It is clear that Granada's translators and intermediaries were well known to Mármol Carvajal, who was even occasionally commissioned to perform Arabic translation, though he did not find great success in this activity. For example, in addition to the Aben Aboo letter, Mármol Carvajal included the text of several other Castillo translations, including other letters from Aben Aboo and from other *morisco* rebel leaders, as well as prophecies, which he translated as *ficciones* (fictions). Many familiar characters from Granada's world of translators are depicted throughout the *Historia del rebelión*, including Alonso del Castillo, Hernando de Barradas, various members of the Mora family, and Alonso de Granada Venegas, the grandson of Granada's original *trujamán mayor*.

Figures connected to the world of Arabic translation, like the Venegas, also used Hurtado de Mendoza's manuscript-in-circulation as a kind of palimpsest on which to inscribe accounts of their bravery and service into history. For example, in a 1619 manuscript copy of Hurtado de Mendoza's *Guerras de Granada*, the actions of both Alonso de Granada Venegas, grandson of don Alonso the first *trujamán mayor*, and Luis Fernández de Córdoba, son of the first Conde de Alcaudete and governor of Spanish Orán between 1518 and 1531 were described in marginal additions.[132] These marginal notations specify that certain "caballeros de Granada" mentioned in the text were in fact these men and their soldiers, and the margins also specify multiple instances when both Granada Venegas and Fernández de Córdoba served as wartime interpreters.[133] Because the information born by marginal notations in the pre-print 1619 copy did not make it into the 1627 print edition, this record of continued language service of both families faded from history. Nevertheless, that information certainly served an important purpose to the anonymous annotator and the men he described. In the absence of more information about the provenance of the Paris manuscript, it can only be speculated that whoever annotated the manuscript was connected to the Granada Venegas, who were in the midst of a campaign for social advancement in the early seventeenth century.[134]

That the Granada Venegas family would have had access to Hurtado de Mendoza's manuscript as it circulated in scribal publication is hardly surprising. He was well acquainted with the *morisco* family and even lived near them in the Generalife as a guest or tenant after his return to Granada in 1569, following the abrupt conclusion to his diplomatic and courtly career. In fact, he wrote the bulk of the *Guerras de Granada* while living in close proximity and regular contact with that family.[135]

Other Alpujarras authors also maintained personal connections to translators like Castillo or members of the bilingual elite like Granada Venegas. These social connections were also employed as "evidence" for the authenticity or legitimacy of the sources they used to write their histories. For example, all of the Alpujarras authors imagined conversations between rebel leaders or "transcribed" their speeches, given in Castilian but imagined in Arabic.[136] This technique, borrowed from classical models of history like Thucydides's "Pericles's Funeral Oration" and the dialogic models of renaissance humanist treatises, was hardly an innovation by the Alpujarras historiographers.[137] Nevertheless, combining purportedly reported speech through the lens of purported translation was an innovation in the way Arabic was used in Spanish literature that was based on models from legal documents and fiduciary translation. This innovation augured the later popularity of fictive translation in literature, as well as historical and doctrinal works, as discussed in the later chapters of this book.

Effectively, reporting speech functioned as an alternative strategy for incorporating Arabic source material and to guarantee authenticity and that of the text based upon those Arabic sources. These imagined speeches and conversations testified to real social relations that affected the course of the war. For example, Hurtado de Mendoza reported a speech made, in Arabic, by one of the *morisco* leaders, Fernando de Válor al-Ṣaghīr (el Çaguer or Aben Humeya in Spanish texts). This speech was purportedly the catalyst for setting off the rebellion when Válor claimed a litany of the injustices endured by *moriscos* under Spanish rule (including proscriptions about language use), and then claimed the title of king of Granada. Though he "recorded" it in his history, Hurtado de Mendoza was not in Granada when this episode supposedly took place. However, it seems that he had an informant who was there or otherwise had access to accurate information and was thus able to relay the content of the Arabic speech "translated" into Spanish. The scene has been corroborated by the transcription of the postwar interrogation of Brianda Pérez, the wife of al-Ṣaghīr's nephew, who described a similar scene in which rebels gathered in an important *morisco*'s Albaícin house.[138] According to Pérez's testimony, Fernando de Válor was declared the rebel king, describing the plan for the first attack, receiving kisses of loyalty from the men and women ready to follow him in to battle, and surrounded by silk banners and two books brought in, from whose "red and green and black letters" were read "cosas de moros."[139] Brianda reported that Spanish military authorities, who must have gotten wind of the plan, then arrived to confiscate Válor's money and supplies, causing him to flee to the house of none other than Pedro de Venegas. Whether or not Venegas was then Hurtado de Mendoza's informant for this episode, these interactions show that relationships, as much as language skill or experiences, underpinned the use of Arabic translation in Alpujarras historiography.

As a member of Granada's aristocratic elite who was well integrated into Castilian court society, Venegas did not publicly support the rebellion. As an acquaintance of one of the rebel leaders and the source of refuge immediately after the "coronation," however, Venegas may have been able to recount some of the scene, including to his neighbor Hurtado de Mendoza. Though Mármol Carvajal's much later account of Fernando de Válor's route to kingship follows more closely the events as recounted by Brianda to interrogators, Hurtado de Mendoza certainly had his sources.[140] The direct route of transmission cannot be confirmed, nor the sources from which he selected the ideas he put into al-Ṣaghīr's mouth, but reading across documents gives some idea how Arabic translation fueled an economy of information in conversation among Granada's elite, which was composed of both *moriscos* and "old Christians."

Indeed, as part of the literary circle that congregated around the Granada Venegas family, Pérez de Hita published the first volume of his *Civil Wars of Granada* in 1595. This first installment was a prose romance that told the fictionalized account of the dynastic and marital strife of the last Nasrid sultans of Granada against the backdrop of the final war with Castile, culminating in Boabdil's surrender to Ferdinand in 1492. Published in 1595, it was a product of the heyday of the late sixteenth-century "moorish novel," a genre that began to flourish a century after the final conquest of the Muslims in Granada.[141] Though it dealt with historical events of relatively recent memory, it was a work of fiction, a status ambivalently underscored by Pérez de Hita's claim to have discovered and translated an unknown Arabic manuscript history, auguring Cervantes's later use of the same device. The second installment of Pérez de Hita's *Civil Wars of Granada*, however, was a real "true history" of the second Alpujarras war.[142] This volume was neither a novel nor a translation (false or otherwise), although some passages were borrowed from other Alpujarras texts such as those of Mármol Carvajal and Hurtado de Mendoza. Published only in 1619, it was Pérez de Hita's own eyewitness account of the Alpujarras war, written as a response to Philip III's expulsion policy, which had begun to take effect in 1609.[143] Like Mármol Carjaval, Pérez de Hita also transcribed full texts of Arabic letters, including from Ottoman rulers in Istanbul and Algiers and from the Moroccan sultan. It is not clear if these letters are related to real texts. If so, they are several stages removed from the original translation. Pérez de Hita's second volume also includes his "translations" of the inscriptions on material and visual objects that circulated as booty or propaganda, including an embossed panel and a painted shield with Aben Humeya's coat of arms: a red lion chained by a Muslim woman, upon a green field (highly significant iconography). In both cases the translations are short romantic odes to a beautiful woman.[144] Pérez de Hita—by trade a shoemaker and designer of elaborate carts used in public festivals, as well as an author of chivalric romances—had an eye for the details of material culture, which at the same time provides an important counterpoint to the other uses of Arabic translation. His case shows that media of translation were clearly far more varied and widely consumed than shown by evidence from the archives of state power.

Whether textual or material, translating Arabic sources to bolster historical and legal arguments related to Spanish sovereignty and identity would become especially important in the final decades of the sixteenth century and into the seventeenth, as will be analyzed in Chapter 5. The foundations of fiduciary translation in *morisco* Granada were based in the work of experts whose work was performative, generative, and fiduciary across diverse institutional settings. That is, translators produced texts and information that were authoritative by virtue of the translator's discursive signals and social status as a trustworthy (*fidedigno*) expert. Although many individual Arabic speakers were subject to restrictive linguistic and cultural policies and to ambivalent attitudes about their Arabic knowledge, many Arabic translators became fiduciaries, who guaranteed the credible transmission of information that could then have a probative effect before the state and other political and religious institutions.

The social reality of translation among Spanish *moriscos* thus shaped the writing of the post-1570s vogue for histories of their present—for which language politics was a key motive and agenda—and their use of Arabic translation with the discourse of "faithfulness" to assure readers of the authenticity of the history. Generations of translation by this time had shaped Late Spanish Arabic and the use of Arabic translation in all kinds of Spanish texts. By the seventeenth century, the *idea* of the translated Arabic text as an authoritative source for Spanish history had been become a literary trope most famously represented by Cervantes's conceit that *Don Quixote* is a translation from the Arabic history of Cidi Hamete Benengeli. However, the effect of long-standing Arabic legal translation practices first on the Arabic language and then on the writing of Spanish historical and other texts was political, and, ultimately, terribly personal. New markets for Arabic translation came to shape competing discourses around the question of whether *moriscos* could be loyal Spanish subjects. Those competing discourses were articulated in terms of language, religion, and history and sought to define identities that were politically intelligible with respect to the Spanish state. The anti-Arabic policies of the early sixteenth century were ultimately reified into language ideologies with devastating effect on hundreds of thousands of Spanish subjects by that century's close.[145] Similarly, the same fiduciary translation that converted Islamic law into Spanish helped underpin justifications for the mass expulsion of *moriscos* between 1609 and 1614. Before that terrible conclusion, however, the practices of fiduciary translation were harnessed and deployed by Arabic speakers working between Spain and North Africa.

Chapter 2

Families in Translation: Spanish Presidios and Mediterranean Information Networks

The tactics that generated Spanish legal instruments and that were based on the social recognition of expertise in Arabic and Islamic law also contributed to the credibility of and opportunities for new generations of translators in Spain's Mediterranean outposts. In Spanish North African garrisons, the social underpinnings of fiduciary translation were transformed into assets through mechanisms analogous to those that ensured the transitivity of legal authority through official translation (*traducción fehaciente*) in Granada. Such assets, in the form of social and sometimes economic capital, were transmitted through institutional and family structures. This chapter traces how the transmission of skills, offices, and authority that were related to fiduciary translation functioned on the outposts of Spain's Mediterranean frontier in the early modern period.[1]

Arabic Fidelities in the Founding of Spanish Presidios, 1497–1535

By the sixteenth century, the Mediterranean was an ancient site of multi-lingualism, language contact, and translation between Arabic- and Romance-speaking powers, institutions, and their agents.[2] Throughout the late Trastámara Reconquista project in Granada (1482–1492), the Castilian monarchs maintained trade and diplomatic relationships with Arabic-speaking Muslim sovereigns and their agents across the Mediterranean.[3] The Catholic Kings continued commercial and diplomatic relationships across the

Mediterranean, from Egypt in the east to Tlemecen across the Strait of Gibraltar, and inaugurated a chain of conquests to establish Spanish garrisons along the North African coast.[4] Their Habsburg successors extended these practices through the end of the seventeenth century, as would the Bourbons after them.

The Spanish presence in North Africa was characterized by a chain of disparate military garrisons, generally headed by a member of the Andalusian nobility.[5] Within a decade of Habsburg ascension, the Orán presidio shifted from being a dedicated military garrison and stopover in the postal and commercial networks that crisscrossed the Mediterranean to becoming a Castilian town, albeit one that never lost its rough military character, complete with royal charter (*fuero*) and a head interpreter (*trujamán mayor*) who oversaw its port in nearby Mazalquivir.[6] These extensions of Spanish administration into North Africa created Mediterranean-wide information networks sustained by translator dynasties whose experiences in fiduciary translation were passed on from generation to generation into the eighteenth century.

Beyond dynastic politics, Iberian garrisons became a forum for diverse formal and informal translation activities performed in a range of sites and institutions. In contrast with those in the *morisco* areas in Granada and Valencia, most records of Arabic-Spanish translation in the North African presidios reflect the oral and ephemeral nature of translation in military, commercial, or political settings. Unlike in the courts and councils of *morisco* Spain, in the presidios the creation of legal instruments through written translation was the exception rather than the rule. Most agreements negotiated between the presidio leadership and local tribes were concluded orally and can only be traced in the Spanish reports sent to the crown or as they appear represented in other correspondence, chronicles, or other narrative sources, including captivity accounts. Of course, the primary institutional sites of written translation activity in Granada—the municipal council, the Royal Appellate Court, the bishop's courts, notarial cabinets, etc.—were also spaces in which oral translation occurred on a regular basis, and this orality left marks in the written record, including the translation of votes made in the council, inventories calculated by tax collectors, witness accounts, and notarized agreements. Likewise, in the presidios, town councils and courts were sites of multilingualism and translation. The demography and political organization of these communities—as military outposts with a small Spanish staff and a large sphere of influence over Arabic-speaking

hinterlands and that provided provisions and security—meant that the bulk
of presidio translation took place "in the field" rather than in institutions of
government, even if it is from the archives of those institutions that traces
of the ephemeral translation are drawn.

Spain's presidio translators played a vital role, often quite literally, in
running the garrisons and the supply, information, and defensive networks
they constituted. The "forgotten frontier" of the Iberian outposts demar-
cated a complex geopolitical arena, with local, imperial, religious, and commercial interests in constant flux and competition.[7] In that arena, translators
simultaneously created and crossed new frontiers in Spanish North Africa at
the same time that they ensured a continuity of administrative practice and
sometimes personnel from Iberian to African settings.

To understand these dynamics, this chapter focuses on the Spanish
Arabic translators of Orán—the largest and one of the longest-lasting Spanish presidios and the one that most came to resemble a traditional Castilian
town—and concludes with additional evidence and discussion about the
functioning of inter-presidio information networks. The theorization of the
office of the Arabic interpreter took place during moments of public conflict
that attracted the attention of the crown or its representatives as they determined who the right officeholder should be based on ever more clearly
defined professional categories and institutions. In these episodes, the qualities and qualifications of specific interpreters were called into question, and
expectations of literacy, fidelity, and experience were articulated. Interpreters (re)established their legitimacy through declarations of personal and
family merit, including service, skill, trustworthiness (*fiel, fidedigno*), and
heritage. These claims were supported by testimony from members of the
community, and sometimes even past and current governors of Orán. This
process of losing, requesting, proving, and gaining or being denied legitimacy as the royal translator was constitutive of fiduciary translation. Unlike
the official translations produced in Granada, fiduciary translation in the
presidios was conducted via reports and memoirs through which imperial
officials communicated about their service to the crown. These reports,
whose ultimate audience was the king, were one forum in which professional categories and characteristics were developed. Meanwhile the social
conduits along which such reports traveled (and which they reflected) and
the editorial spaces they eventually occupied allowed translators to manage
fidelities and patronage across overlapping royal, noble, and municipal jurisdictions and institutions.

Like their colleagues in Granada, official appointments often depended on patronage, while at the same time the translator needed to be deeply embedded in local networks of influence and information. Both patron and local connections were often achieved through family service, reputation, or connections. Since much of the presidio population was bilingual with Spanish, qualified and reliable bilingual officials were primarily needed to manage the presidio's relationships with its hinterlands and foreign merchants or other visitors rather than running government institutions.[8] The former task fell to experienced intermediaries, including Jewish and *morisco* translator families along with so-called "old Christian" families. Eventually Philip II decreed that Orán should employ two interpreters, one Christian and one Jewish.[9] Though their work did not generate the paperwork and legal instruments of *traducción fehaciente,* reading and writing were crucial skills for presidio interpreters. They translated received and intercepted correspondence, as well as writing their own correspondence to their networks of informants in Arabic, Castilian, and Hebrew and their reports in Spanish for the presidio governors and the crown. Translators aided in diplomatic missions, negotiated and liaised with surrounding kingdoms and tribal territories, and maintained a vigorous network of informants, reporting on this ephemeral translation and oral interpretation in official reports and other correspondence. The translator was also in charge of composing the Arabic translations of peace treaties and bilingual passports for safe conduct.

Like many other officials throughout the Spanish monarchy, including the *romançeadores* of Granada, titles and appointments were handed down among family members. For the families of Arabic interpreters in Orán, the pressures to maintain family control over a given office increased, as did competition for that control. Translators and their supporters solved this problem by developing powerful connections that gave them access to public fora (including print markets) in which they could elaborate a discourse of reputation and legitimacy that became inheritable cultural and linguistic capital. That capital, as much as financial capital and the local social capital of varied ethnic and socioeconomic groups, was passed from generation to generation. Discourses of fidelity, service, and skill developed around the Orán translation posts, like the fiduciary discourses and *traducción fehaciente* that had developed in Granada, effectively extending the phenomenon of fiduciary translation across the Mediterranean and into a wider political and social arena.

Translating Conflict: Lawsuits and Reputation Campaigns

As is often the case, the workings (practical and theoretical) of the office of translator in Orán are particularly visible to historians in moments of crisis or conflict that generated a paper trail. Such moments include lawsuits, contentious appointments, and the smear or propaganda campaigns of professional competition in gossip and print. The debates and descriptions of translators and their work in those settings were also opportunities to refine the expectations and professional vocabulary connected to the office, and later generations of translators and their employers relied on many of the same documents that eventually interested modern historians. In the case of the Arabic translators of Spanish Orán, those documents are evidence of the workings of fiduciary translation.

Litigating Translation: Orán's Port Translators, 1512–1533

This extension of Castilian institutions across the Mediterranean included fiduciary translation adapted to a new context. The adaptations were also based on Iberian precedent as well as local experiences. Many different agents facilitated contact between the Iberians and North African communities, including Iberian Jews who had emigrated to neighboring Tlemecen after the 1492 expulsion. In 1512, Sephardic families from Tlemecen were invited to Orán with special permission to reside there and work as Arabic interpreters for the Spanish crown.[10] However, interpreters had been working in Orán since its conquest in 1509 and in neighboring Mazalquivir since its conquest in 1505. For example, in 1508 Ferdinand appointed Miguel de Almenara as the "interpreter of the cities and towns and the locales of the North African Muslims who reside in the borderlands of the town and fortress of Mazalquivir."[11] Almenara already had a record in Ferdinand's service as the Aragonese consul in Orán and Tremeçen and was given his title as interpreter because of the services rendered "en los tratos que ha havido con los moros de allende" (the dealings which have taken place with the North African Muslims).[12] In February 1512, he became one of the *jurados* (nonvoting town councilmen) of the Orán city council.

Another new *jurado* in 1512 was Gonzálo de Alcántara, a Christian lanceman who had participated in the conquest of Orán in the troops of the presidio's eventual first governor, Diego Fernández de Córdoba, the first Marquis of Comares and the Alcaide de las Donceles (a hereditary military honor held by the Fernández de Córdoba family since the fourteenth century).[13] Gonzálo intervened frequently as *lengua* in treaty negotiations with local powers between 1509 and into the 1530s. In 1518 he was put in charge of interrogating Arabic-speaking captives in Orán.[14] Gonzálo may have been related to other bilingual soldiers, like Juan de Alcántara, "now calling himself Yahya," who worked alongside Gonzálo as an interpreter in the 1535 treaty negotiated between the king of Tlemecen and the new governor of Orán.[15] Meanwhile, Gonzálo de Alcántara was taken prisoner by the king of Tlemecen in 1536, but because both sides determined that he had greater value as a free agent, he was eventually released to Orán to continue his military and linguistic service.[16] Alcántara and Almenara, official translators, were thus among the city's first town councilmen, all of whom had been named by the Catholic Kings in 1512 in reward for serviced rendered in the "guerra de los moros de africa enemygos de nuestra santa de catolica" (war against the African Muslims who are the enemies of our holy Catholic faith).[17]

In 1512, Queen Juana appointed as the first official translator of Orán her royal treasurer, Francisco de Vargas.[18] Like the *trujamanía* granted to Alonso Venegas in 1494, Vargas was expected to uphold the office as in "Muslim times" (*tiempo de moros.*)[19] However, Francisco de Vargas was the head of the royal treasury (*tesorero general*)—effectively the chief finance minister—and a resident of Valladolid, five hundred miles away from Orán in the center of the Castilian plateau.[20] Appointing a highly ranked fiscal minister as *trujamán* and *intérprete* of far-off North African presidios was no caprice on the part of the "mad queen."[21] As had been the case on the Castilian-Granadan frontier and during the resettlement of conquered Granada, the role of the fiscal manager and the bilingual intermediary went hand in hand. Vargas was one of the most famous and wealthiest ministers in Charles V's government and one of the key financial managers of the Orán expedition and subsequent provisioning.[22] Nevertheless, he was obviously unqualified to act as Orán's Arabic interpreter, both by virtue of lacking the requisite skills and by the fact that he did not reside in the presidio. Miguel de Almenara, interpreter of Mazalquivir and *jurado* of Orán, instead inhabited Vargas's *officium* as translator in Orán.[23]

As was common practice among high-ranking officials who held more *officia* than they could possibly exercise, it was incumbent upon Vargas to staff the position with an appropriate agent.[24] Almenara was paid 30,000 *maravedíes* per year from Vargas's salary.[25] Vargas himself confirmed Almenara as his *tenyente* (lieutenant) on April 5, 1512.[26] Despite Juana's reservations, that "only you and *not* Miguel de Almenara or others can benefit from the office of interpreter," it was most expedient for Vargas to delegate to the experienced consul and interpreter. Bilingual officials worked alongside other scribes and notaries who must have been called on to engage with translation, including the *escribano de los diezmos e aduanas dela çibdad de Orán*, an office occupied first by Lorenço de Abedano from 1512 to 1534[27] and then the *regidor* Pedro García Camarón after 1534;[28] or the *notario mayor de las cibdades de Orán e Melilla e de las villas de Maalquivir e Caçaça*, Francisco Zapata, who was appointed in 1512[29]; and the *escribano mayor de las rentas de Orán*, Pedro de Velasco.[30]

In the words of Emilio Sola, "In the sixteenth century, the socioeconomic world of the medieval Andalusian frontier seemed to expand across the Mediterranean."[31] The contest over who should hold the *officium* of translator and, more important, who should receive its *beneficium*, became the subject of a multi-decade conflict among distinct constituencies in Orán, reflecting traditional Iberian conflicts between royal, noble, and municipal jurisdictions that had been transplanted to the North African presidios, just as they had been transplanted to Granada. In 1533, a lawsuit was registered by Orán's town council against its port translators, including Miguel de Almenara. The lawsuit reveals a closely knit cohort at the port. For example, the defense witnesses were a roll call of North African fiduciary translation, including Almenara. Along with the merchants' legal representative (*procurador*), Francisco de Madrid, who worked as a translator in various treaty negotiations with Tlemecen, all the defense witnesses had direct links to the world of interpreting and diplomacy. The *jurado* Luis de Hernández and a Muslim ambassador from the neighboring kingdom of Tremeçen were both called as witnesses for Onate and Hernández's defense.[32] The ambassador was most likely the *alcaide* Baudila ('Abd Allah) ben Bogani, the same ambassador who had negotiated a new treaty between Charles V and the king of Tlemecen in March 1533.[33] From among the municipal elites, Pedro García Camarón, *escribano de la aduana* (the scribal notary at the customs house), was called to speak in favor of Onate and Hernández.[34]

Meanwhile, for the prosecution, Diego's eighteen witnesses also represented the multilingual administration of Orán. The first five witnesses were neighboring Muslims, and all provided their evidence via "capitán Gonzalo de alcantara ynterprete," the trusted municipal and military intermediary referred to above.[35] The fifth Muslim witness, Mahamet el Fistelí, *xeque* (sheikh, ruler) of Mazalquivir, shared his name with a prominent *mudéjar* interpreter in Málaga. The next seven witnesses were Jews, all *moradores* of Orán (residents, though without the status of *vecino*). None of these individuals needed an interpreter, and, in fact, at least two, Jacob Alegre and Salomón Ternero, were employed as multilingual messengers across North Africa between 1529 and 1531.[36] The last seven witnesses were Christians, among them one Juan de la Para, whose occupation was listed as "lengua vesino dela dicha çibdad de Orán" (interpreter and resident of the aforementioned city of Orán), and also the abovementioned interpreter, Gonzálo de Alcántara.[37] In this single lawsuit, nearly all the known figures associated with Spanish translation and interpreting in North Africa gathered to give testimony about the office of the port interpreter.

This lawsuit is representative of the ways in which translators in Orán were essential for the running of the port as a major commercial center of Mediterranean trade in addition to their roles in the provisioning and security of the presido. In 1525, Charles V ordered that "all merchandise destined for Algiers or any other place in the land of the *moros*" had to make an obligatory stop in Orán.[38] Any position that controlled this now-bottlenecked trade, like a port translator, would have had an enormous potential for profit. In 1532, when the War Council (*consejo de guerra*) confirmed that Orán was the only legitimate port for commerce with North Africa, the competition for offices that controlled this commerce seems to have intensified.

So it was that, in early 1533, based on reported abuse of the office in Orán and the Kingdom of Tlemecen, one of the *jurados* on the Orán city council, Diego de Castillo, brought a suit against the port interpreters of Orán.[39] As a royal appointment, the post of *trujamán mayor* was overseen by the crown's administrative apparatus, so that complaints or adjustments were first submitted to the Real Chancillería in Granada before reaching the monarchs if higher adjudication was needed.[40] In February 1533, when the lawsuit began, Miguel de Almenara continued to receive a salary related to this position, although in principle it was the *comendador* Diego de Vargas, son of Francisco, who was the titular *intérprete*, having inherited the position from his father in 1521.[41] Charles granted Diego the same *beneficia* that his father and "the other *trujamanes* who worked previously in Orán and the kingdom of Tremecen" enjoyed.[42] Those "other *trujamanes*" included Miguel de Almenara. In 1531, now registered as a *vecino* of the interior Iberian community of Baza rather than of coastal Almería or even Orán, Almenara requested and was granted an official copy of his legitimate appointment as Vargas's deputy for the broadly conceived "office of the interpreter of the towns and villages and other places that are on the North African frontier."[43]

Though Vargas held the royal *officium* and Almenara was his official lieutenant, by 1533 two merchants named Miguel de Onate and Alvaro Hernández actually performed the office, claiming that they did so with the authorization (*poder*) of Diego de Vargas.[44] Whatever the circumstances of this second delegation, the resulting lawsuit is a window into the developing professional expectations and qualifications of the office of Arabic translator and into the significance of the position to royal, municipal, and individual commercial interests operating in Spanish Orán at the beginning of the sixteenth century.

According to the Oranese alderman (and Almenara's colleague on the city council) Diego de Castillo, the delegates Miguel de Onate and Alvaro Hernández were guilty of a number of abuses of their position. These agents had set themselves up in the port of Tlemecen with a group of enforcers (*guardas*) who harassed Jewish and Muslim merchants. The poorly treated Muslim and Jewish merchants "swore to never return to conduct business in this city," a threat that would have had serious financial consequences for Orán's livelihood, to say nothing of the royal fisc. Alderman Castillo portrayed this issue as potential damage to Spain itself, especially considering the structure of the trade embargoes at that time in the Mediterranean: "Your Majesty receives only harm and prejudice against the royal rents."[45]

As port translators with the authority to broker both linguistic and commercial exchanges, Onate and Hernández obliged all of the Jewish and Muslim traders who came to port to register their goods and merchandise. They charged a fee for this required registration, claiming that such payment was part of their rights (*derechos*) and salaries as those who held the *poder* to carry out Vargas's royal appointment as *trujamán*.[46] However, Castillo and his witnesses countered that the *trujamanes* had no such right because the office was predicated on the traditions from "tiempo de moros" (the era of Muslim rule) and previous *trujamanes* had held no such lucrative privilege.[47] To add literal insult to financial injury, Onate and Hernández were accused of mistreating the Jewish and Muslim traders "by word and deed."[48] Abusing or coercing Jewish and Muslim merchants was explicitly prohibited in the international treaties signed between Charles and the king of Tlemecen in 1521.[49] This meant that the dockside quarrels among municipal and royal officials jockeying for position at the edge of Spain's

Mediterranean empire had the potential to set off an international diplomatic incident.[50] In addition, many complained that neither Onate nor Hernández could speak or understand Arabic.[51]

Local contention among professional rivals at the customs house became an opportunity for Orán to articulate its own municipal privileges against the bad behavior of two nominal royal officials. The Orán alderman also protested on the administrative technicality that the royally granted right to collect these fees, which Onate and Hernández claimed to enjoy, had never been presented in writing to the town council.[52] The outcome of this dispute was a lawsuit that was tried first in Orán. This suit was quickly decided in favor of Diego de Castillo, a coup for the local administration, but Onate and Hernández brought an immediate appeal to the Real Chancillería in Granada (in whose archives the trial records have been preserved), which they won in early 1537.

The main complaints issued by Diego de Castillo about Onate and Hernández concerned the improper levying of fees on trade goods, the physical and verbal abuse of the Muslim and Jewish traders, and the inconvenience of *trujamanes* and *intérpretes* who did not know any Arabic. However, the lawsuit and the debates about translators represented far more than whether two unqualified agents had overstepped their boundaries. Diego de Castillo undertook the lawsuit in the name of the city of Orán, as a member of the city council, against abuses committed by agents who were, ultimately, royal appointees. The key to understanding what was really at stake in this lawsuit was revealed in the last questions of Castillo's *interrogatorio* (questionnaire). The first nine out of fifteen questions dealt directly with the abuses allegedly committed by Onate and Hernández, but in question 9, Castillo states baldly that "the aforementioned right of *trujamanería* is in contravention of the liberties and local enfranchisement that had been granted to the city."[53] That is, even if Onate and Hernández had performed their duties as they should have, they were still in violation of the local rights that had been granted by Charles in 1525.

There was an important fiduciary aspect to the work of the port translator in addition to his work brokering among languages. According to Diego de Castillo, the primary function of the *trujamán* in "Muslim times" was to translate contractual terms between merchants both in language and in merchandise. That is, the *trujamán* could help a Muslim merchant and a Christian merchant talk to one another, but he was principally the agent in charge of assessing goods and transactions to make sure that terms were fair. According to Castillo's testimony, these two kinds of "translation"—commercial and linguistic—were the work for which the Orán *trujamán* was paid on commission, rather than a fixed salary based on a royal appointment.[54] This was an argument that attempted to loosen the nominally royal character of the appointment, which explains the success of the defendants in their appeal to the Granada Appellate Court in 1537. The crown may not have been particularly interested in Onate and Hernández or their activities, but it wished to ensure that the rights of royal appointees were upheld.

What was truly at stake was the balance of power between the city's "republican" powers (the term *res publica* appeared frequently in Castillo's arguments) and the jurisdiction of royally appointed officials in the presidio.[55] Wanting to simultaneously assert Orán's municipal privileges and knit the city into imperial networks, Castillo explained what could happen if Charles would intervene on the city's behalf: "If Your Majesty orders that the such rights not be collected in the manner in which they have been collected until the present [that is, falsely, by Onate and Hernández] he will be well served as will be this city and its public good (*res publica*) and all the other individuals who live there and conduct business there will receive great benefits." The position of Arabic interpreter became the site of this contention between local and central powers on the newly forged frontier. This lawsuit was an early example of how the position of Arabic interpreter in Orán would become a point of conflict between royal, noble, and municipal powers.

Treason by Translation: Rescuing Credibility and Reputation Across the Forgotten Frontier, 1555–1593

The Spanish translators in North Africa played an important social and political role in the administration of empire across the Mediterranean, which eventually extended far beyond port transactions. Certainly, ad hoc translations were performed as needed by the peripatetic merchants, friars, captives, renegades, and soldiers who constantly traversed the Mediterranean—as was indeed also the case across the Atlantic and Indian Ocean worlds at the same time[56]—but certain registers of translation had to be protected by ever-stronger bureaucratic and state institutions. Translation eventually came to underpin reputations and other fiduciary qualities, including those of the Spanish king himself. For this reason, important commissions required that the interpreting staff be selected from the noble and military elite, as had also been the case in post-conquest Granada. For example, Gonzálo Fernández de Córdoba (1453–1515), *alcaide* (military leader) of Illora and later Gran Capitán, actually drew up the Arabic capitulations for Granada in 1491 with the help of an interpreter named Simuel (possibly Habenatahuel, one of the Nasrid *trujamanes mayores*). Gonzálo's nephew, Diego Hernández de Córdoba, also contributed important military service in the Granada war and in the conquests of Mazalquivir and Orán, becoming the first governor of the presidio. Diego's son, Luis Hernández de Córdoba, became governor after him and was actively involved in bilingual diplomacy, serving as the interpreter in the 1533 negotiations he hosted on his Andalusian estate with the king of Tremeçen.[57] The third governor of Orán, Martín de Córdoba y de Velasco, the brother-in-law of the previous governor Luis Fernández de Córdoba, all but conducted his own diplomacy with the local chiefs.[58] This model of presidio diplomacy—whereby the governor ran a team of interpreters, intermediaries, and informants who answered first to the nobleman, who then mediated strategic information in his own reports back to the royal court—was followed for many years in Orán. This style of administration eventually led to friction in the mid-seventeenth century between "king's men" and "governor's men" among the translators.[59]

The position of Arabic translator in the North African presidios was thus an important and highly visible political office. Indeed, in some Spanish North African territories, governors performed their own translation work. In some cases, like that of Alvar Gómez de Orozco, el Zagal, the *alcaide* or military commander of Bône, conducted negotiations because of his Arabic skills.[60] Alvar Gómez knew that using his language skills officially would yield a reward from the royal administration, and in 1537 he asked to be paid for his work as *intérprete de la lengua arauiga,* among other *mercedes* (rewards), including that his son be made a page in the royal household.[61] In many local negotiations, the fact that that the royal representative was the same person as the principal negotiator, and that he knew Arabic, eschewed the need for official translations of the kind required by the Real Chancillería in Granada. These translators nevertheless acted in habitually fiduciary roles when negotiating contact, collaboration, and conflict on the frontier.

At the end of the fifteenth and early sixteenth century, bilingualism was common among Spain's warrior nobility, many of whom had cut their teeth raiding along the Granada-Castile border or in the Granada or North African campaigns at the turn of the century, and for whom Arabic knowledge and the tasks of waging war would have gone hand in hand. These generations of frontier aristocracy would prove to be the last in a long tradition of aristocratic multilingualism, and there is no evidence that Martín de Córdoba y de Velasco acted as interpreter while governor of Orán, even if his uncle and cousin had done so when governing before him. Nonetheless, a trusted and, ideally, high-status representative was needed to conduct the local and international diplomatic relations that sustained the presidio system. For this work, Martín depended on a military captain named Gonzálo Hernández.

Hernández was in many ways the ideal person for the job, because he literally embodied both Spanish and North African nobility. His grandfather was a Zayyanid aristocrat from Tlemecen who helped broker the surrender of Orán to the Gran Capitan Gonzálo Fernández de Córdoba in 1509. Shortly thereafter, the son of that aristocrat converted to Christianity with the name Francisco Hernández (probably in honor of the Fernández de Córdoba) and married an anonymous noble Christian woman (*una Cristiana hidalga*) who was herself a member of the Fernández de Córdoba family.[62] Thus Gonzálo was the relative of Tlemeceni and Spanish aristocrats, including the governor of Orán, a count who referred to the translator repeatedly as a relative (*pariente*) in his correspondence with the royal court. He referred to his own brother-in-law, Luis Fernández de Córdoba, the Marquis of Comares, as Gonzálo Hernández's father-in-law (*suegro*). In addition to these ties to local aristocracy, Hernández also held important status in the municipal community of Orán as a councilman. Named as a *jurado* in October of 1534, he received the position when his relative Luis Fernández de Córdoba renounced it in his favor before leaving his post as *capitán general* of the presidio and to make way for don Martin de Córdoba y Velasco, the Count of Alcaudete.[63] Gonzálo Hernández thus joined several other translators who were members of the Orán municipal council, including Miguel de Almenara and Gonzálo de Alcántara, and continued to work collaboratively on translation tasks with those men and others.[64]

Gonzálo Hernández acted as Martín de Córdoba's official Arabic translator until the governor's death in 1558. From this position Hernández played a starring role in the "reputation games" of Spain's North African presidios.[65] During this time, he was the count-governor's favorite emissary, due to his skill and service as well as his family connections. Despite this patronage, Gonzálo ran into problems with other Spanish officials when negotiating a royal appointment as translator and Spanish representative to the Moroccan

Figure 6. Treaty articles stipulated by the last Waṭṭasid Moroccan
sultan, Muḥammad al-Shaykh, in the proposed anti-Ottoman
alliance with the Spaniards to attack Algiers (1557). © España.
Ministerio de la Cultura y Deporte. Archivo General
de Simancas, GYM, LEG, 1318, 88, f. 1r.

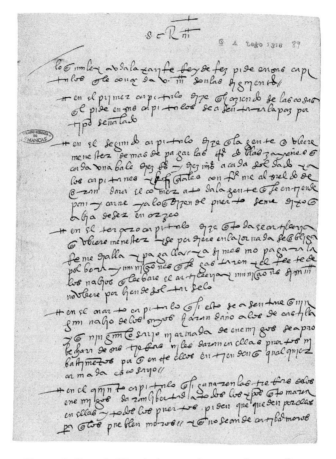

Figure 7. Gonzalo Hernández translation and report from
1557 embassy to Moroccan sharīf. On the verso, Hernández
included additional information, "lo que se me dixo de palabra
que no se puso en los capitulos." © España. Ministerio
de la Cultura y Deporte. Archivo General de Simancas,
GYM, LEG, 1318, 89, f. 1r–v.

sultan, who knew him personally and also trusted him. Although Gonzálo
was ultimately vindicated and re-adopted into Spanish administration as a
valuable agent (even ransomed at one point by Philip II himself), the documents reflecting the debates over his appointment reveal a good deal
about the contested status of Arabic translators within the Spanish imperial

system, and how the position of translator and the discourses of fidelity, credit, and confidence that were connected to linguistic service were used to create, contest, or transmit reputation as a tangible asset for translators and their family members.

In 1555, Gonzálo was denied permission by the Spanish regency court to travel to Fez as Charles V's representative. The object of the mission was to establish an anti-Ottoman alliance with the new ruler of Morocco, Muḥammad al-Shaykh (1490–1557), who had requested that Gonzálo personally be sent to conduct the Hispano-Moroccan negotiations. Gonzálo's candidacy was rejected on the recommendation of Antonio Galíndez de Carvajal, who had been sent to Orán as a royal representative to conduct a regular review of the count's government (*visita*). Neither man appreciated the other, and one avenue that Galíndez de Carvajal pursued to damage the count's reputation was attacking the reputation of his *morisco* relative and interpreter and even restricting the latter's powers and movements. Indeed, as Hernández was ready to set sail for the Moroccan mission, Galíndez de Carvajal stopped the ship's departure at the last minute and hauled Hernández off to jail.[66]

While the governor wrote furiously to the court to have his interpreter released, Hernández remained imprisoned, and Martín de Córdoba sent to Fez the Jewish agent Jacob Cansino and another agent, Miguel Lazcano, who negotiated for several months before leaving without coming to an agreement. Meanwhile, in May, at exactly the same time that the Oranese translators Lazcano and Cansino arrived in Fez, a shipment of mail arrived in Orán by way of Ottoman-controlled Algiers, bringing once again to the fore the problem of trust and translation. Among the letters carried by the Jewish and Muslim passengers, two were intercepted, causing suspicion that some travelers were Ottoman agents. Although a preliminary translation was done by the slave of a resident of Orán, the governor required a more official translation before reporting the evidence to the crown.[67] In an attempt to rehabilitate his interpreter, Gonzálo Hernández—who was also his great nephew-in-law—Martin wrote to the royal court describing the incident and the need for an official translation by a sanctioned translator, that is, someone with the fiduciary qualifications to ensure the translation. Gonzálo was still imprisoned, and so the governor requested a special license for Hernández to make a translation and to interrogate the prisoners captured with the letters. Although there were doubtless additional members of the Cansino family in Orán at the time who could have performed the office, the Count of Alcaudete was anxious to reinstate his relative as a legitimate bilingual agent of the crown and so pled on Gonzálo's behalf that he be given the commission.

Martín advocated for Gonzálo first and foremost using evidence of his experience with confidential matters, in which the latter had displayed both skill and trustworthiness. His qualities as a skilled linguist and trustworthy man (*hombre de confiança*) are repeated throughout the memorial. With casual anti-semitism, the governor even went so far as to say that Gonzálo would be a more reliable choice than the absent Jacob Cansino, who was characterized only as *el judío*, although he reassured his audience that Jacob—currently on an official diplomatic mission—was a perfectly reliable fiduciary translator: "a seruido fielmente" (he served loyally).[68] The count then gave a detailed outline of Gonzálo's parentage on the Muslim side, emphasizing the crucial role of the latter's ancestors in facilitating the transfer of the city to the conquering Cardinal Cisneros and insisting on Gonzálo's relation to a lineage of reliable and effective intermediaries. The governor pointed out that both Gonzálo's grandfather and father had married into Christian families following the conquest and that the father had converted and served the king of Spain as an officer in Orán.[69]

Gonzálo regained royal favor, and he was eventually sent as the royal representative to Morocco once the question was turned over to Philip II in 1556. In 1557 Gonzálo spent the better part of a year negotiating in Fez, reaching an agreement with the Moroccan ruler that would later fall through. Gonzálo then traveled to the Spanish court and gave his report orally and in writing to the regent, Philip's sister Juana (see Figures 6 and 7).[70] This report is a valuable counterpoint to the count's letters of recommendation and shows how Gonzálo fashioned his own reputation through descriptions of his service and fidelity. Though the style of the report is reserved, he made clear his own protagonism and the of his value in service to the monarchy, declaring that "everyone in Ceuta told me that my arrival is the best thing that could have happened."[71] Gonzálo's report reveals fascinating features of how the Moroccan negotiations were conducted and how Gonzálo translated them back to the Spanish court. For example, when enumerating the clauses of the anti-Ottoman agreement to which the Moroccan sultan had agreed, Gonzálo explained that the sultan "told me orally what he did not put in the articles" (*se me dixo de palabra, que no puso en los capítulos*).[72] Thus, part of his translation work was not only to bear and manipulate documents, but to contain and communicate vital strategic information.

Gonzálo's biggest disgrace, and that of Martín de Córdoba, came in 1558, during a battle with Ottoman forces at the nearby port of Mostaganem, which resulted in the former's capture and the latter's death. It had been planned as a joint Hispano-Moroccan attack, but the Moroccan help that Gonzálo negotiated the year before never arrived, and the Ottomans razed the Oranese troops. The governor himself was killed and his son was taken hostage along with the interpreter. It was a devastating encounter for the Fernández de Córdoba family and their reputation as military experts, and even more threatening to the reputation of the monarchy itself, an issue that worried both Charles and Philip considerably. Though apocryphal, Spanish historiographers of the time attributed the emperor's death soon after the battle to despair over the count's defeat by the Ottomans and the concomitant risk of losing imperial prestige.[73] Happily for the new King Philip, who had taken up his father's throne when the latter abdicated in 1556, the shameful defeat made very little echo in the European news networks of the time, so Spanish face was saved before their European rivals.[74]

At the crux of these European-wide reputation games stood the "invisible" figure of Gonzálo Hernández himself, the Arabic translator. The failure of Moroccan support was perceived as a failure of his negotiations and cast doubt upon the guarantees that he offered both the crown and the count after returning from Fez—namely that the Moroccan soldiers would be ready to support the attack on Algiers. Nonetheless, in the near term, it was the reputation of the count that suffered most. After all, finding a trustworthy translator was part of his responsibility as governor, and thus the failures of his fiduciary were left at his own feet. Gonzálo was eventually ransomed by Philip II himself, along with the count's son (also called Martín de Córdoba), and he was sent back to Orán to continue working as a soldier and interpreter, which he did faithfully if not always correctly, being deceived at least once again during his career by two Ottoman spies.[75]

Gonzálo's trustworthiness and reputation had two distinct legacies during the long aftermath of the so-called disaster at Mostaganem. In the first place, just as his position as interpreter was based upon his family connections—both to the Fernández de Córdoba family and through his father, Fernando, who had sometimes worked alongside Gonzálo as an unpaid assistant—he was able to transmit his reputation for skill and fidelity to the next generation. In 1570 Gonzálo's son Luis was named the captain and interpreter of a troop of Spanish soldiers. Luis worked with an anonymous Oranese Jew who assisted him as translator.[76] Though no information has

survived about the Hernández translator dynasty in Orán after Luis's service, it is clear that at that time they were thriving as a family of fiduciaries,
based in large part on the importance of trust in interpersonal systems and
bilingual expertise. This was true for the *morisco* Hernández family, as well
as for the Jewish and Christian families discussed below. Effectively, service,
reputation, and, above all, fidelity became transmissible assets that helped
each new generation secure appointments and rewards (*mercedes*). Families
used linguistic service to advance social status across several generations in
societies in which merits gained force as they were accumulated over a long
period of time.

Second, however, was the effect of Gonzálo's reputation on the later generations of the Fernández de Córdoba family, not only in Orán but also, and
perhaps more importantly, in Spain itself. Ultimately, the memory of Gonzálo's translations and their terrible effect on the Mostaganem campaign would
be rewritten by the family, with the aim of rehabilitating the reputation of
the count, which had been sacrificed for the monarchy's own face-saving in
1558. The reputation game that began in the 1530s with Gonzálo's appointment in Orán thus culminated only in the 1590s, and became an early example of how formerly private documents through which translator reputation
was created and transmitted (legal testimony, letters of recommendation,
confidential reports, etc.) were converted into public print projects for wide
audiences across Spain and even beyond.

Translators Accused: Claims and Counterclaims in Print Histories

Gonzálo's life and reputation were saved in 1561 when he was ransomed by
Philip II from captivity in Algiers. This rescue came at the cost of the reputation of his patron and friend, Martín de Córdoba, who was blamed posthumously for the defeat of the Spanish at Mostaganem by Ottoman Algerian
forces in 1558. Though such aspersions were distasteful to them, the powerful Fernández de Córdoba family suffered no great harm, and generations
of Martín's relatives continued to hold the position of governor of Orán and
other royal titles.[77]

Nonetheless, the count's damaged reputation was eventually salvaged by
the promotion—by his descendants—of a new depiction of Orán's Arabic
translators at the 1558 defeat. In 1593, a decommissioned soldier from Orán,
Balthasar de Morales, published in Córdoba a fictionalized account of the
events of 1558, *Diálogo de las guerras de Orán*. The work was dedicated to

Martin Alonso de Montemayor, the nephew of the deceased and maligned Count of Alcaudete and former governor of Orán who had been killed in 1558. The history of the battle was recounted as a humanist dialogue between three characters, Guzmán, Mendoza, and Navarrete, the latter of whom played the author's roles as a former soldier of Orán and one who knew the truth of the count's qualities and bravery. Morales, through the mouthpiece of the character Navarrete, provided a counternarrative to the *mala fama* that Guzmán and Mendoza had heard about the count's role in the defeat, explaining in detail that "When the count arrived in Orán, a certain Gonzalo Fernandez tricked him by saying that the Arabs wanted [the attack on Algiers], and that they would help him conquer that territory. Since he was such an experienced man and a translator, he said that it would be a good idea to go to two areas called Tacela and Guardáz, which is in the middle of the province, and from there carry out his plans. This was the cause of his defeat, because once he got there the Arabs did not appear."[78]

The count's defeat and consequent loss of reputation was thus rewritten as the fault of Gonzálo Hernández's trickery and bad information. The rest of the dialogue showed occasional examples of Hernández's perfidy but focused on reestablishing the reputation of Martín de Córdoba through careful arguments about what constituted service and honor, and thus reputation, for a Spanish nobleman. Morales, via the character of Navarrete, concluded that the count had fought nobly to the death, by which means he "fulfilled his honor" (*pues cumplió con su honra muriendo*).[79] The count's tragic death in defeat was converted into a mark of honor, whereas his failure as a commander was pinned on the untrustworthiness of the translator Gonzálo Hernández. Throughout the dialogue, the former soldier used similar technical keywords for "service" and "reputation" that had appeared in the correspondence generated by the preparations and fallout of the 1558 campaign. Morales's text stands halfway between the norms of humanist discourse and new norms for historiographical writing that were also being developed during this exact time in the administrative documents of the empire.[80] This was the "paperwork of reputation," which would become the principal currency of the "economy of *mercedes*" in the seventeenth century and was much used by later fiduciary translators.[81] Gonzálo Hernández's case is only one example of how the reputations of Arabic translators were used as currency to advance their own causes, or those of others.

In the seventeenth century, it became ever more common to convert this paperwork of reputation into editorial projects that could prove lucrative and/

or of great political use. This was a strategy used not infrequently by officials working for (or aspiring to work for) the Spanish monarchy, and translators were no exception. Indeed, the dominating translator dynasty of early modern Spanish history, the Gracián, used print regularly to publicize their translations and royal service.[82] For example, Diego Gracián's 1564 edition of the *Peloponnesian Wars* of Thucydides was sent directly to Philip in manuscript.[83] With the translation, he sent a request that he be allowed to retire and that his well-qualified eldest son, Antonio (*tan hábil como yo o más*), inherit his position–and a detailed record of his service to the king to justify the *merced* he was asking for.[84] In the meantime, the paratexts of the print work reveal a long-term investment in the "economy of *mercedes*," including the printing of royal letters to and from Charles, Philip, and other members of the royal family, attesting to the usefulness of the translation (*muy útil y provechoso*) and the quality of Diego Gracián's service.[85]

It was through this kind of discourse and publication project that professional qualifications were established and refined. Diego Gracián used terms like "experience" (*experiencia*), "confidence" (*confianza*), "fidelity" (*fidelidad*), and *secreto*, among others, to describe the work he had performed while secretary of translation (*secretaría de la interpretacion de lenguas*) and to qualify the significance of his work as a translator. These terms would remain keywords for referring to translator service over generations. For example, in 1636, the humanist scholar Vicente Mariner had printed a short text in Castilian and Latin describing the duties, functions, and characteristics of the *oficio del intérprete*, which he dedicated to don Juan Idiáquez, one of the chief ministers of Philip III and patron of the Basque Arabic translator Francisco de Gurmendi (whose work will be discussed in Chapter 5).[86] Mariner described the office of interpreter in conjunction with his translation of excerpts from the Greek collections at El Escorial, many of which have now disappeared.[87] Mariner was above all renowned for his translations of the *Iliad* and the *Odyssey*, and he was also the chief librarian at the royal library in the palace-monastery of El Escorial. There he not only oversaw his own translation enterprises from classical languages, but almost certainly interacted regularly with the Arabic interpreters who were employed there. Mariner's description of the interpreter's tasks and qualifications was self-consciously rooted in classical, and especially Latin, tradition. His reflections on translation advocated a nuanced balance between *ad verbum* and *ad sensum* and echo the many of the themes traditionally expressed in dedicatory epistles and prefaces in Castilian dating to at least the fifteenth century.[88]

Nonetheless, Mariner's articulation of the precepts and best practices of the *oficio del intéprete* was indicative of a new trend of professional declarations that intensified toward the middle of the seventeenth century.

Mariner's prescriptive and theoretical text was issued at nearly the same time that other officially employed translators began to circulate accounts of their services. In 1642, Francisco Gracián Berruguete printed an account of his services and those of his family as royal translators. Drafts of this account had been circulating since 1633.[89] Just four years before Gracián Berruguete's print publication, Jacob Cansino—a descendant of the Cansino sent to Fez instead of Hernández in 1555—also published a similarly titled self-panegyric to the services of his family in Orán.[90] Both Gracián and Cansino adhered to the common format of asking for royal payment or patronage, and both read their qualifications back in time through the biographies of ancestors who had performed the same or a similar office. Though one man worked in the libraries of the royal court and one in the ports and battle-fields of North Africa, both insisted on the range of services that made up their (and their families') careers as translators. These were families of "fix-ers" par excellence, and their activities did not have to take place in liminal border zones but could operate in the very heart of the monarchy as well as at the edges of empire.[91]

The "King's Jews": Service and Virtue Among Orán Translator Families

Working alongside the Christian and *morisco* translators who staffed Orán's institutions from 1509 onward were several families of Jewish trans-lators. Many multilingual agents all across North Africa were Jewish and in 1509 the small Jewish community in Orán was permitted to remain in the city as translators before the Jewish community from Tlemecen was allowed in 1512.[92] Ferdinand granted the Oranese Jews an official title as early as 1514. The first to be granted a royal appointment were the Santorra and Cansino families. Rudi Santorra was the head of the only Jewish family allowed to remain in Orán following the Spanish conquest in 1509, and the Cansino were one of two additional families invited back by royal *cédula* (order) in 1512 to serve as tax collectors to the surrounding communities.[93] Though the Cansinos were not originally named as interpreters, they moved quickly into this role and held on to the office until 1666. What happened to the Santorras between 1512 and 1551, when Jacob appears as a fully invested and official *intérprete lengua*, has not survived in the existing documentation.

The position of Arabic translator in Orán was a contentious position, and the most important qualifications of experience, trustworthiness, and skill were weighed against personal connections, family rivalries, suspicions of disloyalty, and religious stereotyping.[94] The religious identity of the translators of Orán was in fact a component in their professional qualifications from the very beginning of Spanish rule in 1509. Less than two decades after Spain had expelled its entire Jewish population in 1492, the Jewish residents of Spanish Orán were marked in the eyes of other residents by dress, customs, family ties, the physical space that they occupied in the Jewish quarter, and the valuable language skills that many had developed participating in Mediterranean commercial networks or working as translators for other North African powers, like Tlemecen or Morocco.

Meanwhile the community rendered valuable service to the presidio as translators and contributed to the local economy.[95] The third Conde de Alcaudete complained in 1601 that no Christian in Orán knew how to write in Arabic, nor could any access information networks comparable to those controlled by the Jewish interpreters.[96] In 1636 Pedro Cantero Vaca, during an official ecclesiastical review (*visita*), commented at length on the Jewish community, its relationship with the Christians, and the reliability of the translators and determined ultimately that "it is debatable whether the Jews should be allowed to live in this presidio, and there are arguments on both sides."[97] That there was room for debate in the mind of the supervising ecclesiastical official indicates that religious identity, while certainly important, was a secondary consideration to the reliability and usefulness of the community to Spanish power.

The question of the interpreter's religion as a professional *dis*qualification was not seriously raised until 1656, when the idea of expelling the Jewish community from the Spanish territory of Orán was advanced by the then governor, the Marquis de San Román.[98] This debate was latent until his successor, the Marquis de los Veléz, lobbied the queen regent, Mariana de Austria, to expel the Jewish community of Orán in 1669. He justified the recommendation to expel the community using anti-Semitic language, claiming that there were Christians in the presidio who qualified as interpreters.[99] Based on this record, historians have supposed that the Christian interpreter, pulled from the military ranks of the garrison, was supposed to be a kind of check on the Jewish interpreter. In fact, Christian interpreters accessed this office on their own merits and connections and had served as alternative intermediaries for translating correspondence and gathering documentation. Jewish and Christian interpreters worked in tandem, traveling together to reconnoiter surrounding territories, composing and signing reports together, and interrogating prisoners.[100] Though religious identity shaped the social relationships and professional lives of these men, it was far from the most important factor until the mid-seventeenth century crisis and expulsion.

The requisite skills and signs of reliability were most clearly laid out in a series of documents written around the succession of Jacob Cansino to the office of *intérprete lengua* between 1633 and 1634 following the death of his brother Aaron. These documents were part of the paperwork of reputation through which the legitimacy of previous familial appointments was tested and ultimately affirmed, as was the king's privilege to appoint the interpreters of Orán rather than deferring to the advice of his governor. The question of whether skill and fidelity were transferred through family ties or obscured by these connections was argued from both sides, and Jacob Cansino lobbied successfully for his reinstatement as the *intérprete lengua* based on how he was able to present evidence of his family's long service as a natural quality that made him the best candidate for the job.

The Cansino dynasty enjoyed high status and regular employment and remuneration in Orán throughout the sixteenth and seventeenth centuries. The Cansinos' salary vacillated between the substantial amount of twenty-five and thirty *escudos* per month, while the Christian interpreters sometimes went without pay and never made more than fifteen *escudos* per month. Yaho Sasportas, on the other hand, while serving and acting as *intérprete lengua* between 1633 and 1636, was issued forty-five *escudos* a month.[101] The family was expelled from Seville in 1492, at which point Jacob Cansino and his family moved to the kingdom of Tremecén and then to Orán in 1512. Isaac Cansino, Jacob's son, held the office from 1558 to 1599 and was even called to Madrid in 1580. His son Hayam was sent for several months of 1608 to San Lúcar to work with the Duke of Medina Sidonia on negotiations with Morocco over the port of Larache.[102] These interpreters, no doubt through their frequent contact with the Spanish administrators for whom they worked, were well integrated into the mechanisms of the Habsburg imperial bureaucracy from the beginning.[103]

When petitioning the king for money or permissions, members of the Cansino family asked for letters of recommendation from nobles and other important officials. They recorded and reported the exact dates of these letters and all of the royal decrees issued in their favor, demonstrating an aptitude, gained from generations of service, for working within the bureaucratic apparatus. The family paper trail allowed translators to insist on their hereditary service as a reason to request remuneration and job security. This practice served Jacob well when, following Aaron Cansino's death in 1633, the former was unable to become the *intérprete lengua* of Orán. The only other Cansino eligible for the office was Hayan's brother, and Jacob and Aaron's uncle, Brahim. Brahim was deemed unsuitable, not only due to his advanced age, but once it was discovered that he was literate only in Hebrew and had no knowledge of Latin letters.[104]

Yaho Sasportas was appointed as interim interpreter, with his son Jacob as his official lieutenant, since Yaho was himself quite elderly. The office might have passed in this generation to the Sasportas family, who already enjoyed a prestigious reputation as loyal servants of the Spanish crown and reliable and capable translators, were it not for a vigorous campaign launched by Jacob Cansino to win back his rightful office. In 1636, after two years of lobbying in Madrid, Philip IV issued a royal *cédula* reinstating Jacob over Yaho, citing his family's long service as the source of Jacob's rights to the office.

In 1633 Jacob Cansino found himself in prison in the governor's castle in the Spanish presidio of Orán and thus unable to succeed to the post of *intérprete lengua*.[105] His pre-jail activities indicated a promising career as both a member of the Spanish service in Orán—as soldier, translator, captive negotiator, and grain supplier—and an important member of the small Jewish community in the presidio.[106] As he reported to the king in 1626, he had been extensively trained by his father Hayan and, although the official post went to his older brother, he had assisted his father for more than a decade by translating important letters and intervening with timely information in military campaigns, which led to the death and captivity of an "ynfinidad de enemigos" (infinite enemies). His training included the ability to read and write in Spanish, Hebrew, Chaldean (Syriac), Arabic, and "Cetenia" (probably a Berber language).[107] In short, Jacob Cansino painted a picture of a family that was totally integrated into all aspects of the presidio life and that contributed tremendous support to its administrative, military, religious, and social activities, in addition to ensuring the continued supply of grain to the community, one of the most severe concerns in the history of this presidio. Throughout his report he insisted on the quality of reliability and trustworthiness that was demonstrated in each generation. He constructed a service record that could be inherited across generations, which he would invoke even more strongly when his livelihood and personal freedom were threatened.

Jacob faced strong competition. Yaho held an exceptional place in the presidio administration. He had been granted the title of *xeque* and was the acknowledged head of Orán's Jewish community.[108] He was also, in 1626, granted a special privilege to send and receive mail without it passing through the censorship of the interpreter, whose job it was to intercept suspicious correspondence. Thus, Yaho maintained an unsupervised network of informants among Ottoman and North African communities who were not loyal to the Spanish. This license was renewed in 1654 by the governor, the Marquis de San Román, who reaffirmed Yaho's service and credibility and ordered that his freedom to correspond without supervision continue without contradiction.[109] When Yaho became acting interpreter in 1633, he in effect controlled the majority of communication in and out of the presidio.

Jacob's predicament in 1633 launched a flurry of letter writing between Orán and Madrid, leading to Jacob's release and permission to visit Madrid in 1634. Philip IV, who ordered Jacob's freedom, ultimately issued an encomiastic nomination for him to return to Orán in the official capacity of *intérprete lengua* on the merit of his family service beginning with his grandfather (also named Jacob) in the 1550s. Jacob was granted an official license to publish this decree, including royal praise of the Cansino family.[110] The king's official approval was printed and circulated among the reading public of Spain. The problem of Cansino's succession in 1633, however, also opened the floor to debate as to what the most important characteristics were for the Arabic interpreter of Orán to possess, including the matter of blood purity, perhaps setting the foundation for anti-Semitic schemes in the 1650s and 1660s. Though the Cansinos had the support of important Christian officials, the Sasportas enlisted their own advocate to argue that the office should be filled without reference to the family of the applicant and based only on the function of their demonstrated skill in language and reliability as loyal Spanish agents.

This episode reveals a tension between central and local authority—whether the king or the governor should make the appointment for this particular office—that dated back to the original litigation between the town and royal officials in the 1533 lawsuit heard in the Real Chancillería of Granada. In 1633, just after Aaron Cansino's death, a report was submitted

to the king whose title reveals the stakes and strategies of translator appointments: "The Arguments for the Office of Arabic Language: The Governor's
Selection, his ability to make it [considering] the crime of infidelity, as is
beneficial to the Service of His Majesty and the Assurance of the Continuation of these Presidios and their Security."[111] In this title, the language of
fidelity was closely associated with the definition of the translation office.
The claims of generations of individual fiduciary translators and their families had become a tool to delimit an institution.

   This report was in fact a piece of pro-Sasportas propaganda.[112] The
author asserted that only a qualified and discrete person with knowledge of
Arabic should act as interpreter, by which he meant that the intermediary
should report faithfully what was said in Arabic *only* when asked to do so by
the governor.[113] In other words, all mediation was controlled by the governor, not generated by the interpreter as a royally appointed official, whose
agency in that position was severely limited. According to the report, none
of the previous interpreters, whether Jewish or Christian, had worked in an
official capacity, an assertion that the author supported by claiming that the
interpreters went long years without salary. This revisionist recharacteriza-
tion of the sixteenth-century office of the interpreter as purely ad hoc and
unpaid was meant to undermine the dynastic legitimacy of the Cansinos as
hereditary and royally appointed officeholders and the legitimacy of their
position as a royal appointment rather than the governor's selection. The
anonymous author of the 1633 report directly addressed the competition
between the incarcerated Jacob Cansino and the available Yaho Sasportas,
asserting that if Jacob were to remain in the office it would be because his
father had the support of nobles such as the Duque de Maqueda (who also
wrote in support of Jacob's petition for a trading license in 1626), not because
of his actual qualifications. It was, instead, Yaho who possessed the necessary ability, intelligence, and reliability, as well as the experience of information gathering gained during thirty years of service to the Spanish monarch.
The author of the report insisted that Jacob Cansino had shown himself to
be unfaithful, as demonstrated by his current accommodations in the governor's prison.[114]

   In response to these accusations and as a tool to promote his legitimacy,
Jacob turned to print as a vector for salvaging his reputation. In 1638 he
published a translated version (actually transliterated from Ladino) of the
Glories and Grandeur of Constantinople (*Extremos y grandezas de Constantinopla*), by Moses Almosnino.[115] He accompanied his "translation" with a

fourteen-folio piece of pro-Cansino propaganda: "Service Report of Jacob Cansino (of the Hebrew Nation)" ("Relación de los servicios de Iacob Cansino (Hebreo de Nación)"), which repeated many of the qualifications enumerated in the report he had submitted on his own behalf in 1626, namely that he and his family had provided invaluable services in times of war, had ensured the supply of basic goods, and had traveled in the service of the king—Jacob the elder as a royal emissary in 1555 to the king of Morocco, Isaac to the court in Madrid in 1580, and Hayan to Sanlúcar in 1608 to assist with delicate diplomatic arrangements between Spain and Morocco.[116] On top of all of this, they had translated faithfully many important documents. He insisted on his double service as soldier and interpreter, noting that a previous governor had written in 1630 that "he had served with approval in military campaigns as well as in everything concerning the office of the interpreter." Jacob and Aaron's father, Hayan, was wounded in battle, and Jacob cited this sacrifice as a crucial part of his father's merit, and, by extension, his family's merit and his own. Having reported his father's military valor and contributions, Jacob was also sure to insist that his family had only ever fought in the name of peace and the prosperity of the presidio.[117] Jacob himself claimed to have participated in battles as a soldier and, on at least one occasion, to have collected the wounded and tended to them in his home, an image of military service that was repeated by other petitioners to the king, including the Gracián.[118] The men of the interpreter's family, including the interpreter, thus were required to act as soldiers, meaning that they paid to outfit themselves for war with arms and horses and offered their services in battle. A not insignificant number of Cansinos had died while on campaign, serving the Spanish kings.

The *relación* concluded with a reproduction of Philip IV's 1634 appointment of Cansino, in which the king made reference to the right he had demonstrated to office.[119] He ordered Cansino to take charge of the so-called ministry of languages (*ministerio de lenguas*) that was run from the presidio and which by the 1630s served as a crucial node in the networks of information exchange—official, secret, stolen—between the Spanish territories and the Ottoman regencies to the south and east and Morocco to the west. Jacob employed the term *ministerio* to refer to his family's activities since the 1550s, and it was repeated by Philip IV in his appointment letter. Jacob described the death of two of his relatives at the 1558 Battle of Mostaganem—in which Martín de Córdoba had died and Gonzálo Hernández had been captured—equating military service and translation service. By 1636

Figure 8. Jacob Cansino's 1638 edition of Moses Almosnino, *Extremos y grandezas de Constantinopla*, with an extensive paratext relating to the service and patrons of the Cansino family. An engraved frontispiece of the Count-Duke of Olivares is visible through the left-hand folio. © Biblioteca Nacional de España, R/13197.

Jacob had succeeded in converting Ferdinand's 1512 *cédula*, which had mandated only that one out of the three Jewish families permitted to reside in Orán would be interpreters (an office which, as mentioned above, was not even assigned to the Casino family), into a regular institution for fiduciary translation, to be controlled in perpetuity by his descendants, the natural heirs to the office of the interpreter.[120]

Once reinstated, Jacob exercised his office until he died in 1666. It seems that there was another interlude, in 1659–1660, when he found himself again in prison and subsequently exiled, and his son Abraham acted in his stead. Throughout the 1650s both the Cansinos and the Sasportas were working again on reputation campaigns with the goal of securing the appointment as translator. In 1660, however, Jacob was back at his post, having again gained the good graces of Philip IV by virtue of a *memorial* that restated his services and contributions, especially to Christian causes.[121] He even sent a petition to the king, asking for a *merçed* for each of his sons, Hayan and Abraham, who served as his assistants, and reminding the monarch that he had agreed to let him name his successor.[122] Meanwhile, the Sasportas continued to serve as interpreters, without an official title, and as important agents in gathering information from their contacts with the Ottomans.[123]

When Jacob died in 1666, his sons Hayan and Abraham were named as principle and assistant interpreters, respectively.[124] The Sasportas, however, objected and once again tried to take over the office, a contest that caused the exasperated War Council to request the governor to recommend three suitable candidates. The governor, the Marquis de Vélez, found this a good opportunity to recommend instead that the crown consider appointing another Christian as interpreter. He used this possibility as a springboard from which to argue that the Jewish community was a dangerous and unnecessary presence in Orán and that they be expelled as soon as possible with no possibility of return.[125]

Attitudes toward the Jewish community of Orán in the 1660s were, however, much different than they had been in the even in the 1590s or 1640s and '50s. The reputation campaigns of different translator candidates motivated the *Consejo de Estado* (State Council) to examine the legitimacy of the patrimonialization of the office. This inquiry contributed to the ultimate decision to expel, which was supported by the Marquis de los Vélez, who firmly believed that the Jewish community of Orán should be expelled. Marshaling historical evidence to make a legal argument, he wrote repeatedly to the government in Madrid and scoured the city archives of Orán for evidence he could use to show that the Jewish families did not naturally hold the right to live in Orán. He came up with Ferdinand's 1512 *cédula*, which granted the right of citizenship to the Santorra, Cansino, and Benismerro families, and used this document to argue for the illegitimacy of the current community.[126] By late 1668 the governor had convinced the queen regent, who issued the expulsion order promulgated and effected, to the surprise and distress of that community in 1669.

Nonetheless, Mariana of Austria worried that the community could not be expelled without consequences. When a translator was actually found to have done something subversive and subsequently punished, the crown struggled to discipline its agent without breaking the ties of informants he had cultivated. The queen mother was concerned that expelling the Jewish community would leave the presidio without bilingual intermediaries and that the expelled intermediaries could take valuable information with them to furnish to Spanish enemies. However, of most concern to the queen mother as the custodian of the royal reputation, was the fear that expulsion would mean dishonoring the "royal word" as given by Fernando in 1512.[127] Fidelity in translation was indeed supposed to be a two-way street.

Eventually, the order was given and the expulsion of the Jewish community of Orán followed the model of the 1492 and 1609–1614 expulsions. It was not the first program to restrict the residency of the Oranese Jews.[128] Beginning in 1591, and then again in 1646, 1652, and 1655, the Jewish community was asked to provide a list of "newcomers" who could not claim a right to residence based on the permissions of the early sixteenth century or subsequent service.[129] In April 1669 nearly five hundred individuals were loaded onto three boats and sent across the Mediterranean, many settling in the Medici port of Livorno.[130] Though in many ways a shocking decision, given the constancy of royal support for the Jewish interpreters of Orán, Jean-Fréderic Schaub and Jonathan Israel have proposed that it was a minor victory for the royal reputation in view of Spain's declining military hegemony in the rest of Europe and the palace intrigue between the queen mother and Charles II's illegitimate half-brother, Juan José de Austria.[131]

Soon after the events, Luis Joseph de Sotomayor y Valenzuela, a captain in the garrison at Orán, wrote a detailed laudatory chronicle of the expulsion.[132] As was the case following the *morisco* expulsion, Spanish writers connected to the crown found themselves tasked with writing historical accounts to justify the drastic and devastating action of the state upon its own subjects.[133] Indeed, the text manifests an enduring strand of crusading ideology based on the model of the Catholic Kings.[134] However, it was also another medium by which the rhetorics of service and professional rivalry found their way into the Spanish discourse articulated around questions of Arabic translation. For example, Sotomayor framed the episode of the Jewish expulsion as a professional and ideological contest over the office of Arabic interpreter. He explained the history of Jewish service in this office, invoking the former argument about following the models from "Muslim times" (*desde que estas Plaças se ganaron de los moros*) but criticizing this policy as one of "custom rather than necessity" (*mas por costumbre que por necesidad*), since there were now "many Spaniards who could translate with greater merit and fidelity than all of the Jewish translators."[135] As if to model this himself, in his report Sotomayor provided evidence in the form of letters exchanged between the queen, the governor, and the Jesuit *válido* (favorite) Juan Everhard Nithard. Like a skilled professional translator, he claimed to put the documents and information therein "à la letra" (word by word). By this mechanism, Sotomayor promised that his narrative was honorable.[136] The idea of *honorable* translation was a revision of the now-habitual mechanisms of fiduciary translation, compounded with the discourses of service and lineage that had helped convert linguistic service into the basis of a virtuous reputation.

The report primarily offered a powerful and polemical justification for the expulsion, framed in eschatological anxiety about Jewish presence in Spain's universal monarchy.[137] Using a version of the familiar metaphor of the body politic, Sotomayor reproduced a letter from the governor to Nithard, in which (according to Sotomayor's documents) the latter recommended expulsion as the "only remedy" (*único remedio*) by which to "clean this small part of the body of the Church" (*limpiando este pequeño miembro del cuerpo de la Iglesia*).[138] Once again, as had been the case during the terrible answer to the "*morisco* question" between 1609 and 1614, questions of religious orthodoxy and subjecthood were articulated around issues of translation, the metaphor of purgation, and the devastating effect of expulsion.

Translating Toward Nobility: The Connected Histories of Arabic Translators Across the Spanish Presidio System, 1563–1708

The Ennoblement of the Translator: The Sotomayor Family in Orán

Though Sotomayor y Valenzuela's printed account was the product of patronage networks and reputation games connecting Orán all the way to the royal court, his original antipathy toward the Jewish translators struck closer to home. He was probably a relative, either by blood or marriage, of the Arabic interpreter Francisco Fernández de Sotomayor.[139] The Sotomayor were an old Christian translator dynasty in Orán, though their service across the North African presidios has never been studied. One reason for this may be the more impactful reception of the Cansino print materials, which made no mention of the frequent work that members of the two families carried out together. Nevertheless, it is clear from field reports that the Cansino and Fernández de Sotomayor families worked together frequently. One particularly rich anecdote comes from the chronicle of Diego Suárez, in which he describes the capitulation of the Beni Arax in 1570, a local tribe whose loyalties vacillated between Spanish Orán and the Ottoman-held territories (Aaron Cansino was in fact killed in a skirmish against the Beni Arax in 1633). In 1570 they requested an alliance with Orán and aid to rid their territories of Ottoman control. The governor of Orán, Luis Galcerán de Borja, agreed and issued a twelve-part multilingual treaty with the express intention of it being mutually intelligible and recognized by all parties involved: "para que los dichos caudillos moros lo leyesen y entendiesen y confirmasen, otorgándolo todo públicamente y jurándolo delante de treinte testigos, diez cristianos y diez moros principales y diez judíos, todo otorgado ante el notario público del ayuntamiento de Orán y de las lenguas e intérpretes de aquellas plazas."[140] The translators and notaries of the presidio were called on to act as fiduciaries in this diplomatic and administrative process.

Galcerán de Borja not only promulgated the document in three languages and required a large and evenly distributed body of witnesses, but also insisted that the treaty be signed by the capitulating leaders and that they swear their loyalty on the Qur'ān, performing this action of agreement "ante el mismo escribano público del ayuntamiento de Orán y por medio e intervención de las lenguas intérpretes de aquellas plazas, que eran el capitán Gil Fernández de Sotomayor y Isaac Cansino, judío, y de otros muchos cristiano arábigos que a ello se hallaban presentes."[141] Thus a Fernández de Sotomayor and a Cansino were called on in their official capacity and together with the notary to perform a mutually fiduciary testimony for the terms of the treaty.

Despite what seems to have been a regular partnership, the Cansino won the long-term "reputation game," though the Sotomayor and their allies reaped the most long-term benefit for themselves and their lineage. The Fernández de Sotomayor and Navarrete family came to Orán from Baeza in the early sixteenth century and would play a key role in the centuries-long saga about the post of Arabic translator in Orán.[142] Though they initially collaborated with the Jewish translators, ultimately competition between the families would spur the Sotomayor to support the expulsion. In 1563 Gil Hernández de Sotomayor was named a *capitán ordinario* by the king and traveled to Madrid to be invested with the office in front of the *secretario de Guerra*.[143] According to Diego Suárez's chronicle, he held the official title of *intérprete mayor* (chief interpreter) by the late 1560s, working already in tandem with the Cansino family.[144] Gil was also responsible for writing and issuing passports for safe conduct, which followed a specific formula. The passports were written by Gil himself, in the name of the *capitán general* of Orán and the king of Spain, and had to carry an official stamp (*estampa de bula*). They were composed in identical Castilian and Arabic, with the Castilian (*aljamiado*, in Suárez's description) always occupying the top half of the folded page.[145]

Like the Cansinos, and the *morisco* Hernández family, the Sotomayors passed the title of translator among family members. After Gil Fernández de Sotomayor died, the dual office of captain and interpreter was passed to his son, also named Gil Fernández de Sotomayor. This second Gil Fernández is the individual most commonly thought to have been the first Christian interpreter of Orán and probably did not have a salary for that office. When he died, in 1612, his brother, Fernando de Navarrete, took over from 1612 to 1618 and was paid the paltry salary of fifteen *escudos* per month for his duties as an interpreter. He passed the office to his son, also named Gil Fernández de Sotomayor, who may not have received an official appointment until 1629, although he was working as an Arabic interpreter before that time, having learned Hebrew in 1626.[146]

Through the tandem of military and linguistic service, the Sotomayor family rose in status over the century. Between the 1630s and 1650s, the Spanish king Philip IV corresponded directly with members of this family based in Orán, Larache, and Melilla, sending orders for troop movements and payment for services.[147] In 1643 the *intérprete mayor*, Gil Fernández de Navarrete y Sotomayor y de Valenzuela, was made a member of the Order of Santiago, with the supporting testimony of twenty-two witnesses and the then governor of Orán, the Marquis of Visso.[148] He was also granted the governorship of Peñon de Vélez de la Gomera. Many of the witnesses, whose main task was to answer a set series of questions establishing the supplicant's lineage, standing in the community, and *limpieza de sangre* (blood purity), reported knowing Gil Fernández's father, Fernando de Navarrete, and his grandfather, Gil Fernández de Sotomayor, and that all three generations had been the *intérprete lengua de su Magestad*, or the official royal interpreter. However, this office was only listed in a secondary position to the several military titles of each man, and there is no elaboration or description of these men's linguistic skills, although specific physical skills like horseback riding were invoked. The secondary placement of the linguistic office was strategic. Since many of the ordinary avenues for noble advancement were closed to the officers of Orán, they had to prove their nobility on the strength of their military service.[149]

In order to achieve a place in one of the military orders, it was crucial that neither the applicant nor their ancestors have engaged in trade or other "vile" (*vil*) or low-status professions. Perhaps surprisingly, holding the administrative office of translator was not problematic for the Consejo de Órdenes from the standpoint of *limpieza de sangre*, even though the Sotomayors were well known to be adept in Arabic and other languages. Where linguistic knowledge might have been problematic, however, was in its association with a technical or mundane office like a scribe, and so here the Sotomayor were careful to present their Arabic service as a part of the more noble category of military prowess. In fact, though Gil's position was that of translator, he was in charge of military levies in Spain and troop transfer from the peninsula to the presidio, and he received a (much belated) annual salary of fifty thousand *maravedíes* for this part of his service.[150]

While the Sotomayors eventually consolidated their professional and social advancement at the expense of their former Jewish colleagues, their ennoblement for military, and above all linguistic, service to Spain's Mediterranean empire echoes the case of the "old Christian" *morisco* Venegas clan in Granada. The Venegas were incorporated into Spanish aristocratic networks after claiming their hereditary office of *trujamán mayor* in Granada in 1494, eventually becoming the Marquises of Campotéjar in 1643, in exactly the same year that Luis de Sotomayor received his habit as a Knight of Santiago.

Connected Histories of Arabic Translators Across Spain's Atlantic Presidios, 1610–1689

It is impossible to reconstruct the history of the office of Arabic interpreter across all the Spanish North African presidios with the sources currently available. Nonetheless, there is sparse but tantalizing evidence of contact among presidio interpreters through which they forged their own professional information networks—as in the case of Hernández and the Cansino—and also evidence of translator mobility among the presidios. Indeed, the cursus of families like the Sotomayors, translators in Orán for generations and eventually also governors of Melilla and Peñon de la Veléz, are good examples of how families used service and the rhetoric of service to forge their own professional dynasties in Spain's Mediterranean empire.

The Sotomayor were experienced servants of the Spanish crown in presidio government from the 1560s until at least the 1640s. They expanded their family network into Spain's new Atlantic presidios of Larache (1610–1689) and La Mamora (1614–1681) in the seventeenth century. Both presidios outlasted the Moroccan Sa'adi dynasty from whom they had been conquered, which began to cede territories and control to the ascending Alawites in 1659. Compared to Orán, the seventeenth-century Spanish presidios of Larache and La Mamora were small enterprises, notwithstanding their strategic importance because of their position on Morocco's Atlantic coast. Like the other North African presidios—both Spanish and Portuguese—Larache was ruled by noble governors, though the social status of the governors of "minor" presidios like Larache, La Mamora, and Melilla was usually lower than that of, for example, the counts and marquises who ruled Orán. Nonetheless, they had to demonstrate a strong record of loyalty and service, as was the case with the Sotomayor, whose service record once again was at the heart of the history of translation in Spain's Atlantic North African presidios.

The most important western presidio was Larache, governed initially (1610–1614) by Gaspar de Valdes. A *maestre de campo* who had participated in the conquest of Larache, he then became its governor.[151] He proved well equipped to manage the primary problem of maintaining a presidio: ensuring adequate provisions. Though from the crown's perspective the most important priority were fortifications and defense, local presidio government was always keenly aware that food and supplies were paramount for being able to maintain defensive fortifications (as they reiterated frequently in their correspondence with the central administration). Though provisions were supposed to arrive regularly from Spain, often they had to be supplemented from local markets or otherwise, and for both provisioning and defense it was imperative for the governor to establish and maintain relations with surrounding communities. Indeed, most of the international incidents that Larache was involved in, including its loss to Spain in 1689, were the result of something going wrong on a local foraging or hunting party in Moroccan hinterlands.

As was the case in Orán and the other presidios, these vital relationships depended on fiduciary translation, and Gaspar de Valdés relied on a homonym *morisco* as his trusted *lengua*. Though the *moriscos* were expelled from all Spanish territories, in 1613 a dispensation was made for a group of thirty *moriscos* to stay in Larache to work on the fortifications.[152] Several *moriscos* were rebaptized in what appears to have been a sincere conversion to Christianity, including Gaspar de Valdés, named for the governor who was probably his godfather (*padrino*). Presidio staffing included a paid "intér-prete de segunda," occupied by the *morisco* Gaspar de Valdés in 1616.[153] There were also three Jewish families who lived in Larache, though there was never an initiative to install a Jewish community to serve as translators, as was the case a century earlier in Orán.[154] Indeed, the *morisco* Valdés and the Jewish families are important examples of the mobilities that helped staff the presidios. Just as the expulsion of Iberian Jews in the 1490s was one reason presidio administrators were able to rely on a Spanish- and Arabic-speaking population in North Africa, the coincidence of the conquest of Larache in 1610 with the culmination of the *morisco* expulsion between 1609 and 1614 meant that populating the new presidio coincided with the arrival of significant portions of the *morisco* diaspora to North Africa. Once again, at least in the person of Gaspar de Valdés, expulsion and translation went hand in hand.

In addition to Jews and *moriscos*, other bilingual agents aided in translation. For example, Spanish priests who traveled to Larache to participate in captive rendition brought their own interpreters or were selected for the mission because of their skill in Arabic.[155] Soldiers with previous North African experience, like the Sotomayor, also acted as interpreters, along with other military duties. Despite the decades of effort, military support, and diplomacy that went in to securing Larache for the Spanish, Spanish Larache (1610–1689) was in many ways a minor presidio. Like the other presidios, it rarely had access to sufficient supplies (men, food, arms) from Spain and had to conduct raids and foster relationships with its hinterland communities. It was governed by a Spanish nobleman with aspirations in the presidio and elsewhere. In the 1630s, after suffering two decades of harassment from local Moroccan troops and corsairs in the pay of other European powers, the presidio found itself under siege in 1631. The officer credited for saving the presidio through adroit negotiation in Arabic and Spanish, and who was thence granted the position of interim governor, was none other than Fernando de Navarrete de Sotomayor.

Based on his excellent service record (*hoja de servicios*) and especially given his ability to communicate perfectly in Arabic, Fernando Navarrete de Sotomayor was summoned from where he was serving in Orán to Sanlúcar to receive his interim appointment from the Duke of Medina Sidonia.[156] From there he traveled to Larache and was installed as interim governor in September 1631, where he would serve for two years. Just five years later, his relative Luis de Sotomayor, who also had served in Orán and was then the interim governor of the small rocky Spanish garrison at Peñon de Vélez, was summoned to Larache to act again as interim governor. Luis, whose father (also Luis de Sotomayor) had served as governor of Melilla, was eager to convert his interim title to a permanent position. He petitioned the king to promote him from captain to the higher rank of *maestro de campo*, which was the minimum rank needed to become a presidio governor. In his petition—just as the Cansinos and the Gracián were doing at the very same time in print—Luis insisted on the seventy years of service of his father, and his own thirty-six years of service, and emphasized the many times he had proved himself to be loyal and reliable (*acreedor de confianza*) in the king's service.[157] Despite the interest for the present argument about how the rhetoric of service was deployed efficiently by Spain's Arabic translators in the "economy of *mercedes*," Luis was not permanently promoted based on his linguistic service. The last record he generated in Larache in February 1641, requesting more Portuguese soldiers but specifying that no Catalans be sent, was issued just before the new permanent governor took over in July of that year.[158]

Though Luis did not retain his promotion as governor, in 1643 his cousin Gil Fernández successfully petitioned to become a Knight of Santiago based on a similar career and merits to Luis. Both when successful and when not, the movement of members of the Sotomayor family through the presidio system was one more means to unify imperial experiences and administration from the Mediterranean to the Atlantic. This network used linguistic service to make arguments about fidelity and confidence to be deployed in the economy of *mercedes*. Through these arguments these imperial officials bound the frontier to the monarchy through their own family networks.

The Navarrete and Sotomayor were not the only "old Christian" military-translator dynasties who were eventually able to convert generations of family service into titles and reward to the "economy of *mercedes*." Whereas the Sotomayor had worked for generations alongside the Jewish translator families, Diego Merino de Heredía was appointed as translator only after the expulsion of Orán's Jewish community. Like the Cansinos and the Sotomayors, Merino and his family claimed generations of military service in Orán and intermarried with other important families in across the Mediterranean presidio system, many of whom, like Diego himself, were members of the military Order of Santiago.[159] Merino gave an account of his military and linguistic services sometime after 1695 in an undated petition to be assigned the properties of the *sargento general de batalla cabo subalterno* of Orán, whose duties he had discharged during the absence of that official since at least 1688. The rhetoric he used in this petition was reminiscent of the claims of previous translators of diverse backgrounds.[160] Like Jacob Cansino, he invoked military service, danger to himself, and drains on his own properties (*con gran gasto de su hazienda*) in times when the presidio could not pay for the necessary provisions. Like those advocates of Gonzálo Hernández, Merino characterized his expenses and military exploits using the vocabulary of statecraft, especially "aver adelantado el Credito dellas [the presidios], con gran Punto, y Reputacion" as he also claimed to have done while serving in Peñon de Vélez. He had negotiated with "moros de paz" to abandon their loyalty to the Ottoman powers in Algiers and instead become *vasallos* of the Spanish king, under his command, and he had helped suppress dissention and revolt in the presidio, for its *bien común*. His activities are also corroborated by his appearance in Sotomayor's 1670 *relación* leading a company alongside Andres Francisco de Navarrete, another member of the more ancient translator clan.[161] Merino would continue to serve in Orán until at least 1707, when he seems to have fallen out of favor with the new governor, Carlos Carrafa.[162] Nevertheless, Merino's son, Juan Bernardo, also a Knight of Santiago, continued to serve in his father's positions until the Ottoman conquest of the presidio in 1708.[163]

For these connections to function as currency in the "economy of *mercedes*," what happened on the frontier had to matter to those in Spain. As in the cases of Gonzálo Hernández and Jacob Cansino, patronage networks and audiences for Mediterranean information ensured that presidio activities were known in Spain through print markets, with concrete repercussions on the careers and lives of the translators themselves. It was clear to Spanish rulers and governors that interpreters had immense latitude when parlaying with local powers, and their ability to do so for the benefit of the presidio could be coopted. In time, a counter-discourse of betrayal, infamy, and dishonor developed around presidio translators. This is nowhere clearer than in the case in one of the closing episodes in the history of Spain's Atlantic presidios, the loss of the presidio of La Mamora in 1681.

The rise of a new Moroccan dynasty by the final decades of the seventeenth century changed presidio politics and especially the position of the Atlantic outposts. The Alawite sultan, Muley Ismail (1634–1727), was eager to demonstrate his legitimacy through a show of force in expelling the Spanish from Morocco's Atlantic coastline. He was successful in 1681 with La

Mamora and 1689 for Larache. The loss of both presidios engendered a negotiation over captive exchange in which translators were intimately involved, and which will be studied in Chapter 3. However, the siege of La Mamora and its subsequent conquest provides a concluding example of presidio Arabic translators on trial as they have appeared throughout this chapter—both in law courts and in the court of public opinion in the pamphlet campaigns through which supporters and detractors used print to assault the reputation of the translators and their patrons.

The taking of La Mamora by Muley Ismail was above all an opportunity for the new sultan to assert his sovereignty and power. In the spring of 1681 he led approximately fifteen thousand troops to "conquer" the three-hundred-man garrison. By April the presidio could no longer withstand the blockade and so Governor Juan de Peñalosa sent two men to negotiate with the sultan: a provisioner (*veedor*), Bartolome de Larrea, and a captain, Juan Rodríguez, who also served as interpreter.[164] All three hundred presidio soldiers and the forty or more women and children who lived in the presidio as their companions were taken captive by the sultan's forces. The governor, the two mediators (Larrea and Rodríguez), along with some family members and two Franciscan friars, were the only occupants allowed to go free. Upon their return to Spain, Peñalosa, Larrea, and Rodríguez were tried in the noble court of the Duke of Medinaceli and then tried again by the War Council. They were found guilty by the latter of using their position as mediators to exact special privileges. As punishment, Governor Peñalosa was sent into exile in Mazalquivir, Larrea was suspended from office, and Rodríguez was exiled to Fuenterrabia.

In addition to these legal proceedings, the interpreter and his colleagues were also judged in the court of public opinion in a pamphlet campaign that ran concurrently with the two trials. Pamphlets in their favor and against them were published.[165] The language used in one initial accusation—written by a captive soldier in Fez, don Francisco de Sandoval y Rojas—was effusively damning. In addition to calling Governor Peñalosa, "este aborto español," he accused the governor and Larrea and Rodríguez of being friendly with Muley Ismail after previous acquaintance in captivity.[166] This relationship with the Moroccan sultan and the privileged information and status accorded to the translators and governor were understandably anathema to the soldier who had remained in captivity in exchange for their freedom.

Especially significant in this episode was the translator's ambivalent role in sustaining (or sabotaging) the well-being of Spain's presidios in North

Africa. The news and pamphlet campaign about the episode waged a contest over reputation and the question of the right action of the translator, along with other officials. The charge—that the governor, provisioner, and interpreter had cultivated an intimacy with the sultan while their comrades were in chains—was never really fully absolved in public opinion, despite the best efforts of the governor and his supporters. As had been the case with the reputation campaigns in Orán, the figure of the translator provided an expedient outlet for Spanish popular and royal outrage at the loss of La Mamora.

Indeed, the episode shows many parallels with the ways in which, through the publication of the 1593 Morales *Diálogo*, Gonzálo Hernández eventually absorbed the *mala fama* that had originally affected his patron during the later print narratives about his role in the 1558 disaster at Mostaganem. In the case of the pamphlet wars of 1681–1685, the still-living defendants had to suffer the real-life consequences (exile) of actual lawsuits in addition to the verdict of the court of public opinion that had played out in print. However, the way that the hierarchies of service and obligation functioned through professional discourses meant that the translator's reputation was in many ways expendable. Thus, although Arabic translators enjoyed greater professional stability and claims to status based on a recognized vocabulary of the value (and virtue) of their linguistic work, the long shadow of *traduttore, traditore* nevertheless exposed them to blame when something went wrong during an important negotiation.

Professionalization, Patrimonialization, and Inter-Presidio Translation Networks into the Eighteenth Century

Throughout the sixteenth and seventeenth centuries, Spain's presidio translators accessed the "economy of *mercedes*" regularly through a variety of rhetorical and social strategies, especially based on claims about expertise and service. Their work, along with their *morisco* colleagues in Iberia, helped foment the farther-reaching process of the professionalization of the Arabic translator, which really coalesced in the eighteenth century with the institutionalization of translator training programs in the Consejo de Estado, on the one hand, and the regular staffing of expert librarians and cataloguers in the Escorial library and Bourbon Royal Library on the other.[167] Although the most recognizable signs of professionalization stand out in the eighteenth century and are often given as a "late" counterpoint to the professionals working within the Baroque Orientalism of Northern Europe, the process has deep roots in both minority governance and Spain's Mediterranean empire, both of which were outgrowths of enduring crusading ideologies not spent during the final chapter of the Reconquista, which ended in 1492.

The reports submitted by and on behalf of the Arabic interpreters of Orán during these crises of succession are examples of the process of theorizing fiduciary translation and its practitioners that took place around this office from the middle of the sixteenth century to the middle of the seventeenth, a process whose roots were already present in the tensions between royal and municipal officials between 1512 and 1533. It is clear that the office of the interpreter, which required various licenses and the *nombramiento del rey* (royal appointment), was conceived as an important office even at the end of Trastámara rule and throughout the Habsburg period. It required linguistic skills that were considered part of military prowess and experience. Those experiences were a way to achieve nobility (*nobleza*): either the literal *nobleza* of the habit of Santiago, or virtue that could function like *nobleza*, transferable only through family connections. By the 1630s the office took on the professional-ideological characteristics of a "ministry" in the eyes of the interpreter and his patron, the king of Spain. Because of their religion, the Cansinos could never be ennobled or granted membership in a military order, but they created a hereditary professional title in which service became a virtue that functioned much like nobility, just as the "old Christians" Fernández de Sotomayor and Merino y Heredia used their linguistic skills to support their claims to actual nobility.

Chapter 3

Translating Empires: Spain, Morocco, and the Atlantic Mediterranean

The Ottoman-Hapsburg conflicts of the second half of the sixteenth century redefined international politics in the western Mediterranean, inaugurating a new period of inter-imperial relations between Spain and Morocco. Tumultuous dynastic histories on both sides of the Straits of Gibraltar paved the way for frequent diplomatic exchanges between Spain and Morocco, particularly between 1578 and 1614. Throughout this period, local and sovereign rivalries of both the Spanish and Moroccan monarchies combined with complex patterns of trade across the Mediterranean and Atlantic systems, bringing the tactics and texts of fiduciary translation to an audience beyond Iberia and the Maghreb.[1] The vehicular tandem of Spanish and Arabic translation functioned as a formal and informal bridge connecting Moroccan, Ottoman, and diverse European actors through common or competing commercial, political, or legal projects.[2] As drivers of these *langues véhiculaires*, translators navigated what Lauren Benton and Richard Ross have called the "transimperial legal zones" of the early modern world.[3] By so doing, the work of translators between Arabic and Spanish in the western Mediterranean contributed to new elaborations of the law of nations in the early modern period beyond an a posteriori confessionalization of Mediterranean diplomacy.[4] This chapter will study how fiduciary translation—itself the product of centuries of "jurisdictional diversity" in Christian and Muslim territories[5]— provided a path through the "jumbled jurisdictions" of early modern empires.[6]

Increased correspondence (and translation) between Spain and Morocco resulted from a shift in attention of the Spanish crown from the Ottoman eastern Mediterranean to the Sa'adian western sphere. This shift occurred after the Battle of Lepanto (1571) destroyed the Ottoman fleet in Greece and the Battle of Alqazarquivir (1578) in Morocco, which resulted in the deaths of two Moroccan kings and King Sebastian of Portugal. The sixty-year union of the Iberian crowns from about 1580 to about 1640 constituted one of the most significant outcomes of this battle, since Sebastian left no heir other than his uncle, Philip II of Spain. On the Moroccan side, the only royal candidate left standing after the battle was Aḥmad al-Manṣūr, who oversaw a long period of dynastic stability until his sudden death from the plague, in 1603, brought about a new civil war among three of his sons that would last until 1627.[7]

Regular diplomacy thus opened between Spanish and Moroccan courts largely after 1578, though of course occasional cross-confessional negotiations and local agreements had been concluded among Christians and Muslims in the Mediterranean long before.[8] Much of the newly regularized diplomacy was initially related to the thousands of Iberian captives held in Morocco after the battle and to Philip II's long-standing quest to achieve a Spanish presidio on Morocco's Atlantic coastline. As early as 1576, Philip II began to seriously consider how to acquire the Moroccan Atlantic port of Larache (Ar. al-'Arā'īsh), an increasingly valuable site from which to defend the Indies fleet from Moroccan, Ottoman, English, and Dutch corsairs and privateers. Northern Europeans and Ottomans were just as interested in acquiring fortresses along Morocco's Atlantic coast, from which to attack or defend their interests in Morocco (including access to the Indies fleet as it approached Spain with its treasure). Moroccan rulers were able to use these competing concerns to their advantage, as in 1576 when the new Moroccan sultan, 'Abd al-Malik, ceded Larache to the Ottomans to use as a base for Algerian corsairs, making Spain anxious. At the same time that 'Abd al-Malik signed Larache over to the Ottomans, he sent an emissary to Paris and Madrid inviting the French and Spanish (separately) to invade and expel them. This multi-nodal politics would become a hallmark of Moroccan diplomacy and likely allowed the Moroccans to remain independent of any European or Ottoman hegemony.[9]

The outcome of the 1578 war thus inaugurated the construction of an Iberian-Moroccan diplomatic system that required new forms of translation and information gathering, including contact with other European languages like French, English, and Dutch. For Ottoman and North African correspondence (both official and intercepted), presidios were important nodes, as were the noblemen—like the Duke of Medina Sidonia in Andalusia or the Count of Benavente, Viceroy of Valencia—through whose ducal or vice-regal courts western Mediterranean *avisos* were received and processed before being sent to the court in Madrid.[10] Across these conduits, translator practices in Spain and Morocco influenced each other and eventually came to influence how other aspiring imperial powers—like the English, Dutch, French, and even Ottomans—appropriated Spanish-Moroccan practices to consolidate their own Atlantic Mediterranean presence.[11] Analogous to the cases of French and Dutch commercial agents in the Ottoman regencies and Morocco that scholars like Guillaume Calafat have studied, *morisco* and other Spanish-speaking agents in Morocco participated in the construction of a shared diplomatic culture that was shaped by competing imperial and individual agendas, as well as local commitments and knowledge. The intermediaries who could move fluidly between linguistic, social, legal, and political registers, or operate simultaneously across "divers échelons de truchements," had the most success, and many of these intermediaries preferred Spanish as the *langue véhiculaire*.[12] Eventually, Spanish became a link in the chains of translation that bound Iberian, Moroccan, Ottoman, and northern European agents into a Mediterranean commercial and correspondence system.

Morisco Fiduciary Translation in the Mediterranean Diplomatic System, 1578–1588

As in *morisco* government and the presidios, the Iberian-Moroccan diplomatic nexus after 1578 became a fiduciary system founded on credit and credibility, particularly of *morisco* translators and their friends and relations. Indeed, the dynastic upheaval of the late 1570s and early 1580s took place in nearly exactly the same period in which debates over the "*morisco* question" were becoming a political issue of paramount importance in Habsburg Spain following the Second War of the Alpujarras (1568–1571) and its aftermath, to be answered with a blanket expulsion order carried out from 1609 to 1614. The perceived role of the *moriscos* as a "fifth column" for Muslim powers and the increasing pressure on Spain's access to strategic staging posts and natural resources in Morocco from European rivals would ultimately create new professional spaces for *morisco* translators, even as those translators found

themselves with fewer local commissions after the conclusion of the Alpujarras war and the subsequent forced resettlement of Granada's *moriscos* in
Castile.

One way to trace the entanglement of translator trustworthiness with
overlapping commercial and political interests is to map the social aspects
of the exchange of letters that became "objects of translation."[13] The texts
traveled via a specific network of agents and informants with close ties to
both the Spanish and Moroccan courts and local Granada networks. Any
hope of a Hispano-Moroccan alliance took considerable effort and was
forged via the personalities and personal relations of intermediaries. The
majority of this diplomatic correspondence was filtered through a small
group of translators, interpreters, and messengers, all of whom were part of
overlapping personal, as well as professional, networks related to the world
of fiduciary translation.

The first decade of Spanish-Moroccan diplomatic translation, from 1578
to 1588, was carried out principally by two Granadan *moriscos*: Alonso del
Castillo and Diego Marín, who knew one another quite well. In both cases,
their skills and experiences as linguistic intermediaries had been principally
formed in the context of *morisco* Granada before and during the War of the
Alpujarras, which concluded with a program of forced repopulation from
which both Castillo and Marín were exempted. The biographies of both figures are well known in *morisco* historiography thanks to the detailed archival
work of Dario Cabanelas in the mid-twentieth century and the ongoing
research of Mercedes García-Arenal and Fernando Rodríguez Mediano on
the major figures connected to the history of Granada's Lead Books.[14] Here I
wish simply to reexamine some aspects of the biographies and activities of
these well-studied *moriscos* in light of the legacy of fiduciary translation.

Alonso del Castillo's skilled and faithful service in the Alpujarras war
and in the Real Chancillería and Inquisition courts in Granada, his service
in the royal library at the Escorial in the 1570s and 1580s and his connections with important court officials, all made him a primary candidate for
the job of translating the correspondence between Philip II and Aḥmad al-
Manṣūr. This correspondence was motivated by the question of the Iberian
captives and the possibility for the Spaniards to possess the garrison port of
Larache. His personal connections to other *moriscos* across the Mediterranean, such as Marín and his associates, and his local knowledge of Granada
would prove to be assets in international diplomacy.

In the first instance—his experience in the Granada institutions where
fiduciary translation became a dominant mode of producing evidence, like
the Chancillería and Inquisition—Castillo's record of service actually left
him ill prepared to deal with the specialized language of Moroccan diplomacy. Although Castillo had a great deal of experience with Nasrid and
morisco documents, he faced a steep learning curve when confronted with
the technical, though ultimately formulaic, chancellery terms in the Moroccan correspondence.[15] Castillo collected much of the 1578–1588 correspondence in a kind of workbook, and his annotations reveal how much he had
to learn when faced with Moroccan *inshā'* (administrative composition). The
materials collected include not only copies of the Arabic letters and his
translations but also descriptions of the translation process and excerpted
study materials such as word lists and portions of Arabic dictionaries and
maxim collections. Castillo's own marginal notes indicate how he used those
tools to make his way through the complex task of diplomatic translation.

As his ability to negotiate diplomatic registers improved, Castillo nevertheless remained in a key fiduciary position, based largely on his personal
connections across *morisco* society and the court. Those networks were in
some ways more important than his linguistics skills and experiences. In his
workbook, Castillo provides specific information about his translation practices and working conditions. From 1579 to 1581 Castillo worked on Moroccan correspondence in Granada, through the mediation of the president of
the Real Chancillería. The sultan's letters were usually sent across the sea
with an agent trusted by both sides and received by the council of state in
Madrid. There the secretary in charge of Moroccan affairs, Gabriel de Zayas
(until his death in 1593), sent the letters to the archbishop of Granada,
Pedro de Castro (formerly the president of the Real Chancillería, as had
been Castillo's previous patron, Pedro de Deza, to whom the Alpujarras
notebook was addressed), who summoned the *morisco* Castillo to translate
them.[16] The actual mail agent in Spain seems to have been one of Castillo's
neighbors, referred to only as "Amador el correo."[17] The administrative
structure of the monarchy was thus reflected in the socially conditioned
routes of fiduciary translation.

Like Cervantes's fictional translator, Castillo often worked in Castro's
house, as opposed to taking documents home with him, as was his practice in
translation commissions from the Real Chancillería. Under Castro's supervision, Castillo made an initial translation of the Moroccan letters, then he and
Castro worked together to make a revised copy in "clean" Castilian to send

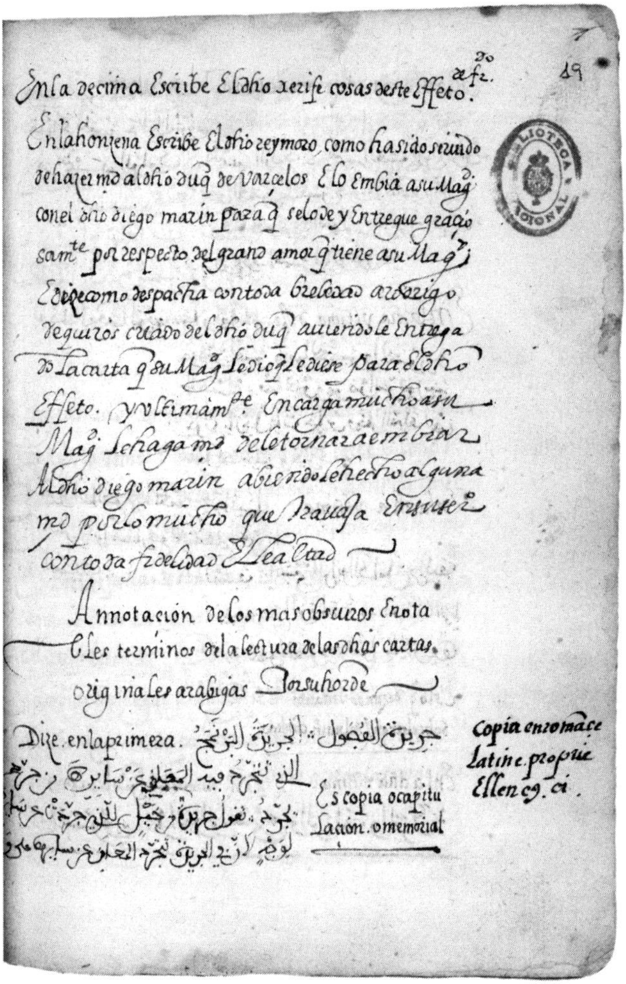

En la deçima Escriue El año xerife cosas deste Effeto.

En la honzena Escriue El año reymozo, como ha sido seruido
de hazerme al año duq de Varçelos E lo Embia asu Mag
conel año diego marin para q se lo de y Entrregue graçio
samte por respecto del grano amor q tiene asu Mag
E çiq como despacha con toda breuedad arbezig
veguios cuido del año duq auiendole Entrega
do la cuita q su Mag le dio q le diere para el año
Effeto. yvltimamte Encarga mucho asu
Mag se haga mo de le tornar a embiar
Al año diego marin abiendo le hecho alguna
mo por lo mucho que ha uida Eruiteer
con toda fidelidad E lea ltad

Annotaçion de los mas obscuros Enota
E les terminos de la lectura de las años cartas.

originales arabigas Consuhorde

Dize. en la primera.

جريدة الفصول · البريق البرنج ·
الد نجح فيه العطيع · رجح
نجح خنل للنجرجة
لوبج لازن البريق نجم العالم

Es copia ocapitu
laçion. o memorial

Copia entromase
Latine propue
Ellen eg. et

Figure 9. In his Moroccan Workbook (c. 1579–1587),
Alonso del Castillo made careful annotations of new words,
particularly early on in the project. This elaborate definition
of what seems to have been for him technical terms that
Castillo expected to encounter regularly in diplomatic
translation indicate that he may have intended to create
a reference work of specialized vocabulary for himself and
perhaps for other translator colleagues. © Biblioteca
Nacional de España, MS 7453, f. 19r.

back to the councils and king. As in the *romanceamientos* that he worked on
in Granada's chancillería, he claimed to have translated the Moroccan correspondence *fielmente*, and he used phrases like "de verbo ad verbum" (word for
word) to assure the fidelity of his translation to the text.[18] The new legal and
chancellery formulae he mastered in diplomatic texts seem to have inspired
him to return to the task of converting Arabic property records, and in 1584,
between Moroccan work, he wrote to his patron, the secretary Zayas, requesting a commission to review all "Arabic property titles that the Muslims of
Granada sold before and after the general conversion to old Christians (*xpianos
viejos*) [so that it may be known] which are true and which are false."[19] Thus,
as he applied the tactics of fiduciary translation to diplomacy, his new expertise gained from diplomatic work affected his translation tasks in Granada.

Like other translators, Castillo's fiduciary position in the diplomatic
system was relational and depended on the actions of other agents working
across the Mediterranean. For example, in 1578 the fiduciary who transported the original exchange between al-Manṣūr and Philip was the Valencian merchant Andrea Gasparo Corso. The Gasparo Corsos were merchants
with factors posted across the Mediterranean, including Ottoman Algiers.
There Andrea and his brother Francisco had met and befriended 'Abd al-
Malik and his brother Aḥmad al-Manṣūr in the 1560s while the latter two
princes were still living in exile in Ottoman territories.[20] They had already
acted as intermediaries between Philip and Uluç Ali, the Ottoman beylerbey
of Algiers in 1569, in the absence of official diplomacy between the Spanish
Habsburgs and the Ottomans.[21] After the Battle of the Three Kings (1578)
and the Iberian Union of the Crowns (1580), Andrea set up an office in Lisbon, from which he became one of Philip's most trusted Mediterranean
intermediaries.[22] Along with their work in the administration of empire, the
Gasparo Corsos were first and foremost merchants, and their political activities were entangled with commercial missions.[23] Formal and informal
diplomacy was thus secured by agents with their own financial stake in the
success of the exchange.

Indeed, one of Castillo's earliest translations from his Moroccan period,
made in 1579, was a travel permit from al-Manṣūr which guaranteed safe
conduct for its bearer.[24] The recipient was Francisco Barredo, a *morisco* merchant and close friend of both Castillo and another *morisco* translator based
in Morocco, the priest Diego Marín, who transported the permit to Spain
to secure its translation. In 1583, al-Manṣūr bought a quantity of jewels and
precious cloth from Barredo and wrote to Marín to have him act as the bank

for this transaction.[25] In this case Marín the translator was acting simultaneously as a commercial and a political fiduciary, beyond his role as linguistic mediator. Meanwhile, the letter was passed along to Castillo, who
dutifully transcribed it among the frenzied but formulaic political negotiations over the possession of the port of Larache.[26] It was common that additional goods and objects moved through diplomatic channels; however, the
presence of this particular letter in the official diplomatic register shows the
ways in which private transactions and patronage were incorporated into
the official correspondence between Philip and al-Manṣūr. It is also indicative of how the burgeoning system of international diplomacy depended on
local networks of agents who already knew and trusted one another.

The key fiduciary of the Barredo affair was Diego Marín, who had served
as the bank for the jewel purchase. All three *moriscos* (Marín, Barredo, and
Castillo) had been involved in the sale and rendition of captives in Granada
during and after the Second War of the Alpujarras.[27] Castillo, who was
already working as a translator, and Marín, who as a bilingual priest in
Granada doubtless also performed translation work as needed among his
parishioners, embodied the overlap between networks of linguistic exchange
and commercial exchange. Marín was eventually captured and found himself
in Morocco when the Battle of the Three Kings took place. Though there
were thousands of Christian captives in Morocco after the defeat of the Portuguese and Spanish troops, Marín had much-needed expertise since he
already knew Arabic and Spanish. He became highly valued by both al-
Manṣūr and Philip as a translator.

Between 1578 and 1588, Philip II and Aḥmad al-Manṣūr corresponded
copiously. In Spain, the Arabic correspondence was translated by Castillo. In
Marrakesh, the Spanish correspondence was translated—most likely *interpreted* rather than translated—by Diego Marín. Marín and Castillo helped
secure their positions as translators through a range of ancillary activities.
For example, Castillo spent the first part of the 1580s in Madrid and the
Escorial, where he continued to translate al-Manṣūr's letters while he
drafted a catalogue of the king's Arabic books. Based on his various services
across the needs of the Spanish monarchy for Arabic translation, Castillo
was finally "received into service" (*recibo en mi seruicio y por mi criado*) and
granted an official appointment as royal translator in 1582 and a regular salary of two hundred *ducados* a year.[28]

Meanwhile, the intervention of translators in conspicuous exchanges
like the Barredo affair is what helped Castillo's translation partner, Marín,

play an even more important part in the negotiations than his superior, the noble ambassador Pedro Venegas de Córdoba.[29] Despite his homonym with the Granada translator dynasty and although he had been the governor of Melilla, Venegas knew no Arabic, unlike some of the other candidates for the position, including Luis del Mármol Carvajal.[30] Ultimately Marín was left on his own in Marrakesh to negotiate the trade of Larache with the Saʻadiens, and after his return to Spain in 1582, the Sultan al-Manṣūr wrote three letters in Arabic directly to Marín. Once again, these personal letters traveled through public diplomatic channels and were incorporated into Castillo's *cartulario*.[31] In these letters, al-Manṣūr indicated the value he placed on the talents and trustworthiness of the Spanish priest.[32]

There is no question that Marín was a valuable intermediary, and he made a personal fortune from his fiduciary position as a credible and trustworthy translator for both sides.[33] The best evidence for how indispensable he became is found in a letter transcribed by Castillo in 1585, when al-Manṣūr wrote to Philip to inform him that he had found out about Marín's death, through poisoning by a rival translator, Jacob Rute.[34] The sudden vacancy left by Marín's death caused al-Manṣūr to reach out to Philip for a very peculiar kind of alliance. The proposition was to train Diego Marín's nephew to replace him as the primary intermediary for *both* monarchies ("our common service"). This proposition reflected expectations in a system ruled by the family dynamics by which the fidelity of one translator could be passed on to his heirs.[35] In effect, the proposition was that Spanish and Moroccan chancelleries would overlap in the person of Marín the younger as a Spanish translator stationed in the court at Marrakesh. Had the initiative gone forward, it would have been a natural development from the syncretic expertise and mutual intelligibility of fiduciary translation across legal as well as linguistic boundaries, as practiced in Granada and the presidios. That is, a Spanish priest recently descended from Muslims had the necessary bilateral linguistic and procedural knowledge to serve simultaneously in the scribal-notarial positions of Moroccan *tarjuman* and Spanish *trujamán*.

Of course, endowing the same person with equal trust from rival sovereigns was an exceptional proposition and probably doomed to failure. In both Spanish and Moroccan courts, translators had access to secret knowledge and also embodied the means to unlock it. Both al-Manṣūr and Philip used codes and ciphers in political correspondence, and tremendous weight was given to the idea of the "secret" in both chancelleries with respect to diplomatic correspondence.[36] For example, throughout his workbook, Alonso del Castillo constantly referred to the "secret" he preserved in performing his task as translator. Across the straits, one of the top Moroccan chancellery officials was the *kātib al-asrār*, or the scribe of secrets, a position held for much of al-Manṣūr's reign by the *wazīr al-qalam* (chief secretary) and *ṣāhib al-turjama* (head panegyrist), 'Abd al-'Azīz al-Fashtālī.[37]

Although no move was made by Philip to appoint Marín's nephew in his uncle's position, the younger Marín seems to have established himself as a kind of Spanish consul in Marrakesh after the assassination of his uncle (although Spain had signed no consular agreement like France and England had with Morocco). The arrangement would prove short-lived. In 1588 English merchants stormed his house in celebration of the news of the defeated Armada, and Marín killed three men. He was jailed for almost twenty years, although the Spanish crown continued to maintain him in relatively comfortable conditions by sending payments to Morocco.[38] Meanwhile, after 1588, al-Manṣūr began a more open diplomatic policy toward Elizabeth and England. Spain's enemy England doubled down on its commercial and political interests in Morocco. Though al-Manṣūr continued to correspond with Spanish agents, in particular about the acquisition of luxury goods like precious gems and artwork, his sovereign politics focused on an alliance with England. The fact that Marín the younger was languishing in jail may have also contributed to the much slower rhythm of Hispano-Moroccan diplomacy in the 1590s and the first decade of the seventeenth century. By 1588, thus, the era of a potential "common service" between Spain and Morocco was over. When Marín was imprisoned, he was removed from the possibility of inhabiting his uncle's position. Like Gonzálo Hernández and Jacob Cansino in Orán, imprisonment was one way of blocking the succession of translator dynasties. There was a vacancy in Spain's new international translation office.

The Spanish Careers of Ottoman Secretaries: Fiduciary Mistranslations

The rhetoric of service continued to circulate alongside and even within translated texts, shaping the future of the office of diplomatic translator. Indeed, the rhetoric of service that Castillo and others used, inflected as it was by the tactics of fiduciary translation, would shape the next periods of diplomatic translation and the position of the translator long after the conclusion of the

morisco period in 1614. Local *morisco* connections and generations of translation practice in minority governance conditioned the first period of the
Hispano-Moroccan diplomatic system, creating patterns that a wider range of
agents would inhabit in the following decades. For example, after Marín's fall
from grace in 1588, al-Manṣūr (or, more likely, his chief minister, al-Fashtālī)
finally conceded a position in the chancellery (*makhzan*) to the enigmatic 'Abd
al-Raḥmān al-Kattānī.[39] This appointment was made despite previous mis-
trust in al- Kattānī, who first arrived in Fez sometime around 1581 claiming
to be a representative of the Ottoman bey of Algiers. At that time, al-Manṣūr's
worries about Ottoman interference in his Spanish politics was at an all-time
high. In 1583, he received a letter from Diego Marín (senior) in Spanish, and
his response was to refuse to read it, because this would have meant asking
someone he did not trust to serve as a translator. Instead, he held one of
Marin's messengers hostage and sent the other one back with the original
Spanish letters and instructions to keep them safe, and to send the same
information back in Arabic. He refused to release the hostage until he received
the Arabic version. As soon as Marín had returned to Morocco, al-Manṣūr
paid off al-Kattānī and sent him back to Algiers.[40]

Al-Kattānī was described in Spanish, Portuguese, English, and Dutch
sources as either an "Andalusi" (*morisco*) or an Ottoman agent (these were
not necessarily mutually exclusive categories).[41] Whatever his background,
al-Kattānī certainly had exposure to fiduciary translation and made use of
typical authenticating formulae as, for example, when translation a letter
from al-Manṣūr to Philip II in 1598 (just before the latter's death):

> This is well and faithfully translated (*bien y fielmente sacado*) from
> a royal letter, signed by the hand of King Muley Ahmet, emperor
> of Morocco, King of Fez and Ethiopia, directed to the King
> Philip, King of the Spains, written in Arabic, whose literal mean-
> ing in translation (*traducida verbo ad verbum*) is the following. . . .
> All of which I, Abderrahmen el Catan, interpreter of these king-
> doms and empire by order of His Majesty [al-Manṣūr], translated
> from Arabic into vernacular Spanish (*español vulgar*) literally (*verbo
> ad verbum*) what the letter contains, and to give faithful testimony
> to this I sign my name (*y en fee desto lo firme de mi nombre*) on the
> aforementioned date, and the date of this letter accords with the
> first days of April 1598.[42]

Al-Kattānī's use of *verbo ad verbum* echoes new choices made by Castillo in the 1580s in his translation of Moroccan correspondence, when he began to append the same Latin formula to his diplomatic work.[43] Unfortunately, we do not have enough evidence about al-Kattānī to speculate about his previous experiences in Spanish institutions, except his use of technical terms which were more likely to have been produced in the chambers of Granada's council, or Chancillería, than in the *makhzan* of Marrakesh.

Whether or not al-Kattānī was an Ottoman diplomat from Algiers, as he claimed, his case is far from the only example of the increasing overlap between Ottoman and Spanish personnel. After 1588, Ottoman expertise permeated Spanish institutions through the activities of Diego de Urrea. Urrea, a Neopolitan renegade and former Ottoman official, is one of the Habsburg Arabic translators who has left the greatest trace across Spanish archives. During the past two decades, scholars like José Floristán and Fernando Rodríguez Mediano have recovered ever more of Urrea's rocombo-lesque life after his reintegration into Spanish Christian courts between Naples and Madrid.[44] There is likely much more waiting to emerge from Ottoman archives about his life as a Muslim in Tlemecen, Istanbul, and Algiers.

Born around 1559 in Naples, Urrea (whose birth name is unknown) was captured by Ottoman corsairs as a child. He seems to have had a brief but spectacular secretarial career in the Ottoman administration, working primarily as a high functionary for the bey of Algiers and as a secretary in Istanbul, and his erudition and secretarial talents were apparently well known across the Mediterranean.[45] He was sent as an Ottoman ambassador to Marrakesh after 1578. There Urrea (at that time called Morato Aga) doubtless met and interacted with Diego Marín. Urrea was on his way from one high posting in Algiers to another in Istanbul when he was captured by Spanish corsairs and brought to Sicily in 1589. From Sicily, he came under the protection of the Spanish viceroy in Naples, who recognized his value as an informant and high-ranking expert in Ottoman affairs. After his acquittal by the Inquisition (where he pled capture and youth as the cause of his conversion to Islam and assured Inquisition officials that he had always desired to return to Christianity and Christian lands), he joined the viceregal household, was baptized as Diego de Urrea, with the viceroy and his wife as godparents, and then sent briefly to the Jesuits to learn Latin. When in 1591 the viceroy of Naples finished his tenure and returned to Spain, he offered Urrea's services to Philip II, who accepted with alacrity.

Urrea was the first Castilian court translator with significant professional experience across Mediterranean courts. This lifelong aptitude in courtly and diplomatic culture may be one reason that he left such a substantial paper trail. After his childhood capture, he was sent to Tlemecen for an Islamic education to, in fact, the very same madrasa as the sons of Aḥmad al-Manṣūr, a personal link that would affect his later translation work. The training he received in the madrasa and in Ottoman service would also affect his professional life in Spain. Like the converted *mudéjar* and Jewish functionaries who found posts in early Castilian administration in Granada, Urrea had the benefit of a profound familiarity with Islamic law.[46]

When he arrived in Castile, Urrea divided his time between teaching Arabic as the newly created chair of Arabic at the University of Alcalá de Henares and, in the Escorial Library, continuing Castillo's work cataloguing and sorting the Arabic materials.[47] He also worked on and off for the Inquisition, as in 1610, when he reported on the testimonies of two Spanish female renegades who came to Spain as part of the retinue of the exiled Moroccan princes (to be discussed below).[48] In 1598 he received a raise in his salary, and his teaching position was transferred to El Escorial, where he was supposed to train others to work as diplomatic translators and librarians for the Arabic materials.[49] One of these disciples—the Basque secretary Francisco de Gurmendi—will be discussed in Chapter 5.

From these materials and his own memory of experiences with Arabic and Turkish books and papers while working as an Ottoman administrator, Urrea wrote at least one book of Spanish political history based on non-Spanish sources, along with several reference works to help his students with their language studies.[50] Urrea arrived in Spain just in time to be pulled into the *plomos* translation project, and indeed it is as a *plomos* translator that Urrea has been productively considered by recent scholars (not surprisingly, he instantly concluded that the *plomos* were forgeries, earning the ire of Alonso del Castillo's patron, Pedro de Castro). At the Spanish court, Urrea styled himself as *Intérprete de las lenguas Arábiga, Turquesca y Persiana*, advertising his ability to manage correspondence from (and for) the entire Mediterranean.[51] Indeed, it was Urrea who double checked the translations of Persian correspondence brought by the English agent Robert Sherley.[52] In the first decade of the seventeenth century Urrea remained in the service of the new Castilian king, Philip III (r. 1598–1621), translating correspondence and other materials for him, including a book of Arabic magic spells sent in 1603 by the king of Bone.[53]

Urrea deployed sophisticated tactics—social and rhetorical—to ensure professional recognition and stability. He was an expert administrator, due to his long experience among the Ottomans, and he acclimated quickly to the Spanish bureaucratic forms (especially the petition and the *relación de servicio*), which he first became acquainted with after his rendition in Naples. He used those forms to connect himself to royal authority through his service record and the support of important patrons. For those, those tactics functioned in much the same way as Castillo's dedications to the president of the Royal Audiencia Pedro de Deza in his Alpujarras workbook and the latter's description of his working relationship with Archbishop Pedro de Castro in the Moroccan workbook. Urrea is not known to have kept a workbook, as Castillo did. Part of the fiduciary status of both translators—doubly essential given the ambivalent attitudes toward *moriscos* and renegades—was the position they established both discursively and socially with respect to their patrons.

Like Castillo, Urrea invoked names in order to inscribe himself into the fiduciary institutions of Spanish administration, which included translation. More so than Castillo—who was always playing catch-up to master Moroccan chancellery forms—Urrea was quite adept at adding or subtracting appropriate chancellery forms (e.g., adding the conventional Spanish formula "I kiss your hands" (*besar las manos*) and subtracting the Islamic invocation "If God wills it" (*in shā' allah*), etc.). Each insisted on his own fidelity and accuracy as a translator and both produced translations that were not always precise. Unlike Castillo's learning curve, however, Urrea's imprecision was tactical, providing another forum for him to generate evidence about his qualifications and service. In fact, his tactical *mistranslations* helped guarantee his position and the reception of his translations as valid diplomatic documents in a set of high-stakes political negotiations. In the next section of this chapter, we will study the bilateral consequences of these political negotiations, which were strongly affected by translation and by the position and experiences of the translators who acted as fiduciaries in the exchanges.

The political negotiations in which Urrea intervened concerned the port of Larache, as was the case with almost all Hispano-Moroccan diplomacy in the late sixteenth and early seventeenth centuries. Philip III saw an opportunity to reopen the question in the context of the Moroccan civil war, which took place between 1603 and 1627. After al-Manṣūr's death from the plague in 1603, a fight for the throne broke out between three of his sons: Muḥammad al-Shaykh (the eldest), Zidān (the ultimate victor in 1627), and Abū Fāris (who was killed in 1608). All three sought European and North African alliances to support their claims and sponsor wars against the others. Despite being al-Manṣūr's oldest son, Muḥammad al-Shaykh never managed to hold firm control over the northern region of Fez, of which he was the nominal ruler, much less the whole of Morocco. Indeed, he entered into the alliance with the Spanish primarily to obtain financial and military support to campaign against his brothers, who ruled from their father's palace in Marrakesh, whereas Muḥammad al-Shaykh had been able to consolidate rule only in the northern region around the former Moroccan capital at Fez.

In 1609 al-Shaykh was chased out of Morocco by his brother Zidān's armies. He threw himself on Habsburg mercy, arriving first in Lisbon and then settling in the Andalusian town of Carmona until 1611. Before his defeat, Muḥammad al-Shaykh ruled Fez and northern Morocco, including the port of Larache on the Atlantic coast. The port was his principal bargaining chip in negotiating for Spanish aid against his brothers, as would become clear in his correspondence with Philip. That correspondence, in turn, became one of Urrea's principal bargaining chips as he negotiated on his own behalf to secure a license to return to Naples.[54]

Urrea used strategic mistranslation in this correspondence in order to strengthen the case that he had been building through the normal channels of petitions and paratexts that structured the "mercy economy." For example, in one of the earliest letters exchanged between Philip and Muḥammad after the latter's arrival in Spain, Urrea used translation to create an inflated sense of his own service in the negotiations.[55] According to the translated text, Muḥammad al-Shaykh expressed his contentment upon Urrea's arrival:

[Urrea's Spanish translation] May your majesty know that the arrival of Diego de Urrea, sent by you, was the perfect cure for all my suffering on account of that which disturbed me, and with his arrival I was relieved of all my nightmares. If only Your Majesty had sent beforehand such a wonderful and loyal servant! If only he had been here since the beginning! What a wonderful, what a loyal servant! He did everything Your Majesty ordered, both in your service and for me so that my kingdom may have peace and relief.[56]

However, in the original text the source of contentment was not Urrea but the arrival of the king's letter and the information contained therein, especially Philip's promised support. Urrea was not mentioned, much less described with encomia, except as the "aforementioned servant":

> [Original Arabic letter] Know that—may God bring victory upon your regard–in the letter that arrived to us was a cure for our troubled destiny, and by it our sorrow was abolished, easily restoring our fate as if it had been as it was at the beginning. And—may God bring victory upon you—that which you permitted be conveyed to us of the good news of our exchange and the strength of our resolution arrived to us, at which time we were reassured by it of your patronage of us and your interest in our affairs. And that is what came from your kingdom, may God make you victorious. And we learned from the aforementioned servant as well, may God make you victorious, about things concealed from us about the source of the betrayal which is the Turks.[57]

The original letter focused on the relationship that Muḥammad al-Shaykh wanted to establish with Philip, whose support and alliance he desperately needed. The translated letter not only reflected those priorities but also promoted the reputation of the translator. Urrea converted Muḥammad al-Shaykh's delight at the arrival of Philip's letter and its contents to delight at Urrea's own arrival and skilled service.

In a subsequent letter Urrea went even further, embellishing Muḥammad al-Shaykh's praise into a testament to his "good service." A few weeks later, Muḥammad wrote to ask Philip to be transported to Peñon de Vélez instead of Tangiers. Then he mentioned Urrea by name as the agent who brought him the articles of the treaty, along with additional messages and information from Philip. Thereupon, the Moroccan prince confirmed that "we had faith in the good advice of your servant" (*taḥaqqaqna min naṣḥ khidmat-kum*)—the object is the advice and not the servant—before moving on to the next topic in the letter. In Spanish, Urrea rendered this as "I certified the good servant that your majesty has in him" (*me he certificado del buen servicio que Vuestra Merced tiene en él*), despite promising in Spanish that he would report "word for word" (*por palabra*) what Muḥammad al-Shaykh communicated to him.[58] Certainly, Muḥammad al-Shaykh's comment reflected the effective work Urrea performed in fiduciary translation and by extension the service rendered to both monarchs. Urrea was still able to guarantee the good faith and understanding of the two parties through his tactical translation of the treaty terms. In addition, Urrea was able to build on Muḥammad's faith in the advice Urrea provided in order to create further evidence about himself to be used in his own petitions for rewards for service rendered. Using the discursive and social tactics of fiduciary translation, Urrea created more currency for his use in the "economy of *mercedes*" and at the same time guaranteed the satisfactory conclusion of the royal negotiations.

These examples are drawn from the earlier letters translated by Urrea for Muḥammad al-Shaykh and Philip III, which may be why Urrea was so anxious to convey to the Spanish king that he was the perfect person for the job, so as to guarantee that he would keep it. In later letters, Muḥammad al-Shaykh was more effusive and specific in his praise of Urrea. After all, Urrea really was his old and trusted acquaintance who performed valuable service for him during the negotiations. These assurances also reflect how Urrea positioned himself as a recognizable fiduciary. For example, in a letter from February 1610, Muḥammad al-Shaykh explained Urrea's trustworthiness:

> God knows that he became the faithful intermediary (*al-wāsiṭa al-ḥaqīqīya*) in all that binds us together, and we did not believe anything brought to us by anyone else (*wa lā amanna shay'an ithā kāna 'alā ghayr yadihi*).[59]

Urrea translated this effective passage nearly literally, using keywords that guaranteed his fiduciary status and the legibility of his service:

> God knows that he [Urrea] has been the true intermediary (*medianero verdadero*) in all that has been arranged (*ordenado*) between Your Majesty and myself, and I have relied on no one but him (*no he fiado de otro sino de el*).[60]

Urrea indeed translated most of the correspondence faithfully. Nonetheless, his administrative competence and varied Mediterranean experiences allowed him to use his translation work tactically for his own agenda. Urrea's work for Muḥammad al-Shaykh demonstrates the tremendous creative power translators had in tasks where they were supposed to invisible.

Ultimately, the outcome of these negotiations was a treaty negotiated and signed between Muḥammad al-Shaykh and Philip III during the winter of 1609–1610, in which Larache was nominally ceded to the Spanish in exchange for military support. The two rulers reached an agreement about their "friendship" (*maḥabba*) in February 1610, though the potential *amistades* between the Spanish and Moroccan rulers had been discussed by their agents since at least 1607.[61] The text was drawn up in Spanish then translated into written Arabic, possibly by Urrea himself based on his formation in Tlemecen and secretarial experiences in Istanbul and Algiers, where Arabic was one of the principal languages used in the Ottoman chancellery. Each ruler—or his amanuensis—commented on the text in his own language.[62] Philip read each article and his response was an opportunity to make an adjustment to the clause, either assuring his commitment to it or changing it slightly.[63] Then, Muḥammad al-Shaykh reviewed the annotated document and showed his agreement to Philip's comments through annotations like "we understand the answer and we are satisfied with it" (*fahimna al-jawāb wa raḍayna bihi*) to demonstrate his accord with each article or the formulaic marginal note "this is correct" (*ṣaḥīḥ dhālik*).[64] When there was more to be said, the notes reflected any adjustment.[65] The translations are unsigned, though Urrea and a Genovese agent in Morocco, Juanetin Mortara, were present at the negotiations.[66]

This process of reading through multiple translations and annotations in different languages introduced the possibility of mistranslation, and indeed it was mistranslation that ultimately ensured the success of the negotiations.[67] The treaty articles that tested confessional boundaries invited the greatest strategic mistranslation. For example, articles 7, 8, and 9 guaranteed Christians exceptional privileges in Muslim lands, including protection of their persons and property. These articles were designed to protect Spanish military and commercial interests, including in any new Atlantic presidios. Especially significant was a promise that Christians would not be taken captive in Muḥammad al-Shaykh's territories. In the robust and long-standing captive economy of the period, this would have meant cutting off a major source of income and an important tool for reciprocity against Christian aggression. Using marginal annotations, Philip agreed with all these provisions as initiated in Spanish. However, in article 11, Muḥammad al-Shaykh asked that the same guarantees be made for his own vassals against Christians (protection of their persons and properties, including against raiding and captivity). This article effectively requested that the Spanish king treat Christians and Muslims equally.

To this, Philip responded in the margins, "That this be conceded and assured in the Plazas (presidios) of His Majesty (Philip) in Berbería, but otherwise our law does not permit it."[68] That is, Philip was willing to concede protection for Muslim life and property in the presidios themselves, but not on behalf the many other Iberian actors involved in raiding and captive trade in Morocco and across the Mediterranean. However, in the translation back into Arabic for Muḥammad al-Shaykh's approval, the second clause about the limits of this guarantee was not translated, only Philip's promise that "nothing bad will happen to anyone in any of Your Majesty's [Philip's] lands, that are part of my [Philip's] territories."[69] The original and the translation carried *nearly* the same meaning—that Muḥammad al-Shaykh's vassals would be protected in Philip's Moroccan holdings—except where Philip, for a small Spanish audience of administrators, had gone out of his way to specify and explain why this agreement was strictly limited and thus likely to be honored only in very specific circumstances. The Arabic translation was phrased with an emphasis on the protection, rather than its limitation. This strategic mistranslation led Muḥammad al-Shaykh to believe that his request was met, without understanding that Philip had placed a significant caveat on his agreement.

The most enduringly important article of the treaty was article 4, by which Muḥammad and Philip agreed that their *maḥabba* would extend to their successors. This clause was an innovation in the way that treaties were traditionally concluded between Christian and Muslim rulers in Iberia and the Maghreb.[70] Most of the agreements signed between Iberian and North African rulers to this point had expired with the death of either of the signatories or had an otherwise limited term.[71] That the *maḥabba* between Philip III and Muḥammad al-Shaykh would carry on after their death was thus a striking agreement, and one indicating a step toward permanent international agreements rather than personal contracts between sovereigns. As Guillaume Calafat has shown, the "léxique de l'amitié" would become a foundation for diplomatic negotiations between European (in this case, French) and Muslim (in this case Ottoman) powers in the later seventeenth century.[72] It was also the clause that would later provide a basis for Muḥammad al-Shaykh's son to mount a case for Spanish favor in the inheritance dispute that will be studied in the next section.

Once the treaty was signed, Muḥammad al-Shaykh left Spain and was transported to the Spanish presidio of Peñon de Vélez in early summer 1610 in anticipation of Spanish support for his campaigns against his brother Zidān. Urrea went with him to help with the final arrangements. The planned capitulation of July 1610 was supposed to be carried out by Urrea and Mortara, who acted as a field agent for Spain's Moroccan affairs and who had worked alongside Diego Marín the younger before the latter's imprisonment.[73] It was Mortara who would eventually secure Marín's release in 1607 as part of the negotiations between Philip III and Muley Xeque.[74] Urrea and Mortara were the Spanish emissaries who would personally "receive" the fortress from Muḥammad al-Shaykh's *alcaide*, the latter having sent the soldiers away on the pretense of giving them their long-overdue payment in Fez.

In spite of the *maḥabba* that had been negotiated between the kings and their successors, the actual rendition of Larache was not so easy for the Spanish to achieve and required an on-the-ground intervention by Spanish translators. Although the exiled Muḥammad al-Shaykh had agreed in writing that the presidio would be rendered to the Spanish, it was his son and rival 'Abd Allah who actually ruled the territory occupied by the presidio when the treaty went into effect. Thus an actual Spanish conquest of Larache had to be organized, even after the signing of the treaty. The Spanish succeeded in taking Larache by force in November 1610.

The 1610 capitulation of Larache—in translation and then, months later, in deed—brought decades of Hispano-Moroccan diplomacy to a conclusion. However, these capitulations and their terms would ultimately serve to renew older patterns of legal translation. Through inter-imperial lawsuits that took place in the context of burgeoning international relations, the tactics of fiduciary translation that had been transplanted from the *morisco* to the Mediterranean context became an important vector to legitimate privileges abroad and assert sovereign claims for multiple constituencies. Fiduciary translation was becoming trans-imperial.

Trans-Imperial Legal Disputes: An Alternative Channel for Diplomacy, 1610–1691

My understanding of "trans-imperial" in the early modern Mediterranean is greatly influenced by the work of Natalie Rothman on Venetian dragomans as "trans-imperial subjects" in Istanbul. These "trans-imperial subjects" were "caught in the web of complex imperial mechanisms [and] at the same time were essential to producing the means to calibrate, classify, and demarcate imperial alterities."[75] This framework can shed light on that web, and how it was mutually constituted by individual action that was conditioned by experiences across a constellation of religious, legal, and linguistic settings that jointly created the "imperial mechanisms" to which Rothman refers. Rothman's paradigm has been adapted by Joshua White in studying "*fetva* diplomacy," in a way that is also useful for understanding the following example from the western Mediterranean context.[76] The fiduciary translation that took place within Mediterranean trans-imperial frameworks sustained inter-imperial systems in the Atlantic Mediterranean in the decades preceding the conventional dating of the development of an international legal system (e.g., the Peace of Westphalia, in 1648). Disputes across Islamic and Christian legal systems arose at the conjunctures of dynastic, military, and political interests. As had been the case in postconquest Granada, translators were needed to convert the validity of religiously grounded legal practices and instruments through the production of official translations (*traducción fehaciente*) and to make the claims mutually intelligible to legal authorities of different religions. As part of these processes, translator tactics once again created opportunities to communicate additional information related to legal, religious, or political claims. In the case of one royal inheritance dispute after the conquest of Larache, the fiduciary translation of a legal opinion (*fatwā*) became an additional venue for cross-confessional legal arguments during diplomatic episodes.[77]

This remarkable case of cross-confessional fiduciary translation involved an inheritance dispute related to Muḥammad al-Shaykh and the very same treaty negotiations that had been concluded in 1610 with Urrea's help. Muḥammad al-Shaykh was assassinated not long after his return to Morocco in August 1613. His son, 'Abd Allah, continued the war with his uncle Zidān, who ruled from Marrakesh. 'Abd Allah and Zidān entered in to a legal dispute over the legacy of Muḥammad al-Shaykh, which was arbitrated by Philip III across religious, linguistic, and legal systems. Fiduciary translation was an important element of the dispute, its resolution, and the long-term political consequences.

Muḥammad al-Shaykh's assassination left a significant portion of his wealth in legal limbo—almost half a million *ducados*, plus three times that amount of value in precious gems. Since Muḥammad al-Shaykh had died intestate, his legacy was governed by a complex and malleable Islamic inheritance system conditioned by custom as well as doctrine.[78] To complicate the matter further, at the time of Muḥammad al-Shaykh's death, the treasure was located in the Portuguese presidio of Tangiers, until it disappeared under suspicious circumstances that instigated a royal inquest of the Portuguese governor of the presidio.[79] Multiple competing dynastic agendas were articulated around this inheritance dispute. At a minimum, the dispute was a forum for the competing claimants for the Moroccan throne, a vector for Philip III's commitment to maintaining a foothold in North Africa through the presidio system, and an opportunity for Portuguese nobility who resented the Spanish king's Iberian hegemony during the period of the Union of the Crowns from 1580 to 1640 to assert their power in the Portuguese presidios.

Both Zidān and 'Abd Allah petitioned the king of Spain in order to recover the lost treasure for themselves, and each portrayed himself as the rightful heir to Muḥammad al-Shaykh. To convey these messages, a range of translation and non-translation strategies were used by Zidān and 'Abd Allah. For example, although Zidān was reported to have "spoken Spanish as fluently as if he had been born in Spain," all of his letters were issued in Arabic.[80] Nevertheless, the Arabic letters were accompanied by Spanish translations made in Marrakesh by the *morisco* translator Aḥmad ibn al-Qāsim al-Ḥajarī. These bilingual chancellery practices echoed the former habits of his brother, Muḥammad al-Shaykh, much of whose early correspondence with Spanish officials was written directly in Spanish—probably by Juanetín Mortara, judging by the handwriting—and signed with Muḥammad al-Shaykh's royal *'alāma* in Arabic.[81]

In substance, each competing monarch invoked the relationship of his father and the diplomatic agreements that had been reached with the king of Spain (Aḥmad al-Manṣūr in Zidān's arguments, and Muḥammad al-Shaykh in 'Abd Allah's). For example, in the first letter that Zidān sent to the Duke of Medina Sidonia in February 1614 to communicate his dissatisfaction with 'Abd Allah's claims, he referred repeatedly to the mutual goodwill and "consideration" maintained between al-Mansur and Philip II via the mediation of the duke (who was the chief minister in charge of North African affairs).[82] He also accused 'Abd Allah of being behind his own father's assassination. Zidān and his translator, al-Ḥajarī, emphasized previous diplomatic accords and the personal relations that helped conclude them, as well as the general principal of international relations: "God has made [possible] conformity and communication between the different nations of the world, even if their laws are different, according to the considerations of good government and the precepts of rule, and thus truth will be achieved in the communication between the kings and governors and important people, both through letters and through embassies, in matters that are weighty and worth considering [carefully]."[83] Effectively, Zidān was insisting on reciprocity in a diplomatic system. This appeal to royal parity and a tradition of diplomatic relations was the foundation for the Islamic legal case he hoped to make intelligible to Philip. ʿAbd Allah also relied on affective and diplomatic language, invoking the *maḥabba* between Philip III and ʿAbd Allah's father, which he ardently wished to renew.[84] However, in translation, this relationship was fashioned as one of service, as for example in spring 1614, when ʿAbd Allah wrote to the Duke of Medina Sidonia to insist that he wished to maintain the written agreement that his father had made with Philip (*kamā kataba li-wālid* . . . *iḥna muwāfiqūn ʿalayhi lā mubaddalayn wa lā mughayarayn*) and asked the duke to write a letter to this effect to Philip on ʿAbd Allah's behalf. The translation, though anonymous, included additional information and phrasing indicative of the creative role of the translator to adapt ʿAbd Allah's message to Spanish expectations. Striking was the use of *merced* (favor) to refer to ʿAbd Allah's requests of both the Duke of Medina Sidonia and Philip III. In this translation, which is one of the least literal in the collection of extant texts, the translator added an assurance of the authenticity of ʿAbd Allah's petition: "And I wrote this letter to Your Excellency in my own hand so that no scribe or other person would take part."[85] Ironically, it seems that this sentiment was added by just such an "other person"—whether by ʿAbd Allah's instruction or the scribe's own initiative is unclear.

Although the agendas expressed in these petitions were political and strategic, their form was legal and religious. The political issue was the system of alliances and rivalries that was articulated through Moroccan foreign relations at this time. Zidān was allied with the Dutch as part of his support and legitimacy against other claimants to the Moroccan throne, including ʿAbd Allah, who was a client and erstwhile ally of the Iberians. The Dutch and the Iberians were nominally in a period of truce after decades of war and rebellion through which the United Provinces had finally achieved recognition of their independence from Spain in 1609. Nevertheless, both the Dutch and the Spanish sought to minimize the success and advantages of the other in Morocco. The legal question, on the other hand, was whether ʿAbd Allah, as his father's heir, was the sole beneficiary of the inheritance that had been left in the custody of the Portuguese presidio. Zidān insisted that the treasure be divided according to the normally prescribed divisions (*partes*). Those *partes* referred to the Qur'ānic "science of shares" (*'ilm al-farā'id*) by which a father's inheritance was divided proportionally among his offspring, wives, and parents (if living). For Zidān, the benefit of following Islamic law in this case would mean that 'Abd Allah would have limited access to his father's funds, which would certainly be spent in the war against Zidān. If divided, the larger portion of the inheritance would go to Muḥammad al-Shaykh's other relatives, several of whom lived at Zidān's court in Marrakesh.[86]

Under Christian law and practice, particularly in Habsburg realms, a father's legacy was governed by primogeniture, as both Zidān and 'Abd Allah were aware.[87] 'Abd Allah anticipated this practice and sought to encourage it by reminding Philip of the transitive *maḥabba* that had been agreed upon between the Spanish king and 'Abd Allah's father.[88] Zidān also invoked diplomatic precedent, specifically the good relations and correspondence between his father Aḥmad al-Manṣūr and Philip III's father, Philip II.[89] In addition, Zidān mounted an Islamic legal argument for the Qur'ānic division and sent supporting documents and translations.[90]

The significance of this case lies in its form and intention, rather than its result. Zidān was not successful in his petition to Philip, who ultimately favored 'Abd Allah and returned some part of the inheritance to him, contingent upon his continuing alliances and "service" to the Spanish king. Once again 'Abd Allah's translator helped him express adequate gratitude for the favor he had been granted, translating 'Abd Allah's report on the news he received from the Spanish court in terms of *merced* and service, ideas that are not present in the original Arabic.[91] It is unlikely that Philip was substantially swayed by the rhetoric of either party; his priorities were the maintenance of the Atlantic presidios and the disadvantage of the Dutch and their allies. Indeed, throughout the discussions of Moroccan affairs among Spanish agents and officials, Zidān was always spoken of as the most likely winner of the civil war.[92] That very respect for his power may have been what cost him a favorable ruling in the inheritance case, since the Spanish would have been loath to provide more resources for the ally of their Dutch rivals. In all cases, the choices of 'Abd Allah's translator inscribed the Moroccan pretender's requests into a familiar vocabulary of service and favor that was eminently recognizable to the Spanish court.

Just as 'Abd Allah's anonymous translator(s) helped him convey, per-haps unwittingly, a message of subservience and gratitude that was appro-priate to the Spanish petition genre, Zidān's translator mediated his patron's message in such a way as to ensure the reception of Islamic legal ideas in Christian chancellery forms. The heart of Zidān's case was a *fatwā* generated collectively by the chief qāḍī and other judges, *'ulamā'*, and *fuqahā'* of Mar-rakesh in October 1614.[93] It was translated in Marrakesh by Aḥmad ibn Qāsim al-Ḥajarī, a Spanish *morisco* who had fled Spain and emigrated to Morocco in 1599 and who already had experience navigating between Chris-tian and Islamic law.[94] Al-Ḥajarī had spent time in Granada and in contact with figures, like Alonso del Castillo and Pedro de Castro, with connections and experience in fiduciary translation. There he witnessed the process of translating and validating Islamic legal information derived from written sources and reinscribing it in the Christian legal system and its archives.[95] In addition, as Isabel Boyano has shown from newly discovered documentation in Granada, al-Ḥajarī did indeed participate in the *plomos* translations, as he later claimed in his autobiography.[96] In Morocco, al-Ḥajarī translated Islamic doctrine into Spanish for exiled *moriscos* then living as Muslims in North Africa after a lifetime without an Islamic education.[97] In 1614, al-Ḥajarī would turn to another form of cross-confessional translation of the *fatwā* and the descriptions of the legal justifications for Zidān's case as they were presented in written form (in Arabic and in translation) in various royal let-ters sent by Zidān to Philip and his councilors.[98] Those texts reveal how fiduciary translation supported bilateral foreign relations in early modern diplomacy.

Al-Ḥajarī's translation tactics indicate that he was aware of the protocol for "converting" Islamic legal knowledge into evidence or arguments that could be used in Christian courts. Like the Granada *fuqahā'* who became councilmen, al-Ḥajarī embodied Islamic and Christian legal expertise and experience, which gave him a special position with respect to Christian institutions. In his autobiographical account of his journey to France and the Netherlands in 1611, which was composed in the 1630s for an Egyptian audience, al-Ḥajarī explained the technical qualifications of his position: "You should know that I am the interpreter of the Sultan of Marrakesh. He who occupies that post must study the sciences (*yaqrā' fī-l-'ulūm*), as well as the books of the Muslims and Christians (*kutub al-muslimīn wa kutub al-naṣrānī*), in order to know what he is saying and translating in the court of the Sultan."[99] The *kutub* (books) of this sentence could refer to a range of legal and scientific works since, as Nina Zhiri has recently shown, al-Ḥajarī was part of a robust and nearly unstudied Moroccan translation movement of European works of science, geography, medicine, and military technology.[100] In his autobiography, al-Ḥajarī was quick to specify that the authority derived from this expertise obtained only before Christian audiences.[101] His role was to conduct *jihād ʿalā dīn* in Christian settings, not the *ijtihād* (legal reasoning) of the specialized and high-status jurists.[102] Nevertheless, the scholarly qualifications that underpinned the *ijtihād* of the *ʿulamāʾ* and *fuqahāʾ* as described by al-Wansharīsī were conceptually analogous to the scholarly qualifications that al-Ḥajarī asserted as royal translator.[103] Being a translator of Islamic legal materials in Christian fora also put him functionally into a sequence of *iftāʾ* (seeking and receiving a legal opinion) by which his translation provided legal information to a Spanish-speaking audience.[104] Al-Ḥajarī was not a *muftī*, nor did he present himself as one.[105] Nevertheless, like a *muftī*, al-Ḥajarī was an "intermediate figure" both between the bundled linguistic, religious, and political systems represented by the Moroccan and the Spanish courts, and between the discursive and hermeneutical interpretative processes that governed making public a legal opinion or an official translation.[106]

In this way, al-Ḥajarī's fiduciary translation in diplomatic encounters was analogous to the translation of Islamic legal documents by converted *fuqahāʾ*—some former *qāḍīs* and *muftīs*—working in *morisco* town councils, appellate courts, and the Inquisition. It was from this position that al-Ḥajarī translated into Spanish the legal opinion of the Marrakesh *ʿulamāʾ* in 1614 and the royal letter drafted by Zidān's chief minister al-Fashtālī. The latter document was meant to insist upon the validity of the *fatwā* in the context of reciprocity and international relations, that is, so that Philip would not only understand the legal argument but also be persuaded that he should consider it before disposing of Muḥammad al-Shaykh's inheritance. Thus there were various levels of legal claims being made by Zidān's party, all of which had to be translated effectively. First was the elucidation by the *ʿulamāʾ* of Marrakesh of Islamic inheritance law and the *ʿilm al-farāʾid* as revealed in the Qurʾān to Muḥammad, which al-Ḥajarī explained in translation was the "ley de los moros."[107] Al-Fastālī and al-Ḥajarī further explained in the royal cover letter and its translation this point in comparison to Christian law.[108] Second was the assertion in the cover letter accompanying the *fatwā* that this legal opinion was legible across religious and sovereign boundaries under the Law of Nations, what in translation al-Ḥajarī referred to as "permitted between 'nations.'"[109] Finally, that Law of Nations was based on precedents of royal correspondence and agreements—and the affective and political bond of *maḥabba*—from which royal reputation (that all-important intangible asset for early modern rulers) could be guaranteed only by respecting the law and property of the other side.

In addition to explaining the technicalities of Islamic and Christian inheritance systems, al-Ḥajarī was sensitive to translating the discursive and social relations that made legal documents valid in distinct ways under Islamic and Christian law. The interdependence of those discursive and social relations was, of course, one of the key attributes of fiduciary translation. The original Arabic *fatwā* was signed by twenty-three judges, including the head *qāḍī* of Marrakesh, Ehmed Benqasim Satibi, and the vice-*qāḍī*, Hebdurrehmén Yborque, the only two whose names and positions were explained by al-Ḥajarī. This collective legal advice bridged the *fatwā* and the *shūrā* (council). Although a *fatwā* is not legally binding, the reputation of the legal elite would have supported the authority behind the legal opinion. Indeed, the first audience for the *fatwā* would have been the people of Marrakesh, who would have learned from it about 'Abd Allah's contravention of legal norms and family responsibility. Like the *fetva* diplomacy that supported Ottoman international relations and imperial governance, Zidān's message was multivalent.[110]

In the Christian system, as al-Ḥajarī well knew, the personal authority of Islamic legal scholars would communicate little, and not only because of the difference in religion. Christian legal norms relied on generating official legal documents whereas Islamic legal norms relied on recognizing a fiduciary system of legal authority. Since al-Ḥajarī was well aware of the Spanish norms, he explained—both in his translator's "preface" and in the Spanish translation—that the Arabic *fatwā* was witnessed by fiduciaries whose role would be intelligible to the Spanish chancellery: "judges and wise men and scribal notaries on the order of the king [Zidān], each one signing by his own hand and writing "So-and-so says or affirms the same" and then placing his seal" (*los jueces y sabios y escribanos del número a pedimiento de su majestad, que cada uno firmó de su mano excriviendo antes "y lo mismo dize o afirma Fulano", metiendo su nombre çifrado en la rrúbrica*).[111] Certainly the moral and legal authority of "judges and wise men" was mutually intelligible. What was particularly significant was al-Ḥajarī's choice to include "scribal notaries" in the list. The *escribano de número* (scribal notary), as we saw in Chapter 1, was an official professional category, requiring an appointment from a governing body and often the passing of an exam. These scribal notaries played an important role in the production of valid chancellery instruments, because their participation and signatures were required for final validation (*anuncio*).[112] This office granted its holder special administrative powers to legitimate documentation through performative discourse, such as inscribing *doy fe* and leaving their scribal seal or mark.

Al-Ḥajarī's inexact translation of the *'ulamā'* position as *escribano* was in fact more "legible" than "scholars" since in Spain it was the *escribano* who had powers to authenticate and legitimate legal instruments. The details of signing, sealing, and validating an oral confirmation of agreement through writing and adjacent performative signs were all discursive stages that would have been recognizable to the Spanish court and chancellery staff, even if the litany of Arabic names, titles, and the legal knowledge and social status of their bearers meant nothing to them. Al-Ḥajarī's description of the kind of officials who signed using Spanish administrative vocabulary was a legacy of the mechanisms of fiduciary translation that had been elaborated in post-conquest Granada and that al-Ḥajarī had witnessed during his time in that city. It was also reflective of his experiences living as a *morisco* in Spain, which had taught him to worry constantly about how Spanish anti-Islamic sentiment would affect the reception of Arabic knowledge.[113] Al-Ḥajarī's long and wide-ranging professional career embodied the ongoing fiduciary translation from Arabic to Spanish after the *morisco* period and across the Mediterranean. This example of unsuccessful "*fatwā* diplomacy" across the Straits of Gibraltar adds to the important conclusions in White's study of *fetva* diplomacy in the Ottoman world, whereby the *seyhülislam* (the "*muftī*" of Istanbul) used legal opinions to negotiate mutual benefits for the empire and its European allies, including not only Venetians but also many of the powers also on the scene in the western Mediterranean, such as the Dutch and French.

Despite al-Ḥajarī's success in rendering the Islamic legal and political claims into legible Christian forms, the Spanish court ultimately "ruled" in favor of 'Abd Allah, Zidān's nephew and rival, who though the weaker ruler in Morocco was in a better position to furnish the Spanish with what they wanted: another fortified garrison on the Atlantic Mediterranean to support the precarious Larache. In August 1614 the Spanish conquered the nearby fortress of La Mamora, preventing Zidān from ceding it to the Dutch as he had promised. Zidān's pro-Dutch policies in this era were also affected by his unsuccessful petitions to Philip III in that same period to return the royal Moroccan library, which had been captured and removed to the Escorial in 1612, sowing the seeds for the ongoing diplomatic incident and translated legal arguments that will be discussed below.[114] As Daniel Hershenzon has shown, the Moroccan library was another vector for inter-imperial and trans-imperial legal discussions. The legal arguments made by Philip's advisors were influenced both by their desire to limit the role of Portugal in Iberian-Moroccan diplomacy and by the question of whether the Spanish capture of the French ship that carried the library had been legal in the first place.[115] Zidān encouraged his Dutch allies to intervene on his behalf with the French, though this avenue was not successful. Meanwhile, both Zidān and 'Abd Allah continued to write and plead their case over the inheritance in Tangiers. By January 1615 the issue was resolved in favor of 'Abd Allah, even though it was Zidān who emerged as the victorious ruler in 1627, and the dynasty was permanently weakened.[116] The issue of the library was on hold as the alliance system shifted across Europe and the western Mediterranean.

Uses of fiduciary translation in diplomatic disputes did not end with the decline of the Sa'adi dynasty. As the seventeenth century waxed and waned, both the Moroccans and the Spanish found themselves competing with other would-be imperial powers in the western Mediterranean. This competition created an increasing need for the circulation of information, some of which continued to rely on fiduciary translation. Portugal, along with its African holdings in Tangiers and Mazagan, had declared its independence in 1640. Although Spain refused to recognize Portugal's independent status until 1668, the union of the crowns was effectively dissolved in 1640, with major consequences for the operation of Iberian presidios. In 1662 the Portuguese princess Catherine of Braganza brought Tangiers to the English as part of her dowry to Charles II of England, allowing the English a strategic possession near the Strait of Gibraltar and facing their rival Spain.

Meanwhile, the new Alawite dynasty—whose success was based upon, among other things, religious legitimacy and the support of religious leaders—was gathering strength. In 1672 the second sultan of that dynasty, Mulay Ismā'īl (1645–1727), took the throne. As part of his consolidation of power in the face of European possessions in Morocco, he sought to take back Moroccan territories under European jurisdiction, including Spanish La Mamora (1681) and Larache (1689), Portuguese Asila (1692), and the now-English Tangier (1684). Only Mazagan was left to a European power (the Portuguese), and this too would be rendered to the Moroccans in 1769.[117]

Spain's defeats at La Mamora and then Larache created additional needs for fiduciary translation between Morocco and Spain. The retaking of La Mamora and Larache allowed the new Moroccan sultan to regain strategic territory and assert his legitimacy and at the same time to reopen dialogue between the Spanish Habsburgs and Morocco. The new dynastic context in Morocco was a motive not only for conquest but also for diplomatic initiatives that depended on translation. Muley Ismā'īl (r. 1672–1727), sent embassies to his rivals France (1681–1682) and Spain (1690–1691). This latter episode was characterized by significant translation activities surrounding the negotiation over Spanish captives from La Mamora (1681) and Larache (1689). Translation would play an important role during Muḥammad ibn 'Abd al-Wahhāb al-Wazīr al-Ghassānī's subsequent embassy to Spain in 1690–1691.[118]

Al-Ghassānī was hardly the first ambassador from a Muslim power to be received at the court of the Habsburgs, and several Muslim princes in exile had lived in Habsburg Spain along with their extended retinues.[119] In 1601, just as the Moroccan embassy was arriving in England, Spain received an imperial delegation from Shah Abbas of Persia.[120] That same year two ambassadors came to the court in Valladolid from the ruler of the North African kingdom of Cuco (Amar ben Amar bel Cadi, in the Spanish sources).[121] Another embassy from Cuco was sent to Valladolid in 1604. During the latter episode, the Arabic-speaking *morisco* Jesuit Ignacio de las Casas interacted extensively with the North African ambassadors, causing him to lament the paucity of Arabic expertise amongst Spain's political officials. One of his principal reasons for promoting Arabic at the turn of the seventeenth century, other than the evangelistic arguments related to the *morisco* mission (which will be discussed in Chapter 4) was the need of the monarchy "not to have only two or four [Arabic] interpreters, but many, of diverse skills, able not only to translate faithfully and discretely the letters and embassies which are brought from other princes in this language, but also to be able to respond with the same level of confidence and security."[122] Indeed, through his conversation with the Cuco ambassador, Las Casas learned of the frustration the latter felt that business could not be conducted quickly, or competently, and that the result could be dangerous. Negotiations were jeopardized by the lack of respect that was felt by Arabic-speaking delegations, and information could be passed or changed that might be harmful to the Spanish king.

Indeed, notwithstanding the intensive translation activities of the sixteenth century, the Habsburg *secretaría de lenguas* still could not count on a regular staff of experts in "oriental" languages until the end of the seventeenth century.[123] When, in 1649, the first official Ottoman delegation arrived in Madrid, the court found itself without a single interpreter equipped to assist during political negotiations.[124] The Spanish Habsburgs were obliged to send to their cousins in Vienna to find out if there was anyone who could mediate with the Ottomans, replicating the collaboration that had taken place around the Habsburg-Safavid diplomatic initiatives beginning in the 1570s. The transfer of translator expertise through dynastic networks was mirrored by the consolidation of translator networks and family connections between the Austrian and Spanish Habsburg realms and beyond.[125]

Meanwhile, by the end of the sixteenth century, Arabic expertise at the disposal of the Spanish crown was limited to the scientific and religious erudition of the handful of Arabic students at the Escorial.[126] Of course, the Arabic patrimony of the Escorial was, in fact, a major part of the diplomatic episode of 1690–1691. In fact, for Muley Ismāʿīl, the primary goal of the embassy was to exchange the Spanish captives for the Moroccan "captives" that had been held in Spain since 1612: the books and manuscripts of the library of Muley Zidān.

The Moroccan ambassador al-Ghassānī was selected for his task primarily because he was considered to have sufficient learning in order to evaluate the Arabic books in the Escorial and thus could ensure that he brought the correct volumes back to Morocco.[127] He took with him his own Spanish interpreter, ʿAbd al-Salām ibn Aḥmad Gassūs, an eminent legal scholar (faqīh) in his own right.[128] This combination of scholarship, diplomacy, and legal and linguistic expertise reflected the fiduciary translation that sustained this example of cross-confessional diplomacy.

On the Spanish side, the ambassador in charge of negotiations in Morocco was, unsurprisingly, a Franciscan with long experience both in captivity and the captive trade, Juan Muñoz.[129] Assisting him in Morocco, and facilitating the interactions between al-Ghassānī and the Spanish court, was the enigmatic "Abdel Messi" (in the Spanish sources), an early member in Spain of the important dynasty of Eastern Christian translators who would work for generations in the Escorial and the Royal Library in Madrid after its founding by the first Spanish Bourbon king in 1712.[130] The installation of this family as royal translators, beginning in 1680 and continuing during the War of Spanish Succession (1700–1714) and the establishment of the Bourbon dynasty, was part of a growing emphasis on professional Arabism in Spain that will be explored in greater depth in Chapter 5. Just as translation was one of the tools of representation available to Muley Ismāʻīl, so too it would be for Philip V (1700–1746).

Already during the reign of the last Spanish Habsburg king, Charles II (d. 1700), Abdel Messi had received the royal appointment of Interpreter of Turkish, Arabic, Syriac, and Chaldean in December 1680. His origins are unclear, though in his appointment as royal translator, he is designated as "born in Nineveh" (which is in modern-day Iraq) and was likely connected to the San Juan family of Iraqi Christians studied by John Paul Ghobrial.[131] In al-Ghassānī's account he is referred to consistently as the Aleppan Christian translator.[132] The latter reflects more about the Moroccan ambassador's mental geography of Syriac Christianity (which extended throughout Mesopotamia) than Messi's actual birthplace.

Al-Ghassānī's impressions of Spain's Arabic translator included those formed during his reception by Abdel Messi's in-laws in Almagro during his journey across the peninsula from Cadiz to Madrid, including a certain cleric (كليرك).[133] Al-Ghassānī's description of the encounter with him was an opportunity to explain to his Moroccan readers that "the cleric is the student who has acquired learning; he is not a friar [فرايلي], though like the friar he does not marry. . . . These clerics are the ones who conduct the *misas*, which means masses, play a musical instrument in their mosques, and recite and chant their prayer books in melodious voices."[134] The Arabic vocabulary and the selective use of Spanish loanwords and their translations in the text is also telling of the way in which legal and linguistic knowledge were entangled in individuals and family networks.

Abdel Messi accompanied al-Ghassānī to court in Madrid and on his return journey to Morocco. Eventually, after al-Ghassānī had returned to Meknes in 1691, Abdel Messi would travel to Morocco in order to conclude the final negotiations. In parallel to Urrea's role at the initial handover of Larache in 1610, Messi traveled to Larache in order to conclude the treaty that returned the now-former presidio to the Moroccans, who had conquered it in 1689, acting alongside the official ambassador, Manuel Viera de Lugo.

Messi was a significant figure throughout this diplomatic episode, and his position in brokering and ensuring the adequate reception of information was noted by the Moroccans. For example, al-Ghassānī recounted how, during his audience with Charles II in Madrid, the ambassador presented the "sultanic" letter to the king who handed it directly to the translator "to translate it into the *ajami* language."[135] According to al-Ghassānī, it was through translation that Charles "felt the weight of the Alawite [the Moroccan ruler]" and his reputation. As was done so many times before, the translator was charged with "conserving the reputation" of his patron and of the state itself through his mediation of legal and political authority.

Messi's extant translation work is a testament to the many continuities and parallels with the earlier episodes discussed in this chapter. For example, in a 1691 letter, Mulay Ismāʿīl described to Charles the arrival of the translator Abdel Messi and the oral negotiations that also took place. Messi himself translated the letter, highlighting his important role in the actual negotiations, rather than that of the actual ambassador, Manuel Viera de Lugo.[136] The content of the letter concerned the ongoing captive negotiations, and in it Mulay Ismāʿīl made two arguments about those negotiations in reference, once again, to (1) previous treaties between Spain and Muslim powers and (2) the opinion of the Moroccan ʿulamāʾ. In his letter, Muley Ismāʿīl invoked the authority of the "ʿulamāʾ/sabios y juezes" (wise men and judges) of his capital at Meknes and rescinded his promise to send back the one hundred Larache captives as his ambassador had confirmed would happen. This was a negotiating tactic that Muley Ismāʿīl hoped would improve his bargaining position for the rendition of either the Moroccan library or a larger number of Muslim slaves in the peninsula.

In the invocation of the anonymous legal authorities of Morocco, the episode echoes the practices of cross-confessional legal disputes that were used in the 1610 negotiations and the subsequent 1614 dispute over inheritance. In fact, Muley Ismāʿīl made direct reference to these earlier episodes as precedents for his negotiations with Spain, claiming that Muḥammad al-Shaykh had made the 1610 agreement only under duress after the Spanish captured his sons and the very same treasure that was later subject to the inheritance dispute. The duress claimed by Muley Ismāʿīl invalidated the 1610 treaty of perpetual friendship (maḥabba)—and its translations—by which "right" the Spanish had claimed the presidio in 1610. According to the ʿulamāʾ of Meknes, since the treaty was not valid, neither was the Spanish occupation, and thus the captives taken during its conquest in 1689 were legitimate prisoners of war and had to be kept as such. He added to this legal and historical argument by invoking the broken mudéjar treaty of Granada from 1492, still a lingering injustice in the Islamic history of Spain that was remembered all too well in Morocco. Muley Ismāʿīl insisted, sovereign to sovereign, that if he were not bound by his law and religion and the council of his legal and religious experts, he would send the captives directly.

Thus he begged Charles to give him some other reason to do so, such as liberating the Zidān library or one thousand Muslim slaves.[137]

Abdel Messi's Spanish translations of these legal arguments about the status of the Christian captives from Larache are one more example of an Arabic translator ensuring the valid transmission of a legal argument made by the king based on the *shūrā* (advice) received from jurisconsults-cum-political councilors. Muley Ismāʿīl turned to legal arguments as diplomatic tactics, expecting the Christian sovereign to understand and accept the premises of Islamic law in translation. There was certainly precedent for that comprehension, including Zidān's petitions, even if not all Moroccan suits before Spanish kings had been successful. Indeed, perhaps in anticipation of the contact between legal systems that would occur during his diplomatic mission, al-Ghassānī showed particular interest in learning about Spanish law (including family law such as marriage and inheritance) during his voyage through Spain.[138] In the "global legal transformation" through which ancient legal pluralities were stretched across a vast scale, cross-confessional diplomacy continued to be predicated on a multi-normative regime.[139] One of the main vectors for this multi-normative regime was fiduciary translation.

The embassy of al-Ghassānī and the correspondence between the two sovereigns (in translation) was a turning point in the foundations of what scholars have categorized as "modern" Hispano-Moroccan diplomacy, which is usually marked as beginning in the 1750s and 1760s.[140] However, official diplomacy between Spain and the Muslim powers had functioned on legal bases before the eighteenth century, even if it was fractured and not always successful. Through the practices and personnel of fiduciary translation, the Spanish language sustained multilateral diplomatic relationships as a Mediterranean lingua franca, like Italian did in the eastern Mediterranean. The legacies of fiduciary translation in the cross-confessional diplomatic system between Spain and Morocco ultimately created more opportunities for translation, and for translators themselves.

Spanish Fiduciary Translation Carries Moroccan News and History Across Europe

Fiduciary translation became part of the habits of the cross-confessional diplomacy that spanned the early modern Mediterranean. As we have seen, that system fostered contact and exchange between distinct political and religious systems and engendered a mutually intelligible set of translation forms and practices by which to negotiate conflict, transmit legal value, or reach individual or sovereign agreements. An additional consequence of the transfer of fiduciary translation practices from the *morisco* to the Mediterranean context was the spread of news and information across Europe about Morocco, North Africa, and the Muslim world.

Arabic-Spanish translation was a key diplomatic tandem in the early modern Mediterranean, reaching its height at the end of the sixteenth century and the first half of the seventeenth. Of course, the reality of the Mediterranean is that it was polyglot. Morocco was the only North African power to have an Atlantic coastline, and beginning in the 1580s it hosted many foreign agents from all over Europe, the Ottoman territories, and other African powers. Almost all of the European agents, who were from England, France, and the United Provinces, used Spanish as the "vehicular language" between Arabic and the language they used in crafting their reports back home.[141] Morocco, on both its Mediterranean and Atlantic fronts, became a major player in the *petite guerre* of corsairing that had been sustained for centuries in the Mediterranean and now had an Atlantic dimension with ships returning from African and American expeditions.

Spanish thus became a conduit for other European powers to trade and treat with Morocco in Arabic. This meant that Spanish was crucial in the chains of translation through which Mediterranean affairs were conducted from the end of the sixteenth century to the eighteenth and that relied on the circulation of accurate news and information. For example, in English correspondence with Moroccan agents and concerning Moroccan affairs, Spanish was used regularly. Even in the period of most intense English-Spanish rivalry, leading up to 1588 and until the deaths of Philip II and Elizabeth (in 1598 and 1603, respectively), the Spanish language underpinned all English-Moroccan correspondence and the activities of English agents in Morocco. This was a conscious and strategic choice. Although advised in 1597 by her ministers not to "lose reputation" by employing the language of an enemy (like Spanish) in diplomatic correspondence, Elizabeth knew that the English could not count on their own language being well enough known to conduct international diplomacy in the Mediterranean.[142] Thus a diplomatic lingua franca was used. In Ottoman affairs, the English diplomatic language was Latin or Italian.[143] For Moroccan affairs, which from the English perspective spanned the western Mediterranean and the Atlantic confluence, this lingua franca was Spanish.

English letters destined for Morocco were sent in Spanish, while those that arrived in England from Morocco were sent in Arabic with a Spanish translation made in Marrakesh.[144] Spanish would have also been a convenient language for Elizabeth, who seems to have known some of the language, perhaps learned from her half-sister Mary, daughter of Catherine of Aragon, or from the many Spanish diplomats and grandees (including Philip II) at court during her childhood. Meanwhile, in England, there was a turn in the language of official diplomacy in 1609—away from an English translation of the Spanish translation, to a Latin and/or English translation made directly from Arabic.[145] This shift in linguistic policy coincided with the development of early English orientalism in the person of William Bedwell.[146] However, this did not stop Moroccans from using Spanish in their English correspondence. Even though Bedwell or other orientalists (of whom there were less than a handful) could translate directly from Arabic, Zidān continued to send Spanish translations from Marrakesh.[147]

Although some of the practices of processing royal correspondence changed at court, Jacobean information networks in the western Mediterranean were nonetheless still dependent on Spanish. For example, the English factor and sometime privateer John Harrison, who undertook no less than eight expeditions to Morocco between 1610 and 1632, used Spanish constantly.[148] As James I and Charles I's principal Moroccan agent, charged especially with negotiating the release of English captives, Harrison used Spanish in Morocco to conduct negotiations with Saletian *moriscos*, with ransomers in Tetouan, and with the agents of Zidān (including the sultan's Spanish-speaking *morisco* secretary, probably al-Ḥajarī).[149] He also brought Spanish materials to Morocco through translation into Arabic.[150] He seems to have served as a kind of procurer of Spanish books—including the Spanish bible of Cipriano de Valera and Spanish translations of the works of John Calvin and Martin Luther—for an eager *morisco* audience in Morocco.[151] One of the most remarkable episodes of the Spanish fluency of this Mediterranean Englishman took place in 1625, when Harrison wrote three different Spanish letters to be copied and distributed across northern Morocco proposing an anti-Spanish alliance: one tailored for a Muslim audience, one for a Jewish audience, and one for the Iberians themselves.[152] Indeed, Harrison, and other agents with long Moroccan experience such as Francis Cottington, manifested the importance of Spanish in their work by frequent use of Spanish loanwords, even when writing to fellow Englishmen. Cottington, one of the pro-Catholic advocates in the English court, spent many years in

Spain, first as secretary to the English ambassador (1609–1611), then as the consul in Seville (1611–1612), and eventually as ambassador (1616–1622 and 1629–1631).[153] From Spain, however, he remained an important source of Mediterranean, and particularly Moroccan, information in England.[154] A successful and well-informed printed history of the Moroccan civil war was attributed to a possible relation, Robert Cottington, about whom little is known.[155]

The example of the English using Spanish for conducting commerce and politics in the western Mediterranean is only one of many. In addition to foreign powers relying on Spanish for the sake of their foreign relations, some Moroccan communities relied on Spanish for their own affairs. The *moriscos* of Salé, for example, and their descendants, maintained the use of Spanish and even Spanish administrative offices in their Moroccan corsair republic.[156] For example, in 1643, "Portuguese" (*converso*) merchants corresponded with Dutch authorities on behalf of the public notary (*escribano público*) of Salé (Morocco), explaining that "We the undersigned certify and authenticate (*damos fe*) to all those who read this, how Muḥammad bin Zayyd, who also signed this paper, is scribal notary (*escrivano público*) of the government of this city of Salé, and in all his acts enjoys complete faith and credit, as a scribe of this kind who is loyal and legal and to be trusted."[157] The continued use of notarial Spanish in Salé, with the fiduciary formulae, by descendants of Iberian Jews in the United Provinces in their transactions with Moroccan Muslim descendants of the recent *morisco* expulsion is highly significant. The sustained use of the notarial office of the *escribano público* in Morocco and the importance of the performative declaration of authenticity that occurred through this kind of fiduciary translation (*damos fe*), an act of legal power through translation, developed in post-conquest Granada before being exported across the Mediterranean and European networks.

The last treaty to be signed between the United Provinces and Morocco in Arabic and Spanish was in 1651.[158] After that, the European diplomatic language used between the Dutch and Moroccan state powers was French.[159] Nonetheless, Spanish continued to be used as the language of business and everyday communication, even by non-Iberian state representatives like the Dutch consul in Morocco, David de Vries, as late as 1655 (and possibly after).[160] In 1682, when a Moroccan embassy arrived at the court of Louis XIV to sign a peace treaty between the two monarchies, the language that was used for one of the drafts was in Spanish (as well as French and Arabic). It is clear that the Spanish text was one of the primary working copies for negotiations since it was annotated throughout in French.[161] Independent of the outcomes related to this treaty, this example shows how Spanish was used in negotiations between Morocco and other European powers (and Spanish rivals) as a diplomatic lingua franca even at the end of the century.

The use of Spanish in translation extended from and sustained European, Mediterranean, and global networks. Other forms of diplomacy throughout the Mediterranean, like the "political economy of ransom," were administrated in large part in Romance languages, including Spanish.[162] Spanish was one of the languages of captivity, but it was also one of the languages by which the economy of ransom was administered.[163] By the seventeenth century, administration of these exchanges and contacts through captivity and rendition reached its height after centuries (if not millennia) of practice. In the seventeenth century especially, Spanish-Arabic translation was one more important vector for this complex system. For example, the account books of the redemptive missionary orders often include the Arabic (or Ottoman) safe conducts granted by North African rulers, with an accompanying Spanish translation generated in the North African chancellery.[164]

The paperwork of captivity was clearly shaped by translation. As Daniel Hershenzon has shown, across the Mediterranean, Spanish captives and their families maintained a continuous flow of Spanish documents with state administration, creating a Spanish-language network for transmitting petitions and information about captivity.[165] In the case of political negotiations, translation provided a parallel forum for the business of captivity, itself often a parallel track for political and commercial negotiations at the individual and state scales.

These examples demonstrate the continuing vitality of Spanish as a legal and diplomatic lingua franca between Morocco and non-Iberian European powers well into the seventeenth century as Moroccan rulers, their agents, and other individuals in contact with European merchants, captives, or others produced Spanish translations or documents directly in Spanish to be sent to France, England, and especially the United Provinces. The endurance of Spanish is a counterpoint to the story of early European orientalism, which was supposedly "flourishing" in those same countries in that period, as a harbinger of later colonialism. That early orientalism did not equip European states with an effective multilingual technocracy as was found in Morocco.

In Morocco, the ability to produce Spanish documents on a mass scale was not so much motivated by an imbalance of power with Europe but was contingent upon the cultural legacy and skills of the Iberian captives and renegades, Moroccan Jews working across Iberia and Europe, and the *morisco* diaspora. Those skills included familiarity with the mutually influential notarial cultures that contributed to practices of fiduciary translation.[166] The continued use of Spanish as a diplomatic lingua franca—which was a legacy of the practices of Arabic-Spanish translation in the Ibero-Moroccan system as it developed at the turn of the seventeenth century—shows that Morocco was not "cut off" from early modern diplomacy or from connections with global empires and did not belatedly gain access to these in the eighteenth century. Similarly, although Dutch, English, and French ships and agents became increasingly present in the seventeenth-century Mediterranean (the so-called Northern Invasion), the continued significance of Spanish (language and individuals) in the western Mediterranean commercial-and-diplomatic-system underpinned even the activities of their rivals in the wars for European hegemony and global empire.[167]

In addition to providing a forum for diplomatic exchange and the continued elaboration of fiduciary translation, the Mediterranean was also where translators gained experience and expertise vital to their professional success and the claims they could make about their service in the "mercy economy." Professional translators used the recollection of Mediterranean experiences to support their *relaciones* and other reports to patrons and the Spanish administration, advertising their skill, expertise, and the strategic information they could contribute to the running of the empire. This experience was one more currency in the economy of *mercedes*. In the meantime, a wealth of Mediterranean experiences circulated in Spain, beginning with the Eastern Reports (*Avisos de Levante*) and Barbary Chronicles (*crónicas de Berbería*) in the 1570s and lasting well in to the eighteenth century.[168] Ultimately, this market for experiences and strategic information would excite interest in historical and political examples from the wider Muslim world, including examples from law and religion, that could be incorporated into Spanish political thought through translation from Arabic and other languages, a phenomenon that will be discussed in Chapter 5.

Meanwhile, in Spain the market for accounts of real-life experience closer to home, including in North Africa and the Mediterranean, continued to thrive. An unknowable number of pamphlet *relaciones* were printed and consumed in Spain that recounted captivity narratives, military service, or news of political events in the Mediterranean.[169] Readers continued to find valuable strategic and polemic information for engaging with Islam and, above all, entertainment. In all cases, the production of these works depended on Arabic translation in some way. This was sometimes direct, as in the case of Leo Africanus, who knew Arabic sources firsthand when composing his Italian history, and Mármol Carvajal, who claimed to rely on Arabic authors while clearly adapting much from his own experiences and his reading of Africanus.[170] In other cases, the North African experiences of Spanish authors were mediated by Arabic speakers or by their own learning of Arabic, though no direct translation is cited in their works, as in the case of the informative captivity accounts of figures like Diego Torres, Antonio de Sosa, Antonio de Saldanha, and Jorge de Henin, and even of Miguel de Cervantes himself.

The market for these kinds of experiences remained open and overlapped with the new markets for Arabic history and political theory. Translators were still among the best equipped to supply such markets, as, for example, in the case of the history of the third Alawite sultan, Muley Ismāʿīl, composed by the second lieutenant (*alferez*) don Joseph de León, the Arabic interpreter of the tiny presidio of Peñon de Vélez (*ynterprete dela lengua Arabiga en dicha Plaza*). This work, completed in manuscript in 1743, serves as a lingering example of the strategies and tactics of Spain's professional Arabic corps before new models were imposed at the end of the eighteenth century.[171] Little is known about the author, other than what he reveals about his twenty years of captivity in the Moroccan capital of Meknes (Mequinez) from 1708 to 1729. The account does not appear to have ever been printed, but it enjoyed some scribal publication and is still extant in at least two eighteenth-century manuscripts housed in the Spanish National Library.[172]

León's account was one among many firsthand reports about Morocco and its sultan. Muley Ismāʿīl ruled for over fifty years, and during this time true and apocryphal stories about him circulated in the reports of captives and diplomatic envoys from France and England.[173] León devoted a chapter to the experiences of Christian captives, including his own experience. León spent the first three years of his captivity in chains before he was determined to be useful and loyal (*considerandome fiel*) and was rewarded with a position in the royal armory. There, having secured the king's grace (*gracia*), he remained in a dignified position until 1728.[174] He used the traditional vocabulary of fidelity and service to describe to Spanish readers his success in a different "economy of *mercedes*": that of the sultan of Morocco. According to León, such a cursus would have been common enough for someone with his qualifications, since "the captives who are recognized as being capable and honorable, and who already speak Arabic (though not write it, since this is forbidden on pain of death), are put to work in the warehouses of the King, guarding them and working in them, among other jobs requiring confidentiality."[175] In this passage, León used the potent ideas of honor (*onra*) and confidentiality (*confianza*) to describe his qualities as they were recognized and rewarded by the Moroccan king as a way to guarantee the transmission of the information and analysis offered in his report.

For Spanish readers, León's work provided a first-person account of Moroccan society, government, and culture in the early eighteenth century, refracted through the opinions of a Spanish soldier and translator with decades of North African experience of interest and relevance in the peninsula. For example, León portrayed the system of advisors and legal experts who counseled the sultan, as had been done in the cases of the council received by Zidān and Ismāʿīl when negotiating for captives and treasure with the kings of Spain.[176] León also described legal norms and offices in relation to familiar Christian vocabulary: for example, "the Head Qāḍī who is renowned like the Pontiff," or explaining in the chapter "How Civil and Criminal Law Is Judged" that "the *talbes* [from Ar. *ṭālib*, student] in the Mosque occupy the same functions as scribes, and just like other [scribes] they issue wills, sales receipts, and other [documents] that are offered, like marriage contracts, and all the paperwork relevant to loans and debt obligations between parties, and all with an authority as witnesses [*testigos*]."[177]

The firsthand account of the presidio translator's experiences in Morocco and knowledge of the Muslim world brought fiduciary translation to new genres and audiences. In over eighty chapters across more than two hundred and fifty folios, León answered his reader's anticipated questions about the geography, history, and culture of Morocco and other parts of the Islamic world, as well as about politics and culture in the sultan's court. Written as a dialogue, the curiosity of his imagined interlocutor also gave him an opportunity to discuss the life of Muḥammad and the early history of Islam in conflict with the Persian and Byzantine Empires and eventually the North African kingdoms it conquered. Surprisingly, there is no account of the conquest of Spain. Indeed, León spent dozens of chapters addressing questions about religious customs and legal frameworks, effectively translating Islamic law and doctrine for Spanish readers.[178] The genre and the readers may have differed from the technical legal and diplomatic instruments that had been received by courts, councils, and kings during the Habsburg period, but results also led to the engagement by Spaniards with ideas and examples derived from Islamic legal practices.

León enjoyed a long and close relationship with Muley Ismāʿīl and his family, and there was much in the sultan's character and actions that he admired. After all, it was Ismāʿīl's curiosity that led to additional professional opportunities for people like León (who identified himself first and foremost as an Arabic interpreter): "In the court there was a man from Salé called Arraez Perez, who was an expert on England and its government after spending time in that country, another Arraez Benasa who had been in France and had similar information about that Kingdom, and a Sevillian called Side Mojamete Andaluz, the interpreter and Physician of the King, who spoke with authority about Spanish affairs, and with these three he [Ismāʿīl] passed the time during unoccupied moments chatting about the governments and the qualities of these powers, since he enjoyed learning."[179] Like others before him, León the translator occupied a position as a trans-imperial expert whose value derived from ambiguous loyalties and experiences. That ambiguity could be transformed into currency in multiple "economies of *mercedes*."

As might be expected in a context where the rhetoric of religious and political rivalry was common, León's descriptions of Muslim law, ceremony, and history offered frequent opportunities for criticism. This was effectively a new kind of polemic, which mixed traditional hostility toward Islam with the burgeoning comparative sciences to create a discourse of civilizational superiority, mediated by the translator's own experience in captivity. Though León's life and work have left little echo beyond the few extant manuscripts of this dialogue, this late example of those syntheses of personal experience and useful information that were the fodder for most *relaciones de servicio* in the seventeenth century, particularly those submitted by translators, is nonetheless a testament to enduring Spanish audience for works written by Arabic translators. These audiences were attracted not only by the exotic but also by the polemical. Although individual experiences across the Mediterranean were as fluid and diverse as ever, León's treatise entered a cultural market where laws, policies, and Tridentine print culture were shaping ever-stricter ideals for subjecthood in relation to language, loyalty, and religion.

Though nominally imposed through univocal orders like royal edicts and the resolutions of ecclesiastic councils, in practice such ideas were disseminated through dialogue, instruction, and, eventually, inquisitorial examination. Indeed, it is no accident that the work is a dialogue between two interlocutors—one anonymous and one being Joseph de León—who in 1743 found themselves in conversation in the Spanish presidio of Peñon. The dialogue was an appealing and familiar didactic format. As had been the case in

Baltasar de Morales's 1593 *Diálogo* between the Orán veteran and residents of
Córdoba, or Juan de Ribera's 1599 *Catecismo provechoso*—a dialogue between
the priest of Guadix and the North African traveler (which is discussed in the
Chapter 4)—conversation provided the occasion for the Arabic interpreter to
showcase his knowledge, experience, and his service and fidelity to Spain and
the crown at the same time that it revealed connections with other legal and
political systems. Like those other dialogues featuring Arabic translators, it
was both informative and polemical about the world of Islam. This was the
other side of fiduciary translation: while it provided the necessary mechanisms
for government and diplomacy across religious and linguistic boundaries,
effectively ensuring at least potential peace and stability at home and abroad,
it also generated material for polemic and normative internal policy, including
in programs of forced evangelization and inquisition.

Chapter 4

Faiths in Translation:
Mission and Inquisition

During the "*morisco* century" (conventionally 1492–1614), different modes of Arabic translation fueled religious debates among Christian elites and institutions, eventually yielding drastic political consequences. One mode was the continuity of a long Iberian tradition of translation of the Qur'ān and other Islamic texts.[1] Translating religious materials from Arabic for polemic purposes began in Iberia in the mid-twelfth century, at which time the Moroccan Almohad Caliphate ruled over a large portion of the peninsula and the Christian kingdoms were far from unified.[2] A competing mode of translating Islamic doctrine and mores into Romance languages was the production of aljamiado literature in the later *mudéjar* periods. This literature, which was closely associated with *mudéjar* Islam and *morisco* crypto-Islam, produced large caches of Islamic doctrine and also the folk knowledge of *mudéjares* and *moriscos*. By the sixteenth century, religious translation activity was motivated and sustained by Europe-wide polemic traditions that developed during an age of new media and new mission fields for reformed Christianities.[3]

Although polemic philology and aljamiado literature were effectively translations of Islamic doctrine that included portions of the *sunna* (Islamic tradition) so often invoked in legal translation as part of the *xara e sinna* (*sharī'* and *sunna*, see Chapter 1), those modes of Spanish translation of Arabic sources had little to do with the practices and personnel of fiduciary translation as they developed in sixteenth-century Iberia. Instead, and somewhat paradoxically, it was the practices and personnel which produced Christian Arabic sources and which were involved in the enforcement of what had been instructed by those translated sources that had the closest structural and discursive connections with fiduciary translation. This chapter will examine the translation of Christian doctrine into Spanish Arabic in the context of the *morisco* mission and the concomitant translation activities that were intended to enforce that instruction through the Inquisition. The chapter concludes with an analysis of the ambivalent legacy of translation's hybrid uses in programs of mission and inquisition in late-*morisco* and post-*morisco* religious writing.

The practices and practitioners of fiduciary translation informed a Christian Arabic translation movement that began around 1500. Significant clerical investment in learning Arabic and producing Arabic materials was meant to guarantee accurate transmission of religious concepts to new Christians (*nuevamente convertidos de moros*). On the one hand, Arabic-speaking priests and their missionary materials occupied a fiduciary position with respect to Christian doctrine and practice and strove to guarantee adequate instruction. On the other hand, the relatively short-lived Christian Arabic translation movement in relation with the *morisco* mission coincided with the spread of the Spanish Inquisition. As Arndt Brendecke has argued, it was that institution whose investigative practices underpinned much of the intellectual and political apparatus that fueled the Spanish empirc.[4] That institution's focus on *moriscos* grew more intense in the 1560s in tandem with the reception of Tridentine policies and royal edicts against Arabic use in Valencia (1564) and Granada (1567). Arabic translators, including clerics who also generated Arabic missionary materials, evaluated Arabic texts, speech, and knowledge within the framework of that specialized legal system. In addition, many Inquisition translators worked as or alongside the *romançeadores* of appellate courts like the Real Chancillería in Granada or the Real Audiencia in Valencia and thus would have been well acquainted with the tactics of fiduciary translation in those sites discussed in Chapter 1. Inquisition translation was thus another form of official translation (*traducción fehaciente*), and like the fiduciary translation of the *romanceamientos*, the process of evaluation through translation performed by translators (*calificar*) created legal evidence in Inquisition trials.

The Inquisition, the production of Christian materials in Arabic, and the designing of a state language policy were all meant to foster *morisco* assimilation to the Christian body politic through the teaching of normative discourses and performances—essentially a kind of social discipline enforced in the vernacular as advocated by the Council of Trent, except that the vernacular was Arabic in translation.[5] Indeed, as L. P. Harvey has observed, *moriscos* were *"also indeed Europeans of their age"* and as such were affected by the fraught relationship between language, subjecthood, and orthodoxy.[6] The sixteenth century was, after all, the age of the ennoblement of vernaculars across Europe under the influence of developing print culture, religious reform, and a flourishing of humanist grammatical projects connected to "national" languages.[7] As Spanish clerics and their translators created Arabic catechisms or interrogated suspected crypto-Muslims, royal language policies shaped broader political debates about what it meant to be a subject of the Spanish crown and whether *moriscos* fulfilled the requirements. An unanticipated consequence of those three interrelated processes was the development of new markets for legal-historical translation in Spanish print culture, fostered by the debates over subjecthood whose parameters were being refined by inquisitors, ministers, and advocates on both sides of the "*morisco* question."

This chapter studies the fiduciary aspects of missionary and inquisitorial translation between Arabic and Spanish during the *morisco* period. Although the discursive and institutional mechanisms for using translation to authenticate a property deed or facilitate diplomatic negotiations were distinct from the religious expertise used to create Arabic Christian materials or identify a Qur'ān, or even to record spoken testimony in an Inquisition trial, Arabic translators across all these sites occupied fiduciary positions in the translation process. Moreover, the use of their translation work in genres related to the instruction and enforcement of religious orthodoxy anticipated the fusion of fiduciary and literary/historical translation that will be explored in Chapter 5.

Together, these final chapters show that the close connection between Spanish governance and Arabic translation did not vanish with the expulsions of Jews, Muslims, and "new Christians" that took place from the end of the fifteenth to the early seventeenth century. Rather, translation adapted to new markets and formats for Arabic expertise, experience, and erudition, first in the debates over the role of the *moriscos* and Arabic in Spanish history and politics, and subsequently in Spanish political thought in contact with a wider international diplomacy. Patterns of Arabic translation in the *morisco* mission and the Inquisition created templates for those later formats, particularly for the direct integration of Arabic speech and text into materials used as legal, religious, or historical evidence in later discourses.

Teaching Christian Orthodoxy Through Translations

Between the period of Christian conquest and conversion in Granada (1492–1502) and the conclusion of the Council of Trent (1545–1563) and its effects on political and religious norms in Spain, a limited corpus of Christian Arabic texts was created through translation. This translation movement was informed by religious reformation projects and missionary experiences across *morisco* areas. Collectively, these texts became an important vector for the linguistic *reducción* of Arabic and the political *reducción* of Arabic speakers, especially *moriscos*. The earliest Christian Arabic texts, produced in the context of Granada's conquest and conversion, shared some of the hallmarks of the fiduciary translation movement taking place at the same time across Granada's secular government institutions. Those hallmarks included (1) translating concepts and texts in *collaboration* with others, (2) an emphasis on clear *understanding* of the source material in the target language—thus a preference for *ad sensum* translation even when it was called *ad verbum*—and finally, in close relation to the previous point, (3) using translation to retain the (legal, religious, fiscal, etc.) *value* of the original materials in a new institutional regime. The Tridentine texts, however, show an increasing emphasis on *instruction* over collaboration, *performance* over understanding, and *imposing new norms* to replace the autochthonous values of Spanish Arabic speakers. Translation was no longer used to guarantee understanding and the legibility of the source values in the target discourse, but rather to produce performances of orthodoxy that could be evaluated by normative institutions from the level of the parish priest up to that of the Inquisition.

The emphasis on performance and evaluation helped transform Arabic materials and information about Arabic speakers into new kinds of evidence in a violent debate about the relationship between language, religion, and subjecthood. Rather than a vector for converting Arabic evidence and authorities into legible precedent in Spanish institutions, as was the case with early fiduciary translation, missionary and inquisitorial translation helped make the case for exclusion. Translation was always an ambivalent process, with many Arabic translators and those connected with them occupying sometimes contradictory positions with respect to understanding or excluding Arabic speech or text. Ultimately, "rhetorics of the expulsion" were based on interactions (real and imagined) between the governing authorities and Arabic speakers, mediated by missionary and Inquisition translators.[8]

The Morisco Arabic Corpus

Immediately following the conquest of Granada in 1492, Castilian clergy were appointed to produce missionary materials to convert the *mudéjares* and provide instruction for those who had already converted. The first archbishop of Granada, Hernando de Talavera (d. 1507), brought a printing press to Granada in 1496 for the express purpose of producing and disseminating a short catechism, "Brief doctrine of what every Christian should know."[9] Talavera's rival, Cardinal Francisco Jiménez de Cisneros, also commissioned an early catechism for Muslim converts, "Instruction in Christian Life" by Antonio García de Villalpando.[10] Despite their stated audiences in Granada, neither work used Arabic or translation to further the missionary goal.

The first Arabic catechism published in the *morisco* context was presented as part and parcel of Pedro de Alcalá's innovative 1505 Arabic grammar, *Arte para ligeramente sauer la lingua arauiga*, of which a second revised edition was published in Granada in 1506. Although the thirty-three chapters of Arabic grammar and the manual for Christian instruction are in fact different works—together with the much longer lexicon that was published at the same time (*Vocabulista arauigo en letra castellana*)—they made up one intellectual and political project, in line with the rise of vernacularism championed by his contemporary Antonio de Nebrija as well as the *morisco* missionary project established by Alcalá's patron Hernando de Talavera.[11]

Alcalá, like other Arabic translators in post-conquest Granada of the 1490s and early 1500s, was in a fiduciary position between languages. He did not wish to erase the difference between Arabic and Spanish, and indeed it was attention to those differences that would ensure correct translation. Like al-Ḥajarī's explanation of his work translating the collective *fatwā* of the Marrakesh *'ulamā'* discussed in Chapter 3, Alcalá explained how he chose *ad verbum* or *ad sensum* translations so as to ensure that the proper meaning was transmitted. For example, when prefacing his catechism, Alcalá warned that

> anyone who reads this questionnaire (*interrogatorio*) and manual
> for confessors (*doctrina de los confessores*) should pay attention to
> the fact that each language has its own manner of speaking, and
> the intelligent man will be sure to conform to each one as well as
> he can. For doing otherwise would be to obfuscate rather than to
> interpret whatever the man was trying to say. For this reason, in

the present questionnaire, many of the questions have a literal
translation that corresponds word for word–since the Arabic could
handle it–while others do not, since it could not, though it is the
same sentence simply rendered in different terms. I have said this
for the benefit of those who are inclined to reproach and not to
defend what their neighbors are doing.[12]

Here Alcalá contributed to the nascent translation theory developing in late
medieval Iberia. Alcalá positioned himself as an expert who could choose
the best means of translation to guarantee understanding across languages.
He defended the natural heterogeneity of language, including to those who
might use such variations to develop a discourse of difference and discrimi-
nation. His remarks about language echo the later pleas of the *morisco* Francisco Núñez Muley in favor of linguistic relativism mentioned in Chapter 1.
Worth noting is that Núñez Muley spent the first part of the sixteenth century in Talavera's service.

The will to continue Arabic evangelization in Granada and in Valencia,
coupled with Tridentine reforms, inspired a second wave of Arabic catechisms in the middle of the century. The figure most closely associated with
the second wave of Tridentine Arabic catechisms was Martín Pérez de Ayala,
bishop of Guadix (Granada) and future archbishop of Valencia. Pérez de
Ayala, who attended the first and second sessions of Trent, wrote a number
of catechisms throughout his life. Two of these were expressly intended for
moriscos, and both were translated into Arabic—in 1554 in Granada and in
1566 in Valencia.

Pérez de Ayala returned from the second session of the Council of Trent
in 1553 after a tour of Italy in the company of the humanist and diplomat
Diego Hurtado de Mendoza, the author of *Guerra de Granada* and himself
an Arabist and collector of Arabic books.[13] Pérez de Ayala's journey to Trent
and back fell in the middle of his tenancy as the bishop of Guadix (1548–
1560). Guadix is a mountainous region in the northeastern part of the province of Granada. The city was surrounded by large noble landholdings,
especially those belonging to the House of Mendoza, the lords of Cenete.
The lords of Cenete had several villages of *morisco* vassals, and there was a
substantial *morisco* population in the city of Guadix itself, many of whom
were subject to the state fiscal regime of tax collection and were active users
of fiduciary translation when bringing suits in the Real Chancillería in
Granada.[14] It is no surprise that Pérez de Ayala was particularly concerned

Figure 10. The woodblock Arabic alphabet in Pedro de Alcalá's grammar and catechism is one of the earliest examples of Arabic printing in Europe. *Arte para ligeramente saber la lengua arauiga emendada y añadida y segunda mente imprimada by Pedro de Alcalá* (Granada 1505), folio c iiii 7 (unsigned). Image courtesy of the Fales Library & Special Collections, New York University.

with *morisco* instruction in these regions, having participated in the Tridentine debates about using the vernacular. Pérez de Ayala's first order of business in 1553, when he finally took up residency in his diocese, was to tour the region on an extended ecclesiastical *visita* and then to convene a synod to elaborate and promulgate his reforms. [15] The argument that underlay this synod was the idea that the converts could not fully assimilate into their new body politic until they learned the "laws" governing religious and cultural practice, as assessed by parish clergy and, ultimately, inquisitors.

To ensure that his parishioners would pass muster, Pérez de Ayala sought to implement the Tridentine prescriptions that encouraged instruction in the vernacular, including advocating the use of Arabic by the clergy. One of the outcomes of the Synod of Guadix was the eventual publishing of its resolutions in Spanish in 1554.[16] Several of the provisions addressed "new Christians" (*nuevos cristianos*), that is, the *moriscos*. At the same time, Pérez de Ayala commissioned an Arabic translation of a short catechism,[17] for which he relied on local translators to render the text into the specific Arabic dialect of the region.[18] The translator was a local secular priest (*clérigo beneficiado*) named Bartolomé Dorador. Such figures were frequently called on to act as translators, including in settings in which they would be exposed to the techniques of fiduciary translation.[19]

What little is known about Bartolomé Dorador paints a portrait of a Tridentine translator between fiduciary models and inquisitorial incentives. Dorador's experiences and expertise were forged by life in *morisco* Granada and in the Spanish presidios in North Africa. He was the grandson, on his mother's side, of Bartolomé Dorador, a relatively high-ranking Spanish officer in the North African presidio of Melilla. He almost certainly learned his first Arabic not in Granada but in North Africa, where he spent several years as a child with his grandfather.[20] Once back in Guadix and ordained, Dorador likely became one of two Arabic-speaking *beneficiados* (parish priests paid by ecclesiastic benefice) that Pérez de Ayala requested of Charles in 1550, although others certainly worked in the villages of the region. After the Second War of the Alpujarras (1568–1571), Dorador became involved in the slave trade of *morisco* captives.[21]

Dorador's translation was never printed or widely circulated. In fact, the only known version is held in the Bibliothèque Nationale d'Alger.[22] It is a surprising text, and not only for being an example of missionary *morisco* translation that ended up in North Africa rather than Iberia. Both the 1505 and 1566 Arabic catechisms were printed in a Latin transliteration of the

Arabic text, with at least partial side-by-side or interlinear Castilian translations, whereas Dorador's translation is in Arabic only, replete with spelling
errors. Despite his orthographic imprecision, Dorador was a fiduciary to a
fault, translating faithfully even when not needed. For example, the prologue, which is in Arabic only, included directions for the clergy and cate-
chists about the reasons for writing and using the short catechism.[23] The
sentiments of this prologue, like the paratexts of translated histories and
relaciones de servicio, were a guarantee to the reader of the authority of the
content as mediated by the translator, although bilingual clergy would not
have needed an Arabic version of this portion.

Dorador seems to have worked closely alongside Pérez de Ayala during
the latter's tenure as bishop of Guadix (1548–1560), accompanying him as
translator for his sermons and translating the *Doctrina* in 1554.[24] Evidence
recently brought to light by scholars from the Guadix archives demonstrates
that Dorador involved himself in translation projects that would support
mission and inquisitiorial programs, going so far as to entrap another
morisco, Diego Çaybon, into dictating Islamic prayers and denouncing him
to the Inquisition.[25] The denunciation claims to report Çaybon's speech
directly and offers a confirmation of Pérez de Ayala's fear that *moriscos* did
not understand the meaning of the liturgy. Dorador reported that Çaybon
asked, "When he [the priest] says mass, why does he drink that wine?" and
then answered his own question with "To do what people are supposed to
do."[26] In addition to reporting Çaybon's speech, Dorador transcribed various
Arabic prayers and explained them using paraphrases that included additional information about the setting.[27] Because his inquisitorial denunciation was effectively legal testimony, Dorador's report and translation bore
several familiar hallmarks of fiduciary translation, such as dates and notarial
marks, as well as the inclusion of "original" evidence and a translation that
explained the value of that evidence. He also described the social relations
and setting ("he came to my house") that supported the veracity of his evidence and translation. This missionary translator used his contacts and
experiences with notarial practices, law courts, and fiduciary translation in
the same year (1554) that he translated Pérez de Ayala's catechism.

When Pérez de Ayala was appointed to the Archbishopric of Valencia at
the end of 1564 after a brief tenure as the bishop of Segovia, he was once
again plunged into the *morisco* mission. In Valencia, the number of Arabic
speakers was at least as high as in Granada, though many more were bilingual, and the regular presence of Muslim captives from North Africa along

with the well-established networks of teachers and preachers sustaining a version of crypto-Islam in that region posed challenges to the clergy who ministered to the Valencian *moriscos*. A high number of *aljamiado* texts circulated among Valencia's *moriscos*.

Perhaps because of this long tradition of contact, the clergy of the Crown of Aragon—of which Valencia was a part—in general adopted an approach to *mudéjar* and then *morisco* conversion that was as polemical as it was evangelical. Two important and popular preachers, Martín García (bishop of Barcelona and participant in the Granada mission) and Joan Martí Figuerola, produced refutations of the Qur'ān and incorporated those arguments into their sermons.[28] Both men knew some Arabic from their work with Juan Gabriel (formerly the *alfaquí* Ali Alayzar).[29] Gabriel had produced a Latin translation of the Qur'ān in 1518 on the commission of Cardinal Egidio de Viterbo. Prior to that he had published an influential anti-Islamic polemic (*antialcorán*) in 1515.[30] Nevertheless, Arabic translation played little role in their preaching to potential or recent converts. The following generation of priests and polemicists in the Crown of Aragon, including Lope Obregón and Bernardo Pérez de Chinchón, relied on the work of Juan Andrés and incorporated Arabic translation into a missionary strategy that relied on disputation rather than instruction.[31]

The tradition of polemic and disputation in the Spanish Levant was displaced by Pérez de Ayala's initiatives when he took up his new position as Archbishop of Valencia in 1564. In 1566 Pérez de Ayala produced a second Arabic catechism (this time in print) that was probably not translated by Dorador, who had remained in Granada.[32] This second catechism was likewise a product of local conciliar debate, and this time the project provoked wider dissemination and a lasting legacy in print. It was printed the same year in which the Roman Catechism of the Council of Trent appeared, as well as the *Manual de confesores y penitentes* (Manual for confessors and penitents) of Doctor Navarrus, Martín de Azpilcueta.[33] The translator is not identified in the printed text, and the author is given only as Pérez de Ayala, who could not have translated it. There is strong evidence indicating that Pérez de Ayala planned to call on the Jesuit Jerónimo Mur to undertake the 1566 translation.[34] In Valencia, the Jesuits established themselves early after their papal foundation in 1540, creating a monastery for members who had taken their vows in 1543. Though I favor the hypothesis that Mur is the 1566 translator, other missionaries and potential translators, like the Arabic-speaking Bartolomé de los Angeles, were also active in the region.[35] If the translator was Mur, however, his work is another example of a missionary translator who also intervened in Inquisition procedures, as will be discussed below.

Whoever the translator was, the 1566 catechism includes a preface, which was addressed directly to the Arabic-speaking parishioners, but given only in Castilian (in contradistinction to the Arabic preface for Spanish-speaking clergy in Dorador's 1554 manuscript). In it, Pérez de Ayala encouraged *moriscos* to take any questions or doubts to their pastors, who had been given a larger catechism to use for explaining more complicated questions.[36] Pérez de Ayala explained: "Although we wrote it [the large catechism] in Castilian, your instructors, and the priests we send to you, will tell it to you in Arabic, for we have chosen them so that they know your language so that nothing may lack in providing you with complete instruction."[37]

It seems that Pérez de Ayala hoped to send out an expert clergy who could guarantee an accurate transmission of doctrine. At the conclusion of the bilingual catechism, the translator spent several lines explaining Arabic pronunciation to the priests who were supposed to be using the manual, and this pronunciation guide reveals a certain linguistic relativism. The translator explained: "Since the Arabic language (like all others) not only has its own characters but also its own pronunciations and sounds of the letters, which cannot always be well substituted with Latin letters, the reader will be well advised of the following rules in order to read and pronounce well *the Arabic words of the Christine doctrine*."[38] Like Alcalá, Pérez de Ayala articulated a theory of language that accepted variation and insisted that correct pronunciation was necessary to guarantee the adequate transfer of meaning. Nevertheless, although Pérez de Ayala and his translator sought to provide the tools by which clergy could engage in an instructive dialogue with their Arabic-speaking parishioners, the content of the catechism and its translation were indicative of new priorities in the evaluation of orthodoxy in Tridentine Spain.

The Marks of Reducción in Spanish Christian Arabic

Talavera and Pérez de Ayala and their translators all participated in a long-term process by which Spain's Arabic speakers faced a political, cultural, and linguistic *reducción*. This term—a false cognate with English "reduction"—at the end of the fifteenth century indicated three mutually reinforcing processes: (1) subjection by military force, (2) the reorganization of political institutions according to the models of those doing the subjecting, and (3) the codification of a language into a series of grammatical principles.[39] It was this last meaning in particular, when combined with the first two, that remade post-conquest societies from the inside out, both in the New World and in Iberia.[40] *Reducción* is clearly visible in the catechetical projects, beginning with Alcalá's joint grammar and catechism, and the results of this *reducción* were transmitted and preserved by the Inquisition, among other institutions.

Translators, official and otherwise, were key figures in the process of *reducción* and, as such, in the running of empire both during conquest and after. Scholars have thus found "conversion" and "translation" to be apt synonyms for the process of *reducción*.[41] Vicente Rafael, for example, used the terms (with the English "reduction") nearly interchangeably in his classic history of the effects of translation in the colonial Spanish Philippines.[42] More recently, the linguistic anthropologist William Hanks has demonstrated how indigenous languages and cultures were "reduced" by colonial (military, missionary, and political) processes. This linguistic *reducción* was also performed by indigenous actors through the use of "reduced" forms of indigenous languages that had been reshaped by generations of language contact and translation with Spanish institutions, a process that took place across the Americas.[43] In his identification of *Maya reducido*, Hanks provides a brilliant template for how to study and understand the mutual influence of language contact, translation, and the mechanisms of colonization (which, in the Spanish case, included mission, conversion, and Inquisition).[44] An analogous, rather than similar, phenomenon is the *árabe reducido* (Late Spanish Arabic), which emerged from the missionary and inquisitorial projects. One goal of this chapter is to understand how the practices and legacies of fiduciary translation shaped *árabe reducido*.

Common to both the American and Iberian contexts, translators faced the issue of how to manage specialized religious vocabulary. The problem was linked to a principal philosophical and practical issue facing theologians during the reformations: How could orthodoxy, or any true belief, be examined and evaluated? Was belief a matter of private thought—inaccessible to anyone outside the individual—or a matter of right actions that could be read by experts (like confessors or inquisitors)? What was the role of language in expressing truth or dissimulation?[45] These questions were closely connected to the problems that fiduciary translation attempted to solve in legal and diplomatic sites, in particular the transmission of credible evidence that created belief about the past and was then used to prescribe and assess future actions. The basic mechanisms of fiduciary translation were thus analogous across legal processes, diplomatic negotiations, and religious instruction. In each of these complex domains, the technicalities of discursive translation were supported by a range of social relations that guaranteed the transmission and enforcement of ideas and values.

Like their colleagues in the Yucatán, *morisco* clergy were faced with the task of translating complex doctrinal concepts, like the Trinity, and practices, like the sacrament of penance (confession).[46] Also, as in the case of *Maya reducido*, the translation strategies of *morisco* officials—notaries and clergy—would leave a linguistic mark on Late Spanish Arabic and later translation practices. In *morisco* Spain, translators had the choice of using Arabic vocabulary that might have Islamic overtones to convey Christian concepts or of importing Romance loanwords into the Arabic translation to mark special concepts. The latter strategy, of course, meant that the neophyte would learn the new concept only as a foreign word, so although the risk of choosing a vocabulary with Islamic overtones might be avoided, there was no way to guarantee that the concept was conveyed. On the other hand, using familiar vocabulary, even if in the "wrong" language, could facilitate understanding.

In general, the catechisms' translators accepted some of the risks of translation. This meant that they sometimes relied on Islamic vocabulary to explain Christian ideas and practices.[47] For example, in addition to using words like *jāmiy'a* for "church" (lit. "gathering place," traditionally meaning the mosque) and *faqīh* for "priest" (lit. a Muslim legal scholar; in Iberia referring to the Muslim elite who may or may not have been distinguished by their legal expertise). These choices were deliberate and they reveal the particularly Iberian dimension of these translations. The general Christian Arabic terms for priest (*qiss*) and church (*kanīsa*) were known and used in medieval Spain—Alcalá even included *caniçe* (church) as the fourth lexical entry for *Iglesia* (church), after *gimie* (*jāmi'/*"assembly," used metonymically for "mosque"), *báyaa* (*bi'a/*"church" or "synagogue"), and *mezgid* (*masjid/*"mosque"). This indicates that the translators of the *morisco* catechisms were conditioned in their choices to select the Arabic terms that would have been most familiar to the *moriscos*. Most significant, however, was the choice of vocabulary that was overtly Islamic for key passages in

the Christian doctrine. Alcalá, for example, used Islamic epithets whenever he referred to *Allah*, which he did not leave as a loanword, *Dios*, like
some contemporaneous American missionaries would do.[48] Instead he used
throughout phrases like "God the mighty and majestic" (*Allah 'azz wa jalla*),
"praise the Lord" (*subhanahu*), and "thanks be to God" (*alhamdulillah*). These
kinds of phrases also appear in Dorador's 1554 translation.[49] Even as late as
1566, the translator retained familiar Islamic epithets, like "God the mighty
and majestic" (*allah azehuguél*), continuing to place these cultural signifiers
in the mouths of the Christian clergy who were meant to read the translated
script.[50] Nonetheless, the 1566 translator made distinct choices from Alcalá
and Dorador, opting more often for a Romance term rather than an "Islamic"
word. That is, where Alcalá in 1505 and Dorador in 1554 used *faqīh* or *salāt*,
the 1566 translator used instead *capellán* and *misa*. Significantly, it is in the
1566 catechism that saints are named for the first time in Arabic.[51] In general, the later translation reflects the generations of missionary translation
that had by that point taken place, including the use of Romance loan words
in Arabic. For example, the 1566 translator used both a loanword for priest
(*capellán*) and the prayer title "*Sanctus*" just before translating the adjective
for saintly (*santo*) into Arabic: "Haté al capelán yecól al sanctus, tecól Cudúç
iléh" (When the priest says the Sanctus, you say, "Holy God"). In Valencia,
the common use of Spanish loanwords in the Arabic text may have been a
legacy of the complex linguistic situation of that region, where Romance
and Arabic speakers lived alongside one another for centuries and maintained a high degree of bilingualism.[52]

Other catechetical projects used Arabic for instructive purposes even
without extensive translation. One of Talavera's successors, another Hieronymite archbishop of Granada, Pedro Ramiro de Alba, produced a Spanish-
language catechism for *moriscos* in 1527. This work was likely a response to
the resolutions of the Capilla Real meeting in 1526 following the inquisitorial
reports about the little assimilation of *moriscos* across Granada.[53] It was in
many ways a typical catechism, except for its references to Islamic practices—
Ramadan (fasting), *guadoque* (ablution), prayers (*salat*)—that appeared primarily as a means to explain to Muslim audiences the errors of past practices
and how their new practices should look.[54] In this text, Arabic loanwords
were used to refer to specifically Islamic concepts—rather than Islamic concepts being used to instruct in Christian practice. The loanwords' appearance
in a Spanish text that was meant to condemn the practices to which the
words referred was another instance of *reducción*.

The most notable difference between the Talavera-sponsored (1505, and to some extent the 1527) and Pérez de Ayala–sponsored (1554 and 1566) projects, however, was the former's emphasis on confession and penance by individual catechumens and the latter's emphasis on collective ritual and liturgy during the mass. Alcalá's project in general emphasized interpersonal dialogue and provided extensive Arabic explanations of certain points of Christian doctrine using key terms borrowed from Islamic theology and doctrine. Using analogy or explanation to communicate the value of concepts had also been used by the *alfaquíes* working as *romanceadores* in the Granada courts at the same time that Alcalá was composing his *Arte*. For example, as we saw in Chapter 1, the notarial scribes of the town council or appellate court regularly explained that the legal value of the translated transactions rested on the *xara e çinna* (*sharī' wa sunna*), a shorthand phrase for Islamic law. Meanwhile, Alcalá used a combination of loanwords, analogy, and metaphor to convey priestly authority, as, for example, when he introduced the most important maxim for new Christians: "The first thing to know is that 'confess' means to 'declare' in Arabic, and every Christian man (and woman) is obligated to confess his or her sins to God and the priest at least once a year. To God, because it is he who pardons sins and no other. To the priest because he is the vicar of God (on earth), for the health of the souls (of his servants), and thus he is like the doctor who cures illnesses (of the soul)."[55]Alcalá's strategic use of loanwords (*al-confessar*), analogical translation (*al-faquí* for priest), and metaphor referring the curative powers of the priest (*bi-ḥāl ṭabīb al-adhī yudāwī al-amrāḍ mīta rūḥ*) were meant to transmit the value of the Christian doctrine to Arabic speakers through a range of references, both Christian and Islamic.

Such an emphasis on the authority of source texts—Islamic or Christian—reflects the importance of guaranteeing understanding and the strategic use of loanwords to ensure acceptance of Christian orthodoxy in Arabic. These strategies were closely related to the ideals of his patron and the head of the Granada *morisco* mission at that time, Hernando de Talavera. Talavera's missionary ideals were in line with those of his order, the Hieronymites, of which Alcalá was also a part. The Hieronymites of the late fifteenth century were highly influenced by Pauline ideals of conversion, by which converts received intensive instruction and were guided carefully to their new belief without compulsion. Talavera seems to have welcomed a certain degree of syncretism in order to achieve true conversions, and his Hieronymite biographers record that the Granada *mudéjares* referred to him

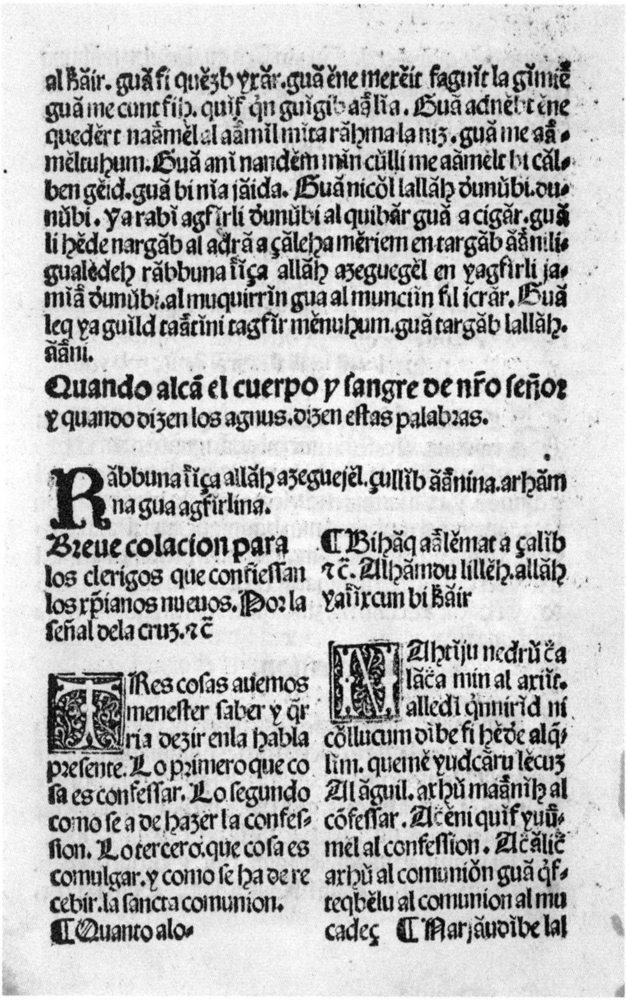

al Báïr. guã fi quĕʒb yrär. guã ëne mexĕir fagnĭt la gĭmiĕ
guã me cunt fiĭ. quiſ ɋn guĭgiⁱᵇ aãlîa. Buã adnĕbⁱⁱ ëne
quedĕrt naãmĕl al aãmĭl mĭta rähⁱma la nĭ₃. guã me aã
mĕluhum. Buã anï nandĕm mⁱⁱn cũlli me aãmelⁱ bⁱ cãl
ben gĕid. guã bi nⁱa ſäida. Buã nicöl lallãh ðunũbi. ðuⁱ
nũbi. ya rabⁱ agfⁱrli ðunũbi al quibãr guã a cĭgär. guã
li hĕde nargãb al adrä a çãleha mĕriem en targãb aãnili
gualĕdeh räbbuna fⁱça allãh aʒeguegĕl en yagfⁱrli ja
miã ðunũbi. al muquirrⁱn gua al munciⁱn fil icrär. Buã
leɋ ya guⁱld caãcⁱnⁱ tagfⁱr mĕnuhum. guã targãb lallãh.
aãni.

Quando alcã el cuerpo y ſangre ðe nřo ſeñoʒ
y quando ðiʒen los agⁿⁱus. ðiʒen eſtas palabʒas.

Räbbuna fⁱça allãh aʒeguegĕl. ɋullⁱb aãnina. arhãm
na gua agfⁱrlina.

Bʒeue colacion para   ℂ Bihãɋ aãlĕmat a çalib
los clerigos que confieſſan   ₹ c̃. Alhãmðu lillĕh. allãh
los xpⁱanos nueuos. Poʒ la   yafⁱxcum bi Bäir
ſeñal ðela cruʒ. ₹ c̃

Res coſas auiemos   Alhxïju nedrũ ĕa
meneſter ſaber y ɋ̃   laĕa min al arïⁱ.
ria ðeʒir enla habla   alledⁱ ɋⁿmirⁱd nⁱ
pʒeſente. Lo pʒimero que co   cõllucum ðibe fⁱ hĕðe alɋⁱ
ſa es confeſſar. Lo ſegundo   lĭm. quemĕ yudcäru lĕcuʒ
como ſe a ðe haʒer la confeſ   Allãguil. arhũ maãnⁱlh al
ſion. Lo tercero. que coſa es   cöfeſſar. Alⁱⁱ ĕni quⁱſ yuũ
comulgar. y como ſe ha ðe re   mĕl al confeſſion. Alⁱ cälⁱĕ
cebⁱr. la ſancta comunion.   arhũ al comuniŏn guã ɋf
ℂ Quanto alo◦   teqbĕlu al comunion al mu
                 cadeç ℂ Marjäuðibe laⁱ

Figure 11. Spanish and Arabic translation in facing columns
in the first pages of the catechetical materials of Pedro
de Alcalá's *Arte para ligeramente saber la lengua arauiga
emendada y añadida y segunda imprimada* (Granada 1505).
Folio aiii verso (unsigned). Image courtesy of the Fales
Library & Special Collections, New York University.

as their *faqīh*. Creating Arabic doctrinal materials and supporting an Arabic-speaking clergy were part of this agenda, and it may explain Alcalá's use of Islamic terminology to convey Christian sacred terms and practices, including confession.

Nonetheless, Talavera did not ignore outward manifestations of faith. In the famous "Instruction de Arzobispo de Granada" to the residents of the Albaicín, which a group of Granada *moriscos* were said to have requested around the time of Cisneros's forced conversions of 1500, Talavera emphasized practice above belief. In this instruction, the first steps Talavera recommended were to "forget all Islamic rituals" and to make sure everyone, including women and children, knew how to make the sign of the cross and how to enter and be in the church, including using the holy water, reciting all the principal prayers, and showing the proper reverence to holy images. In the church, and in the home and the marketplace, Talavera recommended that the new converts imitate their "old Christian" neighbors as much as possible and integrate themselves in Christian social patterns, including joining Christian fraternal orders (*cofradías*), establishing hospitals and other pious foundations, and even in how they dressed and walked and wore their hair. Of course, language was an important part of this performance of Christianity as a guarantee to the sincerity of their conversion. Although Talavera referred to prayers and psalms in Arabic that would be distributed to the *moriscos* (perhaps thinking of Alcalá's work), he admonished them in the same folio to "forget Arabic" as soon as possible and to never speak it in the home.[56]

Later catechisms also emphasized performance of faith in speech and action which depended on translation. Both the 1554 catechism and the 1566 catechisms included the confession formulae like "I am a sinner" (*ana mudh-nib aw mudhniba*) and both specified that the confession was made not only with the priest and god, but also to Mary and Saints Peter and Paul. Dorador provided some instruction though no real explanation: "At the beginning of Mass (*ṣalāt*) you must say the confession (*al-iqrār*) with the priest (*al-faqīh*) like this: I am a sinner; I confess my sins to God the mighty and majestic (*lil-lah 'azz wa jalla*)." He explained the feminine formulation ("anā mudhniba in kāna imratan").[57] The 1566 translator, on the other hand, transcribed the confession prayer only as part of the liturgical recitation during the mass.[58] As reflected in the work of his translators, Pérez de Ayala emphasized making sure that *moriscos* knew what to do during the mass and that they performed the ritual properly. In both the 1554 and 1566 catechisms, there are lengthy explanations of exactly what to do and say, including exactly when to kneel, sit, stand, and perform other actions, that are not in Alcalá's earlier catechism, which devoted its extra pages to explaining confession rather than mass.

Pérez de Ayala was long preoccupied with *morisco* performances of piety at mass. One of the major resolutions of the 1554 synod was Constitution 13, "Of what the New Christians should know and say when they are at Mass." In this constitution, Pérez de Ayala struck at the heart of the Reformation-era question about how belief may be known to ecclesiastical authorities and to society more broadly. He began by commenting on what he observed of *morisco* behavior at mass and what should be done about it:

> Many times we have observed these New Christians at mass, lis-
> tening without any devotion and without saying anything. They
> don't commend themselves to the Lord, they don't beg for his
> compassion for those who are with them in the mass. Even
> though it is impossible for any man to create devotion within
> another, since internal desires belong to God, we are at the very
> least obliged to require them to respond in the posture of their
> bodies, their external actions, and their speech, so that ecclesiasti-
> cal discipline is not perverted. Since the Holy Mass is said before
> all those present (as the holy doctors teach), it seems to be a rea-
> sonable thing that the community [*el pueblo*] conform to the word
> and the intention of the priest who is celebrating it.[59]

In the same resolution, Pérez de Ayala allowed that those who did not know Castilian be allowed to say their part in the mass in Arabic, though this was still measured against standards of orthodoxy. Any deviation from the orthodox version—either by the *morisco* or the sacristan charged with overseeing their performance in the mass—would be fined a *real* for each infraction. Again, in 1566 he insisted that priests should instruct *moriscos* in the following order, making sure that they know "the Pater Noster, Ave Maria, and Credo, the Commandments, the Works of Mercy, and the Confession, because this is the most important. This is what they will be held accountable for by their priests, and by our ecclesiastical visitors. The rest of the doctrine they will learn in time."[60] He then emphasized the correct manner of participating mass that should be inculcated into the *moriscos* in the event of examination. In both resolutions and the translated scripts for mass that accompanied them, Pérez de Ayala indicated that right action would be a proxy for right belief. This kind of examination and the reasoning it was meant to support would become the hallmark of Inquisition interrogations, in which translators played a key role in transmitting witness testimony for evaluation by inquisitors or by themselves evaluating texts and the meaning of their possession.[61]

The emphasis on performing orthodoxy also emerged in translation. For example, following Pérez de Ayala's instructions, Dorador translated a lengthy script for participating in the mass, from a version promulgated in the 1554 synod. He rendered Pérez de Ayala's first-person descriptions following communion into second-person instructions: "Then I return to my seat" (Pérez de Ayala, "me voy hasta mi asiento") to "You go to your seat" (Dorador, "tamshī lī majlasik").[62] As he emphasized the physical performance of attending the mass, he, like Alcalá, chose vocabulary with a familiar, and even Islamic, connotation for the moriscos. For example, after entering the church and using the holy water to bless themselves, Dorador instructed, "You will make a reverence (tasjid) to the altar (al-miḥrab)." The translator acted as a mediator of Pérez de Ayala's direct instructions. For example, Dorado explains, "This is all of what the Christians are required to do when they hear their mass (ṣallātuhum)," before switching into the second person and giving detailed instructions for each action the individual was expected to perform. This short explanation was meant to bring some added degree of understanding to the Arabic-speaking audience, and in these interventions Dorador is a bridge between Alcalá's emphasis on explanation so as to guarantee transmission of orthodox concepts and right practice in 1505 and the 1566 translator's bare directions meant to enforce right action or impose consequences.

Indeed, by 1566, the instructions for the mass had become far more cut and dry, all given in the form, "When the priest says . . ., you say. . . ."[63] Then the catechism continued in Castilian only, instructing the priests to make sure that those in attendance (el pueblo) listen attentively to the mass, with an "honest" posture, and that they were taught the physical script of kneeling, sitting, and standing.[64] There was no space given to an Arabic explanation of the prayers, commandments, or any other part of the doctrine. The Arabic translations were given only to be memorized, repeated, and internalized. What was most important was that these prayers and rituals were correctly performed, not that the moriscos would understand or, privately, accept them.

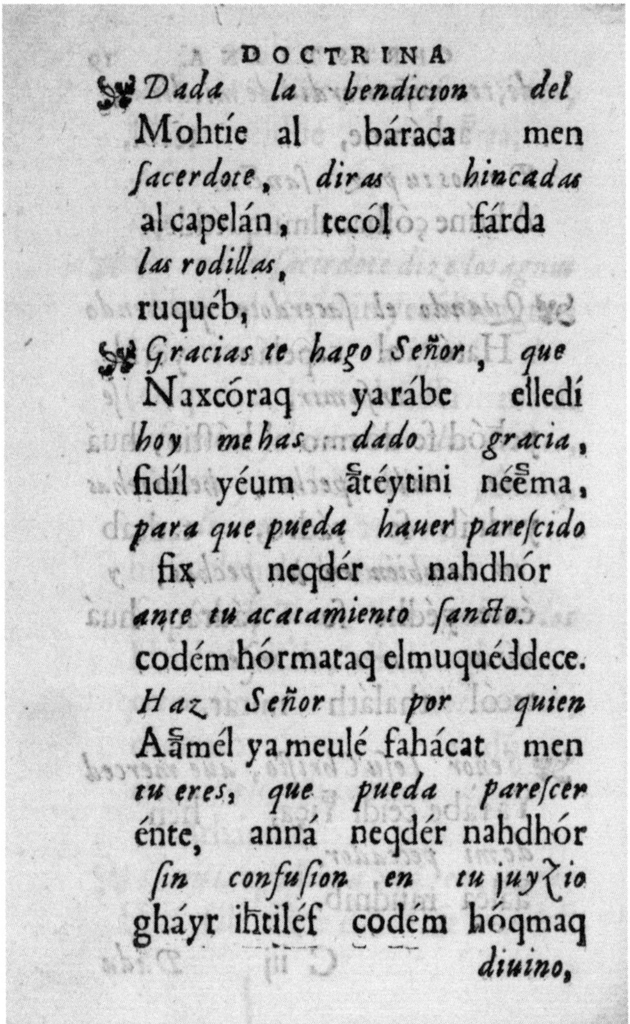

Dada la bendicion del
Mohtie al báraca men
facerdote, diras hincadas
al capelán, tecól fárda
las rodillas,
ruquéb,
Gracias te hago Señor, que
Naxcóraq yarábe elledí
hoy me has dado gracia,
fidíl yéum âtéytini néêma,
para que pueda hauer parefcido
fix neqdér nahdhór
ante tu acatamiento fancto.
codém hórmataq elmuquéddece.
Haz Señor por quien
Aâmél yameulé fahácat men
tu eres, que pueda parefcer
énte, anná neqdér nahdhór
fin confufion en tu juyȝio
gháyr ihtiléf codém hóqmaq
diuino,

Figure 12. An interlineal Arabic translation was printed
with Martín Pérez de Ayala's Spanish instructions to *morisco*
parishioners. Those instructions included the language
of the prayers and the bodily instructions for how to move
during the mass and perform those prayers. Pérez de Ayala,
Doctrina cristiana (Valencia 1566), f. 19v. © Biblioteca
Nacional de España, R/8782.

The three catechisms are indicative of a process of increasing prioritization of right behavior in public, and right collective action, over the impossible goal of regulating personal belief. Alcalá's 1505 translation—with its extensive explanations of the meaning and benefits of Christian practice and heavy use of loanwords—was closest to the approach of the Granada *romanceadores*. Like the *romanceadores*, Alcalá sought to transmit legal value across linguistic, religious, and legal systems by explaining the intent of ritualized uses of information and evidence directly to the "user" of the law (religious or civil).[65] In Dorador's 1554 translation, some explanation was retained, but the emphasis was shifting to a direction that could be ordered and evaluated collectively by the priest in a group setting like the mass. By 1566, the translation became a script intended for public practice and performance, with very little emphasis placed on individual understanding. Comparing the translation and content choices of the three projects demonstrates a gradual shift in emphasis across the overlapping realms of orthodoxy and orthopraxy, the latter being more straightforward to examination by normative institutions. The later 1560s, which coincided with the reception of the final Tridentine resolutions and subsequent consequences for Spanish political and religious institutions, witnessed a definitive shift from fiduciary translation to inquisitorial translation as the dominant mode of Arabic translation in Spain. Nevertheless, some aspects of fiduciary translation were retained in the later regimes of inquisitorial translation, an inevitable product of the overlap of personnel and texts in the later sixteenth century.

Arabic Before the Inquisition: Enforcing *Reducción*

The 1560s were a radical turning point in Spanish-language policies and practices regarding Arabic, Arabic speakers, and Arabic translation. This turn was reflected most saliently in the anti-Arabic edicts across *morisco* areas in Valencia (1564) and Granada (1566). The language politics of the 1560s were themselves inspired by a sense of failure in the *morisco* mission, specifically in *morisco* instruction in and sincere adoption of Christian doctrine. While this failure was attributed in part to the ill-equipped and poorly staffed local clergy, in particular to their widespread lack of Arabic knowledge or Arabic materials to use in instruction, the Inquisition offered a new strategy for enforcing Christian law as performed or expressed by *moriscos*.

In order to process *morisco* testimony along with confiscated Arabic or Islamic texts (not necessarily one and the same), the Inquisition employed Arabic interpreters, translators, and *calificadores* (evaluators).

Also in the 1560s the Inquisition underwent a series of reforms that were motivated and elaborated in large part by the inquisitor general, Fernando Valdés (1483–1568). Among these was the order to restart the mandatory inquisitorial visits that were such an important part of the tribunal's enforcement of orthodoxy. These visits brought the Tribunal into contact with a diverse group of potential penitents, including Arabic speakers. The Inquisition, itself a polynodal organization, approached the problem of evaluating Arabic speech and text in different ways. In the 1560s, tribunals began to focus with new intensity on the possession of Arabic texts—either books, papers, or Arabic inscriptions on small objects such as amulets. They focused on reports of Arabic declarations, Islamic prayers, and exclamations or evidence that an *alfaquí* was teaching with Arabic materials or language.

In Castile before 1570, defendants who needed translators were relatively rare because most *moriscos* there spoke a romance language as their native tongue. Arabic speakers did find themselves occasionally before the Zaragoza, Toledo, and Murcia tribunals, where cases of North African defendants (*berberiscos*) from Orán were tried not infrequently.[66] In Zaragoza for example, where there was no Arabic-speaking staff, inquisitors relied on prisoners who claimed to know Arabic.[67] Inquisitors on Spanish-controlled islands, Mallorca, Canarias, and Sicily, also tried Arabic speakers sporadically in the sixteenth and seventeenth centuries.[68] In Valencia and Granada the need for reliable Arabic translators was greater, and the Granada and the Valencia tribunals used multiple approaches conditioned by the different *morisco* populations they examined.

In Granada, although the relatively young institution was first active in 1498–1499, a permanent tribunal would not be established until 1526. Following Charles V's wedding and yearlong residency in Granada, during which time he asked for reports from the ecclesiastic administration and learned that the new Christians were not successfully assimilated, a permanent ecclesiastic court was established and the first auto-da-fé of the Granada Inquisition was "celebrated" in 1529.[69] Across Spain, the early Inquisition was principally interested in *conversos* (converts from Judaism), so that the first generation of *moriscos* received little institutional attention. The focus on Judaizers shifted to the *moriscos* after Charles V's visit in 1526, and from 1526 until roughly 1580, extant records show that the *moriscos* became the primary target of the office (they constituted 780 of the 998 individuals who were condemned to an auto-da-fé).[70] Confiscation of *morisco* goods, on which the former owners were still taxed, was an extremely lucrative enterprise for the state. Among these goods were often Arabic books or texts, which were transferred to the court for examination.[71] To examine texts and interrogate prisoners, interpreters were increasingly needed in the tribunals of the Inquisition.[72] In 1526, the cathedral set aside a fixed sum to pay the interpreters who accompanied the priests on their *visitas*.[73]

Across this range of activities, Arabic translators knit together Granadan society at all levels across many kinds of jurisdiction and at the same time ensured a tightening of jurisdictional control. Several interpreters are known to have worked for the Granada Inquisition, all of whom served as or alongside notarial scribes in the Real Chancillería and the town council throughout the middle decades of the sixteenth century, and thus would have been well acquainted with the tactics of fiduciary translation explored in Chapter 1. The list of known Inquisition translators includes the well-known examples of García Chacón and Zacarías de Mendoza, as well as Alonso del Castillo, Miguel de Luna, Francisco López Tamarid, and Diego de Guadix. The latter four figures are especially well known in *morisco* historiography for their participation in the translation of the forged Lead Books of Granada after 1588.[74] Though their work for the Inquisition required different discursive mechanisms and social assurances, they all had the tactics of fiduciary translation at their disposal from previous experience.

Archival records for this early period are thin, and there are no extant trial records (*procesos*) from Granada, as in the case of some other more richly documented tribunals (Toledo, Zaragoza, Valencia, Cuenca), which would permit a detailed study of what languages the inquisitors, their staff, and the defendants used.[75] In all cases, confiscation of goods and fining were the most frequent punishment for Islamic practices (609 *moriscos* and 88 non-*moriscos*). Inquisition interpreters like the *moriscos* Francisco López Tamarid (in 1582) and Alonso del Castillo (in 1583) were then called on to evaluate their contents and decide which should be confiscated on the basis of heterodox materials (and thus used in the trial against their owners) and which were scholarly works of medicine, astrology, or history that should be sent to the royal court, where the Habsburgs were building an Arabic manuscript collection.[76]

The few extant translations made by these translators for the Granada Inquisition are known only second- and thirdhand. This transmission reflected the complex legacies of fiduciary translation in Granada. For example, Alonso del Castillo translated three *morisco* prophecies (*jófores*) for the Inquisition on the eve of the rebellion of the Alpujarras. Though the original Arabic and translations are lost, Luís del Mármol Carvajal included versions of his friend Castillo's translations in his work of Alpujarras historiography, *Historia de la rebelión y castigo de los moriscos de Granada*, the same work into which he inscribed Castillo's translation of the Letter of Aben Aboo discussed in Chapter 1. Mármol Carvajal recorded Castillo's commentary on the process of translating these texts for the Inquisition. The manuscripts were in poor condition, and the original language itself was "willfully twisted" (*torcidos a voluntad*) by the unhappy "Moros" who were deprived of their lands and liberty. The translator had to make sense of these confused examples, written in a language he condemned as "mixed up" (*lengua equivoca*). This undermining of the source text was a departure from the discursive and social mechanisms of fiduciary translation that strived to ensure and transmit the value of the original by various means. Castillo's observations then led him to connect the corrupted source text with the religious and political infidelity of the rebels, as recorded by Mármol Carvajal: "It is no wonder that the *moriscos*, who no longer use studies in Arabic grammar, read and understand one thing for another."[77] That is, the later *morisco* generations were missing autochthonous fiduciaries who could create correct Arabic sources that could then be licitly incorporated into Castilian traditions. Thus Castillo and his colleagues were crafting different categories of Arabic sources to be used for different purposes across Spanish institutions. While documents like the property deeds Castillo translated in the 1560s or the diplomatic correspondence he worked so hard to master in the 1580s retained the legal and political value of their original authors, *morisco* folk knowledge was defined as heterodox, infelicitous, and treasonous.

Although the extant records do not permit an analysis of the role of the Granada Inquisition interpreter during trials, some of the Inquisition employees used their titles in other contexts to assert their connection to the Holy Office and the Spanish establishment and to demonstrate their qualifications as professional translators, echoing again the mechanisms of fiduciary translation, where the authenticity of the translation resided in part in the professional status of the translator. This was especially the case with clerics like Francisco López Tamarid, Diego de Guadix, and, of course, the famous *morisco* doctors Alonso de Castillo and Miguel de Luna.

The best-known Granada Inquisition interpreter is García Chacón, who worked alongside the Inquisition visitors in the 1570s and 1580s. Unfortunately, nothing is known about his background or biography, but his activities shed light on the multilingual practices of the Granada Inquisition "in the field," in notable analogy with the fieldwork of tax collectors and the *cabildo* officials involved with the *repartimiento*. Visits were supposed to be a regular practice of each tribunal, but they were expensive and unpleasant for the inquisitors, who avoided doing them whenever possible. After 1560, however, as part of the reforms of the then inquisitor general Valdés, local tribunals restarted this practice. The records of Inquisition visits from 1573 (Guadix), 1581 (Alhama, Málaga, Marbella, Coín), 1582 (Ronda), and 1585 (las Siete Villas, Archidona, Antequera, Loja) describe Chacón in an official role as *lengua* (interpreter), which in itself is an indication of the high number of Arabic speakers who remained in the Granada region even after the forced resettlement following the Alpujarras war ended in 1571.[78] Inquisitorial visits usually lasted from four to six months and were conducted by a team made up of an inquisitor, a specialized "notary of the secret" (*notario de secreto*), a nuncio, a porter, and sometimes a *lengua*. As the Inquisition visit made its way across different regions of Granada, stopping in each town for several days, it would declare its intentions to examine and evaluate the population's heretical behavior by reading aloud the Edict of Faith, usually on a Sunday. The following Monday, Chacón read aloud an Arabic version of the edict, publicizing a written copy of the declaration (*leyóle y publicóle*).[79] The rest of the visitation records—short summaries of the names, residences, crimes, and heresies of the individuals from each town—do not include any references to Chacón's intervention as a translator in individual interviews. Nonetheless, in the visits in which he participated, a larger number of *moriscos* were examined or tried for possessing Arabic amulets, speaking in Arabic, knowing Arabic prayers, and so forth, than in visits in which he did not, meaning that he was probably present to mediate interrogations and testimony.

In general, the practices of Chacón and others, like his colleague Sebastián Merino, who accompanied the 1568 visit, echo those of the municipal translators who accompanied tax collectors or other government representatives charged to investigate or inventory *morisco* communities in the first two-thirds of the sixteenth century. These translators worked in teams, made announcements, interviewed locals, and recorded information for a central administration whose jurisdiction included *moriscos*. Indeed,

Inquisition translators like Castillo were also employed by the Translation Office which was run from the town council (*cabildo*) and served the Royal Appellate Court (Real Chancillería). In Granada, Arabic translators who found themselves in the service of the Inquisition had deep connections to local institutions that relied on fiduciary translation and other forms of bilingual administration.

In Granada, on the one hand, Inquisition archives indicate a continuity in the notarial roles and practices for translators. In Valencia, on the other hand, there is little evidence of an institutionalized position for Arabic translators working as scribal notaries alongside other officials in the *visitas*. This was likely due to the high degree of bilingualism in the region, which meant that many Arabic speakers could perfectly well engage with Inquisition staff in a Romance dialect.[80] Nevertheless, it was the same high levels of Arabic-Romance bilingualism that made the need for Inquisition interpreters and the records of their activities less frequent in Valencia and that simultaneously ensured a high preponderance of trials related to Arabic speech and materials. Paradoxically, the Valencia Inquisition records are the richest extant source for studying how Arabic speakers confronted the Inquisition.[81] The Valencia Inquisition confiscated many Arabic materials and tried Arabic-speaking defendants who needed interpreters (especially women), and to do so they sought out reliable translators whom they then called on regularly even if in an ad hoc capacity.[82] There are three broad categories of Arabic translation represented in Valencia's Inquisition records: (1) the reporting of direct speech and testimony in Arabic; (2) the evaluation and condemnation of Islamic texts like prayers and parts of the Qur'ān; (3) a modified fiduciary translation of "normal" documents of the kind that in Granada were transmitted into Castilian institutions as legal proof and precedent—marriage contracts, property transactions, and so on. In these latter records we observe the strongest linguistic effects of *reducción*.

The Valencia tribunal was established in 1525, just after the Valencian *mudéjares* were converted by force in the aftermath of the Germanías Rebellion.[83] As in Granada, the 1560s opened a new chapter in attitudes toward Arabic that became ever stricter until the edict of expulsion was promulgated in Valencia in 1609. The apogee of Inquisition persecution of the Valencian *moriscos* took place between 1585 and 1595, when over a thousand *moriscos* were tried.[84] Even with this comparative documentary richness, however, complete extant records for the *morisco* period number less than three hundred, including even fewer fully preserved trials. Among these records, only a few dozen recorded translator interventions exist.

Interpreters intervened in interrogations and inspected Arabic materials, which they were allowed to take with them to "translate and evaluate" (*interpretar y calificar*), as Juan Baptista Cabrerizo, "boticario y intérprete" (apothecary and interpreter) did in 1602. Like the Granada *romanceadores*, Valencia's Inquisition interpreters working in a trial context swore an oath to translate "bien y fielmente" (well and faithfully) according to their knowledge—using the trusted formulae of fiduciary translation—or to "tell the truth and keep quiet" (*dezir verdad y guardar el secreto*).[85] Sometimes the interpreters were respected members of the community—like Cabrerizo, whose Arabic knowledge may have come from his trade—and sometimes they were prisoners themselves—like Jaime Paxarico, who took the opportunity of his swearing in as ad hoc interpreter to try to gain some goodwill for his own case, walking a fine line between proving himself useful and maintaining that he did not really know any Arabic at all. Paxarico was imprisoned because other witnesses denounced him as an *"alfaquí* of the sect of Muḥammad, who could read it [the Qur'ān] and read it aloud to the other new Christians (*xpianos nuevos de moros*), and who performed Islamic rites and ceremonies." With such a charge, it is no wonder that he prevaricated when pressed into service as an Arabic translator. When he was brought out of his cell to evaluate a book (*calificar el libro*) in the case of a different defendant, Paxarico swore under oath that "he looked at the beginning of the aforementioned book and having read it very slowly he said that some of the letters that were written inside a box that was painted in green and red and black it said *Book of the Qur'ān*, but for the rest he says that he doesn't know how to read anything other than a few words here and there, which don't make any sense. He says this is because he doesn't really know how to read and the writing is very small and he doesn't understand it."[86] Like Castillo, he cast doubt on the source material in order to signal his own reliability. In spite of these strategic claims to Arabic ignorance, before returning to his cell Paxarico signed his testimony with his Arabic signature.

The primary concern of the Valencia Inquisition was Islamic texts, and, indeed, Arabic Qur'āns or prayers were the most commonly confiscated text. For example, the Jesuit Jerónimo Mur described one crypto-Islamic prayer for the Valencia Inquisition.[87] Mur paraphrased the Arabic dialogue between Gabriel and Muhammad, evaluating it as a "total fable and fiction" (*es todo una fábula y ficción*) in which "Saint" Gabriel denies the Trinity and confirms

Muhammad's prophecy (the Qur'ān). In other cases, Mur examined Arabic medical recipes and charms, as well as commercial and social texts, from merchant inventories to marriage contracts, all of which could have religious meanings in their choices of words, stated intent, or legal formulae. For some of these texts he made a more literal translation, almost always when the content was legal or financial, such as in letters of credit or records of inheritance bequests.[88] This preference for literal translation of legal documents indicated Mur's familiarity with the practices of fiduciary translation in other contexts. Nonetheless, Mur would indicate when legal formulas were problematic, as in the case of his translation of a wedding contract from 1590 that primarily listed gifts and properties to be exchanged. The contract, however, opened with a long Islamic invocation, leading Mur to condemn it as Islamic (*cosa de la seta de Mahoma*), explaining the Quranic provenance of the opening lines. In general, when the text he was tasked to translate was religious, Mur provided a summary and evaluation for the use of the inquisitors. When he offered a detailed description of the contents of the religious materials, he included a warning commentary— "this is all made up" (*todo una fábula*)—to prevent the danger of an unsuspecting reader approaching the ideas with an uncritical or unorthodox eye.[89]

Sometimes the Inquisition interpreters were able to determine whether an Arabic book was dangerous or not. This was the case with the *Urjūzat fi-l-Ṭibb* of Ibn Sina (Avicenna, 980–1037), a prefatory text to his medical textbook, the *Qanūn*. The explanation (*sharḥ*) was written by Ibn Rushd (Averroes) and this particular copy was made by a Valencian *morisco*, Shihāb al-Ru'anī, around the year 1480.[90] By the mid-sixteenth century, the copy of the *sharḥ* found its way into the hands of another Valencian doctor, the *morisco* Miguel Xeb (a possible descendant of the copyist Shihāb).[91] Mur evaluated the book for the Inquisition.[92] His opinion on the work—"I have examined the book and it is fine" (*he visto el presente libro . . . y es bueno*)—is what eventually allowed Archbishop Martín Pérez de Ayala to give its owner, the doctor Miguel Xeb, permission to continue using the book in his medical practice.[93] Indeed, medical texts in Arabic, especially the work of Ibn Rushd, were foundational texts in the Spanish university medical curriculum in Valencia, though they were outlawed in 1565, just before Pérez de Ayala granted a license to Xeb based on Mur's translation.[94] In an example of the close-knit world of Arabic expertise around institutions like the Inquisition and the university, in 1608 another *morisco* doctor Miquel Xep— at only thirty-six year of age, perhaps a younger relative to the 1566 license holder—found himself imprisoned by the Inquisition for attending a Qur'ānic reading. Like Paxarico, he was brought out of his own cell to interpret an Arabic text in the case of another prisoner, Gaspar Febrer. In this instance, the text was a marriage contract, stipulating a dowry (*carta de dote*), whose Islamic content was principally in the preamble, which described an Islamic ceremony and invoked the name of the Prophet ("zeremonias de moros nombrando a Mahoma e ynvocandole y llamándole profeta de Dios"), and in the conclusion of the document, where Muḥammad was again mentioned. This "translation" was more a summary than a literal rendition, with Xep's evaluation and identification of which parts were Islamic. Nonetheless, Xep "signed" the translation in a familiar formula: "This says what the aforementioned half page contained, and it was interpreted according to the practices (*según la práctica que tiene la dicha lengua*) of the aforementioned Arabic language, under oath (*so cargo de juramento*), which was performed, and the doctor Miguel Xep signed it."[95] Even in the cells of the Inquisition, the mechanisms of fiduciary translation reigned.

In other cases, some of the hallmarks of making official translations of legal documents were enacted on documents processed by the Inquisition that were not themselves legal instruments (though their content would be used as evidence against the defendant in his or her inquisitorial trial). In one case, the Valencian doctor Jerónimo Jabar emigrated to North Africa in 1577, supposedly over frustrations related to his medical practice. He was tried in absentia by the Inquisition and ultimately "relaxed by statute."[96] Part of the damning evidence of his intent and commitments was a letter between Jabar and an Algerian friend recounting his emigration. This letter was translated for the Inquisition by the *morisco* Joan Reduan before Sebastián Camacho, "notary of the secret," "who understood Arabic."[97] The translation seems to have been authenticated by Camacho on Reduan's behalf in the later part of 1578: "The translation was made by the abovementioned Reduan, under oath (*so cargo del juramento que tiene hecho*), he said it is true and he signed it with his name."[98] By 1580 the doctor had been found guilty. Using translation, the trial was carried out using the Arabic text as a proxy for the vanished doctor.

Many Arabic speakers in Valencia did not need the services of an interpreter in court since they were able to communicate in a romance language, either Castilian or Valenciano.[99] The Valencia tribunal was itself a more bilingual institution than its counterparts, since from its beginning in 1526 it employed *morisco* informers (*familiares*) who were bilingual, including members of the Abenamir family from Benaguacil, who occupied a position in Valencia similar to that of the Xarafí in Granada (who were discussed in detail in Chapter 1).[100] Some Valencian inquisitors, like Gregorio de Miranda, developed close ties with *mudéjar*-then-*morisco* elite like the Abenamirs. The Abenamirs eventually suffered a fall from grace in 1568, when the inquisitorial informer (*familiar*), Cosme Abenamir, and two of his brothers, were tried by Miranda's colleagues.[101] The agents of the Inquisition and those whom it prosecuted (sometimes one and the same, as in Cosme's case) had deep ties with other sites of translation, though the high degree of bilingualism has made these activities less visible in the archives.

The case of the former *alfaquí* Adam Xubich is emblematic of how an individual might mediate *both* Islamic and Christian Arabic books for very different Spanish audiences. Part of the denunciation that was made against him in the 1530s concerned his reading of Arabic books in the mosque of Algiers. He was charged with recuperating the Islamic books of a deceased Valencian *alfaquí*, Yaḥya Moroni.[102] In 1532 an investigation began into his commercial activities with Algiers, and two other Valencian merchants denounced him for dressing as a Muslim ("ab vestidures de moro") and for going to the mosque in Algiers, where he read Arabic books.[103] Eventually two Arabic letters were confiscated and translated, one by Hieronymo Jabari—about whom little is known, though he may be related to the *alfaquí* Jabar—and one by Xubich himself during the course of his own trial. The evidence of the letters is damning, as Xubich's correspondent seems to have prepared his emigration to Algiers with the permission of Ottoman authorities and requests that Xubich acquire and send the Islamic book collections of deceased Valencian *alfaquíes*. Xubich translated all this information into Spanish, hiding nothing from the inquisitors. This may be an indication of the availability of other Arabic speakers to authenticate his text, or it may be an indication that Xubich had another strategy at hand related to proving his skill as a translator: claiming credit as a loyal subject and fiduciary translator.

Xubich used similar formulations as in 1525 to certify the authenticity of the content of what he translated, formulations that will seem familiar: "This is the translation of the letter that the Father Inquisitor gave me in Arabic, which is the original, translated into Spanish word for word (*palabra por palabra*)."[104] These formulations echo exactly the notarial scripts performed by Arabic translators in Granada looking to prove their reliability to Spanish institutions of power. Indeed, Xubich's inquisitorial charge for the possession of Islamic materials made him a desirable agent for the *morisco* mission. In 1543 he received a copy of the Gospels in Arabic from none other than the bishop of Calahorra, Antonio Ramírez de Haro, who was the commissioner of the newly converted of Valencia.[105] This was the same version of the Arabic Gospels that was lent to the polemicist Pérez de Chinchón by a Valencian inquisitor. The circulation of Christian Arabic materials in Spain and the development of anti-Islamic polemic that would eventually foment debates leading up to expulsion were mediated by a former *alfaqui* first tried, then hired, by the Inquisition as an Arabic translator.

Translators like Xubich helped inquisitors and others evaluate Arabic texts and use that information. An equally important task was the interpretation of oral testimony or other speech resulting from inquisitorial interrogations. When the interpreter facilitated an oral interrogation, the defendant was instructed to say anything they wanted to communicate under their own oath through the interpreter (*por medio del intérprete*). Though direct speech was almost always recorded in Castilian, the interpreter stood between the lines, acting as silent mediator. For example, María Catalán was tried in 1603 along with her husband, in whose possession an illuminated Arabic book was found.[106] In spite of her Romance name, inquisitors communicated with her through their interpreter, the *morisco* Jesuit Ignacio de las Casas ("dándole a entender por el dicho Interprete"). After a long interrogation, during which Las Casas's interventions went unrecorded, María was taken to the next room to be tortured (*cámara del tormento*). The scribe recorded her cries in translation, relying on Las Casas: "She said her arm was broken and she said God be with me Oh merciful father, repeating it in Arabic." Neither María's torment nor the interpreter's job was done at that point, however, because she continued to cry out about the injuries to her arms and hands, pleading for God to be with her, "repeating it in Arabic." The next day she returned for questioning with Las Casas present, where she was condemned to one hundred public lashes and a fine of 10 *ducados* (a typical amount levied on Valencian *moriscos* brought before the Inquisition). The sentence was carried out on September 6, 1604.[107]

Although the traces of translation in the Granada Inquisition reflect strong links to the professional world of fiduciary translation, because of the vagaries of archival preservation very little evidence of the place of fiduciary translation is preserved in Granada's inquisitorial archives. In contrast, in Valencia much of the evidence of fiduciary translation, whether directly connected with the Inquisition or not, has been preserved in the archives of that

institution. Indeed, the Valencia Inquisition would become an important vector for the long-term transmission of fiduciary practices, even though Inquisition translation itself in Valencia is not known to have been connected to the
secular practices of local law courts and government as it was in Granada.

In addition to institutional practices, another way to trace the effects of
translation in Inquisition records is in the language itself. Where the small
morisco Christian Arabic corpus that developed between 1500 and 1566 was
marked by strategic loanword usage, so too was the Late Spanish Arabic
(LSA) corpus, which emerged between the 1560s and the conclusion of the
morisco expulsion in 1614. The evidence of LSA extant in Inquisition and
other Spanish archives attests to a short period of production and use: a
mere half century between the 1560s and the first decade of the seventeenth
century.[108] As L. P. Harvey pointed out in 2005, LSA is a significant and
understudied early written European vernacular that should be recognized
as such, and one shaped strongly by the political dynamics between Spanish
and Arabic speakers in Iberia.[109] More LSA documents have survived from
Valencian institutions than from Granadan ones. Part of this is due to
Granada's distinct demography, with its many Castilian settlers who had no
reason or opportunity to draw up legal documents in Arabic, and to the fact
that the majority of the *moriscos* in Granada were resettled in Castile after
the second Alpujarras war. Those who remained, or returned, were generally well integrated into Castilian institutions and carried out their relationships with those institutions in Spanish. In Valencia, however,
late-sixteenth-century Arabic legal documents survive, sometimes archived
with an accompanying translation.

This sixteenth-century written Arabic vernacular (LSA) is characterized by special features in phonology, morphology, syntax, and lexicon,
including the shortening of long vowels, the confusion of emphatic and
nonemphatic letters, the dropping of the ʿayn, using *mita* or *mata* to signal
the genitive (*iḍāfa*), and using Castilian loanwords.[110] Many of the loanwords
used by LSA texts belong to semantic fields having to do with economic and
juridical institutions, as well as medical, agricultural, and military terms
that were points of exchange with their romance-speaking neighbors.[111]

Particularly significant to the history of Arabic translation in Spain are
the loanwords of institutional terms and related verbs, such as those included
in Table 1. These loan words show how LSA was affected by both sites and
processes of translation that supported linguistic and political *reducción*,
becoming a "reduced" form of the language: *árabe reducido*.

Table 1. Sample Spanish Loanwords in Late Spanish Arabic Related to Economic Transactions and Legal Institutions.

Date	Late Spanish Arabic	Romance Translation	English Meaning	Document Type
1570[1]	وحْدَ[2] بَرَه من الفُرْدي مَةً سِيَدَتَكَ جلنا . . .	Un _albarán_ de la _cort_ de vuestra señoría llegó nos ha venido . . .	A <u>receipt</u> from your lordship's <u>court</u> arrived to us . . .	Debt claim
1608[3]	هذ هوة اِشْشِيو الذي عمل ادك الا اجمعه . . . قيرر منه عام 1608	_Este es la cessió_ que hizo el _Duc_ a la _aljama_ . . . Y se _cobrar_ de ellos	This is the <u>cessio</u> bonorum that the <u>Duke</u> made to the <u>aljama</u> (Muslim quarter). . . . He <u>charged</u> them for the year 1608.	Repossession for debt
1608[4]	هَذِ بَرَ مَتَسُعُد[5]	Este es el <u>albarán</u> de Su'ud	This is Su'ud's <u>receipt</u>	Debt acknowledgement

The corresponding words in each language are underlined.
[1] Barceló and Labarta, _Archivos moriscos_, doc. 83.
[2] See also Harvey, "Arabic Dialect," 113, for the numeral _waḥda_ used as an indefinite article (which Classical Arabic does not have).
[3] Barceló and Labarta, _Archivos moriscos_, doc. 176.
[4] Barceló and Labarta, _Archivos moriscos_, doc. 177.
[5] متا سعد. Here using the Andalusi preposition _matā_ to indicate a genitive relationship normally indicated in Classical Arabic by an _iḍāfa_.

In addition, the process of translating _árabe reducido_ back into Spanish revealed additional linguistic complexities that reflected the long history of language contact between Arabic and Romance languages in the peninsula. In one particularly visible example of this multivalent process, the word _bara_ (بَرَه/بَرَ) appears regularly in LSA texts to refer to a particular deed or receipt or transaction record and was translated as _albarán_, an _arabismo_, or Spanish word derived from Arabic origins. Indeed, the Classical Arabic word to mean an official record or patent, _barā'a_ (براءة) was adopted into Spanish much earlier as the _arabismo_, _albarán_. The "reduced" Arabic (بَرَ), however, was a transcription of the Spanish _arabismo_, that is, a new translation of a Spanish word that had originally been borrowed from Arabic. Indeed, many technical words, especially for legal instruments (like a receipt, _barā'a_), were borrowed into LSA from Spanish (e.g., _cessió_, quitclaim). This is an example of how "reduced" LSA was marked by contact with Spanish and Spanish institutions, borrowing part of its lexical inventory through multiple levels of translation over time. In another case, the use of *qurdī* (القردي) in 1570 was clearly an Arabic transcription of the Castilian word *corte* (court). The Romance translation, more heavily inflected toward Valenciano, rendered this simply as *cort* (the Catalán word for "court"), indicating that such institutional vocabulary was indeed borrowed from systematic contact with hegemonic Castilian and not simply a local loanword (in which case it would have been القرد). By the early seventeenth century, LSA had adopted the term *nuṭārī* for "notary," eschewing the classical *muwaththiq* and the Granadan convention of describing notarial scribes in Spanish using the *arabismo* of *alfaquíes*.[112]

Such linguistic effects of *reducción* are salient in a 1584 correspondence between family members negotiating a captive exchange, in which the writer uses Arabized Spanish code-switching without missing a beat. For example, the letter writer referred to how Don Pedro, the owner of the captive Yusūf (the letter writer's brother), treated him as if he were his own son (*yatrataruk kami walad*).[113] As in early missionary manuals such as that of Pedro de Alcalá in 1505 (*yconfesaru*) and the legal documents (*qubrar*) cited above, the Spanish verb *tratar* (to treat) was incorporated into the Arabic morphology through conjugation (*yatrataruk*). Indeed, this particular word appeared in a variety of contexts, and using Spanish *tratar* in Granadan Arabic is also attested in the Letter from Aben Aboo (discussed in Chapter 1).

One late example of Arabic correspondence produced in Spain is the well-known 1595 letter from a Valencian *morisco* to his father-in-law asking the latter to send him arms.[114] This letter is filled with borrowed Romance terms referring to pertinent institutions—like *abūshṭa* and *qurrū* for *posta* and *correo*, respectively, both referring to the mail system—and instruments, for example the term for "receipt," *bara* (Ar., *barā'a*; Sp., *albarán*), repeatedly used in legal documents. The writer also made reference to the Bank of Valencia (*ṭablā mitā Balnasīa*) and reported some gossip about royal officials: that the secretary Franqueza (*al-Shaqraṭārī Ifranqizzā*) received a *merced* (*mirṣī*) to carry arms. This latter detail shows how *morisco* elites who wanted to get around the royal proscription against *moriscos* bearing arms had access to flexible members of the administration.[115] More significantly for the present linguistic argument, it demonstrates how the vocabulary of Spanish institutions and Spanish power (especially the royal "mercy" (*merced*), upon which the "economy of *mercedes*" ran) was adopted into LSA just as the language and its users were "reduced" (*reducido*) as new subjects of the Spanish state.

Imagined Arabic: Answering the *Morisco* Question in Spanish and Latin Catechisms

The *reducción* of Arabic and Arabic speakers that was achieved through missionary and inquisitorial translation was not only linguistic but also political. Political *reducción* was reflected in the use of and attitudes about Arabic in post-Tridentine Spain that developed in media connected to many who had participated in the missionary and/or inquisitorial projects. The principal media of religious instruction and enforcement in late sixteenth-century Spain remained the catechism and confession, and strong language ideologies about Arabic began to emerge in those genres after 1566. The ambivalent hostility toward Arabic and Arabic speakers that characterized the last decades leading up to the expulsion of 1609–1614 is nowhere clearer than in the post-1566 *morisco* catechisms.

After the Council of Trent and the subsequent language policies of the Spanish crown that limited further Arabic catechetical materials, Iberian traditions of polemic disputation reemerged and combined with the trope of instructional dialogue to generate several distinctive *morisco* catechisms in which translation from Arabic was not performed, but in which the idea of Arabic speech was deployed as an effective narrative and polemic device. For example, in 1568, the *Catecismo provechoso* of the Augustinian Alonso de Orozco appeared in Zaragoza, with another edition in Salamanca in 1572 and a second Zaragoza edition in 1575. Orozco's work was aimed at, and enjoyed particular success with, clergy working among *moriscos* in Aragon and Castile, the latter region having received most of the remaining *morisco* population of Granada after the conclusion of the Alpujarras War in 1571. In his *Catescismo provechoso*, Orozco adopted the common model of the humanist dialogue, which had been deployed to great effect in Pérez de Chinchón's 1535 polemical *Dialogue* between an old Christian Bernardo (likely representing the author) and his friend and recent convert, the former *alfaquí* Zumilla.[116] Orozco likewise cast proxies for himself—an anonymous Augustinian—and a recent convert—a *morisco* named Felipe (perhaps designed to attract the attention of the king). Both of these conversations took place in Spanish. Although the work is billed as a catechism, it functioned primarily in the vein of polemic, and its use of Arabic translation was second- or thirdhand via Orozco's studies of Qur'ān translations and other polemical works.[117] Thus the 1560s witnessed a definitive return of polemic and the appropriation of translation for ideological arguments that had little engagement with actual Arabic speakers.

By the 1580s, debates over the *morisco* question and expulsion quickened, and Arabic translation played a significant role in discussions between clergy and ministers as a symbol of the possibilities and limits of assimilation. On the one hand, anti-expulsion advocates, like the *morisco* Jesuit Ignacio de las Casas, used the promise of Arabic translation to support his arguments about the usefulness of Christian Arabic in teaching orthodoxy. On the other hand, expulsion advocates pointed to translations of North African correspondence—made by Inquisition translators like Las Casas—as evidence of *morisco* perfidy.[118] This "question" was ultimately answered by a royal edict of expulsion, justified according to a decade of legal arguments, leading to charges of linguistic *lèse majesté* against the *moriscos* as a group. Rather than a violation of the majesty of God (*lesae maestatis divinae*), as might have been expected in the context of debates over religious orthodoxy and right practice, the *morisco* expulsion was justified according to a charge of *lesae maestatis humanae*: that is, treason.[119] The Council of State invoked the threat of a conspiracy between *moriscos* and North African rulers and created a political solution to what was usually cast as a religious problem. This was an innovative legal approach that essentially removed the question of *morisco* belief and orthodoxy from the jurisdiction of the Inquisition—where it had been answered on an individual and case-by-case basis for a century—and placed it entirely in the hands of the king's jurists and councilors. On both sides, the tools to make these arguments were provided by translation.

It was in this context that the final *morisco* catechisms were produced— in Latin, Spanish, and Valenciano, not in Arabic. In 1586 Pedro Guerra de Lorca produced *Catecheses mystagogicae pro advenis ex sexta Mahometana*.[120] This was another polemic-cum-catechism, whose first twenty were folios titled "Life of Muḥammad," in which the prophet's false preaching, anti-Trinitarianism, and low morals were highlighted—all traditional tropes of Christian polemic. Guerra de Lorca sprinkled his accusations of Arianism with garbled pseudo-Arabic (e.g., *zurulla* for *rasūl allah*, mistakenly applied to Jesus rather than Muḥammad).[121] Most significantly, the entire chapter "Second Catechism" (of a total of sixteen) was devoted to regulating dress and language as the most important policy to effect the sincere conversion of the *moriscos*.[122] In this section, Guerra de Lorca definitively rejected the possibility that right belief could be achieved without changing external behaviors and attitudes, and he disapproved of translating Christian doctrine into Arabic.[123] The second catechism represented a starkly political argument and called repeatedly on both Philip II and royal and municipal governments to enforce the language laws.[124]

Guerra de Lorca's catechism was firmly in the camp of the Catholic apologists, who thought that purgation was the only cure for Spain's *morisco* ills.[125] According to these arguments, translation campaigns like those of Talavera and Pérez de Ayala had not only been in vain, but had in fact prolonged the malady. Political arguments were also designed for *morisco* audiences in the later catechisms. For example, around 1588 an anonymous author produced the *Catecismo of Sacromonte*, which was intended for the dual audience of clergy looking for tools of disputation and *moriscos* seeking to understand the technicalities of doctrine (whether it reached either of these groups is an open question).[126] This text thus included various political lessons for a prospective *morisco* audience, including a discussion of the relationship between civil, canon, and divine law as a motive to understanding the forms and consequences of sin (cap. 29) and the metaphor of the vassal's loyalty to his prince to motivate the importance of the Ten Commandments (cap. 31bis).[127] Religious instruction in Spanish had become fully indexed to loyal political allegiance.

The *Catecismo de Sacromonte* also included a unique discussion of sins related to language, in which some of the concerns of Guerra de Lorca and others found echoes. The lengthy dialogue was articulated around the instruction of the eighth commandment not to bear false witness: "And thus all sins of language are prohibited to us, because language is the interpreter of reason and understanding. . . . There is no more natural image of man than his words."[128] Echoing Guerra de Lorca's equation of dress and language as the most pernicious outward signs of heterodoxy and infidelity, the anonymous author used the metaphor of dress (*vestido*) to describe how right speech should be formulated and what interior positions it should reflect. Like Lorca's claim that eradicating Arabic would obviate future homicides, the anonymous priest of the *Catecismo* equated those who give false testimony—those who sin in language—with thieves and murderers.[129]

Encoded in the theological claims of the *Catecismo de Sacromonte*'s discussion of the eighth commandment were many of the reforming anxieties about the relationship between internal belief and outward appearance. A strong political argument about the connection between language, belief, and political position was also articulated using keywords of the new political thinking, including some of the elements of moral pragmatism in statecraft that would come to be known as the reason of state, which employed the metaphor of the ship of state: "Like the ship in the middle of an ocean storm, if it is not mastered (*governada*), it will turn over, thus is ungoverned speech (*lengua desconcertada*)."[130] Like other political writing that used the recurring imagery of illness and miasma to make claims about the danger of the *moriscos* and the importance of purging the nation through expulsion, the priest cited Saint James as saying that "an evildoer's tongue is the most pestilent thing in the world. Just as the viper and the basilisk and rabid dogs kill bodies, evil language kills souls and bodies and honor and reputation. Just as they take care to keep the Republic clean of venom and pestilence, so much more should those who govern keep the cities safe from gossipers and bad advisors, just as they guard them from the plague."[131] The *Catecismo de Sacromonte* advanced the growing arguments that indexed Arabic to dangerous and violent uncleanliness, which could only be remedied by government policy. The time for persuasion and accommodation in religious instruction was definitively over. Now language could be only a proxy for Christian orthodoxy, and thus a motive for inclusion or expulsion.

In addition to these familiar tropes, the *Catecismo de Sacromonte* chapters can be read as a gloss on the legacy of bilingual government in Granada itself, where the anonymous manuscript remains in the Archive of the Sacromonte, just outside the city. Bearing witness was, after all, the fundamental function of most of the Arabic translation upon which Granada's government ran for most of the sixteenth century, including the fiduciary translation of the town council and the various law courts. With this in mind, claims like "Infinite good comes from the 'good languages' (or, possibly, good translators, *las buenas lenguas*)" echo the fraught assertions of a *romanceador* like Alonso del Castillo in the midst of the Alpujarras war.[132] Castillo's ambivalent claim that "every Christian tongue (*lengua xpiana*) should give thanks to Your Lordship for such a good and great victory, against such terrible enemies, who spoke that evil language" would have also called to mind the professional category of the interpreter (*lengua*).[133] According to the author of the Sacromonte catechism, the worst kind of "bad language" was that made under oath ("con juramento, o en materia de fee"), calling to mind the vital work of the fiduciary translators in ensuring the right legal value of the Arabic documents and knowledge they transmitted into Castilian institutions.[134] The quality of a translator and his service was all the more paramount in this context—a good *lengua* could heal the world, while a bad one was the seed of all misery.

The final *morisco* catechism produced in Spain was the *Catechismo para la instrucción de los nuevamente convertidos de moros* (1599), by Juan de Ribera (1532–1611), archbishop of Valencia. Juan de Ribera became the archbishop of Valencia after Martín Pérez de Ayala died in 1566, taking the position in 1568 after the interim rule of Fernando de Loáces y Pérez. When he arrived in Valencia in 1568, Ribera was initially sympathetic to accommodation in the *morisco* mission, but in the latter half of his tenure he had a radical conversion to the opposite perspective. Following a 1587 government *junta*—a policy meeting among royal councilors at which the *morisco* question was a central focus—he joined the ranks of the Catholic apologists. From that point on he began to advocate for repressive measures against the *morisco*s and, ultimately, their expulsion.[135]

The 1587 *junta* had directed Ribera to translate from Latin and bring up to date the large catechism that Pérez de Ayala had written to accompany the shorter instructional pamphlet printed in Spanish and Arabic in 1566. Ribera's translation eventually appeared in 1599 in both a Castilian and a Valencian version, published by Pedro Patricio Mey, a member of the Mey printing dynasty, which brought out Pérez de Ayala's Arabic catechism in 1566. There was some debate over whether parts of the catechism should be printed only in Latin since censors determined that there were enough references to Islamic principles that the circulation of such information in vernacular versions was potentially harmful. Ribera advocated for vernacular publication and argued that the Islamic references were common knowledge and were defeated so soundly in the catechism's polemic that it could not possibly be a danger to any Christian reader.[136]

In a prefatory patriarch's letter ("Carta del patriarca," 1599) Ribera described how he carefully gathered Pérez de Ayala's chapters over a period of several months then added and moved some few words and phrases.[137] Overall he painted a picture of minimal intervention, sublimating his role as translator, even if the frontispiece bore his name as sponsor ("impreso por orden del Patriarca de Antochia y Arçobispo de Valencia, don Iuan de Ribera"), rather than Pérez de Ayala's name as author. The latter's original catechism is lost, so it is impossible to compare the source text and Ribera's translation. What is certain is that Ribera translated Pérez de Ayala's project of doctrinal instruction, which used the accommodating power of translation as its central strategy, into an effective and attractive polemic for the Catholic apologists.

Though Ribera's translation moved Pérez de Ayala's text away from its strategies of accommodation, the revised catechism relied on what was becoming a familiar tale: the narration of Arabic translation. Rather than converting a long-lost manuscript, as in Cervantes's *Don Quixote*, the *Catechismo* was written as a conversation between an Arabic-speaking priest near Guadix and a Moor of Barbary. The first dialogue of book 1 is titled: "In which the setting for this catechism is laid out, as the reasoning of a Christian cleric, skilled in the Arabic language, with a Moor of Barbary." The title functions as stage directions for the following dialogue and indicate clearly that the reader should interpret the dialogue as taking place in Arabic, rather than the Spanish or Valenciano in which it was read. The first lines confirm this conceit: "Disciple: Greetings from God, oh Father (*Dios os salude, o padre*). Master: And also unto you, brother. Where on earth [are your from], that you seem so strange to me in your dress and speech."[138] Though speech and dress were again equated, they were not an impediment to dialogue or instruction. As the imaginary conversation advanced, the North African Muslim explained to his gratified listener that he came to Spain expressly to be instructed in and convert to Christianity. At this point there is no question that Arabic is the appropriate conduit for that instruction and conversion. When the disciple asks the master if there is any way to receive instruction, the master explains the risks of receiving instruction in Castilian, "which you don't entirely understand," since much of what the priest would tell the neophyte would be lost. As a solution, the priest explains, "I am his [the head priest's] interpreter. Because many of these newly converted do not understand the vernacular Castilian, I usually preach and translate (*declarar y boluer*) into Arabic what the priest said in the vernacular, in the same order, and without losing almost any point."[139] The two discuss the priest's knowledge of Arabic dialects from Granada and North Africa and even his knowledge of Berber (*Ceneti*) and how he learned them ("I have been more than five years in Africa, where I learned it for curiosity's sake, and I can speak it as fluently as Castilian").[140] Though Ribera used imagined Arabic as a narrative trope to make it attractive to readers of Spanish and Valenciano, the echoes of Pérez de Ayala's use of real Arabic were nonetheless evident.

Based on these characteristics, it may be that the model for the priest character in the 1599 catechism was Bartolomé Dorador, the translator of the 1554 catechism, who also had lived in North Africa. Certainly Pérez de Ayala may have had Dorador in mind when setting out his original contribution, and indeed the dialogue was set in Granada rather than Valencia, on a road not far from Pérez de Ayala's former bishopric of Guadix. However, despite this reference to the *morisco* evangelization in which Pérez de Ayala and Dorador participated in Guadix, the neophyte was not a *morisco*, but a North African. Scholars argue that choosing a North African character, as opposed to a *morisco* from Valencia or Granada, was part of Ribera's accounting to Philip II for the relative lack of success in converting the Valencia *moriscos* during his tenure as archbishop (1568–1611).[141] But this character may also reflect the large population of Arabic-speaking North Africans in Valencia in the seventeenth century, primarily captives, like those who required the translation services of the merchant Alonso de Cantalapiedra in the court of the Baile of Valencia in 1572.[142]

The dialogic form, which was also used to great effect by Pérez de Chinchón, Orozco, and the anonymous author of the *Catecismo de Sacromonte*, was designed to be attractive to clergy trained on patristic sources and humanist texts.[143] It did not, however, please everyone in this audience. The *morisco* Jesuit and defender of Arabic evangelization Ignacio de las Casas loathed Ribera's catechism. For Las Casas, Ribera's polemic was doomed from the start, because it was not based in any kind of real knowledge of Islamic texts or practices, and its imaginary Arabic would do very little in the real-world context of the *morisco* mission. To combat what he viewed as the dangerous policies of Catholic apologists like Ribera, in 1607 Las Casas wrote "Defense of the Arabic Language," addressed to the Castilian Jesuit provincial.[144] In this text, Las Casas made a number of arguments that attempted to recover the value of fiduciary translation. Like the *romanceadores* of Granada, Las Casas insisted that Arabic-speaking clergy be trained as experts in both Christian and Islamic law.[145] He was undoubtedly familiar with the value of those officials and their bivalent expertise since he was born in Granada (*natus Granatensis*) and educated there.[146] His father, Cristobál de las Casas, was a legislative official (*procurador y solicitador de pleitos*), for the Real Audiencia, which employed so many other *morisco* members of the Translation Bureau of Granada.[147]

Las Casas's proposal had wide ramifications. He explained, "The method I have recommended is that young theologians (*theólogos mozos*) of various orders (*Religiones*) and others can learn Arabic in three or four years and with this they will be able to understand it and they will serve the church and these kingdoms not only in this topic but in other ways that I have described elsewhere."[148] Elsewhere in reports to his Jesuit superiors he insisted on the importance of training reliable Arabic translators, among the Jesuits and in Spain, for greater service to the Spanish monarchy and the Church.[149] In addition to the service these Arabic translators could perform in the implementation (instruction) and enforcement (Inquisition) of the *morisco* mission, the same officials could work for the king in his commercial and diplomatic priorities in the Mediterranean. Echoing Ignatius himself, Las Casas supported dialogue with Muslim powers who might ally with the Spaniards in mutual interest in defeating the Ottomans.[150] As an example of the need for the latter, he described speaking with an emissary from the North African kingdom of Cuco in Valladolid in 1604 who was shocked by the lack of an Arabic staff at the royal court. Following Las Casas's conversation with this Arabic-speaking dignitary, he concluded that the *failure* to create a class of professional Arabic experts could be damaging for the king.[151] Like the Catholic apologists, Las Casas made a political argument about the safety of the realm, but unlike those who used language as a motive for exclusion, he insisted that Arabic knowledge was a tool for conserving the monarchy itself.

That Las Casas used political arguments is no surprise given his experiences across the Mediterranean. He cited Spain's presidios—which he visited firsthand while in Orán in 1594–1595 to preach the Easter sermons—reminding his reader that "everyone knows" that the Spanish king rules them and they are Arabic-speaking. He also offered a political argument in dialogue with contemporaneous reason-of-state literature:

> Everyone knows about the presidios, plazas, and cities that our
> King possesses in Africa and its coasts and the kingdoms he has
> on the west coast of Asia and in the east Indies where that lan-
> guage is common and ordinary and native (*natural*) to all of those
> [places]. Who would deny that—in order to defend them and to
> govern them well and to expand his empire and extend the Faith
> to such barbaric peoples (*naciones*)—[he] does not have a need for
> trustworthy and loyal ministers (*seguros y fieles ministros*) who,
> knowing the language well, would not only make it so that the
> vassals would gladly obey their king, but that those who are con-
> verted would be willing to hear the doctrine and follow it.[152]

Next to this passage, a marginal note directed the reader to consult Giovanni Botero's work on universal history, particularly the passage about the Spanish monarchy (*ibi rey cathólico*).[153] Las Casas's argument was that the presidios were, after all, part of the monarchy, and for that reason the king needed good and loyal "ministers," expert in Arabic, to be stationed there. Indeed, several kinds of Spanish official in Orán would have described themselves as "good and loyal ministers," as Jacob Cansino did in his 1638 *Relación*.

It was with the benefit of these experiences, and his rising status in the Jesuit order and other Spanish clerical networks, that Las Casas began to study the *morisco* question in hopes of resolving it. He gathered and reviewed copies of official documents concerning the crown's and Church's uneven policies toward the *moriscos,* and from these he sent memoranda with his arguments to the pope, to Philip III, to the Jesuit superior general Claudio Acquaviva, and to the Inquisition in Toledo to counter the Catholic apologists, who had advocated strenuously for *morisco* expulsion since the 1580s.[154] As a counter-proposal, Las Casas argued for Arabic instruction and the hiring of Arabic speakers in key ecclesiastic and royal posts.

To create this Arabic-speaking corps, the mission needed professors and teaching materials. Las Casas's several visits to Rome meant that he was acquainted with the Christian Arabic materials being printed by the Medici Press (*Typographia Medicea Orientalis*).[155] Las Casas and his fellow Jesuits wanted to buy copies of these texts to bring to Spain but by 1606 could not obtain a license from Philip III for their import and use into the peninsula.[156] Indeed, although in 1610 the pope confirmed the need for Arabic speakers and materials in the Church, by that time the Spanish project to create an Arabic-speaking clergy was on permanent hold as the majority of Arabic speakers were loaded into boats and expelled from Spain.[157]

The *Morisco* Question Answered

The Arabic translation movements in early modern Spain—of Islamic law and of Christian law—had key roles to play in how the *morisco* question was ultimately answered: with expulsion. Hundreds of thousands of Spanish subjects whose language and ethnicity marked them as *moriscos* suffered those consequences. Severe language policies were becoming the terrible norm in early modern European societies governed by orthodox social discipline. The role that linguistic thinking played in humanist philology's service to the state, in translation practices in imperial governance, and in the consolidation of legal and fiscal bureaucracies was paralleled in the debates over religious reform and the new codification of religious instruction during and after the Council of Trent. A preoccupation with language and text was central to most of the reform movements, both Protestant and Catholic, and attitudes toward Arabic (especially as the language of a potentially heterodox community in the *moriscos*) were informed by developing ideas about the connection between language, ethnicity, community, and political participation.

Although it was developments in the catechetical genre that reflected and ultimately supported *morisco* expulsion, the genre did not disappear after 1614. In the seventeenth century, new catechisms were produced with Muslim audiences in Spain in mind. Though the *morisco* population had been expelled en masse, the taking of Muslim captives meant that there was a constant renewal of Arabic-speaking potential converts in Spain. Indeed, captivity and captive exchange became ever more common across the Mediterranean all through the seventeenth century. Though commerce with North Africa after 1534 was briefly prohibited, licenses were regularly granted in Valencia to allow trade whose profits permitted the purchase of Christian captives.[158] There was always also a robust population of Muslim captives in Valencia, as in many port cities in southern Spain, and translators intervened in these commercial affairs. Merchants themselves facilitated Arabic translation in Valencia, a major Mediterranean trading center. For example, the Valencian merchant Alonso de Cantalapiedra (fl. 1547–1616) was also a regular translator.[159] He first appears as a licensed agent to carry and sell goods in North Africa (*Berbería*) on behalf of Pedro de Malea in 1547.[160] In 1567 Philip II ordered the Viceroy of Valencia, Alonso de Pimentel, to pay Cantalapiedra for the more than twenty years of service he had performed as a translator. Cantalapiedra's original *relación* is yet to be found in the archives, but Philip's letter to Pimentel gives a good summary of what the Valencian merchant had described in his petition, which in turns sheds light on how translation functioned in the Valencian courts. Cantalapiedra had apparently explained in his *relación* that "since he [Cantalapiedra] knew Arabic (*la lengua morisca*), whenever there were Turkish or Moorish (*turcos o moros*) captives in the kingdom [of Valencia], who are brought to the city [of Valencia] in order to make their confessions, he is called in to translate (*declarar lo que dixessen en arauigo*)."[161] This document is a rare glimpse of the king's direct involvement with Arabic translation in Valencia. In 1616, he drew up his last will and testament, in which he described some of the redemptions he had achieved in Algiers.[162] This record of Cantalapiedra's work with captives is a testament to an important category of Arabic speakers who began to appear in legal contexts with more frequency by the end of the *morisco* period and remained after expulsion: North African Muslim captives.

It was to this audience across Spanish territories that some later examples of catechisms for Muslims were directed, in which lasting echoes remained of the tension and synthesis between the enforcement of instruction and polemic disputation that had been worked out across the doctrinal treatises and translations during the *morisco* century. In general, anti-Islamic polemic and missionary materials directed toward Muslims and Arabic speakers only became more common in the seventeenth century, as European trade and diplomacy with North African and Eastern Mediterranean powers grew more institutionalized, and Spanish territories were no exception.[163] For example, sometime between 1658 and 1664, the Jesuit Juan de Almarza wrote a catechism for the conversion of Muslims, extant only in a single Spanish manuscript.[164] In 1687, another Jesuit, Tirso González de Santalla, the thirteenth superior general, published *Manuductio ad Conversionem Mahumetanorum* (Handbook to Convert Muslims). Although the handbook contains no passages in Arabic or advice on preaching in Arabic, González de Santalla occasionally used the services of an Arabic interpreter.[165] González de Santalla corresponded frequently with a "Jew from Orán," most likely one of the Sasportas family (who had served as interpreters in the presidio), who came to Spain after the 1669 expulsion from the presidio in order to convert to Christianity.[166] Relying on his experiences in conversation with potential and actual converts, the handbook was also based on his reading of the earlier anti-Muslim polemics.[167] The handbook even featured a reported dialogue between a priest and potential convert in North Africa, the former personified by none other than Ignacio de las Casas. Once again, although the dialogue was reported (nearly a century later) by González de Santalla in Latin, it was described as taking place in Arabic.[168] Imaginary Arabic continued to serve as a powerful tool in polemic in Spanish territories and encounters across the Mediterranean.

As the seventeenth century wore on, the legacy of real and imagined disputation and instruction in Arabic translation remained legible across missionary media targeted toward Muslims.[169] Dialogues were inserted into language learning materials and into performances, both religious and secular.[170] Some high-status converts—including a Moroccan prince who was captured and converted, becoming the Jesuit Baldassare de Loyola— even delivered sermons in Arabic to audiences of Muslim captives in Spanish Naples.[171] The latent echo of generations of Arabic translation in these materials would connect with and influence all genres of Golden Age Spanish literature, teaching new audiences about the memories of Mediterranean and *morisco* encounters. In these genres, the pernicious echo of *árabe reducido* is evident in Cervantes's discussions of the potted etymologies of Arabic loanwords in Spanish (including *alfaquí*, which he does not define) and in the mocking treatment of *morisco* speech, such as Calderón's stereotyped buffoon, the *gracioso morisco* "Alcuzcuz."[172]

Beyond the legacies of material exchange and the popular imagination, Arabic translation continued to play a very real role in the development of Spanish politics and political thought long after the *morisco*-question debates had been silenced. Chapter 5 explores the cultural legacies of fiduciary translation through the vector of Baroque political writing. Against the backdrop of the *morisco* question and expulsion and enduring issues of Mediterranean diplomacy and commerce with Muslim powers, the translation of legal and historical sources in Golden Age Spain took on new urgency for the Habsburgs even as nascent orientalism seemed to be pulled ever farther from the field into the library. Nevertheless, Arabic translation (real and imagined) continued to affect politics and policies through to the conclusion of the Hapsburg period.

Chapter 5

The Legacies of Fiduciary Translation:
Arabic Legal and Historical Sources
in Golden Age Spain

At the end of the sixteenth century and continuing into the seventeenth, Arabic translation in Spain produced new sources upon which to base legal or historical arguments. Historiographers and other writers could hardly avoid dealing with Spain's Arabic past when reflecting upon Spanish identities. Such historical reflections had been promoted during the debates surrounding the "*morisco* question" and became even more common as advisors and politicians considered and sought to explain Spain's declining position in the global political and economic systems of the seventeenth century.[1] This "historical turn" in statecraft was accompanied by a "political turn" in history writing, which also began in the 1580s and which would endure through the next century of European warfare and global rivalries.[2] In this context, later fiduciary translation created a repository of credible legal-historical sources about Muslims in Spain and elsewhere that were used in Spanish politics and popular culture.

In general, seventeenth-century historiography and legal culture in Spain relied strongly on translation, real and imagined. Thus, seventeenth-century Arabic translators found themselves in new positions where they were still required to produce evidence or authoritative knowledge from Arabic sources—or at least pretend to do so. Although the everyday need for Arabic translation to carry out the rule of law over Arabic-speaking minorities waned with the *morisco* expulsion of 1609–1614, by the turn of the seventeenth century, increased diplomatic contact between Iberian and Islamic powers ensured a continued circulation of so-called Eastern manuscripts and other information into Spain, and indeed into all of Europe. Spain's Arabic translators continued to mediate the reception of these legal-historical materials, though increasingly from texts only recently arrived in Spain from Morocco, Persia, or the Ottoman Empire.

The formal requirements for authoritative knowledge from Arabic sources changed at the end of the *morisco* century. The seventeenth century was a time of gradual displacement of fiduciary translation by imagined Arabic—like the instructive dialogues of the late *morisco* catechisms or the frame tale of *Don Quixote*—composed in Spanish for print markets. This imagined Arabic was produced by translators with connections to fiduciary practices and was even generated from real familiarity with actual Arabic texts. Indeed, Arabic knowledge in Spain at this time was sustained through specialized erudite networks articulated particularly around the court, the royal library, and the Jesuit order.[3] However, later translation work with Arabic sources in Spain produced long-form texts that were shaped more by the forms and norms of late Renaissance Spanish historiography and political thought than by institutional needs to guarantee the transmission of legal and political values housed in the Arabic original.

The turn to *ad sensum*, which fiduciary translation had helped bring about through its emphasis on explanation by experts, ultimately yielded translations that were inscribed directly into the forms and references of the target-language tradition. Indeed, whether the *sensum* was actually transmitted *from* the source text was no longer a technical requirement necessitating an expert and fiduciary. Instead, the markets for historical and political examples required information that was already legible to large audiences for whom the trappings of Arabic translation were signals of prestige or exoticism, rather than signals through which the legal or other values of the original Arabic text were transmitted. For example, on the one hand, fiduciary translation in the sixteenth century relied on loanwords from Arabic explained in Spanish and ratified by a team of witnesses. In the seventeenth century, on the other hand, translators produced Spanish texts that, though their sources were Arabic (and sometimes Persian and Ottoman) manuscripts, were crafted to resemble closely other Spanish texts of the same genre. However, rather than using Arabic loan words, it was the imagined Arabic-speaking setting that was used as a rhetorical buttress for political arguments that were made using common Spanish keywords and concepts. Translators effectively rewrote Arabic originals as new Spanish texts rather than producing Spanish translations through which the Arabic original was clearly visible, as it had been in the early sixteenth century, because it was needed to transmit particular information or probative value.

Effectively "domesticating" (to borrow from translation studies) an Arabic text did not obviate the enduring legacies of fiduciary translation, but it did obscure them. This domestication was a counterpart to *reducción*.[4] Where *reducción* dramatically affected the form and references of Late Spanish Arabic, domestication effectively erased many of the Arabic forms and references that had been visible in previous fiduciary translation. The goal was not to disguise Arabic translation as a Spanish original but rather to create a "natural" experience for Spanish readers, who were reassured about the Arabic origins in the title and paratext but who did not find or need the more direct translations and technical explanations to have in themselves a probative value. From domestication, it was a short step to adapting the formulae of fiduciary translation to create imagined Arabic. Whether a catechism, a history, a work of political theory, or an early novel like *Don Quixote*, imagined Arabic came to dominate the presentation and reception of Arabic translations in Spain, particularly at the end of and after the *morisco* period. The domestication of the texts made the original Arabic value less visible, though no less important. The fact that legal, religious, military, and diplomatic translations were already familiar and well-integrated into different institutional contexts, as has been shown throughout this book, might explain how the importance of Arabic and Arabic translation in post-*morisco* Spanish society has been largely missed outside its place as an ancillary to the story of early European orientalism.

Thus, the forms for representing Arabic in translation changed beginning in the final decades of the *morisco* century and lasting through the rest of the Habsburg period. Nevertheless, during the process of producing those translations, Arabic translators from diverse backgrounds relied on familiar practices that were the result of experience in or contact with fiduciary translation, and some of the formulae of those practices remained evident even in the domesticated translations or imagined Arabic. It was also in this period that translators collected a lasting corpus of Spanish Arabic historical sources upon which later writers would rely. This chapter and the short epilogue that follows examine the legacies of fiduciary practices in the writing of Spanish history and the use of translation in Spanish political thought and statecraft.

Fiduciary Translation in Spanish History and Prophecy

Creating Spanish Historical Sources Through Arabic Translation

Though its format and audience were changing, Arabic translation continued to add to the store of materials that could be used in Spain to make legal
and political arguments throughout the *morisco* debates and long after the
expulsion. The work of the Granada *morisco* Miguel de Luna (1550–1615) is
one significant example of the endurance of fiduciary translation for producing legal and historical sources at the end of the *morisco* period, and his work
would leave a long legacy in Spain and across Europe. Luna, like his colleague Alonso del Castillo, was a *morisco* doctor from Granada who participated in many kinds of translation, from history to medicine. Luna's
exposure to the world of fiduciary translation shaped his claims about expertise and his tactics for representing Arabic knowledge in translation. This
influence is nowhere more salient than in his project to ensure the reception
of a new history of Spain.

Among Luna's many activities, his most successful project was perhaps
the publication of *The True History of the King don Rodrigo, in which the Principal Cause of the Loss of Spain is Treated* (1592), whose popularity inspired a
second volume, *The Second Part of the History of the Loss of Spain, and the Life
of the King Jacob Almansor* (1600).[5] Purportedly (though not really) translated
from Arabic manuscripts found in the Escorial, Luna's two volumes describe
an eighth-century eyewitness account of the Islamic conquest and the first
generation of Muslim rule until 763. Luna's narrative of the conquest and
the first decades of Muslim rule in Iberia contained echoes of the real political and military campaigns through which Visigoths and Muslims negotiated new structures of power.[6] He also performed a creative chronological
collapse in the *True History*, particularly in his use of the character of the
Miramolín (*amīr al-mu'minīn*) Iacob Almanzor, effectively inserting an allu-
sion to a later Almohad figure into an Umayyad-era narrative.

In addition to his narrative, Luna provided supporting documentation
throughout the two volumes in the form of transcribed and "translated" letters. Through this presentation and use of "sources," the text offered a substantially revisionist history of the end of Visigoth rule in Spain. It was a
major departure from the romance cycles that circulated in the fourteenth
and fifteenth centuries and that traditionally portrayed the drama of Islamic
conquest with an emphasis on the continuity of Christian legitimacy—that

is, the "real Spaniards" who were pushed into the Pyrenees, from which they would begin "reconquest" centuries later.[7] However, in addition to the useful historical models provided in the lives and deeds of Muslim princes, Luna represented his history to the king as a tool for consolidating political legitimacy by providing important genealogical evidence about previous Iberian Christian kings. In the active markets for genealogical materials in Spain— for proving blood purity or other rights and privileges—and in addition to royally sponsored projects of national history writing, such an assurance could have bestowed great value on Luna's work.[8]

As a work of imaginary Arabic, Luna's *True History* was also an heir to the "fictive translation" trope that became popular in Iberian chivalric romances in the later Middle Ages. Fictive translation strongly influenced the writing of Spanish Golden Age texts, of which the best-known example is the "Arabic translation" underpinning Cervantes's *Don Quixote*, invoked in the opening of this book.[9] Fictive translation underpinned other "moorish novels" like the first volume of the *Guerras de Granada*, which Ginés Pérez de Hita published in 1595 between the publication of Luna's two volumes. Scholars have posited, with good reason, that Cervantes may have had Luna in mind when imagining his fictional translator. However, unlike Cervantes, Luna did not use fictive translation as an attractive narrative device to bring the reader into the world of the text. Rather, he wished that the work be read as a reliable work of history upon which legal and political arguments could be made. For that reason, he presented it using the tactics of fiduciary translation to which he had been exposed in Granada and which he had used in his "real" translation work to guarantee his own fidelity and the accuracy of his work.

Luna used a range of familiar tactics to guarantee the authenticity of his *True History*. These included the tactics of the paratext, in which the siting of the translation and the credentials of the translator were established; the incorporation of translated documents with ancillary explanation like chronological conversions; and the markings of humanist erudition like those that also characterized Castillo's diplomatic workbook (e.g., marginal notes and lexicographical references). Luna used his position as a royal interpreter to guarantee the authenticity of the text on the title page itself: "Newly Translated from the Arabic Language by Miguel de Luna, Granada resident, Interpreter of the King don Philip our Lord." Claiming this official position was the point of departure for the process of translation to follow, echoing the practices of fiduciary translators discussed in Chapter 1.

Figure 13. Alonso del Castillo's transcription and translation of a letter from
al-Manṣūr to Philip II, with an example of his marginal note to explain Arabic
terms from the text. Such notes are characteristic of his Moroccan Workbook
(c. 1579–1587), in which Castillo made marginal annotations about new Arabic
words as he learned them, along with their definitions as found in Arabic
dictionaries. This folio shows Castillo's marginal note for an unfamiliar word
overlined in the text, al-kumkhatu (silk), derived partially from al-Jawharī's
eleventh-century lexical work Ṣiḥāḥ Tāj al-Lugha (also excerpted by Castillo
elsewhere in the manuscript and referenced regularly in the margins).
© Biblioteca Nacional de España, MS 7453, f. 49r.

Luna reiterated his claims to an official position in his dedication to the
king (*Proemio al Rey nuestro señor*). Like most encomia, he used overlapping
motifs from the reports about service, expertise, and experience that also
appeared in *relaciones de servicio*:

It has been sufficiently demonstrated that experience (*experiencia*)—
through the continuous practice (*exercicio*) of mankind—brings the

sciences to perfection and amplifies them. He who pursues them becomes ordained with great virtues, his understanding is elevated to contemplate high-minded and divine thoughts, and finally with these thoughts he finds the means to live in this miserable knot (*nudo*) and avoid drowning in the swamp of blind and monstrous ignorance. It was with this purpose, your Catholic Majesty, that I began as a child to cultivate my abilities (*ingenio*) in the sweet and pleasing (*dulce y sabroso*) exercise of letters, and especially in Arabic (*la facultad Arabiga*), from which I brought to light and rescued the present history. . . . Your Majesty, please receive this small service, as something properly belonging to you, under your protection and support, with which I will be kept safe from my detractors. . . . And may God preserve Your Majesty [and grant you] more Kingdoms, as we your loyal (*fieles y leales*) vassals desire, and as Christendom requires.[10]

Here Luna asserted his fiduciary status using a familiar format and evocative keywords (experience and expertise, service, loyalty, vassalage). The history that followed was thus guaranteed.

In addition to the direct claims that echoed the traditional formulae of notarial translators and the reports of translator service, Luna's paratext also shows transverse relationships with the social bonds underpinning fiduciary translation in Granada. For example, one letter from Joan de Feria, an official of the Royal Appellate Court (Real Chancillería) in Granada, testified to Luna's skill and expertise as an Arabic translator.[11] Feria specified that the latter had "kept the letter and sense as much as possible, following the style of its author Tarif."[12] Those who worked in the Royal Appellate Court in Granada were accustomed to handling translated documents and to using those translations to understand the value of the original sources. As was common in other works of print, Luna's book was embedded in networks of patronage, credit, and support, thus ensuring his access to editors, his approval by censors, and his ability to make claims about his expertise. Those networks were represented in the text itself in Luna's dedicatory letters (to the king, and later to the reader) and in the published letters and sonnets written by other notables in praise of Luna and his translation.

Feria's assurance about Luna's precision in translation reflected other common formulae used in fiduciary translation in which translators promised that the text was "translated faithfully" (*bien y fielmente*) or "word by word" (*de verbo ad verbum*). By the 1580s, when Luna produced his text, keeping the *sense* of the original was also demanded of translators. Luna's close colleague Alonso del Castillo (who often guaranteed his translations using the phrase *de verbo ad verbum*) testified to this exigency when he copied into his diplomatic workbook one of the sentences that he attributed to Marcus Aurelius: "Translators are not obliged to give each word measure by measure, but rather following the sense, translating phrase by phrase."[13] During the course of the sixteenth century, the habits of fiduciary translation across genres promoted a specific form of *ad sensum* translation in which the expertise of the translator was also on display.

The solution to the debate between *ad verbum* and *ad sensum* was further constructed in other parts of Luna's paratext, as, for example, the sonnets of the Golden Age author Juan Bautista de Vivar, who used the poetic format to ask, "Which is of greater esteem, the style or the truth?" His answer was that the author's style and the truth of his work were matched and that he "did not know if it is better to see you [the book] in your original language or in that in which we see you now." This was because Luna was a "faithful interpreter" (*fiel intérprete*) of style and truth, which allowed Vivar to "promise in his name [that of the author] that which he promised by his name."[14] In this claim, two signatures guaranteed the veracity of the work, echoing the traditional assurances of eyewitness testimony. Claims to faithful interpretation (which could take place in collaboration), the guarantee by signature, and the presence of witnesses were all characteristics of fiduciary translation.

Thus, through his translation and selection of original Arabic and Spanish documents throughout the *True History*—many of which were printed in their entirety in the text with explanations in marginal notes—Luna achieved a similar effect to that of the *romanceadores* working for the Royal Appellate Court or the *calificadores* of the Inquisition. His translation furnished authentic evidence from Arabic sources that would be stored and used in Spanish institutions for generations to come. That a printed text like Luna's passed through several censors, included encomia from important officials and literary figures, and was dedicated and addressed to the king himself helped guarantee the authenticity of the history, translation, and texts of the *True History*.

In addition to paratextual strategies, the tactics of fiduciary translation are apparent in the text itself. Indeed, the composition of Luna's fictive translation and the very construction of the historical narrative he provided depended strongly on his familiarity with the mechanisms of fiduciary translation and the formats of cross-cultural diplomacy. Luna incorporated many "translated" documents into his text, primarily diplomatic letters purportedly exchanged between Iberian, North African, and Umayyad leaders in the eighth century. All of these letters were invented, but they were modeled (in translation) on real letters between Muslim and Christian leaders that were exchanged in Iberia in the sixteenth century, of the kind that Luna's colleague Alonso del Castillo worked with during diplomatic commissions.[15]

Luna's invented author, Abulcacem Tarif Abentarique, claimed to be an eyewitness to much of the Muslim conquest of Iberia in the early eighth century. Based on his time with Ṭāriq Ibn Ziyād—the historical general who is thought to have led the first Islamic armies across the Strait of Gibraltar (*Jabal Ṭāriq*)—Abulcacem claimed to offer the most accurate account of the campaign. In addition to what he himself experienced, Abulcacem was inspired by "all the letters and papers that I refer to in this history, which were brought to me personally by the generals who carried out the conquest. Whatever I did not myself see, I informed myself about with great diligence from people whose reports are worthy of belief."[16] This framing, and the supposed documentary base were all invented by Luna. The translation work, however, was in some sense very real, since Luna did produce "Arabic" letters in Spanish based on his experience with Arabic sources and fiduciary translation. From that experience, he created a target text made legible through simultaneous references to recognizable Spanish political concepts and familiar practices of Arabic translation.

The format of the letters was a hybrid of those Luna had probably seen from rebel *moriscos* during the Second War of the Alpujarras (1568–1571) as well as those emanating from Moroccan and Spanish chancelleries; that is, in many ways the letters use conventional Spanish formulae, simply replacing Spanish titles with what Luna imagined to be the analogous Arabic titles.[17] However, the beginnings and endings of the "translated" letters are strongly reminiscent of Castillo's translations of the Alpujarras correspondence and the Moroccan diplomacy.[18] These formulae were doubtless meant to signal to the reader that the text was a "real" Arabic translation. For example, all of the copies of Arabic letters supposedly translated into Luna's *True History* began with some version of "Los loores sean a Dios" (a common translation for *al-ḥamdu lilla*, "praise be to God," or *bi-ismi llāh*, "in the name of God") and a sequence of titles reflecting the military prowess,

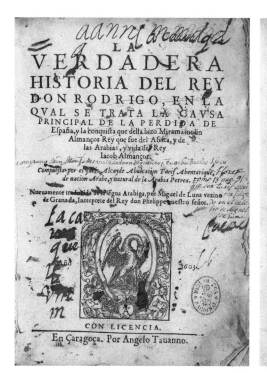

Figure 14. "Translated" letter from an apocryphal Umayyad caliph,
"Miramolin Iacob Almanzor" to his general Muça el Çanhani in North Africa,
c. 713. Marginal notes define the Arabic terms and make chronological
conversions. Miguel de Luna, *La verdadera historia . . .* (1603), f. 13r.
© Biblioteca Nacional de España, R/15600.

position, and lineage of the recipient. The letters likewise give the place and
date of the letter's emission—always according to the Islamic calendar.[19]
Castillo's translations of *morisco* and Moroccan correspondence had introduced the Spanish versions of these conventions to Spanish readers, including Miguel de Luna. Luis del Mármol Carvajal had incorporated some of
Castillo's translations into his later history of the Alpujarras war, making
those formulae available to all Spanish readers.[20] Though one author used
"real" translations to illustrate his history and the other invented his, both
Mármol Carvajal and Luna responded to the market for using translation to
write history and used similar recognizable formats to do so.

Luna's translation games with these letters could become quite convoluted. For example, early on he provided a letter that had purportedly been sent among members of the Visigothic royal family before being captured by the Muslim armies and translated "from Castilian into Arabic" by Abentarique, only to be "translated" by Luna again into Spanish nearly a thousand years later.[21] To assure the reliability of his author—also a translator—Luna created a reciprocal conduit for translation during the conquest, signaling to his readers that Abulcacem had access to "original sources."

Finally, to buttress the credibility of all these documents and many other parts of his narration, Luna turned to another familiar mechanism used by translators and other Renaissance text workers such as philologists and commentators: printed marginal notes. Around the margins of the "translated" letters, notes converted the Muslim calendar to the day and month of "the year of the birth of our savior Jesus Christ." Most of the marginal notes were devoted to explaining the Arabic translation for some Spanish word or concept mentioned in the text. Formally, these marginal notes lent an air of erudition and authority to the work. However, aside from the trappings of expertise, their utility was limited to readers with an interest in Arabic lexicography or in reconstructing the meanings of the imagined Arabic original, since the marginal definitions of Arabic words were not useful for understanding the text itself, which was already in Spanish.

By means of these formal guarantees to the authenticity of Abulcacem's original and the accuracy of its translation (both false, in actual fact), Luna hoped to advance an urgent political argument about *morisco* policies. Central to the argument of his historical narrative was a positive depiction of the first Muslim princes of Iberia, who were able to integrate diverse subjects under just political rule. Luna thus showed how an eighth-century Muslim ruler promised nobility to those in Spain who joined his armies and did not resist his conquest. This was a direct rebuke to Ferdinand and Isabella (and their heirs), since the latter were supposed to have done the same during the War of Granada but had broken their contracts with their subjects repeatedly throughout the sixteenth century.[22]

Luna was not the only writer who thought that compiling Arabic sources was an opportunity to write new Spanish historical narratives. Many Spanish historiographers working at the end of the sixteenth century were simultaneously looking for ways to demonstrate links with a Gothic past and to explain the significance of the Muslim history of Spain.[23] Historians sought out Arabic texts that could provide evidence about this crucial period, and thus Arabic translators became involved with the national historiographic project.[24] Some even worked together in erudite spaces like the Escorial library, where they crossed paths and patronage with other key actors like royal secretaries, including members of the Gracián and Idiáquez families. In such figures, historical expertise overlapped with political counsel at the very moment that history was becoming an auxiliary political science.[25] Translations of Arabic histories were no exception to this trend, even if many of Spain's political "problems" nominally concerned Arabic speakers or Muslims (often conflated in the Renaissance imagination), whether *moriscos*, Ottomans, or Moroccans and other North African powers.

In response to Luna's editorial success, rival royal translators such as Diego de Urrea and the recently arrived Kurdish Marco Dobelio also canvassed the Escorial for early histories.[26] In 1596 Urrea completed a history of Spain based on Arabic and Ottoman sources (using his memory from his library in Constantinople), which was given to the secretary Idiáquez to receive a license for printing (according to the historiographer of Aragon Bartolomé Leonardo de Argensola).[27] However, Urrea's translation is lost and seems never to have been published, perhaps because Urrea became too preoccupied with affairs of the present (like the Spanish-Moroccan diplomacy discussed in Chapter 3). Meanwhile, Dobelio translated a short portion of Abū al-Fiḍā's (1273–1331) *Mukhtasir Tarīkh al-Bashar* (Summary of the history of mankind) concerning the Muslim conquest of Spain, which was meant to provide a counterpoint to Luna's version.[28] Although Dobelio's translation was the most authentic testimony of early Arabic chronicles (and actually a translation), it was Luna's lengthy and vivid fictive translation—presented always as a true history transcribed by a faithful translator—that left a greater mark on Spanish historiography in the seventeenth century, including in translations to other languages and print markets in Europe and the Ottoman Empire.[29]

All of these translations were intended to fuel the late sixteenth-century movement to create a body of knowledge that would sustain the body politic. Indeed, the collaboration between the Neapolitan Urrea and the Aragonese historiographers the Argensola brothers, well studied by Fernando Rodríguez Mediano, is another indication of the way in which the national historiographical project was compiled from multilingual sources that were faithfully translated. Treatises on the body politic and other corporeal analogies for government and the social contract proved to be powerful stand-ins for ideas about subjecthood and identity in Spain.[30] Sixteenth-century writers used many kinds of corporeal and physical metaphors to create ideologies about Arabic and Arabic speakers in Spain, including Alonso del Castillo's description of the language as deriving from the "bowels of the devil" and Luis Joseph de Sotomayor's use of the metaphor of the body to claim that the Oranese Jews were a "mole" on the face of the Spanish Republic.[31] Scholars of political advice literature in the pre-*arbitrismo* (economic reform literature) period also noticed the common trope in advice literature by which history books claimed to be healing objects for both the political and the real body.[32]

The ideational consequence of this metaphor could be taken one step farther for the translators' advantage. If the king translated the medical and political information as he read, or if it was translated for him, could not translation itself constitute a healing practice? Luna made an argument along these lines in the preface to the reader of the *True History*:

> The good interpreter must be wise in all subjects. [Imagine what would happen if] an interpreter were not a doctor who can understand the rules and precepts of Medicine, and the names given by authors for illnesses, simples, and compounds with which they should be cured. I don't know how an interpreter like that, no matter how well he knew the language, could understand the living concepts of the author he is translating and thus be able to translate it in his own version, with the same perfection and knowledge that he would have in his own language, and this same logic holds in the other sciences. What would it be to see a doctor dare to spout theology, or a lawyer interpret medicine. In this I have no doubt that the office of the interpreter is the most difficult of all.[33]

This claim about the necessary knowledge of interpreters and the medical analogy followed immediately from a discussion of translation theory and the distinction between *ad verbum* and *ad sensum*, in which Luna insisted that it was this expertise embodied by the interpreter that allowed him to produce the "difficult and necessary condition" between the two paths (*ad verbum* and *ad sensum*).

Elsewhere the imagery that underpinned Luna's depiction of the best prince and healthiest body politic in his forged translation was the same that informed his work as a medical doctor, although until very recently much less has been known about his work in the field of medicine. For example, a letter

to Philip II written in May 1592 promoting the construction of public baths
for health reasons was recovered in the early 2000s by Fernando Rodríguez
Mediano and Mercedes García-Arenal in the Spanish National Library in
Madrid.[34] This letter advocated reopening public baths as a counterweight to
the popular curative methods of bloodletting and purgation. According to
Luna, bathing upheld what should be the physician's primary principle, pre-
ventive medicine, by allowing toxins to escape bathing bodies gradually via the
pores, without the drastic purges of the Spanish surgeons who, unable to tell
the healthy fluids from the infected ones, drained them all and left the patient
weaker than ever.[35]

This vision of healthy purification as against drastic and dangerous purgation is a clear metaphor for the expulsion of the *morisco* portion of Spain's
body politic. Luna's medical translations were another tactic for expressing
the moral of the *True History*: that indiscriminate expulsion is more harmful than good and that the just ruler "must seek remedies against such
ills."[36] In addition to supporting his medicinal recommendation with Arabic
wisdom, which he explained but left untranslated strategically, so as to lend
an air of legitimacy, Luna historicized the use of baths by Muslims in Spain
and the Ottomans, who were not weakened but strengthened by their use.
When Muslims used baths it was a medical, not a religious, technology that
helped keep their princes and soldiers strong and allowed them to further
their imperial grasp (*ensanchar sus estados*). Arabic medical knowledge had
immediate political use for the Spanish monarchy, even medical knowledge
that seemed to support Islamic practices like bathing, of which the clergy
strongly disapproved (cf. the *guadoque* [Ar. *wuḍū'*], which was condemned in
numerous catechisms). Readopting baths in Spain for medicinal use would
prevent the self-destructive medicine that had deprived Philip of his potential fighting force, since the current state of affairs meant that even the
slightest headache was cause for bloodletting, leaving perfectly healthy men
weakened and unable to bear arms.[37]

Public health was one genre of Arabic expertise of interest to the king,
as was personal medicine. In 1596 Luna was commissioned to translate an
Arabic treatise on gout, a disease afflicting many early modern rulers, including the Spanish Habsburgs.[38] There is little concrete information about this
commission, although an anonymous manuscript copy of a translated treatise
on gout from fifteenth-century Granada resides today in the Real Academia
de la Historia and could be connected to Luna's commission.[39] The translator
included his hope that the medical advice be useful to the king, "as his loyal

vassals wish, and as Christianity requires."[40] The Real Academia copy dates from 1593, and it is likely related to Luna's commission for other medical translations, although a direct connection with the 1596 commission discovered by García-Arenal and Rodríguez Mediano in the Spanish National Library remains speculative at this point.[41] Whatever the connection between the two texts (which will hopefully someday emerge from the archives), the 1593 translation is another example of using translation to make a direct political argument to the king, on behalf of his *morisco* subjects, about the loyalty and usefulness of those subjects *and* their Arabic knowledge and heritage.

Indeed, in Spain as in other parts of Europe, there was a close connection between medical learning and political appointments related to "oriental languages."[42] In Spain, medical learning in Arabic had a regular place in Spanish universities throughout the sixteenth century, both in the medical faculties (especially Valencia) and among *morisco* practitioners like Luna or Castillo.[43] At the very moment that anti-Arabic legislation was reaching a fever pitch, along with quickening anti-*morisco* and pro-expulsion apologetics, Arabic translators from diverse backgrounds struggled to craft legitimate fields of knowledge in practical subjects. Through the tactics of translation, composition, compilation, and intertextuality across these diverse projects, Luna created reliable historical sources upon which to base the legal claims of the *morisco* community for toleration and justice from their king.

Prophecy and Policy: Translating the History of the Future

When the first volume was completed in 1589, Luna's *True History* entered into a complex intertextual argument about history, language, and identity in Spain that was closely bound up with the *morisco* question. Already by the middle part of the sixteenth century, Spanish political thought was marked by profound sensitivity toward the fact that the past was unfixed. This preoccupation with a history that was conceived of as unstable generated a consequent desire for reform through the work of historiographers as well as of other language workers like translators. Such was the urgency to find—or generate—useful materials for this project that a subset of political historical projects in late sixteenth-century and early seventeenth-century Spain were national narratives that, like Luna's *True History*, relied on forged historical sources. Forgeries played a crucial role in the long history of political thought in Spain, and Arabic forgeries and the translation practices that went into their creation, decipherment, and application were no exception.[44] All forgeries, Arabic or otherwise, were intended to rewrite the past so as to create a legal basis for new norms that would favor certain communities.[45] Luna—and almost all of the other Arabic translators in Spain known to have been active from the 1580s until the *morisco* expulsion—was closely involved with one of these forgeries, the famous Lead Books of Granada, known by scholarly shorthand as the *plomos*.[46]

The *plomos* represents, without a doubt, most famous and well-studied episode of forgery and Arabic translation in early modern Spain.[47] The episode lasted for nearly a century, from the unearthing of pre-Islamic Christian artifacts in Granada and its surrounding hillsides beginning in 1588 through the subsequent debate about their authenticity and meaning, which lasted until the Vatican declared them apocryphal in 1682. The "discoveries" of these texts and artifacts were, of course, products of the late-renaissance obsession with antiquities, including a kind of antiquarianism determined to recover sources for Spanish history that could provide evidence for a cultural (and if possible, religious) unity that transcended the period of Muslim rule.[48] For the government of Granada, which in the 1580s and 1590s was still dealing with the legacy of the second Alpujarras war, such pre-Islamic artifacts testifying to the city's early Christian heritage were nothing less than a godsend, and the ecclesiastical elite, like the city's archbishop Pedro de Castro, defended the authenticity of the relics.[49]

These forgeries and their context have received a tremendous amount of scholarly attention over the past two decades since the return of many original artifacts and manuscripts from the Vatican to the Abbey of Sacromonte in 2000 and the discovery of new manuscripts in local archives even more recently.[50] Here I do not pretend to add new archival information to that robust literature—much of which happily includes editions and transcriptions of the documents and artifacts that can be analyzed closely, since the originals are difficult to access—but rather to offer potential new directions in the conversation. We all might look more closely at practices and institutions that seem unrelated to historical forgeries but that strongly determined the form and content of both the apocryphal artifacts and their translation and legacies. In what follows, I aim to connect parts of the *plomos* episode and some of the related work of Miguel de Luna to the practices and legacies of fiduciary translation that have been explored in this book.

Scholars now think that the *plomos* forgers were produced in connection with the educated *morisco* elite of Granada, a social and intellectual set that included figures like the university-trained doctors Alonso del Castillo and Luna (the leading contenders among scholars as the actual forgers), the noble Venegas family, the future émigré Aḥmad ibn Qāsim al-Ḥajarī, and even ecclesiastical elites like the Jesuit Ignacio de las Casas. All of these figures were called on in different capacities to evaluate the *plomos* or to translate them, as were "foreign" experts like Diego de Urrea and Marco Dobelio and their students, including the Basque secretary Francisco de Gurmendi.

In addition to their Arabic knowledge, these figures all shared a background of familiarity with the practices and institutions of fiduciary translation. Many of these translators were simultaneously the products of sixteenth-century humanist and university culture, who participated in diplomatic exchanges between Spain and Morocco, and worked with the Inquisition. Finally, the *plomos* provide examples of the parallel political and linguistic processes of *reducción* through Arabic translation that had begun during the converging processes of conquest, resettlement, and state building and with the ennoblement of Castilian as the state vernacular over the course of the sixteenth century in Spain. As such, the *plomos* provide another example of the ideological and institutional sites that marked Late Spanish Arabic (LSA). Reading the *plomos* in these frameworks helps move beyond the dominating debates about whether the *moriscos* were faithful Christians or crypto-Muslims to reveal a far more complex social reality in which language and translation created opportunities to access as well as barriers to institutions of power. The episode also illustrates how, after two generations of *reducción* had already become encoded in the language of the colonized, Arabic began a new process of domestication that would strongly affect the writing of history and literature long after the *morisco* expulsion.

Like Luna's *True History,* the *plomos* added alternative voices to the prophecies, forgeries, and other sources that influenced the general writing of the history of Spain and the running of its day-to-day politics. From a linguistic perspective, the fact that the texts of the relics were in Arabic, Spanish, and Latin provided Spanish scholars who had differing political agendas a range of possible evidence from which to make linguistic arguments about the writing of Spanish history and the position of different linguistic communities in the body politic.[51] Differences between the "Solomonic" Arabic of the *plomos* and the otherwise non–Classical Arabic of the parchment has been interpreted as either evidence of the lack of Classical Arabic education among the forgers or a deliberate program of inscribing "pseudo-archaic" Arabic to bolster the case that the texts indeed dated from the first century.[52]

There are many texts and many translations related to the *plomos*, a large number of which were studied and published by Miguel José Hagarty in the 1980s. Across the texts, numerous intertextual arguments about Arabic and translation were made. For example, in one apocryphal dialogue between St. Peter and the Virgin, the latter explained why it was that the gospel would be written in Arabic: "The Arabs are among the best of peoples, and their language is among the best of languages. . . . and although they have been great enemies [of Christianity], . . . the Arabs and their language will be those who bring about the triumph of God, his orthodox religion, his glorious gospel, and his holy church in the end of times"[53] This passage, and others like it, have been interpreted by scholars as examples of the dual readings of the *plomos*. For a crypto-Muslim audience, the Virgin's assurance that it would be the Arabs' language and God who would triumph would have read as an immensely gratifying joke on Christian authorities. For those same Christian authorities, the exciting promise of a new gospel sent by the Virgin to Spain itself, whatever the language, would have affirmed Spain's prestigious Christian heritage. Through translation, all sides were able to choose new evidence for their arguments.

In other places, the *plomos* offered an explicit meditation on the ways in which translation itself created authority by making historical information and examples available. For instance, the apocryphal Prophecy of Saint John, which was found early on in 1588 in the Torre Turpiana parchment, is a testament to translation's power as a source of legitimacy and authority.[54] The parchment prophecy took the form of a narrative account supposedly made in the first century AD. In the narrative, Saint Cecilio, the apocryphal translator of the prophecy, was struck blind while returning from a pilgrimage to Jerusalem. The affliction took place on the way to Athens, where he was eventually cured of his blindness after making his confession to the patriarch of that city. During the course of a miraculous mass, a relic of the Virgin was displayed upon which the author said he saw written a Hebrew prophecy that had been translated into Greek by Dionysius the Areopagite, a famous first-century Athenian convert to Christianity.[55] This spectacle of the once-blind Cecilio's witnessing—through reading and the recounting in translation—the apparition of a Hebrew prophecy written in Greek set off a ripple of translations across time, culminating in the *plomos* discoveries and their translation and evaluation by Christian authorities at the end of the sixteenth century.

By design, narrating the performances of translation in the prophetical text took up more space than the prophecy itself, and the translation frames invited endless recurrence through which the secret knowledge was always just one translation away and for which a divinely sanctioned translator was needed. Throughout, the argument made by means of those translation frames was strongly in favor of Arabic's early and legitimate place in Spain, its use by Christians, and its status as a language of "secret" knowledge. As in his *True History* and the medical manuscripts, Luna's message in the *plomos* translations was one of cultural relativism within the framework of political unity and fidelity. He also fueled a developing topos by which Arabic itself became the "bank" (*maṣrāf*) of secret knowledge that could be drawn upon to write Spanish history and design royal policies.[56]

The Torre Turpiana parchment and its translation thus became the key to both the past (history) and the future (prophecy) of the Arabic Christians (*cristianos arábigos*) of Granada. Luna was called on to translate this parchment and the prophecy described within it in 1595. In this episode, the marks of fiduciary translation on the *plomos* project—their forgery, discovery, and their subsequent translation—is especially clear. The form of Luna's paratext is another classic example of fiduciary translation. As with notarized translations performed for the Granada town council and Royal Appellate Court, the *plomos* were also subject to a collaborative process of authentication through translation. For example, before his translation of the text that concluded with the John prophecy, Luna inscribed the following:

> I, Miguel de Luna, resident of Granada and Arabic interpreter, by
> order of his lordship don Juan Mendez de Salvatierra, Archbishop
> of Granada and [member] of the King's Council, translated
> everything written in the abovementioned parchment except the
> encrypted prophecy, which requires more study and consideration,
> which I am continuing to translate. All of which was done in the
> presence of the *Licenciado* [a university degree] Farxado, Chair of
> [Oriental] Languages, in conversation with him to show that the
> translation conforms to the original. And I swear to God and upon
> the Holy Gospels on which I placed my hands that according to
> my loyal knowledge and understanding, according to the rules of

> Arabic grammar, this is faithfully and loyally translated word for
> word, all of which was done in the presence of the *Licenciado*
> Antonio Barba, ecclesiastic judge (*provisor*) working for the arch-
> bishop of Granada, to whom I turned in my translation, signed
> with my name and his name in Granada on March 31, 1588.
> [Signed by Luna and Barba before the witness Montoya the
> secretary].[57]

The mechanisms of fiduciary translation are clear in this passage, including the dating, the description of the exact process of translation and who was present, and the source (or sources) of the commission. In addition, Luna used key phrases in reference to his swearing on the bible, for example, his "faithful and loyal translation," *de verbo ad verbum*. This paratext is structured to assure the reader of the legitimacy of the translation and its sanction by other experts and authorities connected to royal and ecclesiastical power.

During the quasi-legal processes of translating the first of the prophetical texts that would be discovered in Granada, great emphasis was placed on the sense (*sentido*) of the message and the need for an adequate interpreter who could render it *ad sensum*. According to its own text, the message will remain locked away until the appointed time comes when a translator can use the text and its cipher to decode the sense of the text and use it to advise his ruler. In general, by the end of the *morisco* age, an emphasis on *ad sensum* translation gradually helped displace the value of the original in favor of the intelligibility of the translation in the target discourse. This process is also visible in Luna's *True History*; that is, in some ways it did not matter whether or not a real Arabic manuscript was the source of Luna's "translation": the *sense* of the text and of Luna's argument—that good kings enact toleration over diverse subjects—became "true" in Luna's Spanish formulation. Increasing emphasis on the *sensum* of target texts over source texts was a result of the decreasing institutional spaces for fiduciary translation in the face of changing *morisco* policies and demography.

Translating Muslim Mirrors for Princes

Arabic translation in the *morisco* period had a defining effect on the production of Spanish history across a range of genres and media. It is hardly surprising that the question of Spain's Islamic past was closely linked to the *morisco* question. Anxieties about a potentially crypto-Islamic present had an effect on Arabic use and study in Spain. Indeed, one key difference with other early European orientalisms that were developing at the same time was that France, England, the Netherlands, and others were not yet colonial powers ruling over large Muslim populations.[58] Thus much of early northern European orientalism was conditioned by interest that was connected to biblical scholarship, while at the same time motivated by commercial goals and missionary ideals. In Spain the indexing of language and nation was an ideological and politicized process that had begun with the legislation over autochthonous Arabic under the Catholic Kings.[59] However, the growing connection between language and state gained more "scientific" traction through explorations in a nascent historical linguistics that sought to determine the "original" language of "original" Spaniards.[60] For this reason, the concomitant vogues of Spanish antiquarianism and the search for Christian origins motivated projects like the *plomos* and created markets for them and their translators.

Translation strongly affected how "oriental" knowledge—a commodity increasing in popularity across Europe because of trade, missions, and politics—was appropriated and incorporated into Spanish politics via translation. Direct contact with foreign Muslim powers facilitated the acquisition of this knowledge in a range of ways beginning in the latter half of the sixteenth century. The 1570s brought about the resolution of Mediterranean warfare between the Spanish Habsburgs and the Ottomans and the beginning of regular but discrete contact in the 1580s.[61] As discussed in Chapter 3, Portuguese intervention in a Moroccan civil war in 1578 had motivated the opening of diplomatic relations with Morocco. The years 1600–1601 marked the arrival of Safavid embassies to Spain, subsequent to Spanish delegations having being sent to Persia in the 1580s.[62] Texts, translations, and other media of experience arrived in the Spanish court from these sources and others, and most of these sources were channeled into the royal library at the Escorial (Biblioteca Real de El Escorial).

As early as the 1570s, the royal library at the Escorial Palace-Monastery would become the central point of managing both the internal and external governance of Arabic speakers and sources, based first on the collections of Spanish humanists (Juan Páez de Castro and Diego Hurtado de Mendoza), book-buying embassies (Benito Arias Montano), and Inquisitorial confiscations. The Escorial was the repository of the early Spanish histories that were translated by Urrea and Dobelio (and claimed by Luna). In the seventeenth century, the palace-library also came to house "external" Islamic knowledge, which was translated in order to be deployed in Spanish government and administration. With the precipitous decline in "*morisco*" affairs and the lull in official Moroccan diplomacy in the first decades of the seventeenth century, Arabic experts at court were employed primarily for evaluating, cataloguing, and translating the significant Arabic collections of the Escorial. Alonso del Castillo and Diego de Urrea had already made initial catalogues in the 1570s and 1590s, but serious work in the Arabic collections did not really begin until the major (and most famous) infusion of Arabic materials in the form of the captured Moroccan royal library, which was incorporated into the Spanish royal collections in 1612.[63] The infusion of Moroccan texts, the increased exchange between the eastern Mediterranean, and the treasures brought back to Spain by humanist-diplomat book collectors (like Diego Hurtado de Mendoza, Benito Arias Montano, etc.) ensured that Spain's royal Arabic collection would no longer be based primarily upon the spoils of war against the Nasrids, *moriscos*, and North Africans. By the seventeenth century, Moroccan, Ottoman, and Safavid texts flowed into the administrative offices of the monarchy and were translated.[64]

This infusion of Islamic learning into the heart of the Spanish empire had significant consequences for the profession of Arabic translation. Training in Arabic was becoming a regular academic discipline (though it would not be fully consolidated as such until the nineteenth century). For example, Urrea held the chair in Arabic at Spain's flagship university in Alcalá de Henares beginning in 1595 and thereafter trained the Hieronymite monks of the Escorial. This in-house Arabic learning persisted for generations.[65] The translation of political topics from Arabic became yet another avenue for making arguments about Spanish political traditions, including the cherished contractualism (*pactismo*) that characterized the governing of medieval Iberian kingdoms.[66] Arabic sources became well integrated into the compilations of historical evidence and examples used by would-be advisors and reformers (*arbitristas*). Translation of Arabic political thought in Habsburg Spain thus continued to reflect the political language of late Renaissance Europe, especially the traditional vocabulary of contractualism and new ideas about reason of state.[67]

Translation became another forum for constructing and critiquing the contractualism upon which Habsburg rule was based. Habsburg sovereignty over Spanish territories relied upon not only dynastic rights but also the consent of the governed, articulated through the *cortes* system in Castile, the *fueros* of Aragon and the presidios, and other representative mechanisms. This was an age of absolutism, but a negotiated absolutism that yielded heterogeneous rule over diverse territories. This feature of Spanish politics in the early modern period has been studied in terms of the Iberian kingdoms, European territories, and global empire, but the role of Arabic translation in effecting or criticizing this contractualism has barely been noticed.

One of the principal vectors for political language and political theory derived from Arabic sources were the manuals of statecraft in the "mirrors for princes" tradition, which flourished beginning in the later Middle Ages and especially in Baroque Spain.[68] In general, many political models arrived in Spain via translation, and princely manuals were no exception. Spanish kings became translators of classic historical and political works, like Philip IV (who translated Guicciardini).[69] The writing of history and the recovery of potential political models was as true of the European revival of Tacitus that would strongly shape Spanish political thought in the seventeenth century as it was of the circulation of Machiavelli (and the concomitant anti-Machiavellian discourses) and the eventual translation of Persian, Ottoman, and Moroccan political writings.[70] In the following section I offer some preliminary hypotheses about how the translation of Islamic wisdom literature from Moroccan, Ottoman, and Safavid sources was affected by the legacy of fiduciary translation and the transition to imaginary Arabic.[71]

Making Sensum *from Islamic Political Models Through Imagined Arabic*

A contributing factor to the turn toward *ad sensum* translation that Luna preferred was a gradual transition away from incorporating Arabic loan words into translations—a common practice in fiduciary translations and religious texts—in favor of using Spanish key words that may have had little to do with the original Arabic meaning. This turn was in effect a transition from *reducción* to domestication as the mode for adopting and deploying Arabic texts and knowledge for political purposes. For example, Luna's use of a term like *república* in the *True History* connected his "translation" of the chronicle of Islamic conquest to broader readings in political discourse at a time characterized by social, religious, and civil unrest across Europe.[72] This unrest motivated frequent attempts to reform politics, religion, and society, leading to open debate about political and social models and religious ideals. The examples needed for these debates were often derived from translation, and in Spain this included the translation of Arabic sources.

However, to adapt foreign sources from the eastern Islamic world for Spanish debates, a preference emerged for translations that looked very close to domestic discourses.

Luna's choice to use a keyword like *república* in "translation" is highly significant. For him the word was a synonym for government and was frequently associated with the good governance of one of his main characters from the Islamic conquest, Iacob Almanzor: in how he appointed his officials, in how he instructed his son to rule, in how his son reflected on his government after his death, and so on. By using familiar Spanish vocabulary for political concepts and kingly ideals, Luna was also deliberately inserting his *True History* into the lineage of classical political thought in which Plato and Cicero's republics were oft-quoted examples. He even invoked Plato's authority to assure the reader that he had undertaken this project for a higher calling than himself ("según dize Platon, que no nasció el hombre para si solo, saqué aluz esta pequeña obra").[73] In the same sentence Luna had lamented the damage made to "las repúblicas" by those who would criticize his work.

Though it is possible (even likely) that Luna was aware of Platonic thought in Latin translations and its echoes in other Spanish discourses of statecraft, he might also have had access to a Spanish Arabic transmission of Greek political works. One of the most significant commentators of Plato's (and Aristotle's) political thought in al-Andalus was the physician-philosopher Ibn Rushd, known also in his Latinate name as Averroes (1126–1198).[74] Though these texts are no longer extant in Arabic and are known only through medieval Latin and Hebrew translations, it is not out of the question that Luna had access to some Arabic version or knowledge of Ibn Rushd's Arabic commentaries. Indeed, Ibn Rushd is known to have been read by sixteenth-century *moriscos*, as in the case of the Mancebo de Arevalo.[75] For a doctor like Luna, Ibn Rushd's medical writings would have been of great interest. Indeed, Ibn Rushd was the court physician to none other than one Ya'qūb al-Manṣūr (r. 1184–1199). This was the Almohad ruler whose homonymic son would be defeated at the battle of Las Navas de Tolosa in 1212 and whose name in a Renaissance transcription would have been Iacob Almanzor—that is, the same name as Luna's ideal eighth-century prince.[76] It was al-Manṣūr, père, who commissioned Ibn Rushd to make his Aristotelian commentaries, and perhaps also those of Plato.

The creation of the character of Iacob Almanzor is a tantalizing possible clue to Luna's real Arabic sources and how and why he adapted them in

Spanish. Could he have borrowed the name of the patron of one of his intellectual idols to represent the ideal prince's sponsorship of learning (like
Luna's) and also willingness to listen to the voices of experts? Indeed, his
references to the republic are always accompanied with some reference to
Almanzor's interest in scholarship and scholars as part of his strategy for
rule. Little is known about the rule and habits of the real Iacob Almanzor
(Yaʻqūb al-Manṣūr, père), with the exception of his deathbed speech, which
was supposedly transcribed and preserved and reached new levels of popularity in the fourteenth century.[77]

Whatever its source (or sources), the emphasis on republican thought
connected Luna's message to the king about toleration and the keeping of
contracts with his subjects directly to the language of political advice aimed
at the audience of the king himself. Indeed, for a thinker like the Jesuit
Pedro de Ribadeneyra (1527–1611), one of Spain's leading anti-Machiavellian
writers, Plato was the most important source for the Christian reason of
state. Ribadeneyra elaborated on this theme in his 1595 *Treatise on the Religion and Virtues that the Christian Prince should Possess in order to Govern and
Conserve his States, against that which Nicolo Machiavelli and the "politicos" of
our times teach*, insisting that the foundation of this Christian reason of state
was the "conservation of the republic" through sincerity and fidelity (also
keywords in translation).[78]

This reason-of-state discourse was normally advanced through advice
literature for rulers, especially mirrors for princes. Luna's use of *república*
thus connected his historical translation to important contemporary debates
in Spanish political thought. For example, Luna included a "translation" of
what he represented as an eighth-century Arabic letter that referred to the
"prudence" by which Iacob Almanzor ruled his "Repúblicas" and proposed
that he should be a model for "our republics" as a "shining mirror of princes"
(*Espejo resplandeciente de Principes*).[79] The dedication concluded: "Along with
this book you may add the conditions that must be upheld and kept by the
good king in order to be loved by his subjects and feared by his enemies, all
of which can serve as a guiding light for us, with the help of our Lord God,
to reign and govern our kingdoms and republics (*nuestros reynos y republicas*)
so that they will be at peace."[80] Although this letter included the habitual
signals of translation that Luna used throughout his work—the Spanish
versions of the opening invocation "Praise be to God" (*Los loores sean a dios*)
and a Muslim date ("a quatro días de la Luna de Moharran, año de ciento y
diez de la Hixera")—the content and phrasing could have been taken from

any number of Spanish reason of state treatises from the turn of the seventeenth century.

Luna's deployment of "republican" vocabulary throughout the work used imagined Arabic and the formulae of fiduciary translation to signal key contemporary concepts about statecraft and reform to his readers. In Spanish political discourse at the turn of the seventeenth century, the "republic" was a complex signifier.[81] Covarrubias's 1611 definition establishes that the word comes from a Latin cognate meaning "liuera civitas status."[82] In Spain it was sometimes used as a translation of concepts developed elsewhere in Reformation Europe, such as Bodin's *République*.[83] Indeed, the Jesuit and Arabic translator Ignacio de las Casas, in his *Defense of the Arabic Language*, cited Bodin's universal history to support his argument that Spain needed Arabic speakers to promote imperial ventures in Africa and Asia.[84]

Nonetheless, renaissance Spanish use of this term was a concept without a direct Arabic translation until the eighteenth century.[85] The literal meaning of "republic," which of course has classical roots, could be expressed by Arabic words referring to political and civic life in communities, including *siyāsa* (politics), *madīna* (city), or *jāmiʿyya* (society).[86] Spanish translations of Arabic political theory nevertheless used the word "republic" frequently, invoking the range of concepts to which it was indexed. By so doing, however, they were effectively "translating" familiar topoi of renaissance political thought into Arabic wisdom literature for their European audiences. In some ways, investing translated Arabic political thought with a European lexicon was analogous to the tactics and consequences of religious translation half a century earlier.

Luna's "republicanism" thus linked him simultaneously to classical and Arabic traditions as sources for new Spanish policies. What Luna's involvement in both the *plomos* and the production of authoritative historical sources demonstrates is how translators acted as vehicles between recent traditions and classical history and ideas. They were able to do so not from a redoubt of scholarly erudition, but as the heirs to generations of daily practice in which Arabic translation had carried a heavy political significance in legal and diplomatic affairs. Indeed, their interventions in legal, religious, and political discourses shows that they were just as invested in the reformation discourses about law, liturgy, sanctity, and history as any other subject of the Spanish crown whose primary mode of service was scholarship and the management of information.[87]

Luna and his colleagues had a specific political message to convey to the king through the translated tellings of Spain's early Islamic history. This message was the historical precedent for the toleration of different cultural (religious, linguistic, etc.) groups within the same political body, agreed upon through the contractually established mutual agreement between subject and sovereign. Though Luna's text was not an authentic history, in the sense that it did not derive from an actual eighth-century manuscript read and translated by Luna, it nonetheless relied successfully on translation to make historical arguments and deliver political messages. In general, as twentieth-century historians working on Luna have noticed, the class of texts to which Luna's forged "true history" belongs—the *novela morisca*—attempted to advance a critique of anti-Muslim policies of the Spanish state in the sixteenth century and an argument for religious tolerance.[88] The "discovery" and "translation" of this early Arabic chronicle helped underpin the message behind the *plomos* translations, namely that *cristianos arábigos* (Arabic-speaking Christians), like Luna, had inhabited the peninsula before the Muslim invasion of 711, and thus Spanish Arabic speakers had a long history of being Christian.[89] Arabic was not necessarily an index for Islam. Indeed, after the second Alpujarras war and the first edicts of expulsion against the Granada *moriscos*, assimilation was no longer a matter of adhering to administrative norms but instead became an argument for a legitimately plural body politic, one whose regional differences did not render coexistence impossible. Francisco Núñez Muley's 1567 *memorial* had been the rallying cry for this position, and the *plomos*—including the ancillary production and publication of the *True History*—were the most elaborate effort to write those ideas into the physical texture of the past.

Luna's volumes entered the editorial marketplace just as the interest in Spanish history writing was extending to a desire for historical information from outside the peninsula that could situate the Spanish case in a universal and comparative framework. This shift was part of the broader European phenomenon of bringing "Eastern" examples to bear in "Western" political thought.[90] For example, the work of writers like Jean Bodin (1530–1596) circulated widely in Spain despite fears of "Machiavellian" contagion.[91] As early as 1576, Bodin imagined an international framework in which Spain was one among several sovereign powers, along with the kings of France, England, and the Ottoman and Safavid Empires.[92] The following section will explore the burgeoning Spanish market for political advice and historical examples from Muslim powers outside of Spain, a demand that was addressed by Arabic translators still in contact with the legacies of fiduciary translation but whose legibility depended increasingly on "imagined Arabic."

Between Contractualism and an Arabic Reason
of State in a Post-Morisco Age

Luna's *True History* used contemporaneous Spanish vocabularies of contractualism and reason of state to model an ideal prince who did not break his agreements with his subjects and who did not see linguistic and religious diversity as a barrier to political fidelity. Not long after Luna's volumes were enjoying the first reprintings of what would become many editions, a new "Arabic" advice manual was printed, the *Doctrina phísica y moral de príncipes* of Francisco de Gurmendi (1615). Gurmendi (fl. 1607–1621) was a royal secretary of Basque heritage with family connections to the powerful royal minister Juan de Idiaquez (1540–1614).[93] He learned Arabic with Diego de Urrea and Marco Dobelio. He was involved, like Luna, Urrea, and al-Ḥajarī, in the translation of the Lead Books of Granada. He also studied Persian and gained enough competence to translate official diplomatic letters from the Safavid Shah and his ambassadors in 1612 and 1617.[94]

Gurmendi's primary area of expertise was Arabic literature. The capture and incorporation of the Zidān library would make this expertise all the more necessary for the projects of cataloguing and translating the new Moroccan bounty. At this same moment, a new connection between the Spanish Habsburgs and the Safavids was forged, through direct ambassadorial contact beginning with the arrival of the Persian embassy in Valladolid in 1601. A handful of the ambassadorial retinue remained in Iberia after the departure of the ambassador to Goa from Lisbon in 1602 and converted to Christianity.[95] Despite some legal troubles after the separate assassinations of two of their party, these converted Safavid subjects then entered the "economy of *mercedes*" around the court, and at least one of them entered into close contact with Gurmendi, including furnishing one of the laudatory sonnets to the *Doctrina* in 1615.

In his preface to the *Libro de las cualidades*, Gurmendi mentions selecting the book from among the Moroccan volumes.[96] Scholars nevertheless posit that it may have been transmitted to Spain via the Persian delegation.[97] These overlapping translation projects, in concert with his diplomatic activities with Safavid representatives, put the Basque Gurmendi and his translation projects squarely in the center of Spain's Persian and Moroccan diplomatic and intellectual connections, which were also mediated by Urrea, who boasted of Persian competence as well as Arabic from his time as an Ottoman secretary.[98] Like Urrea, Gurmendi's translations have little to do with the longer tradition of anti-Islamic polemic or the *morisco* debates (for and against), even though his expertise and ideologies as a translator and political writer were doubtless shaped by these contexts.

In Gurmendi's translation work, the intertwined strands of Arabic medical, historical, and political knowledge, which had been developing in tandem in the distinct translation projects of figures like Luna and Dobelio, came together. His major work was the manual for kingship, the *Doctrina phísica y moral de príncipes* (1615). He later produced a manuscript translation with the title *Libro de los cualidades del rey*.[99] Both works were dedicated to Francisco de Sandoval y Rojas, the future Duke of Lerma (1553–1625), as the tutor of the future Philip IV. Both texts were supposed to have been translated from Arabic manuscripts found in the Escorial, allegedly from Muley Zidān's library, which Gurmendi had been tasked to catalogue. Scholars have not yet identified the particular source texts for either translation, though the excellent recent thesis by Isabel Llopis Mena suggests that the works were compilations of various texts, including the *Sirāj al-Mulūk*, by the Spaniard al-Ṭurṭūshī (1059–1126); Arabic versions of the Persian political tracts by Miskawayh (c. 932–1030), *Kitāb al-Hukma al-Khālid*; and the *Naṣiḥat al-Mulūk*, attributed to al-Ghazālī (1058–1111).[100] In my opinion, references to the Almohad caliph Yaʿqūb al-Manṣūr (r. 1184–1199) at the end of the *Libro de cualidades* is another testament to the legibility of a cross-confessional western Mediterranean tradition that reproduced his famous deathbed speech until at least the fourteenth century.[101] The enduring tradition, into the *morisco* era, of Yaʿqūb al-Manṣūr's political wisdom seems a likely source from which Luna drew the character Iacob Almanzor to create his apocryphal Umayyad leader in Luna's *True History*. Unfortunately, corroborating the texts that Gurmendi had at hand is made impossible by the record of fire and other destruction at the Escorial library that damaged both the Arabic collections and their records since the seventeenth century.

Although it is not currently possible to identify the exact source text, it is possible to see how Gurmendi made familiar choices in his translations, particularly by using the strategy of domestication with which Luna a decade before had effectively invented a translated history based on his experience with "true" translation. Like Luna, Gurmendi presented his work by assuring his position and expertise, and he likewise used paratexts to map his patronage and social relations and thus gathered more names to guarantee the validity of his work. Juan Bautista de Pastraña wrote one sonnet dedicated to Lerma for Gurmendi's book, which also functioned as an assurance of Gurmendi's expertise and position. He explained what Gurmendi had done, "turning that infidel style into Christian."[102] In another section of the introductory paratext, one of the converted Safavid ambassadors, don Juan de Persia, assured the reader (the king) that he would find material to make legal and political resolutions: "You open a path for monarchs, with which they can establish and maintain their laws."[103] Gurmendi himself assured the reader that he had enjoyed the work of translation into a courtly language that would be recognized by his fellow subjects (ciudadanos estudiosos) as they discovered "the treasures hidden beneath the Arabic language" and who had doubted that "there were books and philosophers among the infidels."[104] The collected voices of the paratext acted—as in Luna's book—as witnesses to the work and credit of the translator.

In spite of presenting the work with the now-customary fiduciary trappings, Gurmendi presented a fully domesticated version of Arabic political thought. This effect was created through familiar references such as key words related to the republic and its conservation and to the virtues promoted by Ribadeneyra's Christian reason of state: prudence, temperance (clemency), courage, and justice (the four cardinal virtues), along with faith, hope, and charity (three theological virtues).[105] Llopis Mena has demonstrated the formal and content relations between Gurmendi's *Doctrina* and sapiental literature across the Muslim world, and it seems certain that Gurmendi did translate from specific Arabic texts into Spanish.[106] Nevertheless, the text that he produced for his Spanish readers was effectively an exercise in European reason of state dressed in an "oriental authenticity." For example, book 2 of the *Doctrina*—whose very title proclaimed it "translated from Arabic"—began its first chapter with the most familiar of images to seventeenth-century European readers: "For the vassals are the body of the Kingdom, and the King is the head of this body, which controls the erroneous or correct movements of the body. And just as a body cannot survive without a head, even less can a Kingdom survive without a King who is noble, strong, prudent, wise, temperate, pious, and just."[107] Not until the end of the fourth chapter, nearly fifteen folios later, would the first reference to an "Eastern" authority be invoked in the text (Khosrow II, sixth-century king of Sassanian Persia), advising no less than a Roman emperor that kingdoms are best conserved by prudence and justice.[108] In the intervening pages the prince was advised to choose his ministers well, to be discrete about his feelings, to act like a "wise doctor" to "conserve the health" of the body politic, and to rule with "*clemencia y misericorida*." Whatever its Arabic origins, the text spoke to Spanish readers in the recognizable vocabulary of reason of state.[109]

Using these Baroque signifiers to translate an Arabic treatise was, in effect, another kind of *reducción* by which the Arabic, Persian, Indian, and Greek voices that emerge in the *Doctrina* were made to speak using the words of Spanish statecraft. For example, the second Abbasid Caliph (Abū Jaʿffar Abdallah ibn Muḥammad al-Manṣūr, 712–775, referred to only as Almansor Rey Árabe and recognizable by his advice to his son "el Muhedi"—al-Mahdī) was made to assert in Spanish that "he who is the head of a republic must not only be good, but seem good."[110] This endorsement of dissimulation—a hallmark of Machiavellian Reason of State—was also useful for translators who had to find new "clothes" for their source ideas. It is likely that this passage was adapted from an Arabic original—it is reminiscent of al-Ṭurṭūshī's discussion "On appearing as a just or unjust Sultan"—but Gurmendi seems to have converted al-Ṭurṭūshī's metaphor of the state as a necklace with the king as the central stone into the Renaissance body politic by which they king was the head of the body of people.[111]

The maxim itself, especially as it appeared in the table of contents at the end of the *Doctrina phísica* (likely the most consulted part of the text), would have been readily interpreted by Gurmendi's readers in the context of anti-Machiavellian arguments.[112] Once again, Arabic translators in Spain were taking part of the Counter-Reformation culture that sought to reform the political foundations of state and group governance. This is one more example of how Gurmendi used Arabic translation and his position within the Escorial library to intervene in the debates over statecraft and policy, including the crucial issue of whether to follow Machiavelli or not.

Even ʿAlī ibn abī Ṭālib–Muḥammad's son-in-law—was made to speak in the *Doctrina* in support of Baroque political ideals. Although his advice was less adapted to Spanish keywords—"The best that can exist in the world is that mankind imitate his creator"—it was nevertheless framed in a classic reason-of-state argument about the importance of reputation, the cornerstone of the conservation of the republic for early modern politicians and political thinkers.[113] In the 1621 *Libro de las qualidades del rey*, Gurmendi

provided a short Spanish manual of Islamic law through his discussion "Of
the Judge and his Qualities" (chapter 7), including quotations and examples
from the writings of or about 'Umar ibn al-Khaṭṭāb (584–644), Mālik ibn
Anas (711–795), Abū Ḥanīfa (600–767), and canonical Islamic historians like
al-Ṭabarī (839–923).[114] Through Gurmendi's translation work, Islamic
administrative and legal norms were again co-opted by the Spanish state
through translation, just as they had been through the fiduciary translation
of Islamic deeds and contracts in *morisco* Granada and Valencia and through
the Spanish adjudication of an Islamic inheritance dispute in Morocco (discussed in Chapter 3). It is significant that Gurmendi's translation of Arabic
political examples and Islamic legal ideas were received in Spain during a
time in which the Spanish monarchy (under Philip II, Philip III, and Philip
IV) was involved in compiling and reforming its legal corpuses.[115] Translators like Gurmendi participated, either directly or indirectly, in debates surrounding such campaigns through their manuscript and published work,
providing materials at the disposition of the men of letters who from spaces
such as the Escorial were in charge of redefining such corpuses.

The ambivalence was clear: Islamic authorities—even the Prophet's own
family—had valuable knowledge to transmit when curated by sanctioned
professionals who could make them speak with the correct vocabulary, *ad
sensum*. Gurmendi's readers recognized this process and its significance. The
final sonnet of the *Doctrina*'s paratext congratulated Gurmendi on "reducing"
the uncouth African language to a courtly speech, marveling at the Platonic
and Aristotelian ideas it contained, "with true and moral lessons that give
reason of state and of government."[116] Far from reflecting a newfound interest
in Eastern models, Gurmendi's translation reflected the ongoing anxiety
about Arabic and Arabic speakers, and the important position of the translator to guarantee the transmission of the sense while making the appropriate
adjustments to the form (domestication).

Gurmendi thus "composed" his translation using "real" Arabic and Persian manuscripts that he encountered in his work in the Escorial library but
heavily adapting their message to the discourses and practices of statecraft
that he was exposed to and participated in at the Spanish court. For example, in the manuscript of the *Libro de las qualidades del rey*, Gurmendi's theory of sovereignty and statecraft was stated clearly from the outset of chapter
1, "Of the King, Prince, or Monarch of a Kingdom or Empire; and of the
Qualities that should be found in the Royal Person," recalling the principles

outlined by Ribadeneyra in his *Treatise on the Religion and Virtues of the Christian Prince so that he can Govern and Conserve his States*:[117]

> The teachings of all philosophers agree that the absolute lord of a monarchy or a republic is called the King and Prince of it, and the conservation of the King and the Kingdom is a reciprocal union and correspondence between the king and his vassals and between the vassals and the king. Both by doing this and by loving their prince, they serve and please not only their natural lord, but also God, who is he who raised Princes above the other creatures of the world. . . . It is from this, say the philosophers, that the happiness of these vassals is derived, in the obedience to their Princes and the prosperity of Kings as they protect (*conservación*) their vassals. Because the King is the living law, distributor of Justice, the North [star] to which all look, and the fundamental eccentric and concentric point around which all divine and human justice revolves. He is God's favorite on Earth, and for this reason his own conservation consists of obeying the King of Kings, who is God.[118]

Although this passage is supposed to be a translation from a work of Arabic statecraft, the argument is fundamentally that of late renaissance reason-of-state literature. Across this ambivalent literature, reason of state was the conservation of the monarchy, and among the anti-Machiavellian strand popular in Spain, the greatest political authority was God.[119] Both sovereigns and subjects owe reciprocal political allegiance as a manifestation of their allegiance to God, which should be manifested through the upholding of their obligations to one another. Like Luna, Gurmendi emphasized the secret and hidden qualities of Arabic knowledge that must be brought to light by a skilled expert—the translator. This ideal is evident in the paratexts of both the printed *Doctrina* and the manuscript *Libro de las cualidades*. For example, at the opening of the *Doctrina*, Gurmendi effectively cast the Duke of Lerma, the king's most trusted royal confidant, as the safe expert through whom the secret knowledge of the Arabs should be transmitted to the king, or to the prince, whose tutor ("ayo y mayordomo") Lerma was when the book was printed in 1615. Gurmendi explained that "although the new means of political government by the Arabs [in itself] invites the reading of the profound maxims that it carries locked up and in code, nothing will satisfy or give greater pleasure to serious and learned men than to see the work come out under the authority and protection of the greatness of your Excellency."[120] Effectively, this was another version of the topos of Arabic as a guardian of secret—and potentially dangerous—knowledge but that nevertheless conserved a wealth of important information and examples locked in its vaults—Luna's *maṣrāf*. Part of the conversion of that wealth through translation and reading, however, was its domestication, first by the translator's choices, and then in the hands of the prince's tutor operating within the domestic spaces for princely education.

Ultimately, translation became a constitutive mechanism for sustaining the Spanish Habsburg "republic." Between organic and mechanistic metaphors of political bodies, conglomerations of families, or the well-ordered system, something had to unify the parts into the whole.[121] This something was the sovereign power of the king and, above him, God, but the mechanism by which the unification took place was translation. This was a unification enforced by temporal as well as divine law. The community was also defined by its outsiders, and language was one way of making this definition.[122] Translators mediated the boundaries of the community by selecting the right metaphor and by ensuring the inclusion of all community members, particularly under the authority of one religious law. Though they made arguments about contractualism that supported toleration, Luna and Gurmendi reflected the same anxiety as a writer like Ribadeneyra about the religious uniformity of the body politic. In essence, translation was a form of sociopolitical and cultural contractualism that accepted diversity while ensuring conformity.

Finally, that Luna and Gurmendi chose to "translate" source texts on which they relied using politically relevant keywords like "republic" was the result of their own tactics of translation. For these professional translators, the function of the translation in the "target" society was much more important than producing an exact equivalent of the Arabic, Ottoman, or invented source text.[123] Arabic translation became, again, a means of creating an authoritative connection between theories and practices of statecraft, such as the argument that a republic ruled by consent was the same as a monarchy ruled by a just prince. However, that these translators were able to make relevant interventions in this discourse was also the result of more than a century of practice by which Arabic translation had been used to effect and break contracts between the Spanish rulers and their subjects. Through all these channels, Arabic translation became a key ingredient in the contractualism that characterized Spanish reason of state at the same time that Arabic speakers were expelled from the body politic.

Imagining Fiduciary Translation

Interest in the learning and practices of the Islamic world grew throughout the seventeenth century, both among Spain's political elite and in the wider audiences for the mass print market. The sixteenth century witnessed an explosion in Spanish history writing and writing about Spanish engagement with Islam in the Mediterranean and North Africa.[124] Inside the administration, this growth in interest and opportunities for contact is reflected in the development of an "Oriental" branch of the State Translation Office (*secretaría de interpretación de lenguas orientales*), beginning with Diego de Urrea.[125] Much of the diplomatic and commercial contact with Islamic empires (especially the Ottomans and Safavids) had been channeled through the aristocratic information networks of Spain's eastern Mediterranean viceroyalties (Naples, Sicily) by information agents and their Eastern Reports (*avisos de levante*). These reports were destined for the administrative elite, but over time they came to shape narrative forms for Mediterranean experiences in all kinds of genres, including accounts of events (*relaciones de sucesos*), captivity narratives, and fictional works in prose and for the theater.[126] Across Spanish society, interest in Spanish Mediterranean experiences was manifested by the editorial success of works like Luis del Mármol Carvajal's *Descripción de África* and other Barbary Chronicles.[127] There was a hunger for translations from and about the Ottoman, Persian, and Moroccan worlds. The Orán interpreter Jacob Cansino's transliteration of Almosnino's *Extremos y grandezas de Constantinopla* (1638), discussed in Chapter 2, was one example of this interest. In addition, works in Spanish about Mediterranean experiences found an eager audience across Europe.[128]

As the market for Spanish information about Arabic-speaking lands and Arabic texts expanded, the professional spaces for Arabic translation in Spain became ever more closely reserved to the protected spaces of royal libraries. As Fernando Rodríguez Mediano and Mercedes García-Arenal have shown, from those spaces, Arabic knowledge did not wane in the later part of seventeenth century Spain, in contradistinction to what was affirmed in 1970 by James T. Monroe's otherwise excellent and important survey on

Islam and the Arabs in Spanish Scholarship.[129] Among Spain's remaining Arabic translators, however, the mechanisms of fiduciary translation from Arabic grew less essential. Though scholars worked in teams and with dictionaries and other materials to verify meanings (of words and texts) and exchanged manuscripts from which they derived greater philological and historical knowledge, their translations no longer affected the legal or political use of Arabic texts on Spanish Arabic speakers. From their libraries, Spanish Arabists in the second half of the seventeenth century worked across an international erudite network that connected Granada and the Escorial to Rome and Northern Orientalists.

Until the 1680s, this correspondence continued to be articulated around the *plomos*, which were subjected to a new translation movement in Rome. Ultimately it was the Islamic terms of the *plomos* texts—evaluated as such by the Maronite translators of the Vatican—that caused their final condemnation by the pope in 1682. The subversive use of *árabe reducido*, which had allowed the *plomos* to function as bivalent texts—with a crypto-Islamic meaning in Arabic and a Christian message in Spanish translation—would become the evidence against their legitimacy. As García-Arenal and Rodríguez Mediano have pointed out, "It is paradoxical and a little sad that those same Christians from the East that Núñez Muley and Ignacio de las Casas invoked to defend their own identity as "Christian Arabs" would be the ones who, to reaffirm their own identity, would point to the Granadans as unredeemable Muslims who could not possibly be integrated into the Catholic world."[130] It was these Maronite Christians and those working with them in Rome who would create a canonical and definitive Catholic Arabic without any of the markings of Islamic loanwords that had characterized the Spanish Arabic catechisms.[131] This was a project of linguistic codification that did not rely on *reducción*.

Meanwhile, in the 1680s as the *plomos* were shut away in the Vatican vault, Luna's *True History* was being defended by its editors and translators across Europe as a unique and legitimate source for Spanish history.[132] A 1687 English translation (from a French translation from the Spanish) emphasized the reliability of Luna's Arabic author Abulcacem because of his eyewitness status:

> This single history may stand in competition with all those of the Greeks and Romans. And indeed, the Circumstances of the Conquest of Spain by the Moors, in the year 712 of our Lord, are so

curious, and the Life of the Caliph Almanzor, under whom this great event happen'd, so fine, that Abulcacem Abentari, who accompanied Tariff and Muca throughout that whole Expedition, may be said to Challenge more Credit than Arrian, who only writ after the Memoires of Ptolomey and Aristobulus, who attended Alexander in his; and that he has all the qualifications necessary to merit the Character of the most perfect of Historians.[133]

Effectively, these were Abulcacem's credentials, upon which the reader could trust the fiduciary position of the historian himself. Other Spanish historians were attributed as commending Abulcacem "as an Author the most worthy of credit they knew."[134] One of those authors cited in 1687—Jaime Bleda (1550–1622), a Valencian historian and stridently anti-*morisco* Catholic apologist—indeed characterized Luna's Abulcacem as just such a fiduciary in Bleda's own *Crónica de los moros en España* (1618):

The Moorish historian Abulcacim Tarif, though a barbarian, demonstrates by his style of writing that he is not recounting falsehoods or second-hand stories, but events that he either witnessed and saw with his own eyes, or heard from serious and reliable individuals who named people, times, and places. All of this can be deduced from his straightforward manner of relating the events of the loss of Spain, not letting love, passion, envy, or ambition prevent him from telling the truth of everything that took place. Because of these guarantors, I venture to follow him in this chapter.[135]

For Bleda, Luna's Abulcacem was a *fiador* (guarantor; in English, a synonym for "fiduciary"). The discursive signaling of "people, time, and place" clearly referred to the information that Luna had inscribed into his imaginary letters and marginal notes, practices that had been inspired by his familiarity with fiduciary translation.

As for the translator, the late seventeenth-century French and English defenders insisted that Luna's past experiences had made him exactly appropriate for his task and that experience was another form of guaranteeing the truth of the text: "Michael de Luna, [Abulcacem's] translator, as he was a Citizen of Grenada [sic], whence the Moors had not long been driven, he could know by Tradition many things that had relation to this history: And in all probability having been chosen by Philip the Second, to be Interpreter of the Arabick Tongue; and having doubtless had a great part in the Scrutiny made after Arabic Books, that compos'd the greatest part of the Escural Library."[136] Though the French and English readers were not thinking of the practices of Granada's Royal Appellate Court when they referred to "Tradition," they intuited that the habits and traditions of *morisco* Granada conditioned Luna's ability to translate (like his connection to the king and thus to the Escorial conditioned his access to the "original" manuscript). Luna's imaginary Arabic was what captured his audience's attention, but the long legacy of fiduciary translation to which he was visibly the heir is what guaranteed the runaway editorial success of Luna's *True History*, both in Spanish and in later translations well into the eighteenth century.

In many ways, the imaginary Arabic that was developed in the 1590s in works like Luna's *True History* (1592 and 1600) and Ribera's *Catecsimo* (1599) and that echoed in later editions and adaptations in the later seventeenth century—whether translations of Luna's *True History* or Tirso de Santalla's *Manuductio ad conversionem Mahumetanorum* (1687)—fulfilled many of the same functions of fiduciary translation, particularly the "recovery" of legal and historical examples to use in political arguments. Fiduciary translation in Spain became permanently inscribed in the records of the past. Meanwhile, across the Mediterranean, it endured in the presidios and *morisco* diaspora. Within Spain's enduring market for Arabic translation, outsiders like Urrea, Dobelio, or Cansino, who were embedded in their own social and discursive fields, found ways to awaken the imagination of Spanish print audiences to news, information, and experiences from the "East" that included strategies of domestication. The social and discursive mechanisms of fiduciary translation were still legible across the frame of imagined Arabic and still guaranteed the information provided (apocryphal or not). However, the very real effects of Philip III's expulsion policies on hundreds of thousands of real Arabic speakers between 1609 and 1614 effectively severed many of the social bonds across which fiduciary translation had functioned for over a century.

Miguel de Luna was among the last generation who could rely on those bonds as a *morisco* in Spain. In 1610 he made a final appeal for clemency from expulsion based on his record of service as a translator and his particular proficiency with the *plomos*. He was keenly aware of his ambivalent position as an Arabic speaker: the source of both his professional qualifications and liminal political status. This awareness did not prevent him from arguing forcefully against linguistic profiling: "Justice means nothing if it is sufficient to say, 'He knows the Arabic language, he is a Morisco, arrest him without hearing him out.'[137] Ironically, the final generation of fiduciary translators in Granada, who had collectively constructed a legal archive based on translation, was also subject to the translation-fueled "justice" that rejected the legal or political value of Arabic fidelity as claimed by the anti-expulsion advocates. Ultimately, Luna and his family were allowed to remain in Spain, and his death, in 1615, was reported as that of a good Christian, with a good Christian burial, echoing the assurances about Castillo's death, in 1610.[138] So too was Luna's work fully absorbed into the Spanish literary tradition, its Arabic origins clothed in new adaptations and imitations, from the multiple translations across European languages into the eighteenth century to provision of a model for Cervantes's narration of the adventures of *Don Quixote*.[139]

Epilogue

Imagining Fiduciary Translation at the End of Imperial Spain

An historian stands in a fiduciary relation toward his readers.
—Augustine Birrell, *Obiter dicta* (1910)

The seventeenth century produced new outcomes from traditional practices of fiduciary translation. Across the complex distribution of power and enforcement in the overlapping jurisdictions across Spanish territories, the discourses about Arabic established cultural hierarchies that used language as an index for religious orthodoxy and political fidelity. The result for individuals was an ambivalent, and sometimes dangerous, cultural status that at the same time fostered access to professional, social, and economic opportunities. The cases studied in this book provide a window into a complex phenomenon by which the political and personal consequences of knowing Arabic in early modern Spain proved to be highly beneficial for a select minority—and consequently devastating for the majority of Arabic speakers and many others.

Not long after Miguel de Luna published his continuation of the True History of King don Rodrigo—*Segunda parte de la historia de la Perdida de España* (1600)—Miguel de Cervantes embarked on the publication of the two volumes of his great novel, *El ingenioso hidalgo don Quijote de la Mancha* (1605 and 1615), which appeared just before and just after the *morisco* expulsion of 1609–1614. In both cases, Luna the historian-translator and Cervantes the novelist-historian used fictive translation to incorporate new Arabic sources into Spanish narratives. Cervantes's fictional Arabic author,

Cidi Hamete Benengeli, and the *morisco* translator in Toledo succeeded in embedding the legacy of Spain's Arabic translators into the text of one of the greatest and most successful works of world literature.[1] Scholars posit that the anonymous *morisco* translator of Toledo could well have been based on Miguel de Luna himself.[2] Cervantes perhaps played on Luna's own game of writing "true history" from forged translated documents. As he described the results of the month spent alongside the *morisco* in his house translating the manuscript he had found in Toledo, he listed the few variations he had been able to discern in the *morisco*'s translation in comparison with his other source text. Having verified these small differences created by his translator, Cervantes assured the reader: "There were some other small issues, but none of great importance and that don't effect the true telling of the story (*verdadera relación de la histora*), and none is bad so long as it is true (*que ninguna es mala como sea verdadera*)" (*DQ* bk. 1, chap. 9). That is, small foibles of translation do not affect the truth of the source, and truth can even be created in translation, as in the case of these "small issues" (*menudencias*) that diverged from Cervantes's knowledge of the text but that he allowed could perfectly be true.

Both Luna and Cervantes had great success in translation, creating an echo of Spanish Arabic translation across world literature and European histories of Spain. Throughout the seventeenth and into the eighteenth century, Cervantes's "Arabic translation" was translated into all the major European languages in innumerable editions. Meanwhile, Luna's "true history" had an important effect—again, through translation—on the reception of the history of Spain and the Islamic conquest in Europe throughout the seventeenth century and into the eighteenth. Luna's political argument for toleration against the "despotism" of the Habsburgs was adapted in French and English translations. His text became fodder for Enlightenment writers like Montesquieu who perpetuated the anti-Spanish Black Legend through critiques of Spanish decline and fanaticism (of which the Inquisition was a particular target).[3]

Though Luna's True History was discredited along with the *plomos* at the end of the seventeenth century, the market for "Eastern" knowledge established by Gurmendi's domesticating translations endured in Spain.[4] In 1654 and 1658 a final Eastern "mirror" was published in Spain, which revived the professional markings of the fiduciary translators. This was the *Espejo politico y moral para principes y ministros y todo genero de personas*, a version of the *Tales of Calila wa Dimna*, translated from Ottoman Turkish by the Ragusan interpreter, Vicente Bratutti. Brattuti was a state translator for the Austrian Habsburgs until 1649, when he moved from the court of Vienna to Madrid in advance of the Ottoman embassy, though the Ottoman delegate also proved to be an Italian speaker.[5] Brattuti also translated three volumes of Ottoman history into Italian and Spanish.[6] Like other translators who had reached print markets, including Luna, Gurmendi, and Cansino, Brattuti contributed to the repository of "credible" legal historical sources about Muslims by translating works of history. Once in Madrid, he switched from Italian to Spanish to publish and promote histories of the Ottoman Empire and Ottoman Egypt.[7]

During all this time, Brattuti remained on the payrolls of both the Austrian and Spanish Hapsburgs, and what little is known about his biography reveals an international network of translators connected by family and other bonds that spanned the Habsburg and Ottoman courts.[8] Brattuti's translations of Ottoman histories and traditional Arabic political advice literature are an example of how translators, like many subjects of the dynastic continuum of the Habsburgs, moved with ease between states and performed different tasks as either diplomatic translators or translators of histories. Other translators did the same, like the Neapolitan-Ottoman renegade Diego de Urrea, the Kurdish Iraqi Marco Dobelio, and the Scot David Colville.[9] In another example, the Flemish would-be *arbitrista* Jorge Henin (who was connected to the archducal court in Brussels), worked as an *alfaqueque* (captive redeemer) in Istanbul and Marrakesh before becoming a translator and advisor to the Moroccan Sultan in the 1610s and aspiring to become one of Philip III's advisors thereafter.[10]

The seventeenth- and eighteenth-century translations, retranslations, and new editions of old translations carried with them the lasting effect of the technical fiduciary translation movement that had begun in *mudéjar* Granada after 1492 across Europe. Brattuti's Spanish translation of an Ottoman *Kalila wa Dimna* (Madrid 1654 and 1658) was even translated into Latin in a Frankfurt library by "an admirer of Hobbes" in 1725.[11] In Spain itself, the actual relics of fiduciary translation—the *romanceamientos* of Granada—circulated through the hands of law clerks who used them to build cases in eighteenth-century lawsuits. In those lawsuits, evidence and arguments were sometimes printed in pamphlet form, effectively translating the *romanceamientos* and other Arabic information from the sixteenth century and earlier into Spanish editorial markets of the eighteenth century. Meanwhile, in the newly established Bourbon Royal Library in Madrid and in the Escorial, state-employed Arabic translators and librarians worked through the Arabic collections in the Escorial and Madrid Royal Palace to locate valuable medieval Spanish texts in Arabic that could be translated for the benefit of the nation. These included especially medical, agricultural, and engineering works. For example, the Spanish treasury minister Pedro Rodríguez, Count of Campomanes (1723–1802)—an aspiring Arabist and translator of a portion of the Andalusi agricultural manual *Kitāb al-Filaḥa* (Book of agriculture, 1751) who collected Marco Dobelio's original manuscript translation of the early account of the Islamic conquest of Spain, also still in the Campomanes archive—used Marco Dobelio's version of Abū-l-Fidā's account of Islamic conquest to work on his own translation, on commission from the newly created Academy of History (Real Academia de la Historia).[12] In 1796, Faustino de Borbón (b. 1755), an Arabist and *escribiente de árabe* in the Royal Library in Madrid, published his *Cartas para ilustrar la historia de la España árabe* (Letters illustrating the history of Arab Spain). These newly translated Arabic sources were intended to replace those provided by Luna as the definitively authentic historical documents dating from the eighth century and related to Visigoth, Islamic, and Asturian history. Faustino's *Cartas* were meant to be a contribution to the revival of the knowledge and greatness of medieval Spain, with special focus on its Islamic and Arabic components, although their historical perspective was criticized by Faustino's successors.[13]

Indeed, Arabic remained one of the languages most critical to the theory and practice of Spanish statecraft all throughout the eighteenth century. Though international diplomacy between Spain and Morocco paused during the War of Spanish Succession and Bourbon transition (1700–1714), a renewed period of Spanish Arabic practice and translation opened in the 1750s, especially during the reign of Carlos III (r. 1759–1788). During this period several proposals were advanced for founding a Spanish school for Oriental languages (*lenguas orientales*) on the model of the Venetian *giovani di lingua*, the French *jeunes de langues*, and the Austrian *Sprachknaben*.[14] It was also during this period that the Maronite Miguel Casiri produced his Escorial catalogue, *Bibliothecae arabico-hispanae escurialensis*.[15] Meanwhile, Casiri's colleagues among the Arabic scribes (*escribientes de árabe*) of the Escorial and the Royal Library in Madrid worked their way through the cataloguing and translation of Spain's Arabic patrimony.[16] In addition, at the end of the 1750s, diplomacy with Morocco reopened as Spain sought a Mediterranean alliance against the English stronghold at Gibraltar. Though there were no official embassies between Spain and Morocco between al-Ghassani's visit in 1690–1691 and that of Aḥmad bin Mahḍī al-Ghazāl in 1766 to negotiate for captive Muslims and Islamic books trapped in Spain, trade and correspondence continued across the Strait.[17] In 1766 a new episode in the history of translation in Hispano-Moroccan diplomacy took place during the treaty negotiations and mutual embassies between Meknes and Madrid from 1765 to 1767.[18] This episode motivated calls for increased Spanish expertise in "critical languages" like Arabic, Ottoman, and Persian, bolstering the arguments for founding a state-sponsored program to train young interpreters, *jóvenes de lenguas*. Similar proposals and projects would be launched throughout the final decades of the eighteenth century, until being put on hold by the Peninsular Wars (1808–1814) and their aftermath.

Presidio politics also remained a vital political topic shaped by the transmission of strategic information gleaned by translation, including during the Ottoman conquest of Orán in 1708, Spain's reconquest of the presidio in 1732, and the final loss of that Spanish territory in 1792. The Ottomans and Spanish Bourbons signed a treaty in 1782, but it did not put an end to hostilities between Spain and the Ottoman regencies.[19] Meanwhile, the continuing Spanish efforts against the *petite guerre* of Mediterranean piracy and in defense of the increasingly precarious presidio system, including constant Moroccan pressure on Ceuta and the Ottoman attempt to capture Melilla in 1774, culminated in the spectacle of the unsuccessful sieges of Algiers in 1783, 1784, and 1785 before the final signing of a treaty with Algiers in 1785, which was renewed in 1786.[20] Napoleon's Egyptian expedition in 1798–1801 put new pressures on both Ottomans and Spanish Bourbons, although this was a process already underway through the activities of figures such as the French interpreter and orientalist Venture de Paradis (himself a product of France's *jeune de langue* program and who had worked across North African from Morocco to Egypt).[21] All of this made for new configurations in the Mediterranean alliance system and new opportunities for Spanish-Arabic translation.

The effect of Spain's Mediterranean politics in the eighteenth century, along with the legacy of Spain's Arabic history in translation as transmitted and retranslated during the *Ilustración* (Enlightenment), would revive old tropes and practices of Arabic translation in Spanish culture, eventually resurrecting the legacies of both fiduciary translation and imaginary Arabic. The most well-known and clear-cut example is the *Cartas Marruecas* of José Cadalso, which was published posthumously and serially beginning in 1784 in the periodical *Correo Madrid*.[22] Cadalso's work was printed in toto for the first time in Madrid in 1793 and then in Barcelona in 1796. It was also in 1796 that Faustino de Borbón published his *Cartas para ilustrar la historia de España árabe* and demolished Luna's reputation.

The *novela morisca* and other Golden Age literature, especially the work of Cervantes, continued to have a strong influence on late eighteenth-century authors like Cadalso.[23] That influence was effectively a new vector for fiduciary translation in Enlightenment Spain that brought with it the legacies of the Mediterranean and *morisco* practices and settings. Cadalso's fictive premise was that a friend had died and left him some mysterious manuscript papers, among them *Letters written by a Muslim [moro] named Gazel Ben-Aly, to Ben-Beley, his friend, about the uses and customs of the ancient and modern Spaniards, with some of Ben-Beley's answers and other related letters*.[24] These documents reflected Gazel's journey around Spain, his impressions recorded in letters sent to Morocco, and his dialogue with a Spanish friend. For Cadalso, a major figure in Spain's literary scene during the reign of Charles III (r. 1759–1788), the fictive translation of the *Cartas* was an opportunity to showcase the Spanish history and character favorably in comparison with those of other societies, whether imagined Islamic societies or neighboring European societies like Bourbon France.

Many scholars have failed to recognize that the Moroccan ambassador, Aḥmad ibn Mahdī al-Ghazāl, upon whose embassy Cadalso's imaginary Moroccan traveler is based, actually did write an Arabic-language account of his journey (*riḥla*) across Spain, his impressions of the "uses and customs of the Spaniards," and what he could glean about Spanish history.[25] Cadalso did not consult this *riḥla*, which was dedicated to and destined for the Moroccan sultan Muley Muḥammad ibn Abdallah (r. 1757–1790), and his *Cartas Marruecas* owes more to Spanish traditions of travel literature.[26] In addition, the trappings of fiduciary translation evident in Castillo and Luna's sixteenth-century work (real and fictive)—Islamic invocations, dates, titles, and so forth—are no longer present. Nevertheless, the publication of the "letters" of the imaginary Moroccan in a Madrid newspaper—along with Cadalso's use of the trope of fictive translation and his commentary on it—indicates the degree to which Arabic translation was taken for granted by writers and readers as a source for Spanish texts and political arguments.[27]

As García-Arenal and Rodríguez Mediano have demonstrated, Spain's seventeenth-century Orientalism was characterized by an increasing ideological separation between Arabic and Islam.[28] However, Arabic knowledge in eighteenth-century Spain was still articulated along religious lines, though by this time it was a language of mission rather than crusade, and religious mission was fully intertwined with commercial and political interests. Many Arabists in the eighteenth century hailed from Eastern Christian families who established professional dynasties in Spanish royal libraries following the reconciliations of the Maronites, Armenians, and others with Rome after the Council of Trent. They circulated on the routes of Iberian empire that spanned the Mediterranean and reached into the Indian Ocean, including Portuguese fortresses in the Persian Gulf, through which Iberian-Safavid diplomacy was channeled. For example, Faustino was the son of Domingo Muscat Guzmán—whose name indicates a possible origin in Oman, part of the Portuguese sphere of influence from the Indian Ocean—who also served in the royal library as an Arabic translator in the 1770s.[29] Domingo, Faustino, and other Eastern Christians, like the Maronite Antonio Banha Menna, joined the San Juan family and Miguel Casiri—the most important Arabic bibliographer at the Escorial—during the eighteenth century.[30] While most Arabic experts working in Spain in the eighteenth century were eastern Mediterranean immigrants or their descendants, Spanish Franciscans also upheld long traditions of Arabic teaching and use in their mission in the Holy Land and while working on captive redemption in Morocco, effectively spanning the Mediterranean with a network of native Spanish priests who carried out parts of their mission in Arabic and in translation.[31]

In addition to Spanish-Moroccan diplomacy, Spanish Arabism enjoyed a renewal at the court of Charles III, whose ministers and academies supported translations of Andalusi scientific texts (eventually yielding another forgery scandal).[32] However, the late eighteenth-century translation of Andalusi sources was not simply a feature of the desire of Enlightenment Spain to prove the excellence of its medieval heritage against the example of either absolutist decline under the Habsburgs or the putative modernity of the French Bourbons. Neither were the Andalusi translations that enjoyed such wide popularity in print simply a feature of a proto-Romantic Enlightenment nationalism in Spain, or the result of a concomitant secularization of Spanish Arabism in line with new geopolitics in which ascendant European powers were striving to take as much power as possible from an "Islamic Mediterranean."[33] Rather, even at the close of the Spanish imperial period and in full *Ilustración*, the translation movement that took place under Charles III, including Faustino's debunking of Luna's "true history," was part of the still-ongoing process of generating and compiling autochthonous sources for use by the Spanish state of which Luna's work had itself been a product.

The work and legacy of fiduciary translation and Arabic translators left indelible marks on Spanish culture and society. There is no more visible trace of fiduciary translation than *Don Quixote*. In Cervantes's concluding paragraphs, Don Quixote died peacefully surrounded by his friends, with his will and testament faithfully executed by the priest and scribe. The saga concluded with Cidi Hamete Benengeli hanging up his pen.[34] The death of the main character at the conclusion of the second volume (1615), the witnessing of the will, and the hanging up of the pen to rest for all time (*luengos siglos*), so long as perverse and presumptuous historians (*presuntosos y maladrines historiadores*) did not take it down to profane it, was all meant to seal the writing of Don Quixote's history (and its translation from Arabic) and leave a credible record of the knight's deeds along with the perils of reading the wrong thing. This record yielded untold iterations of transmission, always retaining the authority of the Arabic text in translation, its Arabic author, and between every line, its *morisco* translator.

Abbreviations

Works frequently cited have been identified by the following abbreviations.

ACA   Archivo de la Corona de Aragón
ADMS   Archivo del Ducado de Medina Sidonia
AGS   Archivo General de Simancas
AHN   Archivo Histórico Nacional
AHUV   Archivo Histórico de la Universidad de Valencia
AME   Archivo Municipal de Éjica
AMGR   Archivo Histórico Municipal de Granada
AMMu   Archivo Municipal de Murcia
ARChG   Archivo de la Real Chancillería de Granada
ARSI   Archivum Romanum Societatis Iesu
ARV   Arxiu del Regne de València
BL   British Library
BnF   Bibliothèque Nationale de France
BNA   Bibliothèque Nationale d'Alger
BNE   Biblioteca Nacional Española
BRP   Biblioteca del Palacio Real
BUG   Bibliothèque Universitaire de Genève
BZ   Biblioteca Zabálburu
CCA   Cámara de Castilla
GA   Guerra Antigua
LSA   Late Spanish Arabic
OM   Ordenes Militares
PUL   Princeton University Library
RAH   Real Academia de la Historia
RGS   Registro General del Sello
SIHM   *Sources inédites de l'histoire du Maroc*
SN-AHN   Sección Nobleza Archivo Histórico Nacional
SP   State Papers (English)

Notes

The following Spanish words and abbreviations are used in the notes with archival sources: año (year); bis (copy); caja (box); cap., capítulo (chapter); céd, cédula (royal order); doc., documento (document); envío (dossier); exp., expediente (file); leg., legajo (file); ley (law); lib., libro (book); núm., número (number); partida (part); pieza (artifact); sig., signatura (quire); título (title); tomo (volume).

INTRODUCTION

1. Venuti, *Translator's Invisibility*, 1 and passim.
2. Elliot, "Europe of Composite Monarchies," 57–58.
3. Cervantes, *Don Quixote*, f. 32v.
4. An overview on Iberian medieval multilingualism is in Gallego, "Languages of Medieval Iberia." On the complexity and fluidity of political, religious, and linguistic identities in medieval Spain, see Catlos, *Kingdoms of Faith*.
5. A comprehensive study of mudejarism as a European phenomenon is Catlos, *Muslims of Medieval Latin Christendom*. See also Márquez Villanueva, "On the Concept of Mudejarism," 23–50; and Nirenberg, "Bibliographic Essay."
6. This kind of indexing is part of an ideological process by which "linguistic features are seen as reflecting and expressing broader cultural images of people and activities" which results in political and personal consequences. This process has been studied intensively by semioticians and linguistic anthropologists. See the discussion in Irvine and Gal, "Language Ideology and Linguistic Differentiation," especially 37.
7. Mary Louise Pratt defined "contact zones" as "social spaces where cultures meet, clash, and grapple with each other, often in contexts of highly asymmetrical relations of power." These historical spaces also offer a useful way of understanding interaction among speakers of different languages outside of the "utopian" speech communities through which modern linguistic theories and political identities have often been imagined. Pratt, "Arts of the Contact Zone," 34 and 37.
8. García-Arenal, "Religious Identity," 500.
9. For a recent review of *morisco* historiography, see Colás Latorre, "Treinte años."
10. This possessive impulse spanned Spanish society from the peasant who "drank" a *jofor* to the king's Arabic collections in the Escorial. On the talismanic place of Arabic across Spanish society, see López-Morillas, "Language and Identity," 199.

11. On the development of privileged discursive practices as they took on religious and political meanings in the context of religious wars and state building, see Bauman and Briggs, *Voices of Modernity*, 5–10.

12. See Nalle, *God in La Mancha*; Christian, *Local Religion*; and Rowe, *Saint and Nation*.

13. Indeed, the model for this translator is probably identifiable with the *morisco* translator Miguel de Luna. García-Arenal, "Miguel de Luna," 262.

14. On the diverse multilingualisms of the early modern Mediterranean into which the Spanish cases must be situated, see Dursteler, "Speaking in Tongues."

15. Folger, *Writing as Poaching*, 21 and passim.

16. Analogous studies whose authors and conclusions have provided valuable interlocutors and models for my approaches are Rothman, *Brokering Empire*; and Yannakakis, *Art of Being In-Between*.

17. In recent translation studies scholarship in Renaissance topics, the idea of "strategies" is preferred to describe "the rhetoric of self-representation and self-promotion—including self-effacing statements—used by translators and printers to secure their social and financial success." See Rizzi and Troup, "Introduction," 6.

18. Certeau, *Practice of Everyday Life*, 33–35. Certeau's ideas have informed Yannakakis's studies of the bilateral agency of native intermediaries who carried out translation work in colonial Oaxaca and Folger's analysis in *Writing as Poaching* of the mechanisms for individual reward across Spanish American imperial structures.

19. Feria García and Arias Torres, "Un nuevo enfoque," 207.

20. Arias Torres and Feria García, *Los traductores de árabe*, 19–21. On the practical aspects for contemporary translators charged with creating legally valid instruments through "official translation," see Mayoral Asensio, *Translating Official Documents*, 1–4 and passim. See also Woolard, "Introduction," 11, 14, for the language ideological uses and critiques of parts of Speech Act Theory.

21. For example, see the discussion in Bourdieu, *Language and Symbolic Power*, 72–76.

22. Bourdieu, *Language and Symbolic Power*, 79.

23. A useful comparison could be made with the *viri fidedigni*, whose attributes and actions helped shape the norms and institutions of the medieval English church and who have been recently studied by Ian Forrest, *Trustworthy Men*, 5–6 and passim. This status—which was as important in commercial as in ecclesiastical courts—derived from the Roman procedure by which adjudication was based on *reduction ad arbitrium boni viri*.

24. Bourdieu, *Language and Symbolic Power*, 72.

25. Extremera Extremera, *El notariado*, 63–78.

26. See the overview of the elaboration of notarial theory and practice from the thirteenth century through the seventeenth in Nussdorfer, *Brokers of Public Trust*, chapter 1, "The Jurists: Writing Public Words."

27. Wiejers, "Some Notes," 85–88.

28. A useful analogy of credit/credibility practices from commercial contexts (which of course overlapped with many other realms) could be the bills of exchange discussed by Francesca Trivellato, whereby "someone who was legally or socially recognized as a merchant scribbled a few coded words before adding his (or, more rarely, her) signature." See Trivellato, *Promise and Peril*, 2 and passim.

29. For recent interventions in the long-running debate among economic historians about the role of institutions in agency relations, see the discussions of how agency relations in Mediterranean, Indian Ocean, and global networks were characterized and enforced through business

correspondence and various kinds of contracts in the work of Jessica Goldberg, which is based on eleventh-century Geniza documents, and of Sebouh Aslanian, which is based on Armenian archives now located in European collections. Goldberg, *Trade and Institutions*, 180–84 and passim; Aslanian, *From the Indian Ocean*, 169–73 and passim.

30. Recent important collections on linguistic and cultural translations of religious, scientific, and political texts in the early modern period have been edited by Simon Ditchfield, Peter Burke and R. Po-chia Hsia, Karen Newman and Jane Tylus, Andrea Rizzi, and Anne Coldiron. Contributors to these collections are advancing a dynamic field of early modern translation history that connects local practices and institutions to global networks and imperial powers.

31. Though I do not wish to push the analogy too far, useful comparisons might be made between the ambivalent representations of Arabic-speaking *moriscos* in Spanish literature and the deployment of representations of other minorities across European genres that helped spread and maintain pervasive discriminatory attitudes about non-Christian "others." See, for example, the important recent thesis of Francesca Trivellato concerning the reasons for which the "legend of the Jewish invention of bills of exchange emerged and evolved as part of the collective suspicion produced by forced baptism, acculturation, and assimilation—three very different phenomena, but all accompanied by apprehensions about moral contagion and the subversion of the moral order." Trivellato, *Promise and Peril*, 7.

32. Wiejers, "Some Notes," 85.

33. See especially Rodríguez Mediano, "Fragmentos del Orientalismo," and García-Arenal and Rodríguez Mediano, *Orient in Spain*.

34. Hershenzon, "Doing Things with Arabic" and "Traveling Libraries"; Zhiri, "Captive Library."

35. On Arabism and biblical scholarship in early modern Europe, see Jones, "Learning Arabic," 87–88 and passim.

36. In the fields of literary and intellectual history, Fuchs in *Exotic Nation* and Kimmel in *Parables of Coercion* have advanced our understanding of how discourses of otherness helped marginalize and eventually exclude those deemed to be *moriscos* in early modern Spain, in contradistinction to earlier acceptance or interest in cultural forms marked as Islamic.

37. Dew, *Orientalism*, 4–5.

38. Toomer, *Eastern Wisdome and Learning*; Bullman, *Anglican Enlightenment*; Ghobrial, *Whispers of Cities*. See also the many important studies by Alistair Hamilton, including *William Bedwell the Arabist*.

39. Burman, *Reading the Qur'ān*. On the reception and translation of early modern Qur'āns, see Tommasino, *Venetian Qur'ān*; and Bevilacqua, *Republic of Arabic Letters*.

40. Some of these new polemic attitudes were devised through European Renaissance historiographical projects that attempted to write Ottomans into a universal history premised upon classical and biblical sources. See Meserve, *Empires of Islam*; and Bisaha, *Creating East and West*. On fears about Ottoman-*morisco* collaboration, see Hess, "Moriscos."

41. For example, Loop's study on the oriental scholarship of the Swiss scholar Johann Heinrich Hottinger (1620–1667) builds a case for the role of Arabic knowledge in confessional polemics between Protestants and Catholics. Loop, *Johann Heinrich Hottinger*.

42. See Heyberger, *Les chrétiens du Proche-Orient*; Girard, "Le christianisme oriental"; Ghobrial, "Migrations."

43. This is also true in recent Mediterranean studies more broadly, as in Mallette's erudite *European Modernity*. See, for example, Lopez Baralt, *Islam in Spanish Literature*, 30, on how

contemporary Spanish literary writing dealing with Spain's Islamic past have been influenced by Said's thesis.

44. Fuchs, *Exotic Nation*, 3.

45. Rather, she asserted, Spanish perspectives on language and identity were based on experiences "at home," with immediate consequences for the lives and futures of Arabic-speaking subjects in Spain, as well as the elaboration of the Spanish past for Spanish editorial markets and political uses. García-Arenal, *Is Arabic a Spanish Language?* First delivered as the James K. Binder lecture in 2014.

46. García-Arenal and Rodríguez Mediano, "Sacred History, Sacred Languages."

47. For a thorough state of the question and comprehensive bibliography, see Amelang, *Historias paralelas*. French scholarship in this field has been equally robust and impactful, in particular regarding questions of language use and other cultural practices of religious minorities. See Vincent, "Reflexión documentada." See also the collected volumes organized by Vincent and his colleagues, Jocelyne Dakhlia and Wolfgang Kaiser: Dakhlia and Vincent, *Les musulmans dans l'histoire de l'Europe*, vol. 1; and Dakhlia and Kaiser, *Les musulmans dans l'histoire de l'Europe*, vol. 2; and the recent book by Valensi, *Ces étrangers familiers*.

48. García-Arenal, "Religious Identity."

49. For a state of the field on this topic, see the valuable contributions collected in García-Arenal and Wiegers, *Expulsion of the Moriscos*.

50. On the ways that seventeenth-century Spanish historians used language ideologies to argue for national genealogies, see Woolard, "Bernardo de Aldrete." On the episode of the Lead Books, see Harris, *From Muslim to Christian Granada*; and García-Arenal and Rodríguez Mediano, *Orient in Spain*. See also the work of authors collected in Barrios Aguilera and García-Arenal, *Los plomos del Sacromonte*. In addition, see the valuable discussion of forgery and history writing in late Renaissance Spain by Olds, *Forging the Past*.

51. Monroe, *Islam and the Arabs*; Rodríguez Mediano, "Fragmentos de orientalismo"; Rodríguez Mediano, "Diego de Urrea en Italia"; Rodríguez Mediano, "Sacred Calendars"; and most recently, García-Arenal and Rodríguez Mediano, "Arabic Manuscripts."

52. See Brendecke and Martín Romera, "El *Habitus* del oficial real."

53. During what John Headley has identified as the "administrative threshold" at the turn of the sixteenth century, notaries and "super-clerks" (secretaries) responded to increasing demand for paperwork processing in the running of larger and more complex polities, displacing the traditional medieval office of the chancellor with a range of professions. At this same time, "the signature came to compete with the regime of the seal" (the chancellor's regime). Headley, *Emperor and His Chancellor*, 15, 18. The "faith-making" power of Arabic translator signatures was no different.

54. Reiter, "In Habsburgs sprachlichem Hofdienst."

55. Though the Spanish and Portuguese empires continued to be administered separately, the Habsburg king was nonetheless in charge of both systems until the Portuguese revolt of 1640, and nominally until papal recognition of the new Portuguese monarchy in 1668. Important work on the cultural translations that occurred during diplomatic, commercial, and military contacts (including conflict) in the Indian Ocean world has been done by Sanjay Subrahmanyam, who raises the useful heuristic (key in translation studies) of commensurability in early modern encounters. Subrahmanyam, *Courtly Encounters*, 6–7 and passim.

56. Cáceres Würsig, *Historia de la traducción*, 151–60.

57. Venuti, *Translator's Invisibility*, 5–14.

CHAPTER 1

1. "Carta de como quieren y mandan sus Altezas q[ue] sean tratados los nuevamente conuertidos e doctrinados," BNE, MS 7881, ff. 25v–26v, quoted in Pereda, *Los imágenes de la discordia*, 276.

2. Documents 11–17 in Gallego Burín and Gámir Sandoval, *Los moriscos*, 172–82.

3. On the ambivalence of Romance *alfaquí* from Arabic *al-faqih* (jurisconsult) or *al-ḥakīm* (wise man, judge, sometimes used to refer to a medical doctor in the Iberian contexts), see Burns, *Islam Under the Crusaders*, 222, 253–54.

4. Abad Merino, "La traducción de cartas árabes," 488–89.

5. ARChG, Expedientes, caja 4343, pieza 29.

6. See the overview of the "Legal Revolution" in early modern Spain in Kagan, *Lawsuits and Litigants*, 17 and passim.

7. For overviews of *mudéjar* governance, see Catlos, "Ethno-Religious Minorities" and the later chapters of Harvey, *Islamic Spain*.

8. Catlos, *Victors and the Vanquished*, 163–65.

9. Miller, *Guardians of Islam*, 82–83; Burns, *Islam Under the Crusaders*, 249.

10. See Echevarría Arsuaga, "De cadí a alcalde mayor," parts 1 and 2; Molénat, "Alcaldes y alcaldes mayores"; and Mata Carriazo, "Alcalde entre los cristianos."

11. Ferdinand continued to rule his *mudéjar* subjects in Valencia according to long-standing tradition. Meyerson, *Muslims of Valencia*, 6 and passim.

12. For example, those studied in Burns and Chevedden, *Negotiating Cultures*.

13. On the extension and expansion of the professional offices around the chancellery, including the establishment of the royal appellate courts and their staff, see Headley, *Emperor and His Chancellor*, 23.

14. Coleman, *Creating Christian Granada*, 77.

15. *Trujamán* is a loanword from the Arabic *tarjumān* (as is the Ottoman *dragoman*), meaning "translator," a common term in medieval Iberia—in both its Arabic and Romance versions. See sources listed in Dozy, *Supplément aux dictionnaires arabes*, vol. 1, 143–44. In 1495, Nebrija included the entry "Trujaman en arauigo. interpretes.etis." Nebrija, *Vocabulario español-latino*, f. CIv.

16. The paucity of Nasrid sources makes it difficult to conclude whether Alonso's Muslim name was indeed 'Alī 'Umar (two *isms*, that is, two given names) or if it is missing patronymics by which one of those *isms* would be part of a *nasab*, the compound patronymic, and whether the normal fifteenth-century Spanish transliteration, *al-Nayyar*, should be read as *al-Najjār* (the carpenter) or *al-Nayyir* (the luminous one).

17. On the entangled Nasrid and Castilian noble lineages of the Granada Venegas, see Seco de Lucena Paredes, "Alamines y Venegas."

18. AMMu, Cartularios Reales, 1453–1475, ff. 255v–256r, doc. 70 in *Colección de Documentos de Murcia*; AGS, RGS leg.1476–VI, 428.

19. "que vuestro poder oviere." That is, the kings specify that no one *but* Israel or one of his deputies had the right to *dar fe*. AMMu, Cartularios Reales, 1453–1475, ff. 255v–256r, doc. 70 in *Colección de Documentos de Murcia*.

20. On the Xarafí working with Ibn Kumisha and in the household of Muley Haçcen, see López de Coca Castañer, "Granada en el siglo XV."

21. In the same document Boabdil requested *mercedes* for the *mudéjar* family of the Mora, Ibn Kumisha, and al-Malih, the primary negotiators of the final capitulations. *CODOIN* 8: 465–80. Ysaque de Perdoniel was a loyal agent to al-Mallāḥ, who recommended to Zafra that the former be put in charge of the customs house. See Gaspar Remiro, *Los últimos pactos y correspondencia*, 69.

22. AGS, RGS, leg. 1494–II, 20. In 1500 don Alonso submitted the appointment to the municipal council: AMGR, Libro del Cabildo 1, f. 154r–v [May 22, 1500], doc. 204 in Moreno Trujillo, *La memoria de la ciudad*, 349.

23. AGS, RGS, leg. 1494–II, 20.

24. AGS, RGS, leg. 1495–VIII, 19.

25. García Luján, "Geneología del linaje," 19.

26. In 1490, a member of Simuel's family was given special permission to remain in Guadix and retain ownership of their houses and properties. Fernando granted the *merced* because "Symuel, mi yntréprete de lo arávigo, vuestro hermano" had asked. Archivo Histórico Municipal de Guadix, Pieza 5/3, doc. 1 in Espinar Moreno et al., *La ciudad de Guadix*, 47–48. In 1491, Simuel himself, "intérprete de su magestad," was given special permission to live in Málaga with his family. Cruces Blanco and Ruiz Povedano, *Inventario de acuerdos*, 191.

27. AGS, Patronato Real, leg. 11, 3, 2.

28. On this term in *morisco* scholarship, see Vincent, *El río morisco*, 92–93.

29. García Luján, "Geneología del linaje," 13–43.

30. González Vázquez, "La academia Granada-Venegas," 413–28. On the Granada Venegas *tertulia* as the founding sponsor of the *plomos* forgeries, see García-Arenal, "El entorno de los plomos."

31. Moreno Trujillo, *La memoria de la ciudad*, 16–17.

32. Libro I, f. 171v [January 5, 1501], doc. 277 in Moreno Trujillo, *La memoria de la ciudad*, 383.

33. On those Nasrid *fuqahā'* who remained in Granada, see Galán Sánchez, *"Fuqahā'* y musulmanes vencidos."

34. The original ordinances from 1500 are reproduced in the later text of the *Ordenanzas de Granada de 1552*, f. 3v. Quoted in López Nevot, *La organización institucional*, 310–12.

35. AMGR, Libro del Cabildo 1 (1497–1502); Moreno Trujillo, *La memoria de la ciudad*, 24–35 and passim.

36. AMGR, Libro del Cabildo 1, f. 105v [November 27, 1498], doc. 123 in Moreno Trujillo, *La memoria de la ciudad*, 267–69.

37. Lope was not the only magistrate (*procurador*) to act as interpreter. SN-AHN, Bornos, caja. 113, doc. 1, ff. 72–75; Libro del Cabildo 1, f. 162v [November 10, 1500], doc. 213 in Moreno Trujillo, *La memoria de la ciudad*, 364–66.

38. Cabrillana, *Almería morisca*, 42.

39. AGS, RGS, leg. 1494–X, 295 and 386.

40. AGS, RGS, leg. 1498–VIII, 214; AGS RGS, leg. 1498–X, 272; AGS, RGS, leg. 1498–VIII, 126; AGS, RGS, leg. 1498–XII, 271. For a later example, see Osorio Pérez and Peinado Santaella, "Escrituras árabes romanceadas."

41. AGS, RGS, leg. 1501–II, 29.

42. AGS, CCA, céd. 5, 46, 2.

43. AMGR, Libro del Cabildo 2 (1512–1516), Libro del Cabildo 3 (1516–1518), Libro del Cabildo 4 (1518–1522). There is an edition of Libro 2 in the series Monumenta Regni Granatensis Histórica: Guerrero Lafuente, *La memoria de la ciudad*.

44. Appearing in over a dozen documents from 1512 to 1517 in Guerrero Lafuente, *La memoria de la ciudad*; and García Valenzuela, *Índices de los libros*.

45. Venegas "dyxo quel commo ynterprete mayor desta cibdad lo avya por bien," that is, in his capacity as the chief interpreter he approved Aguilar's appointment: AMGR, Libro del Cabildo 2, f. 26v, January 7, 1513; Guerrero Lafuente, *La memoria de la ciudad*, doc. 24, 134–36.

46. AMGR, Libro del Cabildo 2, f. 352r, doc. 349 in Guerrero Lafuente, *La memoria de la ciudad*; and doc. 736 in García Valenzuela, *Índices de los libros*.

47. This was a similar salary to that received by other administrative roles like that of the *almotacén* (regulator of the market) or the majordomo who kept the council itself running smoothly. For comparison, Alonso Venegas received twenty thousand *maravedíes* simply to travel to the court on behalf of Granada in 1517.

48. AGS, Estado, leg. 1, "Capitulaciones con moros y caballeros de Castilla," in *CODOIN*, 8: 439–37.

49. In 1473 Isabella named Abrahen Xarafi as the *alcalde de las aljamas de Avila y Aranda*. This Abrahen Xarafi was also an *alfaquí* and doctor (*fisyco*). Archivo de la Real Chancillería de Valladolid, Ejecutorias, caja 39/7, edited by Azcona, *Isabel la Católica*, 193. Quoted in Molénat, "Alcaldes y alcaldes mayores"; and Echevarría, "De cadi a alcalde mayor."

50. AGS, RGS, leg. 1488–V-15, 170.

51. Arias Torres and Feria García gathered a state of the art bibliography in 2004, "Escrituras árabes granadinas romanceadas. Subsequent documents have been published, primarily in article appendices. A useful recent bibliography is in Zomeño, "Los notarios musulmanes," 206–9. See also the overview of Crespo Muñoz, "Acercamiento al estudio."

52. Arias Torres and Feria Garciá, *Los traductores de árabe*, 19–21. This study builds on their 2005 article, Feria García and Arias Torres, "Un nuevo enfoque"; and Feria García's doctoral dissertation, "La traducción fehaciente del árabe."

53. Docs. 3, 4, and 5 in Santiago Simón, "Algunos documentos."

54. One notable exception is the collection in SN-AHN that I have studied elsewhere: Gilbert, "Transmission, Translation."

55. See Zomeño on these kinds of documents, the few that are extant, and the notaries who produced them: "From Private Collections"; and "Los notarios musulmanes."

56. "Shāhid."

57. On the distinction between *kātib* and *muwaththiq* in the *mudéjar* context of the Crown of Aragon, where multilingualism and pluriculturalism affected notarial and other scribal practice since at least the thirteenth century, see Burns, *Jews in the Notarial Culture*, 33–43 and passim.

58. https://www.ilm-project.net/en/front

59. Arié, *L'Espagne musulmane*, 319–20.

60. On this transition and the monetary policies of the Catholic Kings, see Gilbert, "King, Coin, and Word."

61. *Siete partidas*. Partida 3, título 16, leyes 24–26.

62. See Perry, "Jewish *translata* documents from medieval Catalonia."

63. See Tyan's entry on *'Adl* in the *Encyclopedia of Islam* (*EI*), 2nd ed.

64. Moreno Trujillo, *La memoria de la ciudad*, 16.

65. Moreno Trujillo, *La memoria de la ciudad*, 422.

66. Seco de Lucena, "La escuela de juristas," 26–27.

67. The *fatwā* was recorded in the legal compilation of a contemporaneous Granada *faqīh*, the *muftī* Muhammad ibn Yusuf ibn Abi Qasim al-'Adari al-Mawwāq (d. 1492). Miller, "Muslim Minorities," 273–74.

68. Don Andrés's *carta de regimiento*—promulgated by Hernando de Zafra on behalf of the Catholic Kings on November 30, 1500—was reproduced in the *cabildo* records when don Andrés was incorporated into the council on February 23, 1501: AMGR, Libro del Cabildo 1, ff. 180v–182r [February 23, 1501], doc. 240 in Moreno Trujillo, *La memoria de la ciudad*, 401.

69. "E asy firmaron de sus nombres dos alfaquíes escrivanos públicos." Arabic text, facsimile, contemporary Spanish translation, and Xarafi's *romanceamiento* in Molina López and Jiménez Mata, *Documentos árabes*, doc. 4, 13–16.

70. *Siete partidas.* Partida 3, título 9, ley 1.

71. On the diplomatics of chancellery documents in late Trastámara and early Habsburg Spain, including the use of formulae and professional titles, see the works of Martín Postigo, especially "La cancillería castellana," 358–62.

72. Molina López and Jiménez Mata, *Documentos árabes*, 13–16.

73. Molina López and Jiménez Mata, *Documentos árabes*, 13–16.

74. See López de Coca Castañer, "Granada en el siglo XV" and Malpica Cuello and Trillo San José, "Los infantes de Granada."

75. López de Coca Castañer, "Granada en el siglo XV," 626.

76. Documentary appendix, López de Coca Castañer, "Granada en el siglo XV," 612–25.

77. Malpica Cuello and Trillo San José, "Los infantes de Granada," 376.

78. Malpica Cuello and Trillo San José, "Los infantes de Granada," 379–380.

79. Malpica Cuello and Trillo San José, "Los infantes de Granada," 392.

80. Burns, *Islam Under the Crusaders*, 226–28.

81. "Que es persona vien esperta en la dicha lengoa [*sic*] arábiga e en nuestra lengoa [*sic*] castellana y son personas que saben la xara çuna de los moros, e que sabren vien declarar e interpretar las dichas cartas de arábigo en nuestra lengoa e letra castellana." AGS, Casas y Sitios Reales, leg. 10, f. 197, quoted in Malpico Cuello and Trillo San José, "Los infantes de Granada," 376.

82. On the development of the professional and conceptual tandem of *officium* and *beneficium* in medieval Iberia, see García Marín, *Oficio público en Castilla.*

83. See Francisco Nuñez Muley's report of their service in Charles's service in the *comuneros* revolt.

84. *Morisco* representatives had pleaded for stays of implementation and had even offered payments. For the record of the 1522 payment of 60,000 *ducados*, see AGS, Estado, leg. 27, núm. 318.

85. Coleman, *Creating Christian Granada*, 7.

86. For example, *Pareçer de la Inquisición sobre algunos capítulos presentados por los moriscos a Carlos V*, AGS, Cámara de Castilla, Diversos de Castilla, 8, núm. 85, February 4, 1539, *Españoles trasterados*, 83–84.

87. Garrido Atienza, *Los alquezares de Santa Fe*, 48.

88. Archivo de la Alhambra, L-77-2, doc. 4 in García Pedraza, *Actitudes ante la muerte*, 2: 940–48.

89. SN-AHN, Osuna, leg. 1868, docs. 1–3.

90. See Gilbert, "Transmission, Translation," esp. 368–72.

91. Very little is known about Juan Rodríguez's life and activities, despite the relatively high number of extant translations. See the documents dating from 1531 to 1561 in Osorio

Pérez and de Santiago Simón, *Documentos arábigo-granadinos romanceados*. On his activities in the *marquesado* de Cenete between 1549 and 1550, see Gilbert, "Transmission, Translation."

92. According to the town council minutes, Venegas ordered that the municipality name a new Arabic translator to replace the deceased Juan Rodríguez ("cabildo se llame por nombre un romançeador de escritpuras arabigas en lugar de Juan Rodriguez falleçido"). AMGR, Libro del Cabildo 5, f. 270r.

93. See Espinar Moreno and Quesada Gómez, "Documentos árabigo-granadinos." Castillo also translated for the Real Chancillería in the 1550s. See the document discovered in Abad Merino, "La traducción de cartas árabes."

94. Abad Merino, "La traducción de cartas árabes." On Alonso del Castillo's activities, see the comprehensive Cabanelas, *El morisco granadino*, and new information added in García-Arenal and Rodríguez Mediano, *Orient in Spain*, 95–120.

95. In 1555 and 1556 the Mora family was still working as *cabildo* interpreters. Jiménez Vela, *Índices de los libros de cabildo*, doc. 355; 1556 Marzo 3, AMGR, Act Cap. 55, fol. 73r–74v.

96. In 1521 Ambrosio's papers were deposited into the collection of another notary by his wife, doña Mayor de Mendoza Xarafi, indicating that the line had died out. Feria García and Arías Torres, "Un nuevo enfoque," 223.

97. AMGR, Libro del Cabildo 5, f. 73r.

98. In addition to Alonso del Castillo, who was appointed in September 1556, Diego Hernández Malaquí was granted his usual two thousand *maravedíes* in annual salary for his position as "lengua y intérprete" at the council meeting of December 18, 1556, and again on April 19, 1566. AMGR, Act Cap. 55, fol. 350r–354v, doc. 457 in Jiménez Vela, *Índices de los libros de cabildo*, 301 and doc. 507, AMGR, Act Cap. 56, fol 138r–139v.

99. García Pedraza, *Actitudes ante la muerte*, 2: 457–85.

100. See García Pedraza, *Actitudes ante la muerte*, 2: 473–74; and Obra Sierra, *Catálogo de protocolos notariales*, passim.

101. Albarracín Navarro, *El marquesado de Cenete*, 13–19.

102. See García Pedraza's major study on *morisco* Christianity, *Actitudes ante la muerte,* 2: 325–35. See the many references to lawsuits, testimony, and legal instruments that involved Arabic speakers in García Valenzuela, *Índices de los libros.*

103. On religious dissimulation, including *morisco taqiyya*, see Catlos, "Ethno-Religious Minorities," esp. 371. See also O'Banion, "'They will know our hearts.'"

104. For example, Viguera Molins, "Partición de una herencia"; and Pascual Cabrero, "Pleito por la herencia."

105. *Capítulos acordados en la Junta de la villa de Madrid sobre la reforma de las costumbres de los moriscos de Granada (1566),* in Mármol Carvajal, *Historia del rebelión* , libro 2, cap. 6; original in Simancas, AGS, RGS, leg. 1566–11, 17. Emphasis added.

106. Article 5 concerns dress; article 6, the customs for weddings and other celebrations; article 7, public baths; article 9, the *gaçis*, or captives from North Africa; and article 10, the rights of *moriscos* to own black slaves.

107. Garrad, "Original Memorial," 199.

108. Garrad, "Original Memorial," 201–8; and Harvey, *Muslims in Spain*, 212. See also documents 21 and 24 in Gallego Burín and Gámir Sandoval, *Los moriscos.*

109. The erudite posthumous study of this *memorial, To Live Like a Moor,* by Constable appeared just as the present book was completed. Although the planned chapter on language did not end up in Constable's final work (p. xv), the entire study is an important compliment to the discussions in the present analysis.

110. Núñez Muley, *Memorandum*, 92–94. Square brackets in original. Similar arguments were put into the mouth of a relative of the *morisco* leader of the rebellion in Diego Hurtado de Mendoza's account of the war. *Guerra de Granada*, lib. 1, cap. 7.

111. Núñez Muley, *Memorandum*, 95.

112. Núñez Muley, *Memorandum*, 98. Cleverly, Núñez Muley used the same argument to return to the more personally problematic question of Arabic names, noting that "if we are to cease using Morisco surnames, to whom will they send the tax bill?"

113. Mármol Carvajal, *Historia del rebelión*, lib. 3, cap. 4.

114. Abad Merino, "La traducción de cartas árabes." See also Rodríguez's retranslations of Xarafi texts in the SN-AHN, Osuna collection.

115. See Castillo, *Sumario*, for the full title.

116. Castillo informed Deza in his prologue that the Arabic originals had gone with a version of the same summary for Philip II the previous year, a manuscript that seems to have been lost. Castillo, *Sumario*, 10.

117. Castillo, *Sumario*, prologue to the first letter, 14.

118. Castillo, *Sumario*, 11–12.

119. Hess, "Moriscos," 13.

120. Torres Palomo, "Sobre la carta de Abenaboo," 128.

121. [Original Arabic]

وذِممتي وكِنْ انْتَ تَرِيد **تَتُرَطل** فذي المبرَك مِئن سُلْح كُلّ مَتعمِلْ تَعْملْ مَعي

"and on my honor, if you wanted to negotiate in this blessed [opportunity] of arms all that you would negotiate, you negotiate with me." AME, Fondo Marquesado de Peñaflor, de Cortes de Graena y de Quintana de las Torres, lib. 93, núm. 246.

[Castillo's Spanish translation]

y fe y si tu quisieres **tractar** *en estas bendictas pazes lo que tratares tratar has conmigo*

"and **by my faith**, if you were to wish to **negotiate** in these blessed peace talks, what you would try to negotiate you would do with me." AME, Fondo Marquesado de Peñaflor, de Cortes de Graena y de Quintana de las Torres, lib. 93, núm. 245.

122. See the many excellent works of Rodríguez Mediano on this topic, beginning with "Fragmentos de Orientalismo."

123. On a "juridical turn," which took place in the 1640s in Spanish history writing, see Valledares, "Juristas por el rey."

124. On Alpujarras historiography, see Kimmel, *Parables of Coercion*; and on *Crónicas de Berbería*, see Martínez Góngora, *Los espacios coloniales*.

125. Mármol Carvajal, *Historia del rebelion*, lib. 9, cap. 9.

126. On translation as domestication, see Venuti, *Translator's Invisibility*, 19, passim.

127. Mármol Carvajal, *Historia del rebelion*, lib. 1, cap. 16.

128. The canonical texts of Alpujarras historiography would be (1) Mármol Carvajal, *Historia del rebelion*; (2) Hurtado de Mendoza, *Guerra de Granada*; and (3) Pérez de Hita, *Segunda parte de las Guerras civiles*.

129. On this intertextuality, see Kimmel, *Parables of Coercion,* 117–37 and passim.

130. On the capture of books and manuscripts by Spanish soldiers on the 1535 Tunis campaign, see Martínez de Castilla Muñoz, "The Qur'anic Manuscripts of Charles V."

131. Pérez de Hita, *Segunda parte*, ff. 139v and 288v.

132. BnF, Espagnol 334, 1619, f. 26, f. 92v, passim.

133. As "que se avia platicado [marginal note: "por don Alonso de Granada Venegas"] con los moros," BnF, Espagnol 334 1619, f. 96v.

134. García Luján, *Documentos de la Casa de Granada*, 16–17; and Peinado Santaella, "Los orignes del marquesado de Campotejar," 271.

135. Spivakovsky, "Some Notes," 213, 218–25.

136. For example, Pérez de Hita, *Segunda parte*, 51, cap. 8, 554.

137. Hurtado de Mendoza's devotion to Thucydides is well known, and it is no surprise he would choose *The History of the Peloponnesian War* as a model for describing the civil war between *moriscos* and royal forces in Spain. See Vivar, "Tucídides y *La Guera de Granada*," 1819. Before and after the Second War of the Alpujarras, *The History of the Peloponnesian War* was an extremely popular object of translation in Habsburg Spain. Hurtado de Mendoza was also one of Spain's best-known early Tacitists. See Bravo, "La présence de Tacite."

138. Torre y Franco-Romero, "Don Diego Hurtado de Mendoza," 385–91. Quoted in García-Arenal and Rodríguez Mediano, *Orient in Spain*, 83.

139. Torre y Franco-Romero, "Don Diego Hurtado de Mendoza," 388.

140. Mármol Carvajal, *Historia del rebelion*, lib. 4, cap. 7. Reference in the margin note in Hurtado de Mendoza, *Guerras de Granada*, 1627, BnF Espagnol 334, 11v.

141. Soledad Carrasco Urgoiti, Francisco Marquez Villanueva, and Juan de Mata Carriazo, have all noted the parallels with the medieval *romance frontizero* or frontier ballad. The "moorish novel," however, did not exist until at least 1560 with the publication of *El Abencerraje*. Carrasco Urgoiti, *El moro de Granada*, 47–69. Barbara Fuchs argues that the connection between the *romance frontizero* and the "moorish novel" is indicative of a longer hybrid continuity: *Exotic Nation*, 102–16.

142. The full title of the first 1595 Zaragoza edition was *Historia de los vandos de los Zegríes y Abencerrages Cauualleros Moros de Granada, de las Guerras Ciuiles que huuo en ella, y batallas paratuculares que huuo en la Vega entre Moros y Cristianos, hasta que el Rey Don Fernando Quinto la ganó. Agora nuevamente sacado de un libro Aráuigo, cuyo autor de vista fue un Moro llamado Aben Hamen, natural de Granada. Tratando desde su fundación. Traduzido en castellano por Gines Perez de Hita, vezino de la ciudad de Murcia.* The second volume, also called the *Guerras civiles* and published ever after jointly with the first volume, is titled *Guerras civiles de Granada y crueles bandos entre los convertidos moros y vecinos cristianos* (1619).

143. AGS, Estado, leg. 2638, (impreso), *Bando de la expulsión de los moriscos, publicado por el marqués de Caracena, virrey de Valencia.*

144. Pérez de Hita, *Segunda parte*, ff. 139v and 288v.

145. A recent language-ideological approach to studying the discursive tactics and cultural practices of the *moriscos* is Barletta, *Covert Gestures*.

CHAPTER 2

1. On medieval precedents of multilingual military and diplomatic agents working in family networks across the Mediterranean, see Fancy, *Mercenary Mediterranean*, 90–92 and passim.

2. Wansbrough, *Lingua Franca*.

3. For example, in 1483 Ferdinand as king of Aragon signed a treaty of alliance with the king of Tunis. Doc. 36 [May 23, 1483] in Torre, *Documentos sobre relaciones internacionales*, vol. 1.

4. On the Iberian conquest of North African holdings in the fifteenth and early sixteenth century, see Hess, *Forgotten Frontier*. The longest-held Iberian possessions in North Africa were Melilla (1497 to present), Orán (1509–1708, 1732–1792), Peñon de Vélez (1507, 1520, 1564 to present), Larache (1610–1689), and La Mamora (1614–1689). The longest-held Portuguese presidios, which were governed separately during the Iberian union of 1580–1640, were Mazagan, 1502–1769; Tangier, 1471–1661 (went briefly to the English as Catherine of Braganza's dowry until the 1684 conquest by Alawites); Ceuta, 1415 to present (Spanish).

5. Gutiérrez Cruz, *Los presidios españoles*, 66–78.

6. In 1514 the crown ordered that the Fuero de Málaga be applied in Orán as the Fuero de Orán. Gutiérrez Cruz, *Los presidios españoles*, 102.

Charles V's 1525 *carta puebla* to Orán repeats the privileges and obligations of the medieval Andalusian plazas frontizeras and was renewed by Philip II in 1565 and Philip III in 1611. AGS, Libros de Privilegios y confirmaciones, lib. 313, artículo 2, doc. 326 in *Colección de privilegios*, 498–502. See also Francisco Alijo Hidalgo, "Privilegios a las plazas frontizeras"; and Jiménez Alcázar, "La frontera de allende."

7. Hess, *Forgotten Frontier*, 40–41.

8. Compare a 1520 letter from the Corregidor of Orán opposing sending soldiers from Orán to the Netherlands, arguing that "it would be best if they were retained here, since they were raised in [Orán], they know and speak the language of the Moors, and can render more useful services than the recruits coming from Spain." Charles approved the suggestion. See doc. 7 in Primaudaie, *Documents inédits*, 28–29.

9. "Un judío es siempre lengua intérprete de la arábiga con un cristiano. de la Arábiga una es Christiano otra de esta Nación por dictamen de la procedencia del gran Monarcha Phelipo Segundo y porque entran en la Berbería y tienen mucha comunicación y correspondencia con los moros reciuen de ellos mas auisos que el Christiano y del mismo oficio ambos son de mucha confianza y estimación y de interese." Jiménez de Gregorio, "'Relación de Orán,'" 102. In 1601 the governor made a similar argument that "por las mismas causas que no ocurren en los christianos que aunque se supone mayor fidelidad en ellos no pueden tener las ynteligencias que los judíos." AGS, Guerra, leg. 586, s.f., in Alonso Acero, *Orán-Mazalquivir, 1589–1639*, 212.

10. A history of relations between two of these families, the Cansino and the Sasportas, is in Schaub, *Les juifs du roi d'Espagne*.

11. "Intérprete de las çibdades e villas e lugares de moros de allende que están en la frontera de la villa e fortaleza de Mazalquivir."

12. In 1502, Miguel de Almenar [*sic*] was the consul in Tremecén. Doc. 48 [Nov. 20, 1502] in Torre, *Documentos sobre relaciones internacionales*, 6: 316. In 1505, Miguel de Almenara, as a vecino de Almería, was the consul de Castilla residing in Orán. Gutiérrez Cruz, *Los presidios españoles*, 108.

13. Before moving to Orán, Alcántara had lived and worked in Málaga, where he was granted territories near Velez Málaga. AGS, CCA, Personas, leg. 1, f. 447.

14. Doc. 6 in Primaudaie, *Documents inédits*, 24.

15. "Todos los quales dichos capítulos y escritura que de suso va aquí escrita y declarada por los yntrépetes [*sic*] Gregorio [*sic*] de Alcántara y Estevan Martín y Juan de Alcántara, que ahora se dize Yahya, secretario del señor Rey." "Capitulación entre Muley Baudila, ben Reduan

y el Conde de Alcaudete (Campo cerca de Orán, 24 junio, 1535)," doc. 6 in Mariño Gómez, *Carlos V*, 40–41.

16. "Lettre de Moulaï Mohammad au Comte d'Alcaudete (Tlemecen, 12 juin, 1536)," doc. 83 in Primaudaie, *Documents inédits*, 224; "Capitulación entre Muley Baudila, ben Reduan y el Conde de Alcaudete (Campo cerca de Orán, 24 junio, 1535)," doc. 6 in Mariño Gómez, *Carlos V*, 40.

17. AGS, RGS, 1512-2, núm. 179 [February 18, 1512]. See nos. 180–183, 191, and 197–202 for the other appointments. Two Alcántaras, caballeros moriscos, received payments from the crown as early as 1468. One was Fernando de Alcántara, "que llamaban cuando moro Yuça Mondejar," and the other was Juan de Alcántara. See AGS, Escribanía mayor de rentas, Quitaciones de Corte, leg. 1, núm. 41 and núm. 62.

18. The 1512 *cédula* to Vargas specifies that "vos solo o a quyen vuestro poder ovieree no el dicho miguel de almenara ny otros puede ni podiadan usar el dicho oficio de yntérprete e trujamán en la dicha çibdad de Orán e Reyno de tremeçen." AGS, RGS, 1512-2, núm. 185.

19. AGS, RGS, 1494-II, f. 20; AGS, RGS, 1495-8, f. 19.

20. Vargas also oversaw the taxation of the goods that left Spain (via Málaga, for example) with the "cristianos nuevos" who were moving "de allende." Bejarano, *Documentos del reinado*, doc. 416, 83. Additionally, he oversaw the royal payments to the duke of Alba for the tenancy of Bugía. Gutiérrez Cruz, *Los presidios españoles*, 90.

21. Juana granted a monopoly of all trade with Orán and the surrounding territories to Alonso Sánchez, treasurer of Valencia, in 1510, rescinding the position in 1511. La Véronne, "Les villes d'Andalousie, 15.

22. Commenting on the professional accumulation of Francisco de Vargas throughout his career, Charles V's *cronista* recorded that "tiene tantos oficios que sólo él tiene de salarios tanto como todo el Concejo." Carande, *Carlos V y sus banqueros*, 85.

23. Gutiérrez Cruz, *Los presidios españoles*, 108.

24. García Marín, *El oficio público*.

25. March 7, 1512, ARChG, leg. 221bis, sig. 2, ff. 22r–24r.

26. ARChG, leg. 221bis, sig. 2, f. 24v.

27. AGS, CCA, Oficios, [March 20, 1512] "Lorenço de Abendano Escribano de la Aduana de Orán."

28. AGS, CCA, Oficios, 23-1, núm. 146 [March 20, 1512] and 240 [February 11, 1535] (old foliation). The transfer of office actually occurred several months earlier in November 1534. AGS, RGS, 1534-XI [November 1534], s.f.

29. Gutiérrez Cruz, *Los presidios españoles*, 99.

30. Gutiérrez Cruz, *Los presidios españoles*, 100.

31. Sola, "Carlos V y la Berbería," 431.

32. ARChG, caja 221bis, pieza 1, f. 20v.

33. It may be that the ambassador passed through Orán on his way to Spain, or it may be that another ambassador is referred to. In any case, the ambassador was not ultimately called as a witness. See doc. 5, "Capitulación (1533)," 28–37. And although Francisco de Madrid proposed Baudila as an initial witness for the defense, he seems to have been replaced by Hernando de Alcalá, an *escribano público* who was present at other treaty negotiations resulting in the generation of bilingual texts. Doc. 3, "Capitulación (1521)," in Mariño Gómez, *Carlos V*, 7 and 26.

34. AGS, RGS, 1536-XI [November 1536]; García Camarón had been appointed as regidor on March 22, 1532. AGS, RGS, 1532-III [March 1532]; ARChG, 221bis, sig. 1, f. 5v [May 19, 1533].

35. In the *interrogatorio*, those witnesses who did not know Castilian were "preguntado por lengua del capitan Gonzalo de alcantara ynterprete." ARChG, leg. 221bis, sig. 2, f. 31r.

36. Both Ternero and Alegre were involved in the 1521 treaty between the king of Tlemecen and the governor of Orán, Ternero as "judió aljamiado, enbaxador e vasallo del Señor Rey de Tremeçen," and Alegre as "judío, yntérprete aljamiado." Gonzálo de Alcántara was also present in the capacity of principal interpreter. See "Capitulación entre el Rey de Tremecén y el segundo Marqués de Comares (Orán, 1 octubre 1521)," doc. 3 in Mariño Gómez, *Carlos V*, 7–26; doc. 14, "Lettre de Jacob Alegre écrite en hebreu," c. 1531. Primaudaie, *Documents inédits*, 43–44.

37. ARChG, 221bis, sig. 2, ff. 31r–65v.

38. La Véronne, "Les villes d'Andalousie et le commerce avec la Berbérie (1490–1560), in *SIHM: Archives et bibliotheques d'Espagne*, 2: 16. Also, docs. 5 and 7 in SIHM: *Archives et bibliotheques d'Espagne*, 1: 44–52 and 57–60. See also Mariño Gómez, *Carlos V*, lxx–lxxii for a discussion on the changing policies of allowing and prohibiting commerce.

39. Although he had been dead for more than a decade, this would not be the first time that the management of one of Francisco de Vargas's offices was the subject of *mala fama*. Vargas had a reputation for corruption. See the summary of the contemporary chronicler Galíndez de Carvajál, quoted in Carande, *Carlos V y sus banqueros*, 85.

40. In 1514, via the Real Chancillería, the queen still received complaints that the office was not paid correctly. AGS, CCA, Libros de Cédula, lib. 34, f. 211.

41. Diego's appointment by Charles is detailed in the lawsuit. ARChG, leg. 221bis, sig. 2, ff. 9v–10r.

42. The privileges according to Vargas in 1512 and that were then devolved on his son in 1521 included the specification that "gozeys de todas las otras honras e mercedes e franqueazas prerrogativas que son gozados [por] los otros ynterpretes e trujamanes q hansydo en los dichos rreynos agora e podays llevar e llevadays todos los salarios e derechos etc que los dichos trujamanes ynterpretes moros solyan llevar en la dicha çibdad de Orán syendo la dicha çibdad de moros asy de los mercaderias e cosas contratads y comprados e vendidos como de todas las otras cosas abyan en tiempo de moros." "Título de yntérprete e trujamán de Orán para el Liçençiado Vargas," AGS, RGS, 1512-2 [February 1512], núm. 185.

43. ARChG, leg. 221bis, sig. 2, f. 22r (copy). This document referred to Francisco de Vargas as the officeholder, although a provision was made for the arrangement to continue with whoever took over the office after him.

44. ARChG, 221bis, sig. 2, ff. 14v–15r.

45. "juran de no volver a contratar en esta çibdad. . . . Su Magestad es deservido en daño e perjuycio de sus rrentas rreales." ARChG, 221bis, sig. 2, f. 29r.

46. "Desimos q devida a vra merced nos deve dexar gozar libremente della conbransas de la trujamanía desta çibdad conforme al uso y constumbre q hemos tenydo en la dicha cobrança y ansy mysmo otras personans en nonbre del liçenciado Francisco de Vargas tesorero que fue de su magestad . . . e ansy mysmo por el dicho comendador diego de vargas hijo del dicho liçenciado francisco de vargas en cuyo nombre cobramos los dichos derechos dela usa trujamanía e por su poder." ARChG, 221bis, Sig. 2, f. 14v.

47. ARChG, 221bis, Sig. 1, 4v and Sig. 2, f. 29v.

48. ARChG, 221bis, Sig. 2, f. 30v.

49. In 1521, it was decided that "los mercaderes moros y judíos ni otras personas ni a las mercaderías que fueren del dicho Reyno de Tremeçén o salieren para él, no se puedan detener; ni hazer agravio a los mercaderes." See "Capitulación (1521)," doc. 3 in Mariño Gómez, *Carlos*

V, 18. This was reconfirmed in 1536, "Asiento y capitulación de paz entre el Conde de Alcaudete, en nombre del Emperador, y el Rey de Tremecen, Muley Mohamad (Haste, 17 junio, 1536)," doc. 8 in Mariño Gómez, *Carlos V*, 58.

50. The Kingdom of Tlemecen abutted the Oranese hinterlands, and its sovereign swore regular fealty to the Spanish monarchs via bilingual treaties beginning in 1517, with friendly relations already underway by 1511. Mariño Gómez, *Carlos V*, cxiv–cxxxi. On Orán's relationship with Tlemecen, see La Véronne, *Rélations entre Orán et Tlemcen*.

51. The lawsuit began on February 6, 1533, and sentence was handed down on April 26, 1533. The appeal was issued on May 19, 1533, and the final resolution was concluded on February 27, 1537. ARChG, 221bis, sig. 1 and 2.

52. ARChG, 221bis, sig. 2, f. 7r.

53. "El dicho derecho de la trujamanería es ya sydo contra la dicha libertad e franqueza [granted to the city]." The *previllegio* to which Castillo refers is most likely the Privilegio á la ciudad de Orán e á la villa de Mazalquivir, issued by Charles V on May 5, 1525. Published in *Colección de privilegios*, 498–502.

54. According to the seventh question in the *interrogatorio* prepared by Castillo, the witnesses were to confirm or deny whether "los trujamanes que a abido en tiempo de moros en esta çibdad eran e fueran de lengua arabiga para entremeterse e ser enterpretes quando eran llamados entre los xpianos que aquy contratavan con los moros e judios que no sabian la lengua de xpianos e para poder entender asy mysmo a los moros e judios tratantes e que el tal ynterprete e trujaman que ansy se hallava conçientar e convenyr e ygualar quales quieres mercaderias e contrataciones con quales quier personas e davan e pagavan por razon de su trabajo de averse hallado presente al ygualar de las tales contrataciones de mercaderias." ARChG, 221bis, sig. 2, f. 29v.

55. Since 1514, on the precedent of the fuero de Málaga, the council members were chosen from, literally, a hat (*insaculación*). However, by the 1530s, some of the *jurados* were chosen instead by election: Gonzálo de Alamos (AGS, RGS, 1532-XII [December 1532]), and Alonso Villollos (AGS, RGS, 1535-XI [November 1535]).

56. On translation across the global Portuguese empire, see Couto, "Role of Interpreters." In the Canary Islands, see Sarmiento Pérez, *Cautivos que fueron intérpretes*.

57. See "Capitulación entre el Virrey de Sicilia, en nombre de Carlos V, y el rey de Túnez," doc. 15 in Mariño Gómez, *Carlos V*, 80. This *jurado* Luys Hernández de Córdoba is difficult to identify. He may indeed be Luis Fernández de Córdoba, Marqués de Comares, the capitán general and governor of the presidio, although he may have only been part of his household or otherwise associated with him (thus the similarity in name). In October 1534, Luis Hernández renounced his position as jurado on the city council of Orán, shortly after the capitán and governor renounced his charge on June 1. AGS, RGS, 1534-X [October 1534]. It is unlikely but not impossible that a marquis and the governor of the presidio would have held a position as jurado on the city council (he probably would have been a higher-ranking regidor). Even more confusing, there is a record of a Luys Hernández absent from Orán in February and March 1533 while in Espejo (the estate of the nobleman Luis Hernández de Córdoba) helping to negotiate the treaty between Charles and the king of Tlemecen: "[the Tlemçeni ambassador] dixo lo siguiente por lenguas de Andrea Bives y Luys Hernándes, al Marqués de Comares, en presençia de my Francisco de Maçuela, escrivano público de la dicha villa." See "Capitulación entre el embajador del Rey de Tremeçen y el Marqués de Comares, gobernador y capitán general de Tremecén y Ténez (Espejo, 14 marzo, 1533)," doc. 5 in Mariño Gómez, *Carlos V*, 35.

58. Liang, *Family and Empire*, especially 157–63.

59. On June 14, 1536, the new governor, the Count of Alcaudete, interviewed representatives sent in an embassy from Ben Redouan to negotiate for certain hostages who had been left in the city some time previously. The four interpreters who were present to facilitate the negotiations were Gonzálo Hernández, *jurado*, and Alonso de Cabra, Juan de Medina, and Juan de San Pedro, *lenguas intérpretes de la dicha ciudad*. Doc. 74 in Primaudaie, *Documents inédit*, 225–26.

60. "Capitulación de los criados y mensajeros del Rey de Tremeçen con el Conde de Alcaudete (Orán, 12 enero 1545)," doc. 25 in Mariño Gómez, *Carlos V*, 129.

61. AGS, Estado, leg. 30, doc. 26.

62. This version of Gonzálo Hernández's family history was recounted by the conde de Alcaudete in a memo that was also intended to function as a letter of recommendation to Charles V for the services of the translator. AGS, Estado, leg. 479, f. 191.

63. AGS, RGS, 1534-X [October 1534].

64. In 1536 at a captive exchange, Gonzálo Hernández, Alonso de Cabra, Juan de Medina, and Juan de San Pedro were all named as "lengua e intérprete" of Orán, though Gonzálo performed the active work between the parties. "Procès-verbal de la conférence qui a eu lieu entre le comte d'Alcaudète et les cheikhs arabes du parti de Ben Redouan, pour la reddition des otages (14 Juin, 1536)," Primaudaie, *Documents inédits*, 224–29.

65. See Gilbert, "Juegos de reputación."

66. AGS, Estado, leg. 479, ff. 189–190v.

67. AGS, Estado, leg. 479, f. 187.

68. AGS, Estado Leg. 479, f. 191r–v.

69. Gonzálo's father, Francisco, also worked as an interpreter until the 1570s, sometimes alongside his son. AGS, GA, leg. 81, no. 85, f. 317.

70. AGS, Estado, leg. 481, f. 133, doc. 118, "carta del conde de Alcaudete a la princesa regente, 14 Septiembre, 1556," in *SIHM: Archives et bibliotheques d'Espagne*, , 2: 368–69; AGS, Estado, leg. 485, f. 273, extract from "Cartas de Gonzálo Hernández a Muley 'Abd Allah, al alcaide al-Mansur, y al alcaide de Tetoun, más la respuesta del alcaide de Tetouan," doc. 119 in *SIHM: Archives et bibliotheques d'Espagne*, 2: 370–76.

71. AGS, Estado, leg. 468, s.f., docs. 113–124 in *SIHM: Archives et bibliotheques d'Espagne*, 2: 399.

72. AGS, Estado, leg. 468, s.f., docs. 113–124 in *SIHM: Archives et bibliotheques d'Espagne*, 2: 396.

73. Luis Cabrera de Córdoba, in his *Historia de Felipe II*, described the count's excellent reputation and its close association with the reputation of the king, referring to "sus grandes méritos y servicios" and claiming that when the news of the Mostaganem defeat arrived, "entristeció a Castilla, y al emperador agravó la enfermedad, y murió." See the discussion in Schaub, "El lado oscuro," 443–44.

74. Rodríguez-Salgado, *Changing Face*, 282–85.

75. Veronne, "Nouvelle note," 146. Isaac Cansino was also present and fought at this battle. AGS, Cámara de Castilla, leg. 1154, año 1627, núm. 49. Suárez Montañés, *Historia del maestre*, 182.

76. "Nombró el Maestre por cabo y lengua de esta gente al capitan Luis Hernández, natural de Orán, hijo del capitán Gonzálo Hernández, nieto del moro alcaide de una de las puertas de la ciudad de Orán, el que hizo el trato con el alcaide de los Donceles y de Mazalquivir para entregar a Orán al rey de España." Suarez Montañés, *Historia del maestre*, 341. Later in his

chronicle, Suárez Montañés describes this *judío* as part of Luis's regular entourage. Suárez Montañés, *Historia del maestre*, 350.

77. On the career of this family in Orán and elsewhere, see Liang, *Family and Empire.*

78. "Que cómo el Conde llegó a Orán un Gonzálo Fernández engaño al Conde diciendo que los alárabes lo deseaban, y le ayudarían a tomar la tierra. . . . Que como hombre tan práctico y lengua, le dijo que sería muy bien ir a una provincia que se llama Tacela y á Guardáz, que es el riñón del reino, que desde allí haría sus negocios; esto fue la causa de su perdición, que salido allí los alárabes no vinieron."

79. Morales, *Diálogo de las Guerras de Orán*, 356–57.

80. On the development of the crossover between historiographical forms and administrative practice, see the discussion in Folger, *Writing as Poaching*, 4–9. For an overview in the Mediterranean context, see Tarruell, "Circulations entre Chrétienté et Islam."

81. On the use and form of soldier writing (in the market for mercedes and for wider literary audiences), see Martínez, *Front Lines.*

82. Cáceres Würsig, "Breve historia."

83. Salamanca, Juan de Canova, 1564.

84. AGS, Estado, leg. 144, f. 331.

85. On the rhetorical, social, and professional strategies of this family, see Gilbert, "A Mediterranean Family Business."

86. Idiáquez died in 1614, so the text was probably composed sometime earlier but not published until 1636.

87. Andrés, *Catálogo de los códices*, 534.

88. See the anthology of translator prefaces in Santoyo, *Teoría y crítica.*

89. "RELACION DE LOS SERVICIOS de don Francisco Gracián Dantisco Verruguete, intérprete de las lenguas de todos los Consejos y Tribunales de su Magestad y de su padre, y passados." RAH, Salazar y Castro, E-21, ff. 64r–65v. He had first circulated the same text as a manuscript petition beginning in the 1630s. AHN, Consejo, leg. 4426, exp. 1634.

90. "RELACION DE LOS SERVICIOS de Iacob Cansino (Hebreo de nacion), vezino de Orán, Lengua y intérprete del Rei nustro señor en las plazas de Orán y Mazalquivir, y los de su padre, abuelo, y bisabuelo." Cansino, "Relación de los serviciosdel traductor."

91. On the fixer, see Stahuljak, "Medieval Fixers."

92. Gutiérrez Cruz, *Los presidios españoles*, 96.

93. Caro Baroja, *Los judíos en la España*, 1: 215–16.

94. Indeed, most scholarship about Arabic translation in Orán has focused on Jewish communities: Schaub, *Les juifs du roi d'Espagne*; Alonso Acero, *Orán-Mazalquivir*; Israel, "Jews of Spanish North Africa"; Israel, *Diasporas Within a Diaspora.*

95. In 1520, the anonymous *corregidor* (royal representative) warned that it would be wrong to chase Jews from Orán since they were so useful in commercial activity. Doc. 6, Primaudaie, *Documents inédits*, 30. In 1516, Lope Hurtado de Mendoza also argued that the Jewish community of Orán must be allowed to practice their religion or else they would leave the city and take their trade with them. Gutiérrez Cruz, *Los presidios españoles*, 96.

96. Alonso Acero, *Orán-Mazalquivir*, 212.

97. "El punto sobre si conuiene que los judíos estén en aquellas plazas es disputable y no faltan motiuos por una y otra parte." Jiménez de Gregorio, "'Relación de Orán,'" 102. Cantero Vaca's ecclesiastic visit was likely related to the fact that Spain's North African presidios had been recently incorporated into the Dioceses of Cadiz and Málaga.

98. Schaub, *Les juifs du roi d'Espagne*, 126–27. This same Marquis de San Román continued to employ many Jewish interpreters. See various documents in BL, Additional MSS 28,441, ff. 25, 221, 302.

99. He argued that "despues de naturalizados ya los Españoles en el Pais y comerciando con los Moros se hicieron practicos en el hablar, y escriuir la lengua Arabiga; y deuiendo cesar la asistencia de tan dañosa gente, auiendo cesado la causa de su introducion." See Díaz Esteban, "Una vacante de intérprete." Jonathan Israel also discusses this episode and the second expulsion. See Israel, *Diasporas Within a Diaspora*, 163.

100. See, as examples, BZ, Altamira, 287, GD. 2, doc. 19; RAH, Salazar y Castro, K-64, ff. 156–157, ff. 221r–v; K-65, ff. 178r–v, ff. 193r–195, ff. 214r–215v. There are many more in the BZ, RAH, and BL.

101. Cansino, "Relación de los servicios del traductor"; Prieto Valenzuela, "Informe sobre el oficio de intérprete de la lengua arábiga en Orán. Por Felipe Prieto Valenzuela," 1633, RAH, Salazar y Castro, K-64, f. 93–95. Israel notes that the interpreter salaries were "equivalent to that of a senior officer in the garrison." Israel, "Jews of Spanish Orán," 240. The king took an interest in making sure that his interpreters were well paid. In 1655, most likely following complaints that payments were being issued in the cheaper *vellón* rather than in silver, he ordered the governor of Orán, at that time the Marquis of San Román, to supervise the payments issued by the presidio's *tesorero*. He held that the interpreters should be paid in the same fashion as his other soldiers and insisted that even the younger members of the interpreter's family had a "right" to be paid. "The King to San Román about Interpreter Salaries," October 4, 1655, BL, Additional MSS, 28, 441, f. 302.

102. Cansino, "Relación de los servicios del traductor."

103. García-Arenal, Rodríguez Mediano, and El Hour, *Cartas marruecas*, 19.

104. Schaub, *Les juifs du roi d'Espagne*, 65, 85–86.

105. Schaub, *Les juifs du roi d'Espagne*, 66. Cansino had (once again) annoyed the current governor by appearing not to support his appointment.

106. As early as 1626, while his brother Aaron still held the post that had been passed to him by their father Hayan, Jacob submitted a successful appeal to the king to allow him a license to trade, a frequent appeal made by other Jewish families in North Africa. Jacob Cansino, "Memorial expediente de Jacob Cansino Hebreo, vezino de Orán," AGS, Cámara de Castilla, Memoriales, September 31, 1626; Israel, "Jews of Spanish North Africa." A prominent part of his argument for why he should be granted the license to trade was that a similar license had been given to his cousin, Yaho Sasportas. By 1627, Philip IV had granted him a place in the cavalry of Orán. Cansino, "Relación de los servicios del traductor."

107. Cansino, "Memorial expediente de Jacob Cansino Hebreo, vezino de Orán," AGS, CCA, leg. 1154, año 1627, núm. 49.

108. Israel, "Jews of Spanish Orán," 239.

109. Israel, "Jews of Spanish Orán," 242.

110. Almosnino, *Extremos y grandezas* (1638), f. 8.

111. "Causas que se dan para que el oficio de lengua Arauiga: La selección del General, y puede promouerlo por delito del infidelidad que es conuiniente al seruicio de Su Magestad y a los asiertos de la suçecion destas plaças y seguriadad dellas." Prieto Valenzuela, "Informe sobre el oficio de intérprete de la lengua arábiga en Orán. Por Felipe Prieto Valenzuela." RAH, Sálazar y Castro, K-64, ff. 93–95. Other historians who have made use of this document have characterized it as anonymous and undated, although it is referred to in the preceding document (f. 92)

from 1633 as Prieto Valenzuela's discurso being sent from Orán to Madrid in order that it may be read to the king.

112. Prieto Valenzuela records that a royal *cédula* of 1514 gave permission to "vezindar" the Cansinos and Benismeros, with the Cansinos in charge of "seruir de lengua." He ignores the Santorras. RAH, Sálazar y Castro, K-64, ff. 93–95.

113. "El oficio de lingua Yemtrepete [*sic*], Propía Cosa es Ynterpretar de Vna lengua a otra. Y si remirase a este fin solo qualquiera que supiese hablar La arauiga, lo puede, ser Y el general valerse de quien mexor le pareçiese en qualquiera Ocasion suponiendo que siempre elixirias para esto la persona demas Secreto que enq[ue] lo a la interpretaçion Vasta para dezir lo que el moro, En arauigo, Y responder lo que el general mandare, siendo fiel ala interpretacion." Prieto Valenzuela, "Informe sobre el oficio de intérprete de la lengua arábiga en Orán. Por Felipe Prieto Valenzuela." RAH, Sálazar y Castro, K-64, ff. 93–95.

114. RAH, Sálazar y Castro, K-64, ff. 93–95.

115. On Almosnino and the significance of this unique early modern Ladino print book in Spain, see Borovaya, *Beginnings of Ladino Literarture*, 105–6.

116. Israel, "Jews of Spanish Orán."

117. "Siempre ha procurado la quietud y concordya del rreyno y que los vasallos cumpllesen con sus obligaçiones y trujesen la provisión de la gente de guerra a muy moderados precios." Cansino, "Relación de los servicios del traductor."

118. RAH, Sálazar y Castro, E-21, ff. 64–65v.

119. "Iacob Cansino . . . vino a esta Corte à cosas de mi seruicio, me ha representado el derecho que tiene à este officio, por auer continuado en su familia de mas de cien años a esta parte sucesiuamente de padres à hijos, auiendo muertos algunos en mi seruicio." Cansino, "Relación de los servicios del traductor."

120. Alonso Acero, *Orán-Mazalquivir*, 207.

121. La Véronne, "Interprètes d'arabe à Orán," 118.

122. Since the original *nombramiento* of 1636 had not specified the right to name his successor, Jacob included a copy of the 1640 *cédula* in which the king referred to "haviendole yo echo m[e]r[ce]d de que nombrasse dos hijos suyos, para que le ayuden en el exerçiçio de su oficio, lo hizo a Hayan y Ysac Canssino, suplicandome sea seruido de mandar, que el hijo mayor que ha de seruir sus ausençias, y enfermedades, goze de ocho escudos, y el otro de seis." "Sobre aclarar a Hayen Cansino el goçe de 8 escudos de suledo al mes que auia goçado en estas plaças," April 26, 1666, BUG, Coll. Éd. Favre, vol. 57, ff. 133r–v.

123. La Véronne, "Interprètes d'arabe à Orán," 119; Israel, "Jews of Spanish Orán," 242.

124. La Véronne, "Interprètes d'arabe à Orán," 119; BUG, Coll. Éd. Favre, vol. 57, ff. 129–135v.

125. Sotomayor y Valenzuela, *Brève relation*, 37–45.

126. Israel, "Jews of Spanish North Africa," 82.

127. Sotomayor y Valenzuela, *Brève relation*, 47. See also Caro Baroja, *Los judíos en la España*, 1: 217.

128. For a comparison of the events, see Schaub, critical introduction to Sotomayor y Valenzuela, *Brève relation*, 7, 13–14.

129. "Denunciation de Isaac Cansino, lengua ynterprete of Orán, espía del rey de Argel y de España," 1591, AGS, Guerra y Marina (GM), leg. 339, núm. 178.

130. On the expulsion, see also Sánchez Belén, "La éxpulsion de los judíos." On the immigration of North African Jews in Livorno, see Trivellato, *Familiarity of Strangers*, 93.

131. On these theories, see Schaub's critical introduction to Sotomayor y Valenzuela, *Brève relation*, 23.

132. Caro Baroja, *Los judíos en la España*, 1: 215–19; Sotomayor y Valenzuela, *Brève relation*.

133. On the historiography justifying the morisco expulsion, see Harris, "Forging History"; and Feros, "Rhetorics of the Expulsion."

134. Schaub, critical introduction to Sotomayor y Valenzuela, *Brève relation*, 10.

135. Sotomayor y Valenzuela, *Breve relación*, 1670, ff. 1r–v.

136. "las causas que justifican esta demostración, las quales pongo à la letra, que si à su lado se escurieceren mis escritos, quedarán honrados por lo menos." Sotomayor y Valenzuela, *Breve relación*, 1670, f. 2v.

137. On the eschatological arguments throughout Sotomayor's book, see Schaub, critical introduction to Sotomayor y Valenzuela, *Brève relation*, 16.

138. Sotomayor y Valenzuela, *Breve relación*, 1670, f. 5r.

139. The *hoja de servicio* for Sotomayor and Valenzuela is in AGS, GA, Servicios, leg. 57, f. 73, See Schaub, critical introduction to Sotomayor y Valenzuela, *Brève relation*, 10.

140. Suárez Montañés, *Historia del maestre*, 339–40.

141. Suárez Montañés, *Historia del maestre*, 340.

142. García Carraffa and García Carraffa, *Diccionario heráldico y geneológico*.

143. "Nombrmiento de Gil Hernández de Sotomayor como capitán ordinario," AGS, GM, Libro-Registro 28, ff. 69v–70v, August 9, 1565.

144. See the episode described above in note 51. Suárez Montañés, *Historia del maestre*, 340.

145. Suárez Montañés, *Historia del maestre*, 390. In other parts of the chronicle he uses the term *aljamiado* in a way that seems that he intends Hebrew. Suárez Montañés, *Historia del maestre*, 340.

146. This lineage is sketched out in Prieto Valenzuela, "Informe sobre el oficio de intérprete de la lengua arábiga en Orán. Por Felipe Prieto Valenzuela." RAH, Salazar y Castro, K-64, f. 93–95. Alonso Acero cites a memorial from the governor, the Marquis de Velada, in 1626, which—in addition to describing the "necesidad de persona capaz en muchas lenguas," referring to the work done by Aaron and Jacob Cansino—notes that "El Capitan Gil de Navarrete, también lengua de V.M. en estas plaças aprende aora la hebrea y sabe mucha parte della." From BZ, Carpeta núm. 256, ff. 74r–v, see also Alonso Acero, *Orán-Mazalquivir*, 213.

147. *Catálogo de los documentos*, 14, 21–22.

148. Gil Fernández de Navarrete y Sotomayor y de Valenzuela, son of Don Fernando de Navarrete y Sotomayor and Leonora Anna María de Valenzuela. "Expediente de Prueba de Caballeros de la Orden de Santiago Gil Fernández de Navarrete y Sotomayor y de Valenzuela, Capitan de Caballos-lanzas españolas en Orán y Gobernador de Peñon," April 1643, AHN, Ordenes Militares, Caballeros Santiago, exp. 2997. Gil Fernández de Navarrete, trans., "Traducción de una carta en árabe, escrita por Lajadar Benbumediem, cabeza de la parcialidad de Ulad Garrab, que escribió a los de parcialidad aconsejánoles lo que deben hacer frente a los españoles. Original firmado por su traductor Gil Fernández de Navarrete, caballero de Santiago e intérprete mayor de la lengua arábiga por Su Majestad." (Orán, n.d.), RAH, Salazar y Castro, K-65, f. 85r.

149. "Como en estas plazas no ai officios anales ni otros q en q se pueden haçer a estos patronos de hijo dalgo sino los de jente de guerra en q se an ocupado el Pretendiente y sus

pasados." "Expediente de Prueba de Caballeros de la Orden de Santiago Gil Fernández de Navarrete y Sotomayor y de Valenzuela, Capitan de Caballos-lanzas españolas en Orán y Gobernador de Peñon." AHN, OM, Caballeros Santiago, exp. 2997.

150. See *Catálago de los documentos*, 21–22.

151. RAH, Catálogo de la colección "Pellicer" antes denominada "Grandes de España," vol. 1, Madrid 1957, 394.

152. Lapeyre, *Geografía morisca*, 197.

153. Saint Cyr and Joulia, *Larache*, 269, 345.

154. Malagón Pareja, "Larache en el sistema," 532–33. On the petitions of Jewish translators wishing to reside in Larache and Ceuta with their families and work as intermediaries, see Schaub, critical introduction to Sotomayor y Valenzuela, *Brève relation*, 15–16.

155. For example, in 1630, Fr. Antonio de Quesada, captive, went to Larache to negotiate a rendition since he had learned Arabic while captive. Saint Cyr and Joulia, *Larache*, 173.

156. Saint Cyr and Joulia, *Larache*, 183.

157. Saint Cyr and Joulia, *Larache*, 196.

158. Saint Cyr and Joulia, *Larache*, 199–200.

159. Diego's 1671 *expediente* is AHN, Ordenes Militares, Caballeros_Santiago, Expediente 5240, where he was described as "Capitán de Caballos-lanzas y lengua-intérprete de Orán."

160. *Relación de méritos de Diego Merino y Heredia, caballero de Santiago* (s.f., post-1695), BNE, MS 17605, ff. 261r–2r.

161. Sotomayor y Valenzuela, *Breve relación*, f. 20r.

162. On how Merino y Heredía and other officials were affected by the factionalism of pro-Bourbon versus pro-Austrian parties during the War of Spanish Succession and how these played out in the presidios and Orán in particular, see Seneschal, "El cambio dinástico," 344.

163. "Relacion de servicios de Don Juan Bernardo Merino de Mendoza, Cavallero del Orden de Santiago, y de los de su padre, el Maestro de Campo Don Diego Merino y Heredia, Cavallero del la misma Orden." AGS, GA, leg. 44, 26–27.

164. On this episode, see Saint Cyr and Joulia, *Larache*, 251–52.

165. *Aviso verdadero y lamentable relacion, que haze el capitan don Francisco de Sandoval y Roxas, Cautivo en Fez, al Excelentisimo señor Don Pedro de Aragón, dandole quenta de las sacrilegas acciones que han obrado los perfidos Mahometanos con las Santas Imagenes, y cosas Sagradas que hallaron en la Mamora: Entrega de dicha Plaça: Trato que hizo el Governador della con los Moros; y lo demas que verá el Curioso* (Madrid 1681); *Respuesta que da la verdad a vna carta que con nombre del Capitan Don Francisco de Sandobal y Rojas, fu [sic] fecha en Fez à catorze de Mayo deste año de ochenta y vno, parece averse escrito— segun la imprenta— al Excelentissimo señor Don Pedro Antonio de Aragon, y se ha impresso en Madrid, y Sevilla, dando cuenta à Su Excelencia de la perdida de la Mamora. Dirigida a el mismo excelentissimo señor, en defensa del Maestre de campo Don Juan de Peñalosa y Estrada, Governador que fue de la dicha plaza, etc.* (Cádiz, 1681); *Informe juridico militar, en defensa del Maestro de Campo Don Juan de Peñalosa y Estrada, Governador que fué de la Plaça de San Miguel ultramar, conocida vulgarmente con el Nombre de Maamora-Y en que se defienden tambien D. Bartolomé de Larrea, Veedor de aquella Plaça, y el Capitan Juan Rodriguez, en la Causa Criminal, que se sigue contra ellos por el señor Fiscal del Consejo Supremo de la Guerra, que los supone culpados en la pérdida de aquella Fuerça* (n.p., 1681).

166. *Aviso verdadero y lamentable relación que haze el capitán don Francisco de Sandoval y Rojas, cautivo en Fez, al Excelentísimo señor Don Pedro Antonio de Aragón* [. . .]. c. 1681, f. 2r.

167. García Ejarque, *La Real Biblioteca*.

CHAPTER 3

1. Yahya, *Morocco in the Sixteenth Century.*

2. On the rise of the *langues véhiculaires* in tandem with state and international systems in the later Middle Ages, see Grévin, *Le parchemin des cieux.*

3. Benton and Ross, "Empires and Legal Pluralism," 9.

4. Calafat, "Les interprètes de la diplomatie," 381.

5. On Iberian "jurisdictional diversity," see Burns, *Islam Under the Crusaders*, 249 and passim. Enduring practices in pluri-confessional societies—like the Ottoman Empire—where multiple confessionally derived legal regimes operated and were valid are discussed in Barkey, "Aspects of Legal Pluralism," 84–86.

6. Describing the "constructive function" of "jumbled jurisdictions" across imperial claims and agents are Burbank and Cooper in "Rules of Law," 282–83.

7. On this figure, see García-Arenal, *Aḥmad al-Mansur.*

8. On the frequent cross-confessional negotiations between Spanish agents and North African powers before the Ottoman possession of North African regencies in 1517 and the consolidation of the Sa'adi dynasty in the middle of the century, see Escribano Páez, "Negotiating with the 'Infidel,'" 193 and passim.

9. For an excellent discussion of al-Manṣūr's flexible politics of self-representation vis-à-vis the Spanish and Ottomans, see Cory, *Reviving the Islamic Caliphate.*

10. On this genre as developed in the east beginning under Charles V through the Viceroyalty of Naples Mediterranean, see Sola, "Los avisos de levante," 207–30.

11. Wansbrough, *Lingua Franca*, in particular chapter 2; Hoenerbach, "Some Notes"; Hoenerbach, "El notariado islámico y el cristiano."

12. Calafat, "Les interprètes de la diplomatie," 410.

13. Flood, *Objects of Translation.*

14. The most recent synthesis of scholarship on both men is the recent reedition and translation of García-Arenal and Rodríguez Mediano, *Orient in Spain.* Among Cabanelas's work that is still very useful is "Diego Marín"; "Otras cartas"; and "Pedro Venegas de Córdoba."

15. On Castillo's learning curve, the materials he had at hand, and those he created himself, see Gilbert, "Arabic from the Margins."

16. On the career of Pedro de Castro, see Harris, *From Muslim to Christian Granada*, 40.

17. BNE, MS 7453, f. 5r; f. 63r–v.

18. e.g. BNE, MS 7453, f. 5r.

19. BNE, MS 7453, ff. 62r–63r.

20. On the relationship of the Gasparo Corso family and the exiled Sa'adī princes, see Oliver Asín, *La hija de Agi Morato*, 8–14 and passim. In 1577 they sponsored the publication of a panegyric poem in Valencia about 'Abd al-Malik's qualities. (He was just about to usurp the Moroccan throne from his nephew al-Mutawakkil and doubtless wished to sow the seed for a warm Iberian reception to a potential alliance.) On this text and its publication, see García-Arenal, "Textos españoles."

21. La Véronne, "Les frères Gasparo Corso."

22. See, for example, the correspondence between Andrea Gasparo Corso and the royal secretary Mateo Vázquez in 1580 in which Andrea recounted events in Lisbon and his own service. ADA–PL, caja 115, docs. 133, 136, 144, 160, 161, 173.

23. For example, in 1580 Andrea wrote to Vázquez to complain that he had still received no salary for his royal service (despite repeated petitions) and that he could not get any ready money from the family firm in Valencia. ADA, caja 115, doc. 173.

24. BNE, MS 7453, Castilian summary f. 11r; Arabic text, f. 270.

25. The episode is described in Cabanelas, "Diego Marín," 15–16.

26. Only the Arabic text is extant in Castillo's *cartulario*, which Cabanelas published with his translation in "Diego Marín," 16, 29. For a detailed description of the negotiations during the reigns of Philip II and his son Philip III, see García-Arenal, Rodríguez Mediano, and El Hour, *Cartas marruecas*.

27. García-Arenal and Rodríguez Mediano, *Orient in Spain*, 129–30.

28. BNE, MS 7453, ff. 18v–19r.

29. According to Matias Venegas, Diego Marín rode at the left-hand side of Pedro Venegas in official ceremonies. See Guillén Robles, "Una embajada española," 54. Marín's role was not that of subordinate or functionary. As Cabanelas says in slightly different ways in various articles, Marín benefited from "las ventjas que le confería su conocimiento de la lengua árabe y de las costumbres musulmanas, cualidades que llegaron a hacerlo tan imprescindible para el monarca español como estimado por los sultanes 'Abd al-Malik y 'Abd al-Mansur." Cabanelas, "Pedro Venegas de Córdoba," 135.

30. Luis del Mármol Carvajal, author and *veedor* of Granada, pleaded with Philip to grant him a position as ambassador to Morocco on the basis of his loyal service and especially his skill in translation. Having acquitted himself well in the service of the Spaniards in North Africa and Granada, he sent three letters to the king reminding him of his services to his country and asking for various rewards. In particular, in 1575, having recently published his *Descripción general de África* in 1573 out of his own pocket, he asked that the king include a copy of the work in his royal library at El Escorial, reminding Philip of some battlefield translation he had done: "hizo traducción de las letras Arabes que estan en el Estandarte que se ganó en la batalla naual." See "Memorial de Luis de Marmol a Felipe II pidiendo diferentes Mercedes" (1575), in Mármol Carvajal, *Descripcion general de África*, 37. Although Philip was inclined to give Mármol Carvajal the posting, his advisor Juan de Silva talked him out of it, based on the argument that the ambassador should be a person of more "calidad." See *CODOIN*, vol. 43. The letter in question is "Copia de carta de don Juan de Silva á S.M., fecha en febrero de 1579" (128–129). For more on Marín, see García-Arenal, Rodríguez Mediano, and El Hour, *Cartas marruecas*, 47–61. Also, "se ha mandado a P[edr]o Venegas de Cordoua mi Criado que os lo declarara por medio de Diego Marin q[ue] por Vuestra orden Va en su compañía." AGS, Estado, leg. 206, s.f.

31. Although Marín was not regularly called on to do written translation (Alonso del Castillo translated this correspondence from Spain), it is clear that he knew how to read Arabic. When Marín was loaned to the Duque of Lisboa in 1580, the duke reported that he received a letter pertaining to the question of the Moroccan princes in Portugal and that "Hésela dado a Diego Marín para que la traduzca." CODOIN, 32: 543, reproduced in Cabanelas, "Diego Marín," 11.

32. In one letter, al-Manṣūr reproaches that Marín's *compañeros* have come without him. Since their letters are in Castilian, and al-Manṣūr trusts only Marín, they must send a representative back to Spain to get the translations from Marín, holding the other representative hostage until the safe return of the letters in both languages. Cabanelas, "Diego Marín," 15.

33. On the profits made by Marín, and other priests, as facilitators in the slave trade after the war of the Alpujarras, see García-Arenal and Rodríguez Mediano, *Orient in Spain*, 123.

34. Rute first arranged for Marín to be shot but, when this failed, poisoned his rival. See García-Arenal, Rodríguez Mediano, and El Hour, *Cartas marruecas*, 61. Both Marín and his merchant friend Barredo were poisoned to death within a couple of years of one another—Marín supposedly by a rival translator, and Barredo by rival merchants.

35. "[P]ues ciertamente comprabaréis su eficacia en nuestro común servicio y la natural habilidad con que se desenvuelve." Translated by Cabanelas in "Diego Marín," 27. There is a theory that this nephew could be a son though al-Manṣūr always refers to the younger Marín as a nephew, *walad akhik* or *ibn akhik*. See BNE, MS 7453, f. 64r.

36. Mouline, *Le califat imaginaire*, 221–29.

37. The biography of al-Manṣūr's chief translator and head of the chancellery, which included the office of translation, gives this title for 'Abd al-'Azīz al-Fashtālī. In al-Maqqari, *Rawdat al-'As*, 112.

38. "El Consejo de Estado a 6 de Ag[os]to 1600 por Diego Marín, que esta preso en Marruecos," AGS, Estado, leg. 2471.

39. On this figure and the other Spanish translators at the court of al-Manṣūr, see Gilbert, "The Circulation of Foreign News," 64–66. On the "translation movement" of European texts at the Saadi court, see Zhiri, "Task of the Morisco Translator," 14–15.

40. On al-Kattānī's first stay in Fez and Marrakesh and his subsequent dismissal, see the account of the Portuguese captive Antonio de Saldanha, in Saldanha, *Crónica de Almançor*, 70–79.

41. In addition to Saldanha's account, al-Kattānī appears in the reports and accounts of Dutch agents in Morocco and in translated correspondence to England and Spain. See Gilbert, "Spanish Translators," passim.

42. RAH, Salazar y Castro, F-33, ff. 33r–34r. "Este es traslado bien y fielmente sacado de vna carta Real misiva firmada de mano del Rey Muley Ahmet emperador de Marruecos Rey de fes y etiopia dirigida al Rey Phelipe Rey de las espñas escrita en letra y lengua arauiga cuyo tenor traducida verbo ad verbum es este que se sigue. . . . Lo qual yo abderrahmen el catan interprete por su magestad en estos Reinos ei mperio. Traducuda de lengua arauiga en español Vulgar Verbo ad Verbum como en ella se contiene y en fee desto lo firme de mi nombre fecho ut supra concuerda la fecha d esta carta con los propios dias de Abril de mill y quinientos y noventa y ocho Abdurrahmen El Catan."

43. BNE, MS 7453, f. 5r, c. February 1580. "y luego el lunes proximo sigue en todo el dia Romançe otra carta arabiga del dicho Xerife la qual un dia antes embio su megestad al dicho señor president de manera que son onze cartas las que en todo el dicho tiempo romançe y de todas saque diez hojas de borrador y en llimpio ocho hojas despues que de verbo ad verbum con ayuda del dicho señor presidente las corregí."

44. His own account of his biography is found in various letters to the Consejo de Estado, including one dating from September 11, 1601, and another from November 6, 1603. AGS, Estado, leg. 2741. Most recently, for synthesizing recent scholarship, see Floristán, "Diego de Urrea."

45. On Diego de Urrea's career in Constantinople, Ottoman Algiers, Sicily, and Castile, see García-Arenal and Rodríguez Mediano, *Orient in Spain*, 225–44.

46. "Razon es dezir quien es Diego de Vrrea, es natural a lo que el dize del Reyno de Napoles: tomaronle los Turcos tan niño, que le criaron en su ley y costumbre muchos años, y en ellos atendio a la lengua Arabiga, la Logica, y Philosophia con muchas ventajas, enterrãdose muy bien del Alcoran y su Maldita Theologia, por tanto estremo, que no vuo Moro que se le

auentajasse, y aun después en la Almahala de Muleixeque se ordenò, que nadie disputasse con el." Rojas, *Relaciones de algunos svcesos prostreros*, f. 63r.

47. AGS, Cámara de Castilla, Personas, lib. 28-1; AGS, Estado, leg. 1701, s.f. The raises kept coming, see throughout AGS, Estado, leg. 2471, for the year 1601. This didn't stop him from complaining about being paid too little: see the letter of September 10, 1602, in the same legajo.

48. AGS Estado, leg. 220, s.f., Carta de Urrea February 5, 1610. "he hecho la diligencia acerca de las dos renegadas que tiene el alcaide Budemir como vuestra magestad me lo mando, sacandolas de su casa, y ponendolas [sic] en otra y en presencia del comisario del santo oficio y de dos familiars y un notario se pregunto a cada una por si, con toda la nidustria [sic] possible y respondieron en lengua Arabiga porque no saben otra, que eran criadas en Fez muy niñas y que no sabian otra secta sino la mahometana y que no querian ser xpianas, y se [sic] con ellas todo quanto se pudiera hacer, y se dio parte desso al santo officio en Sevilla y assi se las lleva consigo el dicho alcaide Budemir. Nuestro señor guarde la Real persona de vuestra magestad. De Carmona, 5 de febrero de 1610. [firma] Diego de urrea."

49. AGS, Estado, leg. 1702, s.f.; AGS, Estado, leg. 2741, letter from September 11, 1601. He again asked for permission to leave the court, having trained replacements at least for Arabic: "antes de Usar de la liçençia [to return to Naples] dexara en San Lor[enz]o algunos frayles que podrán seruir a VMd en los papeles arauigos pero no en los Turquescos y Persianos."

50. García-Arenal and Rodríguez Mediano, *Orient in Spain*, 229.

51. AGS Estado, leg. 2471 [May 17, 1601], and elsewhere. BRP, 2/2154, doc. 27 (1603).

52. AGS, Estado, leg. 22o, s.f. Carta de Urrea, January 25, 1610.

53. "Certifico y hago fe yo Diego de Urrea criado del Rey N.S. Interprete de los papeles Arabigos, Turquescas, y Persianas, que por mandado de su M.d he visto el libro intitulado, Luz resplandente, compuesto por Ahmed natural de la Ciudad de Bona en Africa. Trata muy doctamente todo lo que es arte magica, hechicerías, y otras suporsticiones; y el dicho libro es tal, que no hallo pueda aprovechar para ninguna cosa, sino es para un a chimenea, pues todolo que trata son hechicerías, arte magica, y supersticiones, que hazen con palabras del Alchoran [sic]: y para que se sepa lo que contiene, y cumplir con lo que su M.d me manda, he puesto parte de las cosas, q trata, que son las siguientes. . . . Esto, y otras cosas se mejantes a estas es lo que contiene este libro, y por la verdad lo firme de mi nombre. En Valladolid a diez y siete días del mes de Julio de mill y seiscientos y tres años. Diego de Urrea [firma]." BRP, 2/2154, doc. 27, ff. 27v–30r.

54. Simancas is full of petitions from Urrea asking to be allowed to leave the cold winters of Castile and retire to Mediterranean Málaga, or better yet, to his hometown of Naples, for health reasons. AGS, Cámara de Castilla (Memoriales), leg. 1068, doc. 36. Urrea eventually petitioned for the right to return to Naples in 1611 and from there had an interesting Italian career as an expert informant to Roman and Neapolitan orientalist and academic circles, as Fernando Rodríguez Mediano has shown. "Diego de Urrea en Italia."

55. AGS, Estado, leg. 256, 74. See García-Arenal, Rodríguez Mediano, and El Hour, *Cartas marruecas*, 266–76. English translations from the Spanish and Arabic by Gilbert.

56. "Sepa Vuestra Magestad que la venida del dicho Diego de Urrea emviado por su real orden fue una cura muy acertada para quitarme todo el dolor que tenia de algunas cosas que me desconfiavan y perturbavan, y con su venida tomé aliento de todas mis congoxas y pesadumbres. ¡Oxalá Vuestra Magestad me huviera emviado antes tan Bueno y fiel criado! ¡oxalá huviera venido luego del principio! ¡o qué Bueno, o qué fiel criado! él ha cumplido todo lo que Vuestra

Magestad le mandó, assí para las cosas de su real servicio como para que mi reyno tenga paz y sossiego y descanso." AGS, Estado, Leg. 256 f. 74. See García-Arenal, Rodríguez Mediano, and El Hour, *Cartas marruecas*, 266.

57. اعلم، نصركم الله، ان نظركم في رسله الينا صادفت دواء المنا و نفست به كربتنا فيا له من رسل لو كان من
اوّل، فحصل عندنا، نصركم الله، ما ادنته بتبليغه الينا من الخير فيه انجلي غيارنا و اشتدُ حزمنا حين تحققنا منه توجهكم الينا واهتمامكم بامورنا، فذالك هو المظنون من سلطانكم، نصركم الله، و تلقينا من الخديم المذكور أيضا، نصركم الله، ما كان غائبا عنا من مكآنُهُ معدُن الغدُر الذين هم الترك.

58. AGS, Estado, leg. 494. See García-Arenal, Rodríguez Mediano, and El Hour, *Cartas marruecas*, 282–86.

59. AGS, Estado, leg. 256, 75. See García-Arenal, Rodríguez Mediano, and El Hour, *Cartas marruecas*, 290–96.

60. AGS, Estado, leg. 256, 75. See García-Arenal, Rodríguez Mediano, and El Hour, *Cartas marruecas*, 290–96.

61. Spanish reports about negotiations with Muley Xeque discuss potential *amistades* since at least 1607. See AGS, Estado, leg. 206, s.f., "Copia de carta de Juanetin Mortara para el duque de Medina Sidonia y su fecha en Larache a 10 de noviembre de 1607."

62. Arabic facsimile and contemporaneous Spanish text in *El perfume de la amistad*, 242–49.

63. For example, in the simplest cases, his approval was recorded as "Your Majesty was content about it and said it was fine" (*Que Vuestra Majestad estava contento dello y lo dava por bien*).

64. On the use of this phrase in lieu of royal signature in the Moroccan chancellery, see Castries, "Les signes," 234.

65. As following article 2, in which Muḥammad explained "We understand the answer of the Sulṭān Filīb (Philip), may God preserve him, to the abovementioned second article, and the switch [in the plan]." (f.1v).

66. Rojas, *Relaciones de algunos svcesos prostreros*, f. 65v. On Mortara, see the introduction to García-Arenal, Rodríguez Mediano, and El Hour, *Cartas marruecas*, 78–88 and passim.

67. This process of negotiating by translation and mistranslation recalls the treaties drawn up between Charles V and North African powers such as Tunis in the first half of the sixteenth century. See the discussion in Boubaker, "L'empereur Charles Quint."

68. Doc. 1 in appendix, García Figueras and Saint-Cyr, *Larache*, 413. Translated by Juanetín Mortara.

69. *El perfume de la amistad*, 246.

70. On Habsburg-Sa'adī diplomacy in this period, see Bunes Ibarra, "Entre la paz y la guerra," 68–91.

71. See the example from 1249 in Burns and Chevedden, *Negotiating Cultures*, 49–50.

72. See the comments and bibliography in Calafat, "Les interprètes de la diplomatie," 375–76.

73. On the varied career of Mortara, see García-Arenal, Rodríguez Mediano, and El Hour, *Cartas marruecas*, 26–27 and passim. On his work with Marin, see García Figueras and Saint-Cyr, *Larache*, 54.

74. AGS, Estado, leg. 206, s.f. Carta de Felipe III a Muley Xeque, January 25, 1607.

75. Rothman, *Brokering Empire*, 11–15.

76. For an exploration of "fetva diplomacy," see White, "Fetva Diplomacy."

77. On cross-confessional diplomacy, see the special issue of *Journal of Early Modern History* edited by Van Gelder and Krstic, especially their "Introduction," as well as the discussion in Rothman, "Afterword."

78. On the distinction between the normative "law" as expressed in legal theoretical writings and the practice and implementation of law with custom and other norms as "system," see Powers, "Islamic Inheritance System," 11–29.

79. The Portuguese governor, Alfonso de Noronha, appropriated some part of this sum for himself, allegedly in repayment to a debt, and all but fifty thousand *ducados* of the exiled sultan's treasure disappeared, yielding a royal inquiry that exposed ongoing tensions between the Portuguese and Spanish interests in North Africa despite (or because of) the Union. García Figueras and Saint-Cyr, *Larache*, 127.

80. "el dicho çidan habla tan claro español como si se hubiera criado en españa." Reported by Juan Castellanos de Herrera in a *Relación de las cosas de Marruecos* to the duke of Medina Sidonia. AGS, Estado, leg. 206, s.f., November 11, 1607.

81. Many examples are in the Estado section of the AGS. See, for example, AGS, Estado 206, núm. 3, and throughout AGS, Estado 207 (not foliated). On the use of the *'alāma* by Sa'adi rulers, see Castries, "Les signes," 236–39.

82. "teniendo consideración y rrespcto a lo que en tiempos pasados se tenia con mi señor padre, emperador de estos rreynos, que está en gloria, de comunicación por cartas, y del buen rreçevimiento que hazía a las cosas y propósitos que se tratavan en su alta presençia por parte de Vuestra Exçelençia, y que las cosas y negoçios del rrey de España y propósitos suyos corrían por manos de Vuestra Exçelençia, los quales rreçevía con amor y voluntad grande." See García-Arenal, Rodríguez Mediano, and El Hour, *Cartas marruecas*, 338.

83. "Dios, aquel que a puesto entre las naciones del mundo, aunque sean sus leyes diferentes, conformidad y comunicación considerada por el buen govierno y preceptos del rejimiento, y por los rreyes y governadores y jente principal de la qual proçede y se alcança la verdad en lo que entre ellos se comunicare, asi por cartas como por embaxadas, en los casos substanciales y de consideración." See García-Arenal, Rodríguez Mediano, and El Hour, *Cartas marruecas*, 337.

84. AGS, Estado, leg. 255. See García-Arenal, Rodríguez Mediano, and El Hour, *Cartas marruecas*, 346.

85. AGS, Estado, leg. 256. See García-Arenal, Rodríguez Mediano, and El Hour, *Cartas marruecas*, 340–43.

86. AGS, Estado, leg. 495. See García-Arenal Rodríguez Mediano, and El Hour, *Cartas marruecas*, 337–39.

87. AGS, Estado, leg. 260. See García-Arenal Rodríguez Mediano, and El Hour, *Cartas marruecas*, 367–72.

88. ADMS, leg. 2409. See García-Arenal Rodríguez Mediano, and El Hour, *Cartas marruecas*, 335–36.

89. "teniendo consideración y rrespecto a lo que en tiempos pasados se tenia con mi señor padre, emperador de estos rreynos, que está en Gloria, de comunicanción de cartas." ADMS, leg. 2409. See García-Arenal Rodríguez Mediano, and El Hour, *Cartas marruecas*, 335–36.

90. "[Referring to Muhammad al-Shaykh's other children and his wives] y cada uno de los hijos y hijas y las dos mujeres eredan y tienen parte conosçida en nuestra ley en la hazienda del muerto, de la manera que Dios lo tiene declarado a cada uno de erencia en su santa escriptura, y no es dado en nuestra ley que ninguno de los erederos tome más de su derecho que le está declarado y le pertenesçe por justiciar y no más." ADMS, leg. 2409. See García-Arenal Rodríguez Mediano, and El Hour, *Cartas marruecas*, 335–36.

91. AGS, Estado, leg. 255. See García-Arenal Rodríguez Mediano, and El Hour, *Cartas marruecas*, 359–62.

92. E.g., AGS, Estado, leg. 255, núm. 173. Letter from the Duke of Medina Sidonia.

AGS, ‏"قد وجهنا اليكم بكتاب كتبه علماء ديننا وقضاء بلادنا وفقهاؤها وبينوا لكم فيه حكم الله تعالى"‏ .93
Estado, leg. 260. See García-Arenal Rodríguez Mediano, and El Hour, *Cartas marruecas,* 371.

94. Al-Ḥajarī was particularly able to perform the task that Zidān asked of him because he had direct experience with Christian courts. In 1611 he had traveled to France in order to advocate before a Christian judge on behalf of *moriscos* now living in Morocco who had been the victims of robbery aboard the French ships that the Spanish crown had contracted to carry them away during the expulsion. In his account of this experience, al-Ḥajarī depicts his discussion with numerous Christian legal experts, such as the judge in Rouen. al-Ḥajarī, *Kitāb Nāṣir al-Dīn,* 126–27 of translation.

95. For example, when submitting his documentation about the theft of *morisco* properties by French ship captains to the royal council (*diwān al-sulṭānī*) upon arriving in Paris. al-Ḥajarī, *Kitāb Nāṣir al-Dīn,* 129 of translation, 77 of Arabic original.

96. Boyano, "Al-Ḥaŷarī y su traducción," 146–47.

97. Zhiri, "Task of the Morisco Translator," 20–21; and Epalza, *Los Moriscos,* 161–63.

98. Despite conventions of privileging oral testimony over written evidence, early modern Muslim courts, such as the Ottoman *Kadi* courts, accepted a variety of written documents as evidence at different stages of adjudication. For a general discussion, see Ergene, "Evidence in Ottoman Courts," 417–72; and White, *Piracy and Law,* 236.

99. al-Ḥajarī, *Kitāb Nāṣir al-Dīn,* 155 of English translation, 118 of Arabic original.

100. Zhiri, "Task of the Morisco Translator," 14–19.

101. "When I am in the presence of the scholars of our [own] religion, I am not able to talk about the [religious] sciences." al-Ḥajarī, *Kitāb Nāṣir al-Dīn,* 155 of English translation.

102. When describing his efforts to present and defend Islamic ideas before Christian judges or other interlocutors, al-Ḥajarī described his actions as *jihād* rather than *ijtihad*. al-Ḥajarī, *Kitāb Nāṣir al-Dīn,* 118, 121, and passim of Arabic original.

103. Powers, "Legal Consultations (*Futyā*)," 88–90 and passim. Powers cites a passage from the famous fatwā collection of al-Wansharīsī: "The prerequisites of being a *muftī* are that a person be knowledgeable of the law with regard to primary rules, secondary rules, disagreements, and [legal] schools; that he possess the tools of independent reasoning (*ijtihad*) in their entirety; and that he be familiar with whatever he needs to derive judgements, namely, grammar, biographical information, and commentary of the verses that were revealed with respect to the laws and the narratives contained in them" (88; *ijtihād* is in parentheses in the original).

104. On *iftā'* as one of the "modalities of transmitting the outcome of *ijtihād* from the domain of the legal profession down to the public," see Hallaq, "'Ifta' and Ijtihad," 33–38 and passim.

105. On the diverse roles and activities of *muftīs* in Islamic history, see Khalid Masud, Messick, and Powers, "Muftis, Fatwās," 3–32.

106. Messick, *Calligraphic State,* 135–51 and passim. On the "intermediary problem" in the construction of global imperial legal systems, see Burbank and Cooper, "Rules of Law," 282.

107. AGS, Estado, leg. 260. See García-Arenal, Rodríguez Mediano, and El Hour, *Cartas marruecas,* 368 and 373.

108. ‏"أَنْتُمْ في دينِكُم و شريعتكم لا يَرِثُ الأَ الكبير فقَط، و نحْنُ في ديننا و شريعَتنا يَرِثُ الكبيرُ و الصَّغِيرُ"‏ was translated as "porque los Cristianos de España por su ley se lo dan al grande de los hijos solamente, y nosotros en nuestra ley y justicia ereda el grande y pequeño." AGS, Estado, leg. 260. See García-Arenal, Rodríguez Mediano, and El Hour, *Cartas marruecas,* 368 and 371.

109. In Arabic, ‏"أَمَّا بَعْدَ حَمْدِ الله الذي جَعَلَ بين عبادِه من الأمَم ان اخْتَلَفَتْ في الأدْيان"‏, translated by al-Ḥajarī as "Y despuès de las alabanças a Dios, aquél que a permitido entre las naçiones, aunque

sus leyes sean diferentes." AGS, Estado, leg. 260. See García-Arenal, Rodríguez Mediano, and El Hour, *Cartas marruecas*, 367–72.

110. White, "Fetva Diplomacy."

111. AGS, Estado, leg. 260. See García-Arenal, Rodríguez Mediano, and El Hour, *Cartas marruecas*, 373–76.

112. See the studies on the Castilian Chancellery by María Ángeles de la Soterraña Martín Postigo (1959–1967) discussed in Chapter 1.

113. Indeed, he tried to hide the fact that he knew Arabic when traveling in Granada in the 1590s, fearing that "the Christians kill and burn everyone on whom they find an Arabic book or about whom they know he reads Arabic." al-Ḥajarī, *Kitāb Nāṣir al-Dīn*, 88 of English translation.

114. See Hershenzon, "Traveling Libraries"; and Zhiri, "Mapping the Frontier."

115. Hershenzon, "Traveling Libraries," 20–22.

116. AGS, Estado, leg. 260, Arabic only. See García-Arenal, Rodríguez Mediano, and El Hour, *Cartas marruecas*, 380–82.

117. On the translation activities underpinning this diplomatic episode, see the detailed studies by Feria García, "El tratado hispano-marroquí (I), (II)."

118. The most in-depth study on the role of translation and translators during this episode, which relied on bilingual documentation from the Council of State in the Archivo Histórico Nacional, remains Arribas Palau, "De nuevo sobre la embajada." An earlier study, which relied on Spanish-language archives in the ACA, studied the negotiations but not their linguistic aspect: Vernet, "La embajada de al-Gassani."

119. See Alonso Acero, *Sultánes de Berbería*.

120. On English-Moroccan diplomatic relations, see McLean and Matar, *Britain and the Islamic World*, 42–78. The Persian embassy was the result of joint diplomatic initiatives between the two Habsburg courts—the Spanish Habsburgs in Madrid and the Imperial Habsburgs in Vienna—to forge an anti-Ottoman alliance with the Safavids. On these initiatives, see Gil Fernandez, *El imperio Luso-Español*, 57–136. On the role of the English merchant brothers Anthony and Robert Sherley in Safavid correspondence and travels in Europe, see Subrahmanyam, *Three Ways to Be Alien*, 73–130. See also the contributions in García Hernán, Cutillas Ferrer, and Mathee, *Spanish Monarchy*.

121. On this episode and Philip's embassy to Cuco in response, see Saint-Cyr, *Felipe III y el Rey de Cuco*; and Planas, "Une culture en partage."

122. El Alaoui, "El jesuita Ignacio de las Casas," 21.

123. On the later development of the "Oriental" branch of the State Translation Service (translators working for the departments of the Secretaría de Estado rather than the Secretaría de Interpretación de Lenguas), see Cáceres Würsig, *Historia de la traducción*, 151–65.

124. On this embassy, see Conde Pazos, "La embajada turca," 10–17.

125. For example, Reiter shows the connections between the (purported) Ottoman representative Allegretti and the Ragusan translator Brattuti, who had been sent from Vienna to serve as intermediary for him. Reiter, "In Habsburgs sprachlichem Hofdienst," 198.

126. See Hershenzon, "Doing Things with Arabic."

127. Matar, "Muḥammad ibn 'Abd al-Wahhāb al-Wazīr al-Ghassānī," 485.

128. On the qualifications of these men, see Zhiri, "Mapping the Frontier," 968–71.

129. Arribas Palau, "A propósito de una carta," 565–69.

130. García Ejarque, *La Real Biblioteca*, 519–20.

131. Ghobrial, "Secret Life of Elias."

132. English translation in Matar, *In the Lands of the Christians*, 153 and passim.

133. Note that al-Ghassānī used the Arabic transliteration of Spanish words for priest—*clérigo* (cleric) and *fraile* (friar)—rather than *faqīh* or *qiss*. al-Ghassānī, *Riḥla al-Wazīr*, 83.

134. English translation in Matar, *In the Lands of the Christians*, 139.

135. English translation in Matar, *In the Lands of the Christians*, 153–54.

136. "me dixo vustro criado Don Abel Missi lo que deseavais de mi, y lo que me pedís en vuestra carta, que es la libertad de los cien cristianos, sobre lo qual hemos avisado de los que se ofrece antes de esto." García Figueras and Saint-Cyr, *Larache*, 449.

واللقى الينا خديمكم دون ابيل مسيح ما في خاطركم و ما طلبتوا منا فا هذا الماية من النصاري الذي وقع الكلام قبل هذا

Facsimile of the original Arabic letter in al-Tāzī, *Al-Mūjaz fī Tārīkh al-'Alāqāt*, 101.

137. García Figueras and Saint-Cyr, *Larache*, 450; al-Tāzī, *Al-Mūjaz fī Tārīkh al-'Alāqāt*, 101.

138. English translation in Matar, *In the Lands of the Christians*, 133–34, 152, passim.

139. Benton and Ross, "Empires and Legal Pluralism," 13. Scholars of legal pluralism and multi-normativity disagree about the best ways to characterize the range of jurisdictions and practices that conditioned legal activities in the early modern period, but both formulations are helpful in this case. On the concept of multi-normativity, see Duve, "Was ist Multinormativität?"

140. Windler, "De l'idée de croisade." On the role of translators in these negotiations, see Feria García, "El tratado hispano-marroquí (II)."

141. On the status of Spanish as a Mediterranean diplomatic lingua franca, in the vehicular sense of the term, and in contrast to the use of the Mediterranean lingua franca, in the linguistic sense of the term, see Dakhlia, *Lingua Franca*, 242–55; and Mallette, "Lingua Franca." See also Mouline, *Le califat imaginaire*, 224. Mouline predicts a chain of translation performed both in and out of the Moroccan chancellery: Arabic to Spanish to other European language, and vice versa. This certainly is borne out in English documents that were received from Morocco in Arabic and Spanish versions and that only once having arrived in England were translated into English. For example, from Zaydān to James I, National Archives, SP 71/12, parte 1, f. 270.

142. *SIHM: Archives et bibliothèques d'Angleterre*, 2: 117–18.

143. *SIHM: Archives et bibliothèques d'Angleterre*, 2: 40 (1590).

144. For example, *SIHM: Archives et bibliothèques d'Angleterre*, 2: 18, 68, 149, 210, 479.

145. This direct translation from Arabic was made by the early Cambridge Arabist, William Bedwell. *SIHM: Archives et bibliothèques d'Angleterre*, 2: 426.

146. On this figure, see Hamilton, *William Bedwell the Arabist*.

147. As in the case of the letter sent in 1614 to James I, *SIHM: Archives et bibliothèques d'Angleterre*, 2: 479. There is little evidence of William Laud (1573–1645) working as a diplomatic translator. Edward Pococke (1604–1691) would have been equipped and perhaps inclined to intervene in this kind of work after his stay in Aleppo as an English factor in the 1630s, but there is also no evidence extant in the state papers. On early English orientalism, see Toomer, *Eastern Wisdome and Learning*.

148. "Les huit voyages au Maroc de John Harrison," *SIHM: Archives et bibliothèques d'Angleterre*, 2: 441–48.

149. *SIHM: Archives et bibliothèques d'Angleterre*, 2: 446, 567–568, 575. On the *morisco* Salé, see Maziane, *Salé et ses corsairs*, 240–44, on relations with the English.

150. Zhiri, "Task of the Morisco Translator," 20–24.

151. García-Arenal and Rodríguez Mediano, *Orient in Spain*, 147.

152. *SIHM: Archives et bibliothèques d'Angleterre*, 2: 567–68.

153. See the brief biography in *SIHM: Archives et bibliothèques d'Angleterre*, 2: 423. See also Tobío, *Gondomar y los católicos ingleses*, 94, 122, passim.

154. See, for example, the Spanish loanwords in his reports about commercial relations between Moroccans and English and Spanish, respectively, as well as reports about the civil war and the *morisco* expulsion. He was also informed and reported to England about the rendition of Larache and Muḥammad al-Shaykh's affairs. *SIHM: Archives et bibliothèques d'Angleterre*, 2: 423–25 and passim.

155. *A true historicall discourse of Muley Hamets rising to the three kingdomes of Moruecos, Fes, and Sus. The dis-vnion of the three kingdomes, by ciuill warre, kindled amongst his three ambitious sonnes, Muley Sheck, Muley Boferes, and Muley Sidan. The religion and policie of the More, or barbarian. The aduentures of Sir Anthony Sherley, and diuers other English gentlemen, in those countries. With other nouelties* (London: Thomas Purfoot, 1609). The catalogue of the Huntington Library, where I consulted this volume, notes that "Ro. C." (as the dedication is signed) may be a fictitious person. However, the use of the name Cottington as the real or fictive author indicates some knowledge of Moroccan affairs.

156. On the history of this republic, see Maziane, *Salé et ses corsaires*.

157. "Nos los abaxo firmados sertificamos y damos fe a los que el presente vieren, como Mohamed ben Çayde de quien va firmado el papel dessottra parte, es escrivano publico del gobierno desta ciudad de Sallé, y a sus autos se le ha dado entera fe y credito como ttal escrivano fiel y legal y de confianssa." *SIHM: Archives et bibliothèques des Pays Bas*, doc. 10, 5: 33.

158. Al-Shādhalī, *Nuṣūṣ*, doc. 26, 233–37.

159. But at this time, Spanish-Dutch relations improved in the aftermath of the Peace of Westphalia (1648), and there was frequent correspondence between Madrid and The Hague, including about joint anti-French initiatives in the Mediterranean to combat corsair raiding. See Herrero Sánchez, *El acercamiento hispano-neerlandes*, 377–90.

160. *SIHM: Archives et bibliothèques des Pays Bas*, doc. 5, 6: 37. On the use of European vernaculars as communication modes between non-native speakers, see Planas, "L'usage des langues," 21.

161. *SIHM: Archives et bibliothèques de France*, 1: 541–47.

162. On the economy of ransom, see Kaiser and Calafat, "Economy of Ransoming"; and Hershenzon, "Political Economy of Ransom."

163. For example, in an English-captive account, the captive recounted how "I remember, indeed, that during my Abode at Sally, as I was one day walking without the walls, an ancient Grave Man met me, whose looks commanded more than ordinary respect, and speaking French, or mixed Spanish, he desired me to turn back with him into the Fields." The captive learns that the man wants to learn about Christianity, and so "I endeavored as well as I was able in that language to explain to him the Tenor of our Law." *An Account of South-West Barbary*, 67–68.

164. BNE, MS 3837, "Libro de la redención de cautivos que hicieron en Argel los Mercedarios Calzados y los Trinitarios Descalzos de las Provincias de Castilla y Andalucía, en el año de 1713," ff. 1 r–v; BNE, MS 3589, "Libro de redención de cautivos hecha en Argel en 1724," ff. 1r–2v.

165. On the "economics" of this information system, see Hershenzon, "'Para que me saques Cabesa por cabesa . . . .'"

166. Hoenerbach, "El notariado islámico y el cristiano," 113.

167. For a critique of this paradigm, see Greene, "Beyond the Northern Invasion."

168. On the *crónicas de Berbería,* see Martínez Góngora, *Los espacios coloniales.*

169. See, for example, the reports collected by Ignacio Bauer Landauer in vol. 2, *Marruecos,* of his *Pápeles de mi archivo: Relaciones de África,* though the other volumes are also good examples.

170. On Mármol Carvajal's borrowing from Leo, see Rodríguez Mediano, "Luis de Marmól lecteur de León."

171. See Cáceres Würsig, *"Jeunes de langues,"* on Venetian model, beginning in 1781.

172. BNE, MS 10513, and BNE MS 8920. According to the *Inventario General de Manuscritos,* 142, the latter's provenance is Serafín Estébanez Calderón. A third manuscript is listed as being located in the Library of Bartolomé March (20-1-22). See Aguilar Piñal, *Bibliografía de autores,* 236. BNE, MS 10513 was edited with a brief introduction by La Véronne, *Vie de Moulay Ismāʿīl.*

173. On these accounts, see Julien, *History of North Africa,* 247–51.

174. BNE, MS 8920, ff. 4r–v.

175. "Los cautibos que se reconocian aviles, y onrados, y que ya hablaban la lengua arauiga (excepto escriuir que esto se celaua con pena de la vida) se les emplaua en los Almacenes del Rey para su resguarda y trabajo, y otros usos de confianza." BNE, MS 8920, f. 248.

176. León reported that "tambien hay talbes particulares que son doctores de la ley: de los que unos residen en la corte al lado del cade principal, y forman tribunal para la decision de los casos de apelación, y demás prouidencias que emanen de el cade principal, y tambien para satisfacer al rey en las dudas que se le ofrecen un punto de religion." BNE, MS 8920, ff. 116v–117r.

177. BNE, MS 8920, f. 116r, f. 151r.

178. Muslim practices, like prayer (*ṣalā*) and the holy month of *Ramaḍān* are described using Christian vocabulary like "mass" (*misa*) and "Easter" (*Pascua*). He even explained—in answer to the question "what are the principal precepts which they must observe in accordance with their religion (*ley*), without which they would find themselves in a state of sin?"—that the Muslims observed the same Ten Commandments (*decálogo*) as the Roman Catholics, excepting that concerning fornication. BNE, MS 8920, f. 102r.

179. Ismāʿīls international politics is decidedly isolationist: "His reason of state (*razón de estado*) is to conserve the opulence and the peace in the territories under his dominion." León explains that Muley Ismāʿīl does not send or receive regular ambassadors, and that only English and Dutch have consuls in the ports for purely commercial matters. "Havia en la corte un saletino llamado Arraez Perez, que hauiendo estado en Ynglaterra hera practico de aquel pays, y si govierno, otro Arraez Benasa que estubo en Francia, y tenia yguales noticias de aquel Reyno; un Sevillano llamado Side Mojamete Andaluz, interprete, y Medico del Rey que halava con propriedad de las cosas de España, y con estos tres se divirtia los ratos desembarrazados hablando del Govierno y calidad de estas potencias, pues era inclinado a sauer." BNE, MS 8920, ff. 185v–188r. León discussed the career of the renegade from Seville briefly in an early chapter on the Sultan's health, explaining that the former was elevated by the king's grace (*gracia*) to be his interpreter, doctor, and *valido* (favorite) in reward for his skill as a doctor and apothecary who had cured the king during a rare severe illness. BNE, MS 8920, ff. 14v–15r.

CHAPTER 4

1. Arias Torres, "Bibliografía sobre las traducciones."

2. Burman, *Reading the Qur'ān,* 6–9 and passim.

3. On changes in the seventeenth-century field of Christian Arabic translation, see Heyberger, "Polemic Dialogues," 513 and passim.

4. Brendecke, *Empirical Empire*, 35–37 and passim.

5. Near the conclusion of the council, it was decided that the clergy must adapt their prayer and instruction: "to the mental ability of those who receive [the sacraments] . . . and in the vernacular language, if need be and if it can be done conveniently, in accordance with the form which will be prescribed for each of the sacraments, by the holy council in a catechism, which the bishops shall have faithfully translated into the language of the people and explained to the people by all parish priests. (Session 24, Chapter VII)." *Canons and Decrees of the Council of Trent*, 199–200.

6. See Harvey, *Muslims in Spain*, 135 for Harvey's emphasis of this important point.

7. Burke, *Languages and Communities*, 61 and passim.

8. Feros, "Rhetorics of the Expulsion," 60.

9. BNE, Incunable 2489; Talavera, *Breue y muy prouechosa doctrina*.

10. Carrasco Machado, "Antonio García de Villepando."

11. Gilbert, "Grammar of Conquest."

12. "Deve mirar qualquier persona que leyere el presente interrogatorio y doctrina para los confessores que cada uno de las lenguas tiene su manera de hablar y con aquella se deue el hombre cuerdo conformar quanto buenamente pudiere porque de otra manera mas seria enfuscar que interpretar lo que onbre quiere dezir. E por esso en el presente interrogatorio muchas de las preguntas van asi al pie de la letra sacadas parte por parte en l arauia porque lo sufrio la lengua. y otras no asi porque no lo sufrio la lengua. mas solamente la misma sentencia aunque por otros terminos y lo presente sea dicho por aquellos que son inclinados a reprehender y no a defender las obras de los proximos." Alcalá, *Arte para ligeramente saber*, 50–51.

13. Gutierrez, *Españoles en Trento*, 264–79, 774–93.

14. Gilbert, "Transmission, Translation."

15. Asenjo Sedano, "Estudio preliminar," xlvi–xviii.

16. On the context and consequences of the synod, see Gallego Burín and Gámir Sandoval, *Los moriscos* and a facsimile of the synod's resolutions in Pérez de Ayala, *Sínodo de la Diócesis*.

17. BNA 1389 (Christian mss. 3).

18. Although originally from Andalucía, he did not know Arabic himself, and in 1548, when Charles V made clear his intention to name Pérez de Ayala as bishop of Guadix and Baza, Pérez de Ayala demurred that he did not, in fact, know Arabic or *morisco* customs. Pérez de Ayala, *Autobiografía*, cited in Torres Palomo, "Don Martín de Ayala," 510. Even before he was able to take up his episcopal residency, he requested in 1550 that Charles grant him two benefices for Arabic-speaking clergy. See Garrido García, "El uso de la lengua árabe," 127. Pérez de Ayala continued to mandate the use of Arabic among his clergy throughout the synod: "Mandamos que estas dos ciudades Guadix y Baça, se junten todos los nuevos Christianos los domingos de los aduientos y delas quaresmas/o alguna fiesta que ocurriere entre semana, en vna yglesia la que fuere mas accommodada para que todos ellos puedan conuenir y juntarse, y tengan sermon en arauigo acerca dela doctrina y evangelio que occuriere, no auiendo en todas las parrochias hombres doctos y arauigos que los puedan enseñar. y esto hagan los prelados con intérprete/o pongan quien lo haga, porque nunca lo an tenido hasta nuestro tiempo, y es gran daño delas almas delos dichos nuevamente conuertidos no auerlo" (*Sínodo de la Diócesis*, Titulo I, Constitución II).

19. Garrido García, "El uso de la lengua árabe," 129. Lanteyra was one of the villages held in the *señorío* of the Marquis of Cenete. For more on the bilingual priests in Cenete, see Gilbert, "Transmission, Translation," 455.

20. Torres Palomo, "Bartolomé Dorador," 15–16.
21. Garrido García, "El uso de la lengua árabe," 130 and references.
22. BNA, MS 1389 (Christian mss. 3).
23. See Torres Palomo, "Don Martín de Ayala," 515–17.
24. Garrido García, "El uso de la lengua árabe," 128–29.
25. Garrido García, "El uso de la lengua árabe," 131–33.
26. "Dixóme que quando dezia missa para qué bebía aquél vino i él mismo me respondió diziendo para cumplir con las gentes lo avía de azer." Archivo Histórico Diocesano de Guadix, caja 83, leg. 11, pieza C. See Garrido García, "El uso de la lengua árabe," 134–37, transcription and photographic reproduction of the document.
27. "Domingo, día de San Hierónimo postrero día de septiembre vino este dicho moro a mi casa i tratamos en muchas cosas que me dixo fue que procurase el Alcorán que era libro de Dios i palabras suias i que Dios lo avía hecho i se lo avía dado a Mahoma, me dixo así:

"قرآنا ليس بمخلوق عربيا لا دخلة و لا خرج الى كلم ربي الاعز

See Garrido García, "El uso de la lengua árabe," 136–37.
28. Starczewska and García-Arenal, "'Law of Abraham.'"
29. García-Arenal, Starczewska, and Szpiech, "Perennial Importance."
30. Ryan Szpiech, "Preaching Paul."
31. Bunes Ibarra, "El enfrentamiento con el Islam."
32. During the second war of the Alpujarras, Dorador participated actively in the slave trade of captives taken during the conflict, and he remained in Guadix, where he died sometime after 1598. Garrido García, "El uso de la lengua árabe," 129–30. Torres Palomo made use of an *expediente de limpieza de sangre* from 1587, housed in the Granada Cathedral archive, that reconstructs his family history but left a lacuna between 1554 and 1587, which Garrido García has been able to fill using the archives in Guadix. See Torres Palomo, "Bartolomé Dorador," 14–16.
33. The Tridentine Profession of the Faith was translated itself into Arabic by Gianbattista Eliano Romano in 1564. Balagna Cousou, *L'imprimerie arabe*, 27–30. Both of these latter works were what have become known as "large catechisms," certainly a Counter-Reformation genre modeled on the extended catechism of Peter Canisius (*Summa doctrinae cristianae*, 1555). O'Malley, *Trent*, 263.
34. Though the translation is unsigned, Mur was certainly at the front of Pérez de Ayala's mind in with respect to the *morisco* mission and its materials in Valencia. In 1565 he requested of Francisco de Borja—Duke of Gandía and superior general of the Jesuit order—that Mur occupy the Arabic chair at the University of Gandia to train missionaries. Medina, "Jerónimo Mur," 688. Mur indeed returned from Rome to Valencia in 1565.
35. Haliczer, *Inquisition and Society*, 247.
36. "Epistola," in Pérez de Ayala, *Doctrina cristiana*, ff. 3r–v.
37. "Y aun que la escriuimos en lengua Castellana, pero declaranosla en Arauigo los Catechistas, y predicadores que os embiaremos; los quales hemos escogido tales, que sepan bien vuestra lengua, por que no falte nada para vuestra cumplida instruction." "Epistola," in Pérez de Ayala, *Doctrina cristiana*, f. 3v.
38. My emphasis. "Porque la lengua Arauiga (como todos las demas) tiene no solamente proprios characteres, pero aun proprias pronunciaciones y sonidos de letras, que no se pueden bien suplir con letras Latinas estara el lector auisado con estas reglas siguientes para saber bien

leer, y pronunciar las palabras Arauigas desta doctrina Christiana." "Reglas para saber leer las dictiones Arauigas desta doctrina," in Pérez de Ayala, *Doctrina cristiana*, ff. 22r–v.

39. Nebrija's 1495 Latin definitions of *reducir* were *redigo* (derived from *ago*), and *reduco* (derived from *duco*). Among the definitions of *redigo* in the *Oxford Latin Dictionary* are "to drive back, repel an enemy," "to gather crops," "to convert," and "to bring (into a condition, usually with some form of limitation)," whereas the meanings of *reduco* are more closely related to "return" and "restoration."

40. See Gilbert, "Grammar of Conquest."

41. Rafael, *Contracting Colonialism*, 229 (index). See also the discussion of the concept in Gilbert, "Social Contexts, Ideology and Translation," 233–34.

42. Rafael, *Contracting Colonialism*, passim.

43. For a comparison from Nauhatl societies, see the discussion of "Stage 4" in language adaptations in Lockhart, *Nahua After the Conquest*, 318–25.

44. Hanks, *Converting Words*.

45. In the case of Catholic Europe, the problem of mental reservation inspired innovation in linguistic thinking to explain the separation between uttered and interior realities. In a world where the intervention and enforcement of the Inquisition and other courts could demand the justification of others' interpretations of ones thoughts and speech, the Augustinian theory of language, which explained linguistic truth to be a function of the speaker's intention rather than the interlocutor's interpretation, was no longer an adequate paradigm with which to confront the place of *correctio fraterna* (the biblical injunction to privately correct a colleague one knows to have sinned) and the secret of confession when orthodoxy and heterodoxy were now judged by human courts as well as (presumably) divine. Tutino, *Shadows of Doubt*, 20–21. The new conception of the relationship between language and interpretation found among the Spanish scholastics continues to preoccupy translation theorists to this day, as exemplified by the influential (and much debated) theories of George Steiner, that all communication, and even the very process of individual understanding, is translation, and that this broadly conceived act of translation is part of the core of human instinct: the desire to keep meaning private while participating in society. See Steiner, *After Babel*, 222.

46. On the translation of such terms, Hanks, *Converting Words*, 157–63 and passim. Of course, the formal and conceptual relationships between Quiché Maya and Spanish and Andalusí Arabic and Spanish are quite distinct.

47. For example, in Pedro de Alcalá's 1505 work, *Arte para ligeramente saber la lingua arauiga*, some extensive parts of the religious manual designed for Castilian priests were *only* in Granadan Arabic. Alcalá used the Islamic Arabic phrase, "*azza wa jalla*" (lit., "mighty and majestic," used in reference to Allah) throughout the Christian prayers in reference to both God and Jesus, and this phrase remained in Mur's 1566 text. This phrase, loosely translated as "great and glorious," is one of the characteristic descriptors of God (Allah) in the Islamic tradition. Likewise, in 1505 Alcalá made frequent use of the phrase *alhamdulliah* to evoke sincerity and emotion in the Arabic texts intended for the new Christians. This latter phrase had vanished by 1566, but the use of both phrases reveals at least some familiarity with Islamic concepts among the Arabic-speaking priests and a willingness to accommodate those concepts in evangelization.

48. For example, in some Quechua missionary translations *Dios* was retained as a loan translation. See Durston, *Pastoral Quechua*, 214 and passim.

49. BNA, MS 1389 (Christian mss. 3), ff. 33v–34r.

50. Pérez de Ayala, *Doctrina cristiana*, f. 7v.

51. Pérez de Ayala, *Doctrina cristiana*, 7v. Could this be an influence from Mur's Roman experience learning Arabic among Eastern Christians?

52. Bilingualism was especially common among males, and there was a higher degree of monolingualism among females. Ciscar Pallares, "'Algarabía' y 'algemía,'" 136 and passim; and Haliczer, *Inquisition and Society*, 248.

53. On the life and context of Ramiro de Alba's work, see Resines, *El catecismo de Pedro Ramiro de Alba*, 16–17 and passim.

54. "No han de guardar los que fueron Moros el Viernos como solían; ni las pascuas de Ramadán. . . . No han de hazer guadoque mayor ni menor, que es lauatorio para hazer la çala. . . . No han de hazer la çala las veces como lo manda el Alcoran, ni hazia el alquible, ni con las inclunaciones y ademanes con que solía hazerla; sino quando quisieren rezar en la iglesia, o en casa o en el campo, pueden hincarse de rodillas y juntar las manos, o assentados, o passeando podran rezar en todo el tiempo que quisieren no rezando oraciones del Alcoran, sino las de la yglesia que arriba están dichas," ff. 44v–45r. See Resines, *El catecismo de Pedro Ramiro de Alba*, 85.

55. My English translation is a composite of the Spanish and Arabic text, given here:

> Quanto a lo primero, es de saber que confessar quiere dezir manifestar en Arauia y es que todo cristiano o cristiana es obligado a confessar sus pecados a dios y al clerigo vna veç enel año a lo menos. A dios: porque el es el que perdona los pecados y no otro. Al clerigo: ca es vicario de dios en la tierra, para salud delas animas y es asi como fisico que cura los enfermedades.

(Following Alcalá's idiosynchratic Arabic transliteration system): "Narjan dibe al agual. Tahtiju tedrú énne al confessar maanih bal Aarabia alicrár, gua huet, énne cúlli Niçráni yégib aalih icrár bi ḍunúbu al calil márra fa cené, lalláh azéguegélguá lal faqui. Lalláh liénne hu cadir aalél gofrán a ḍunúb gua me gáiru. Lal faqui liénne hu kalifat aláh li menfaat 'iibédu, liénne hu bahál tabib aleḍi ydagui al amrád mita roh." See Figure 11 for the original Alcalá transcription.

Alcalá, *Arte para ligeramente saber*, 33.

56. "Instrucción de Arzobispo de Granada en respuesta a cierta petición que hicieron los vecinos del Albaicín sobre lo que debían hacer y las prácticas cristianas que debían observar s.f. (c1500)," reprinted in Azcona, *Isabel la Católica*.

57. BNA, MS 1389 (Christian mss. 3), ff. 33v–34r.

58. Pérez de Ayala, *Doctrina cristiana*, f. 7v.

59. "Delo q an de saber y dezir los nueuos Christianos quando estan en missa." Pérez de Ayala, *Sínodo de la Diócesis*, f. 54v.

60. Pérez de Ayala, *Doctrina cristiana* (1566), f. 21v.

61. On the effect of the Inquisition on book culture among the *moriscos*, see Fournel-Guérin, "Le livre et la civilization écrite," 242.

62. BNA, MS 1389 (Christian mss. 3), ff. 32v–35v. Pérez de Ayala, *Sínodo de la Diócesis*, ff. 73v–74r.

63. Pérez de Ayala, *Doctrina cristiana*, ff. 14v–20v.

64. This script was translated into Arabic in 1554 but not in 1566. BNA, Christian mss., f. 32v; and Pérez de Ayala, *Doctrina cristiana*, 73v.

65. As I have argued elsewhere, Alcalá likely had extensive interaction with the same group of *alfaquíes* who worked as *romanceadores*. Gilbert, "Grammar of Conquest," 16.

66. In Toledo Inquisición, 191, exp. 2. On Murcia, see Blázquez Miguel, "Catálogo de los procesos inquisitoriales."

67. Labarta, "Notas sobre algunos traductores de árabe," 115–17.

68. In the Canaries, AHN, Inquisición, 1825, exp.16; in Mallorca, AHN Inquisición, 1711, exp.13; in Sicily, AHN, Inquisición, 1747, exp. 8. See the bibliography on the Inquisition in the Canaries and Sicily in Sarmiento Pérez, "Interpreting for the Inquisition," 70–74.

69. The Inquisition was established in 1526 with a three-year grace period, which is why the first trials and punishments were delayed until 1529. Garrad, "La inquisición," 63–65.

70. Garrad, "La inquisición," 68.

71. Ron de la Bastida, "Manuscritos árabes," 210–15; García-Arenal, "La Inquisición," 57–71.

72. Garrad, "La inquisición," 65.

73. The daily salary was 136 *maravedíes* in 1526. García Pedraza, *Actitudes ante la muerte*, 471.

74. For more information about the *plomos* translators, see García-Arenal and Rodríguez Mediano, *Orient in Spain*. On the other names, see Vincent, "Reflexión documentada," 739.

75. The documentary base of the Granadan Inquisition is far less rich than those of the other tribunals, since most of the documents were destroyed in the nineteenth century. See Vincent, "Le tribunal de Grenade," 199.

76. Ron de la Bastida, "Manuscritos árabes," 210–15; García-Arenal, "La Inquisición," 57–71.

77. This was, and is, a common complaint about polyvalence in Arabic and the ambiguity of diacritic marks: "La lengua araviga es tan equivoca, que muchas veces una misma cosa, escrita con acento agudo, o luengo, significa dos cosas contrarias." Mármol Carvajal, *Historia de la rebelión*, book 3, chapter 3.

78. The records of the meetings and edicts of the Capilla Real in 1526 mention the information from ecclesiastical visits, but there is very little detailed information about these visits from the first period. The first extant records of the ecclesiastical visits begin in 1560 and have been recently published as part of the Monumenta Regni Granatensis Historica series. See García Fuentes, *Visitas de la Inquisición*.

79. García Fuentes, *Visitas de la Inquisición*, 123.

80. Ciscar Pallares, "'Algarabía' y 'algemía.'"

81. Haliczer, *Inquisition and Society*, 3–4.

82. Labarta, "Notas sobre algunos traductores," 101–34. The *morisco* Jesuit Las Casas complains about the lack of adequate staff and the tendency to use inappropriate or unreliable people to do the translation. El Alaoui, "Ignacio de las Casas," 21.

83. García Carcel, *Orígenes de la Inquisición Española*, 121–24; Haliczer, *Inquisition and Society*, 245–48.

84. Haliczer, *Inquisition and Society*, 265–66. This is comparable to the figures for Granada from 1550 to 1580; see Garrad, "La inquisición," 63–77.

85. AHN, Inquisición, leg. 550, exp. 11, s.f., on Cabrerizo, see Labarta, "Notas sobre algunos traductores de árabe," 107–8.

86. AHN, Inquisición, leg. 550, exp. 11, s.f.

87. "Comentario sobre una oración mahometana llamada de Guesen," BNE, MS 12694, núm. 57, ff. 1r–4v.

88. See the edited texts throughout the documentary appendix in Barceló and Labarta, *Archivos moriscos*.

89. Doc. 148, Barceló and Labarta, *Archivos moriscos*, 320.

90. PUL, Garrett Islamic MS 526H.

91. Skemer, "Arabic Book," 115.

92. Though Ana Labarta identifies Mur's tenure as the primary Inquisition translator and *calificador* of texts as beginning in 1575, in the obituary written upon his death, in 1602, his pastor Francisco Boldo claims that he had served the *santo tribunal* for more than thirty years. ARSI, Historia Societatis 177, tomo 2, núm. 93, ff. 201r–v.

93. PUL, Garrett Islamic MS 526H. See Skemer, "Arabic Book." Like the Dorador Algerian manuscript discussed below, this manuscript had an unknown trajectory until its discovery in an Islamic country by European scholars in the nineteenth century.

94. On the outlawing of Arabic in the medical faculties, see García Ballester, *Los moriscos y la medicina*. This example of collaboration between Mur and Pérez de Ayala reinforces the likelihood that it was indeed Mur who Ayala tasked with the translation of the catechism in 1566 (above).

95. Labarta, "Notas sobre algunos traductores," 119.

96. Labarta, "Traductores en la Inquisición," 124–31.

97. Barceló and Labarta, *Archivos moriscos*, 242.

98. Barceló and Labarta, *Archivos moriscos*, 243.

99. Ciscar Pallarés, *La justicia del abad*, 165–66.

100. On this family, see Barceló and Labarta, *Archivos moriscos*, 89–91. At least two generations served in this office as Inquisition familiar: ʿAbd Allāh b. Ibrāhīm, qaḍi, who converted with the name Jeroni in 1526, and his son Cosme, whose eventually fell afoul of the Inquisition in 1567 and again throughout the 1570s.

101. Bernabé Pons, "Aspectos lingüísticos."

102. AHUV, Varios, caja 5/2, doc. 64 in Barceló and Labarta, *Archivos moriscos*, 205–8.

103. AHN, Inquisición, leg. 5312, exp. 8, f. iiii r.

104. AHUV, Varios, caja 5/2, doc. 64 in Barceló and Labarta, *Archivos moriscos*, 207.

105. BRP, 2/2241, doc. 27.

106. On both cases, see Labarta, "Los libros," 74.

107. AHN, Inquisición, leg. 550, exp. 11.

108. Harvey, "Arabic Dialect1595."

109. See Harvey, *Muslims in Spain*, 135 for Harvey's emphasis of this important point.

110. See the many works of Federico Corriente on Andalusi Arabic, most recently Corriente, Pereira, and Vicente, *Aperçu grammatical*.

111. Barceló and Labarta, *Archivos moriscos,* 119–20.

112. Barceló and Labarta, *Archivos moriscos*, doc. 171, 337–38.

113. Corriente, Pereira, and Vicente, *Aperçu grammatical*, 253.

114. Edited and studied by Harvey in "Arabic Dialect."

115. Harvey, "Arabic Dialect," 104–5.

116. Pérez de Chinchón, *Antialcorano*.

117. See the study and edition of Resines, in *Obras completas de Alonso de Orozco*, 695–843.

118. As in the case of Mur's translation of the 1588 letter with "News from Algiers" to a Valencian correspondent or his 1582 Arabic copy of a letter from Valencian moriscos to sympathizers in Algiers. Barceló and Labarta, *Archivos moriscos*, doc. 124, 174–75.

119. Benítez Sánchez-Blanco, "Religious Debate in Spain," 102. See also Feros, "Rhetorics of the Expulsion."

120. See Busic's excellent dissertation and edition, "Saving the Lost Sheep."

121. Guerra de Lorca, *Catecheses*: "Deum magnum ab omnibus colendum quasi pro certo symbolo, Alla Quibir, suis proposuit, mysterio Triadis in personis subsistente procul reiecto& milles ab eo aduirato. Nam filium, vnicum scilicet patris verbum, ab ipso gentium, non tamen eidem consubstantialem, praedicauit, voce Arabica Zurulla, quasi flatum seu verbum patris, eum vocitans, vere cum Arrio consentiens, a quo hunc errorem cum alijs multis Mahomedus percepit impius," f. 17v.

122. Guerra de Lorca, "Catechesis secunda, de habitu & lingua relegandis," in *Catecheses*, ff. 23r–33v.

123. Guerra de Lorca, *Catecheses*, ff. 31v–32r.

124. Guerra de Lorca, *Catecheses*, ff. 33r–v.

125. See Magnier, *Pedro de Valencia*, 119–36.

126. "Este es un catecismo util para todos los fieles Christianos, porque contiene una compendiosa y substancial declaracion de la doctrina Christiana, y especialmente muy prouechoso para los Christianos nuevos de Moriscos, y para convertir a Moros porque el estilo es por via de disputa en defense de nuestra santa fe catholica contra la secta de Mahoma. Va escripto en diálogo entre un sacerdote y un Christiano nuebo de morisco al que llama Novicio. Resines," Catecismo del Sacromonte," 44–47, on the problems of dating and authorship.

127. Resines, *Catecismo del Sacromonte*, 254–55, 262.

128. Resines, *Catecismo del Sacromonte*, 262.

129. "Relegata a finibus Hispaniae Algarabia, in illa pax multa esset, vna fides, actionum puritas, ac tandem multa clancularia homicidia vitarentur." Guerra de Lorca, *Catacheses*, f. 33v. "Peccan gravisimamente los testigos falsos que suelen ser homicidas y ladrones." Resines, *Catecismo del Sacromonte*, 311.

130. "Como la nao en medio de la tempestad del mar, si no es governada, da al traves, assi es la lengua desconcertada. Que haze naufragio y destruye todos los bienes." Resines, *Catecismo del Sacromonte*, 311–12.

131. "La lengua del malo dize Santiago que es la cosa mas pestilencial del mundo, pues la vivora y el basilisco y los perros raviosos matan a los cuerpos, y la mala lengua mata a las animas y a los cuerpos y la honrra y fama, etc. Como tienen cuydado los que gobiernen de limpiar las republicas del beneno y pestilencia, assi la avian de tener y mucho mayor, de guardar las ciudades de los murmuradores y malos consejeros, como quien las guara de la peste." Resines, *Catecismo del Sacromonte*, 310.

132. "Infinitos bienes an de venir al mundo mediante las buenas lenguas, pues por la predicación del Señor y de los apostoles vino la salud al mundo, y de las malas lenguas vienen infinitos males, como se manifiesta en la persuasion de la serpiente a nuestre madre Eva, y de todos los ereticos, y infieles, y malos consejeros, y detractors, etc." Resines, *Catecismo del Sacromonte*, 311.

133. "E toda lengua xpiana deve agradecer a V.S. tan grand bien e tan grand victoria, como ha havido de tan capitales enemigos, que aqueste mal language hablaron." Castillo, *Sumario e recopilación*, 11.

134. Resines, *Catecismo del Sacromonte*, 310.

135. On Ribera's radical shift, see Ehlers, *Between Christians and Moriscos*; and Benítez Sánchez-Blanco, *Heróicas decisiones*.

136. Ehlers, *Between Christians and Moriscos*, 119–20.

137. "Así fue menester gastar algunos meses en disponer las materias y capitulos, y assi mesmo en añadir y mudar palabras y clausulas para mayor claridad de la doctrina." Pérez de Ayala and Ribera, *Catechismo*, 2.

138. Pérez de Ayala and Ribera, *Catechismo*, f. 1r.

139. Pérez de Ayala and Ribera, *Catechismo*, f. 6r.

140. Pérez de Ayala and Ribera, *Catechismo*, ff. 6r–v.

141. Ehlers, *Between Christians and Moriscos*, 120–22.

142. On Cantalapiedra's activities, see his petition to Philip II for payment as captive translator. SN-AHN, Osuna, caja 418, d. 519, f. 1r. For example, in 1572 Cantalapiedra was called on to translate in the criminal trial of two "*turcos*," Mustafa and Bellí. ARV, Real Audiencia, Procesos Criminales, Letra G, núm. 215, ff. 48r–53v. I am grateful to Professor Jorge Catalan of the University of Valencia for this reference.

143. "Carta del Patriarca," in Pérez de Ayala and Ribera, *Cateschismo*, f. iir–v.

144. He did not name names, but he clearly intended Ribera among others when he criticized the Valencian clergy not only for baptizing by force but for (in 1608) "no averles dado la doctrina competente hasta aquí" (not giving them adequate instruction until now), and because this instruction is an obligation, not doing it is "worse than a mortal sin." El Alaoui, "El jesuita Ignacio de las Casas," 21.

145. El Alaoui, "El jesuita Ignacio de las Casas," 22.

146. ARSI, Shedario Unificato, Las Casas, Ignatius de.

147. El Alaoui, *Jésuites, morisques et indiens*, 113. His mother's name was Gracía Mendoza, and she was likely part of one of the many *morisco* families to adopt the surname of the principal noble family of Granada and its capitán general.

148. Benítez Sánchez-Blanco, "De Pablo a Saulo," 420.

149. In Rome, where he joined the Jesuit order in the 1570s, Las Casas was set to study classical Arabic (*fuṣḥā*) in addition to his native Granada dialect. While in Rome, he worked on translating the Council of Nicea into Arabic, along with another Spanish Jesuit, Francisco Torres. Medina, "Jerónimo Mur," 688. It is not known if Torres himself knew any Arabic.

150. El Alaoui, *Jésuites, morisques et indiens*, 65–66.

151. "¿Quien no ve que, siendo el que es [the king], tiene obligación de tener no sólo dos y quatro intérpretes sino muy muchos, unos major que otros, aptos no solamente para interpretar fiel y seguramente las cartas y embajadas que de otros príncipes desta lengua le trahen sino para poder responder con la misma confiança y seguridad a ellos? Bastaba esto sólo para mover a su Magestad a dar luego traça cómo se executasse, aviéndo provado la falta que a avido assí con los que vinieron y vienen de África, del Cuco, y otros, como los Persianos." El Alaoui, "El jesuita Ignacio de las Casas," 21–22.

152. "Todo el mundo sabe los presidios, plazas y ciudades que tiene nuestro rey posee en el África y sus costas y los reynos que tiene en la costa occidental del Asia y en la India oriental donde esta lengua es común y ordinaria como natural casi de todas ellas pues, ¿quien negará que para poseerlas seguramente, governarlos dichosamente, y dílatar más su imperio y estender la fe en tan bárbaras naciones no tiene necesidad de seguros y fieles ministros que, sabiendo bien la lengua, no solamente hagan que obedezcan los vasallos con gusto y contento sino que los que son convertidos oygan de buena gana la doctrona evangélica y se muevan a seguirla?" El Alaoui, "El jesuita Ignacio de las Casas," 22.

153. "[Nota en el márgen: Véase a Joan Botero en la *Relación universal del mundo*, ibi, rey cathólico]." El Alaoui, "El jesuita Ignacio de las Casas," 22.

154. See Magnier, *Pedro de Valencia*, 119–36.

155. The first texts produced on the Medici Press were an Arabic version of the Gospels (1590/1591), followed in 1592 by three books on the Arabic language itself: the *Ajumurriyyah*, the *Kafiyyah*, and an anonymous *Alphabetum Arabicorum*, later thought to be a product of the

Press's founder Gianbattista Raimondi. See Jones, "Learning Arabic in Renaissance Europe," 167–70; and Jones, "Medici Oriental Press." Jones notes that, also in 1592, an Arabic grammar appeared in Frankfurt an der Oder. The Medici Press, which lasted only until 1614, filled its later roster with technical Arabic books of grammar, geography (al-Idrisi), or mathematics (Euclid and Avicenna) rather than religious texts. This gap was filled by Arabic books imported from the East and, later on, by the press of the Propaganda Fide, which was established in 1622. See Henkel, "Polyglot Printing-Office."

156. Various requests (none granted) by the Jesuit Francisco de Quesada to Philip III advocating for Arabic printing in Spain and the purchase of Arabic books in Rome are in ACA, leg. 669, núm. 24.

157. El Alaoui, "El jesuita Ignacio de las Casas," 24.

158. Pardo Molero, "Mercaderes, Frailes," 181.

159. Alonso Cantalapiedra shared his name with a better-known (though perhaps lesser) Arabist of the mid-sixteenth century, working with a very different kind of Arabic in a very different context. This was the Salamanca Hebraist Martín Martinez de Cantalapiedra, who used the 'Ajurrūmiyya to teach university students the rudiments of Arabic grammar, though without their having necessarily mastered them. There is no discernible family link between these homonymic individuals, but the coincidence of their names, chronology, and very different Arabic knowledge is a testament to the wide range of Arabics used in Spain in the mid-sixteenth century. On this figure, see Bataillon, "L'arabe a Salamanque," 1–17; López-Baralt, "A zaga de tu huella"; and most recently, Martínez del Castillo Muñoz, "Teaching and Learning of Arabic."

160. ARV, Real Chancilleria, Diversorum Lugartenientiae, 1425, fol. 31r–32r. See Pardo Molero, "Mercaderes, Frailes," 181.

161. Philip granted him the small annual salary of twelve escudos, specifying "as is the custom for the Arabic interpreter (como se acostumbra por intérprete de la lengua morisca)," in addition to a bonus of five sueldos per captive confession, the same amount usually paid to owners when their slaves made a confession. SN-AHN, Osuna, caja 418, d. 519, f. 1r.

162. ARV, Manaments y Empares, 1616, libro 5, ff. 2r–v.

163. Colombo, "Jesuits and Islam"; Heyberger, "Polemic Dialogues"; Valensi, Ces étrangers familiers; and the recent volumes of Les musulmanes dans l'histoire de l'Europe, edited by Jocelyne Dakhlia and Bernard Vincent—vol. 1, Une intégration invisible (2011) —and by Jocelyne Dakhlia and Wolfgang Kaiser—vol. 2, Passages et contacts en Méditerranée (2013).

164. Colombo, "Juan de Almarza."

165. See Colombo, "'Even Among the Turks,'" 26.

166. García-Arenal and Rodríguez Mediano, Orient in Spain, 324–25.

167. Especially the Confusión de la secta mahomética y del Alcorán by Juan Andrés (1515). See Colombo, "'Even Among the Turks,'" 36–41.

168. "Colloquium inter Patrem Ignatium de las Casas & Mahumetauum quendam: ex quo probatur, Mahometanos solo rationis ductu posse cognoscere Alcorani falsitutes. Pater Casas. Mihi Tripolim versus pergenti se adiunxit Maurus ex comitatu & iam mihi propior factus benevolé; vrbaneque salmem mihi impartiuus est: dixit que mihi, audivi te Idiomate Arabico loquentem, qua propter placet mihi tecum sermonem facere." González de Santalla, Manuductio ad conuersionem Mahumetanorum, 2: 387.

169. González de Santalla used dialogues and the idea of a dialogue throughout the Manuductio, and meanwhile his colleagues included dialogues in Arabic and Turkish grammars and in sermons and plays. Colombo, "'Infidels' at Home," 206 and passim. Bilingualism in the

bagnos was common across the Mediterranean. See Calafat and Santus, "Les avatars du 'Turc,'" 487–88, 502–4.

170. Colombo, "'Infidels' at Home," 200–206.

171. Colombo, "Muslim Turned Jesuit."

172. Cervantes, *Don Quixote*, book 2, chapter 62; Pedro Calderón de la Barca, *Amar después de la muerte* (1677). The "morisco gracioso" was a common stereotype in Golden Age theater, including in the works of Lope and Calderón. Bergman, *Art of Humour*, 129–39.

CHAPTER 5

1. On the literature of political and economic advice that reinforced the narrative of decline as it sought to reform the Spanish government, see Gil Pujol, "Spain and Portugal," 438–39.

2. On this political turn in Spain, see Kagan, *Clio and the Crown*, 207 and passim. For a discussion of the turn in general in the Renaissance, see Popper, *Walter Ralegh's "History of the World,"* 11 and passim.

3. Rodríguez Mediano, "Fragmentos de orientalismo," 243–76.

4. Lawrence Venuti describes the translation theories using the example of translating Catullus into English: "The canonization of fluency in English-language translation during the early modern period limited the translator's options and defined their cultural and political stakes. The translator could choose the now traditional domesticating practice, an ethnocentric reduction of the foreign text to dominant cultural values in English; or the translator could choose a foreignizing practice, an ethnodeviant pressure on those values to register the linguistic and cultural differences of the foreign text." Venuti, *Translator's Invisibility*, 68.

5. Luna, *La verdadera historia*; Luna, *Segunda parte de la historia*.

6. For an overview of this period, see Kennedy, *Muslim Spain and Portugal*, 1–37, 309; and Catlos, *Kingdoms of Faith*, 21–57.

7. Fernández Albaladejo, "Entre godos y montañeses"; Rodríguez Mediano, "Al-Andalus, ¿es España?"

8. On the genealogical markets, see the study in Soria Mesa, *La biblioteca genealógica*, 13–28.

9. Marín Pina, "El tópico de la falsa traducción," 542–43.

10. Luna, *La verdadera historia*, Proemio.

11. Feria was also the author of *Dialogismo y lacónico discurso: En defensa de las reliquias de San Cecilio que se hallaron en la Iglesia mayor de la ciudad de Granada*, and thus was connected to the world of *morisco* intellectuals who produced the *plomos* forgeries (including Luna). García-Arenal and Rodríguez Mediano, *Orient in Spain*, 183.

12. Letter to the Reader from Joan de Feria, in Luna, *La verdadera historia*, ff. 4r–v.

13. BNE, MS 7453, f. 255r.

14. Verses (Redondilla) of Joan Bautista de Vivar, in Luna, *La verdadera historia*, ff. 6r–7r.

15. Cf. Castillo letters from BNE, MS 7453, ff. 2r–62r and passim.

16. "En aquella sazon estaua yo con el Tarif en la prouincia de Granada. Junto con esto me dio nueuo aliento auer juntado todas las cartas y papeles que refiero en esta historia, los quales me fueron entregados por los mismos generales que se hallaron en aquella conquista, y lo que

yo no vide me informe dello con mucha diligencia de personas principales dignas de ser creydas sus relaciones." Luna, *La verdadera historia*, f. 5r.

17. Many of the phrases are simply conventional patterns found in royal orders. For example, when Almanzor appointed Tarif/Ṭāriq to head the Iberian campaign, his letter of appointment included the phrase "auemos tenido por bien de nombrar y señalar, como por la presente nombramos y señalamos por nuestro alcayde y Capitan general y caudillo mayor noble" (Luna, *La verdadera historia*, ff. 12v–13r); another example is in a public letter from the general Abdalaziz to the people of Fez: "Hazemos saber a los alcaydes y capitanes y a los ofifciales de la gente de guerra deste dicho reyno de Fez, y a todos los demas sus naturales moradores estātes y abitātes en el . . . ." (Luna, *Segunda parte de la historia*, f. 51); and in another letter from the same general, Abdalaziz, writing back to the Umayyad caliph in Damascus, in which he calls himself "presidente del supremo Consejo de Guerra, Alcayde y Capitan General de su armada de mar." (Luna, *Segunda parte de la historia*, f. 73r).

18. E.g., Castillo, *Sumario é recopilación*, 44 and passim.

19. For example, the concluding affirmation that a letter was sent "De nuestra Alta presencia y real palacio de Albaçatin, a quatro dias de la Luna de Rageb, año de ciento y dos" (Luna's "translation" Luna, *Segunda parte de la historia*, f. 25v) is formally similar to what would have been the translation of an actual Arabic letter from late sixteenth-century Morocco: (from al-Manṣūr to Elizabeth, *SIHM: Archives et bibliothèques d'Angleterre*, v. 2, plate 4) "ṣadara 'alā al-maqām al-'ālī al-mawlay al-amāmī al-ṣulṭāni" or (al-Manṣūr to Philip, BNE, MS 7453, f. 68v) "fa kitābna hadhā ilaykum min ḥaḍaratna al-'āliya." These letters all used Islamic chronology.

20. From the *morisco* rebels: "Los loores á Dios del estado grande, venturoso, renovado por Muley Mahamet Aben Umeya" (lib. 6, cáp. 31); and in two letters from Aben Aboo to the Ottomans in Constantinople and Algiers: lib. 8, cáp. 8. and lib. 9, cáp. 10.

21. "Carta escrita por la Reyna Anagilda, madre del principe don Sancho, al Rey don Rodrigo." [Marginal note:] "Esta carta fue traduzida por Auentarique de lengua Castellana en arauiga e aora se boluio a traduzir de arabigo en romance." Luna, *La verdadera historia*, f. 7v.

22. See García-Arenal and Rodríguez Mediano, *Orient in Spain*, 161–62.

23. Fernández Albaladejo, "Entre godos y montañeses"; Rodríguez Mediano, "Al-Andalus, ¿es España?"

24. Ecker, "'Arab Stones.'"402.

25. See Kagan, *Clio and the Crown*; and Grafton, *What Was History?*

26. On Dobelio, see García-Arenal and Rodríguez Mediano, "Los libros de los moriscos."

27. García-Arenal and Rodríguez Mediano, *Orient in Spain*, 234.

28. García-Arenal and Rodríguez Mediano, *Orient in Spain*, 263 and passim.

29. Bernabé Pons, "Introducción," 36–37.

30. García-Arenal and Rodríguez Mediano, *Orient in Spain,* 167.

31. Castillo, *Sumario é recopilación* 12; and Sotomayor y Valenzuela, *Breve relación*, 11

32. On the imbrication of medicine, history, and political council in French and Spanish courts, see Montcher, "La historiografía real"; and Soll, "Healing the Body Politic." The appropriation of classical medical metaphors for statecraft was also prevalent in the Ottoman Empire. See Ferguson, *Proper Order of Things*, 5.

33. Luna, first letter to reader, *La verdadera historia*, f. 2v.

34. Iverson, "El discurso de la hygiene"; García-Arenal and Rodríguez Mediano, "Médico, traductor, inventor," with a reproduction of the manuscript on 226–30.

35. "Tambien tienen el principado entre estas medicinas las que sacan del cuerpo los malos umores sin diminucion de la sustancia y umedo radical y no las que enflaquecen y gastan la virtud: por cuya causa aunque las sangrias y purgas que usan los medicos en nuestra España hazen prouecho al parecer de presente, son malas y dañosas por ser venenosas medicinas." BNE, MS 6149, quoted in García-Arenal and Rodríguez Mediano, "Medico, traductor, inventor," 226.

36. García-Arenal and Rodríguez Mediano elegantly unpack all the ways in which Luna uses the physical body as a stand-in for the body politic in this letter in *Orient in Spain*, 166–70.

37. "auerlos quitado de España ha sido causa que apenas le duele a un ombre la cabeça quando le mandan sangrar 5 y 6 vezes: por que no ay otro remedio en caso necessitado: y quedando tullido de los braços para no poder mandar las armas y tan flaco y debilitado el cuerpo que no es para seruirse asi en los dias de su vida." BNE, MS 6149, quoted in García-Arenal and Rodríguez Mediano, "Medico, traductor, inventor," 228. The Arabic translation is my own.

38. Instituto Valencia de don Juan, envío 92, tomo 1. See García-Arenal and Rodríguez Mediano, *Orient in Spain*, 170. Also Iverson, "El discurso de la hygiene."

39. RAH, 2/MS 118, *Contra la enfermedad de la gota, i como se ha de curar este mal terrible. Compuesto por el doctissimo varon Animar guan, El guixtati Medico de Camera del Rey de Granada llamado Mulei Abulhacen. Traducido de Lengua Arabiga en Castellano. Por mandado del Rey n[uest]ro S[eñ]or Phelippe 2.o año 1593.*

40. RAH, 2/MS 118, f. 2r.

41. Nonetheless, nineteenth-century Spanish historians of medicine thought it was Luna. See Sánchez Quintanar y Sánchez-Nieto, *Biblioteca Médica Hispano-Lusitana.*

42. See Dew, *Orientalism*, 26.

43. García-Ballester, "Circulation and Use."

44. See the discussion in Olds, *Forging the Past*, 126–43 and passim.

45. For example, the *plomos* helped authenticate the Christian character of Granada and thus its right to the privileges of Christian subjects. This was an argument promoted by "old Christian" settlers throughout the sixteenth century and that was codified in local historiography in the beginning of the seventeenth, after the conclusion of the *morisco* expulsion (from Granada in 1571; from Spain in 1614). See Harris, "Forging History."

46. As an introduction to the basic events and the immense recent bibliography on the *plomos*, see the entry by Bernabé Pons on the Lead Books of Sacromonte in the recent volume of *Christian-Muslim Relations: A Bibliographical History*, vol. 6.

47. A defining study of the potential forgers, their motives, and their context was published in Spanish in 2010 and again in English translation in 2013, offering, among other conclusions, a synthesis of the extensive scholarship on this episode. Mercedes García-Arenal and Gerard Wiegers, *Orient in Spain.*

48. Rodríguez Mediano, "Al-Andalus, ¿es España?"

49. See Harris, *From Muslim to Christian Granada*, 44 and passim.

50. Drayson, *Lead Books of Granada*, 2; Boyano, "Al-Ḥaŷarī," 137–38.

51. Woolard, "Bernardo de Aldrete," 458.

52. Koningsveld, "Le Parchemin et les Livres," 174–75; Hagerty, "Transcripción, Traducción, y Observaciones," 2.

53. Hagerty, "Transcripción, Traducción, y Observaciones," 127.

54. The text has been recently edited and published by Koningsveld and Wiegers in "Five Documents."

55. The way that the wise philosopher is characterized differs in Arabic and Spanish. In Arabic, Dionysio is characterized as "the pious and eminent philosopher, the glory of God"

using terms (*ṣāliḥ, fakhr al-dīn*) with Islamic overtones. In Spanish, he is "the servant of God, the most wise philosopher," which has Christian overtones (*siervo de Dios*). See Koningsveld and Wiegers, "Five Documents," appendix, doc. I, 219–20.

56. وترجمته بلاسان الحالي اعجمي و عليه اشتحرنا شرحا محط بالاغز المذكور عربيون المصراف في جزيرة اشبنيه" Koningsveld and Wiegers, "Five Documents," appendix, 220. Luna translated *al-ghaz al-madhkūr ʿarabiūn al-maṣrāf fī jazīrah Isbanīa* as "el secreto ya dicho en Aravigo, lenguajes [with previously referenced 'lenguaje común español'] usados en la tierra de España." Koningsveld and Wiegers, "Five Documents," appendix, 221.

57. Yo Miguel de Luna vezino de Granada interprete de lengua Arauiga por mandado de su señoria Don Juan Mendez de Saluatierra Arçobispo de Granada del consejo del Rey nuestro señor, traduxe todo lo questaua escripto en el pergamino susodicho except la çifra de la prophecia por que require mas estudio y consideraçion laqual boy traduziendo todo laqual se hizo en presençia del licenciado Faxardo cathedratico de lenguas [orientales] comunicando con el la dicha traduction laqual es conforme al original. Y juro Dios y a los sanctos euangelios en que puse mis manos que a mi leal saber y entender sigund el termino gramatico arabe esta fiel y lealmente traduzida de verbo ad verbum todo lo qual se hizo en presençia del liçenciado Antonio Barba prouisor deste arçobispado de Granada a quien yo se lo entregue y lo firme de mi nombre y el dicho prouisor en Granada a 31 de março de 1588 años.

Miguel de Luna
El licençiado Ant. Barba
Ante my: El doctor Montoya Secretario

(From Koningsveld and Wiegers, "Five Documents," appendix, doc. I, 219–20.)

58. On the early development of Northern European orientalism, see Jones, "Learning Arabic"; and Toomer, *Eastern Wisdome and Learning*. For a recent study of French orientalism as a feature of Baroque commerce, see Dew, *Orientalism*. See also the discussion in this book's Introduction.

59. See García-Arenal, "Religious Identity," 500 and passim.

60. Woolard, "Is the Past a Foreign Country?," 67–70; and Woolard, "Bernardo de Aldrete," 451, 459, passim.

61. On this policy shift, see Rodriguez-Salgado, *El paladín de la cristiandad*.

62. See particularly the works of Gil Fernandez and Floristán. For a bibliography about these relations, see Floor and Hakimzadeh, *Hispano-Portuguese Empire*.

63. On this episode, see Hershenzon, "Traveling Libraries."

64. There was a range of imperial and administrative languages used across the Islamic world, including Persian among the Safavids and Ottomans and Ottoman Turkish across the Ottoman Empire and its North African regencies. However, classical Arabic learning was a foundation of these Islamic empires and also in Morocco. This classical Arabic foundation was sometimes mediated by translation into Persian or Ottoman.

65. *Memoriales sepulcrales.* See Hershenzon, "Doing Things with Arabic."

66. *Pactismo* is often associated with the particular rights and privileges of non-Castilian kingdoms (e.g., Navarre, Aragon), but even in Castile (which included Granada) the idea of a contract between subject and sovereign was a powerful source of political legitimacy in the Habsburg period. On this idea as found in the Spanish Scholastics, see Hamilton, *Political Thought*, 40–43.

67. Gil Pujol, "Spain and Portugal," 441–57.

68. Feros, *Kingship and Favoritism*, 21–31.

69. On the place of history and translation in the education and statecraft of Spanish kings, including their own translations, see Montcher, "La historiografía real," 46–51.

70. On Spanish tacitism and translation, see Martínez Bermejo, *Translating Tacitus*. On the European reception of Tacitus, see the articles collected in Merle and Oïffer-Bomsel, *Tacite et le Tacitisme*. A short overview of Machiavelli in Spain is in Bleznick, "Spanish Reaction to Machiavelli"; and see also Puigdomènech, *Maquiavelo en España*.

71. Scholars have begun to explore this question in the context of a Eurasian transmission of ideas between the classical age and the Renaissance. See the introduction and articles collected in Biasiori and Marcocci, *Machiavelli and Islam*, 1–15.

72. Gil Pujol, "Concepto y práctica."

73. Luna, *La verdadera historia*, f. 3v.

74. On Ibn Rushd's commentaries on Aristotle's *Ethics* and Plato's *Republic*, see the discussion and bibliography in Black, *History of Islamic Political Thought*, 122–26. Aristotle's *Ethics* was available to translate, but not the *Politics*, which would only be "discovered" a few decades later by Aquinas in France. Thus Plato's *Republic* (in Arabic, *Kitāb al-Siyāsa*) was used to supply the "practical" examples of rule to supplement Aristotle's theories in the *Ethics*.

75. On Mancebo's reading of al-Ghazālī, Ibn Rushd, Ibn al-'Arabī, etc., see López-Baralt, "Moriscos," 481.

76. On the historical Ya'qūb al-Manṣūr and later Christian adaptations of his "legend," see Alvira Cabrer, "La imagen del *Miramolin*," 1004–1010. The name or sobriquet al-Manṣūr/ Almanzor—literally meaning "the victorious"—was quite common. The still-reigning Moroccan sultan Aḥmād al-Manṣūr (d. 1603), for example, might have also been called to the minds of Luna's readers, or even the famous warrior and political councilor Muḥammad ibn Abī Amīr al-Manṣūr, who lived at the end of the Cordoba caliphate. On this figure, his legend, and later echoes, see Echevarría Arsuaga, *Almanzor*.

77. Kennedy, *Muslim Spain and Portugal*, 248.

78. For example, "Pero no es menos dañosa esta hypocresia y simulacion para la vida humana, e infame para la reputacion del mismo Principe, y perniciosa para la conservacion de su estado, que es aborrecida de Dios. Porque la perfidia es hija legitima de la simulacion, por la qual todas las cosas del mundo se arruinan, y se sustentan por la verdad y fidelidad. A esta fidelidad llama Ciceron unas veces seguridad, otras fundamento de justicia, otras conservación de las Republicas. Platon dize que es verdadera firmeza, pura sinceridad, y clara filosofia." Ribadeneyra, *Tratado de la religion*, 230–31.

79. Luna, *Segunda parte de la historia*, f. 2v. On the second volume of *La verdadera historia* as a mirror for princes, see García-Arenal and Rodríguez Mediano, *Orient in Spain*, 161–62; López-Baralt, *Islam in Spanish Literature*, 213–15; and Kerlin, "True Mirror for Princes," all of whom follow and expand upon the work of Francisco Márquez Villanueva. See Márquez Villanueva, *El problema morisco*, 45–97.

80. Luna, *Segunda parte de la historia*, ff. 2r–3v.

81. Gil Pujol, "Concepto y práctica"; and Herrero Sánchez, "La Monarquía Hispánica."

82. The "*republico*" was "a man occupied with the public good" (*el hõbre que trata del buen publico*). Covarrubias, *Tesoro de la lengua española*, sec. R, f. 9.

83. Braun, "Making the Canon?"

84. See the marginal note in BL, Additional MSS, 10238, f. 216r.

85. Contemporary Arabic uses *jumhūriyya*, while Dozy translates both *mashayikha* and *al-shawwar* as *république*, according to his nineteenth-century understanding of the terms.

Supplément aux dictionnaires arabes, 1: 799 and 810. In addition to the Andalusi and early modern Moroccan usage for this political concept, Dozy's dictionary and other works of nineteenth-century orientalism (e.g., Lane's *Arabic-English Lexicon*), which are essentially lexicographic surveys of extant texts, offer no other direct translation for "republic" in Arabic. On the *jumhurriyya*, see Lewis's entry "Djumhūriyya" in the *Encylopedia of Islam*, 2: 594.

86. Indeed, the most usual translation of Plato's *Republic* was simply *Kitāb al-Siyāsa* [The book of politics].

87. For a comparison of the way that Tridentine reforms fueled history writing, including local erudition, see Ditchfield, *Liturgy, Sanctity, and History*, 5 and passim.

88. Monroe, *Islam and the Arabs*, 7–9.

89. See the study by Bernabé Pons in "Introducción," xiii–xxxiii.

90. Le Thiec, "L'Empire ottoman."

91. See Braun, "Making the Canon?," on how the Inquisition's censorship of Bodin offered an alternative means for interested readers to learn about it.

92. "If the prince is an absolute sovereign, as are the true kings of France, Spain, England, Scotland, Ethiopia, Turkey, Persia and Muscovy, whose authority is unquestionably their own, and not shared with any of their subjects, then it is in no circumstances permissible either by any of their subjects in particular, or in general, to attempt anything against the life and honor of their king, either by process of law or force of arms, even though he has committed all the evil, impious and cruel deeds imaginable." Bodin, *Six livres de al République*, book 2, chap 5.

93. See Floristán, "Francisco de Gurmendi."

94. Gil Fernández, *El imperio Luso-Español: Tomo II*, 211, 418–19.

95. Gil Fernández, *El imperio Luso-Español: Tomo I*, 57–136.

96. "De toda la librería que se tomó a Muley Zidán y está en mi poder, aunque ay muchos libros de filosofía y medicina y otras faculdades de no poca consideración, ninguno me pareció más a propósito para ponerle en la lengua castellana para que VEx pudiese pasar los ojos por él, que este que trata de modo del gobierno de aquellos Reynos que por ser tan estraños a los nuestros en todo, podrá la novedad servir de divertir y recrear el ánimo a V Ex y de dar a conocer el mío, que es y ha sido siempre de hallar algo con mi pobre ingenio que poder ofrecer a los pies de V Ex." Gurmendi, *Libro de los cualidades*, f. 4r.

97. Llopis Mena, "Teoría política árabe," 168 and passim.

98. AGS, Estado, leg. 220, s.f. Urrea report to the Consejo de Estado on January 25, 1610, vouching for Robert Sherley and the Persian letters he brought with him.

99. A valuable critical edition of both texts with a study of the author and his contexts is Llopis Mena, "Teoría política árabe."

100. Llopis Mena, "Teoría política árabe," 177–217. See also Rodríguez Mediano, "Fragmentos de orientalismo," 258. The source of al-Ṭurṭūshī's manuscript was likely the Moroccan library, rather than a copy circulating in Iberia (though it is always possible that there was a copy of the *Sirāj* in the Nasrid books that Cisneros transferred to the Complutense). Many early modern Moroccan scholars, such as Ibn Khaldūn and al-Maqqarī, were vitally interested in the works of al-Ṭurṭūshī and other Andalusi thinkers. See the preface in Alarcón y Santón's translation of the *Sirāj*, xv.

101. Gurmendi "translated" the deathbed speech of "el califa Ebi Yusuf Jacob Almansor" at the end of chapter 33 of the Libro de las qualidades, ff. 95v–96r. Later reports of this deathbed speech are found in the Bayān of al-'Idhārī (c. 1312). Kennedy, Muslim Spain and Portugal, 248.

102. "De Ivan Bavtista de Pastrana, Contador de su Magestad, al Excelentísimo señor Duque de Lerma, dando noticia del Autor. Soneto: . . . Criandose en Madrid de pequeño/Con

el dueño de Idiaquez peregrino/Sea en la lengua Arabiga ladino/Y entienda al Afro, Assio [*sic*], y al Isleño/Raro aprender de lenguas, pues en suma/Las traduze y entiende, y aun comenta/Y aquel estilo infiel buelve Christiano/Señor Excelentissimo esta pluma." Gurmendi, *Doctrina phísica*, paratext f. 4v.

103. "Don Ivan de Persia a Francisco Gurmendi, y a su libro de Dotrina [*sic*] de Principes traduzido de Arabigo en Español. Soneto: . . . A los Monarcas abres un camino/Con que establezcan y conseruen leyes." Gurmendi, *Doctrina physica*, paratext f. 5v.

104. Gurmendi's "Letter to the Reader": "Con gusto me ocupè [*sic*] en la traduzion desta sentencias poniendolas en estilo y lenguaje que gozzassen dellas nuestros Cortesanos y Ciudadanos estudiosos, para que se aduierta y note, que tesoros estan escondidas debaxo de aquel idioma Arabe, y para satisfacer a los que ponen en question, si ay libros y Filosofos entre aquellos infieles, porque saquen de aqui el dolerse dellos, y pedir a Dios, que es la verdadera sabiduria, los trayga en conocimiento de la verdad." Gurmendi, *Doctrina physica*, paratext f. 7r.

105. Gil Pujol, "Spain and Portugal," 441.

106. Llopis Mena, "Teoría política árabe," 168–73 and passim.

107. "Porque los vassallos son el cuerpo de vn Reyno, y el Rey la cabeça de esse cuerpo, y corre por quenta de la cabeça el mouimiento errado, o acertado del cuerpo, y ansi como vn cuerpo no puede permanecer sin cabeça, mucho menos vn Reyno sin vn Rey noble, fuerte, prudente, sabio, clemente, piadoso, y justo." Gurmendi, *Doctrina physica*, f. 94v.

108. "Escriuio vn Emperador de Roma a Cosdrue Rey de Persia preguntandole, que con que tenia y conseruaua su Reyno? Respondiole: Con no afloxar y desfallecer en lo que mando y prohibo, con no hazer al côtrario de lo que prometo, proueo y gouierno por razon y no por passion, castigo por culpa y no por yra, compro los corazones cô amor y no por temor y espanto, y imprimo en sus almas de mis vasallos el temor y respect que me deuen, sin vsar en lo que pueden y valen de agrauio ni tirania." Gurmendi, *Doctrina physica*, ff. 108r–v.

109. Gurmendi, *Doctrina physica*, ff. 100v, 101v–103r, 106 r–v.

110. "Tabla de las sentencias y cosas notables que contiene este libro," Gurmendi, *Doctrina physica*, 161r–164v. This idea appears in chapter 4, "Concerning diverse attitudes appropriate to Kings and Good governance," of the *Doctrina physica*: "El que es cabeza de una república, no sólo ha de ser bueno, sino parecerlo." Gurmendi, *Doctrina physica*, f. 111r.

111. al-Ṭurṭūshī, chapter 39, "On appearing as a just or unjust sultan" (*Fī mithal al-Sulṭān al-ʿĀdil wa-l-Jāʾir*). *Sirāj al-Mulūk*. For al-Ṭurṭūshī, the beauty of the necklace depends on its central stone, while the unjust ruler is like a thorn in the foot (*shawka fī-l-rajal*). Alarcón, *Lámpara*, vol. 2, 48.

112. Gurmendi, *Doctrina phísica*, 161r–164v. On these ideas, see Truman, *Spanish Treatises on Government*, 28–29 and passim.

113. "Otro Poeta dixo: Si quieres hazer vna Buena obra, hazlo presto. Y verdaderamente el beneficio y merced hecha a quien se deue y lo merece con equidad y prudencia, si es Gloria en la vida, es Gloria y fama en la muerte. Dezia el Rey Ali bin Ebi Talib: Lo major del mundo y que puede auer en el es la obediencia y imitación de la criatura al criador. Guardete pues de desobedecerle, o de no imitarle, que perderás el mayor beneficio de todos que es el premio que tiene guardado en el Parayso." Gurmendi, *Doctrina phísica*, f. 77r.

114. Gurmendi, *Libro de las cualidades*, ff. 33r–7r.

115. Guilarte Zapatero, "Un proyecto para la recopilación."

116. "De Don Jvsepe dela Cerda y Baçan. Soneto: Reduzir a lenguaje Cortesano/Politico Español, cuerdo y medido/Del Afro inculto el metodo Escondido/Iuntando lo scientifico a lo

vrbano./Ver lo dificil de Platon tan llano/Y a Aristoteles verle aquí entendido/Lo Etico a sup unto reduzido/Lo sentencioso, prouechoso y sano./Facilitar las ciencias al mas rudo/Con lecciones morales verdaderas/Y dar razon de Estado y de gouierno/Solo Gurmendi conseguirlo pudo/Como maestro en lenguas estranjeras/Haziendo el nombre de su libro eterno." Gurmendi, *Doctrina phísica*, paratext f. 6v.

117. "Del Rey, Príncipe, o Monarcha de un Reyno o Imperio y de las qualidades que deven concurrir en la persona real." Gurmendi, *Libro de las qualidades*, f. 6r.

118. Gurmendi, *Libro de las qualidades*, ff. 6r–v.

119. See Bireley, *Counter-Reformation Prince*, 48–50 and passim.

120. Gurmendi, *Doctrina phísica*, ff. 3v–4r. Dedicatoria a Lerma: "aunque la novedad del modo de gobierno político de los árabes convide a la lección de él, ninguna cosa agradará y satisfará más a los hombres graves y doctos, para entender que este libro lleva en sí, encerradas y cifradas, altas y profundas sentencias, que verse salir a luz debajo la autoridad y protección de la grandeza de Vuestra Excelencia."

121. On the changing metaphors for political communities from the late Middle Ages through the seventeenth century, see Maravall, *Teoría del Estado,* 97–112.

122. Maravall, *Teoría del Estado*, 105–6.

123. These professionals are essentially using what translation studies refers to as skopos theory. See Munday, *Introducing Translation Studies*, 72.

124. See Bunes Ibarra's exhaustive study, *La imagen de los musulmanes.*

125. On this Oriental branch, see Cáceres Würsig, *Historia de la traducción*, 151–64.

126. This is the argument in Sola, "Los avisos de Levante," 207–30.

127. Martínez Góngora, *Los espacios coloniales.*

128. This was true not only of Spain. For example, the famous "prince of the Republic of Letters," Nicolas-Claude Fabri de Peiresc in Marseille, sought information from and about the Islamic world, including reports and historical accounts written in Spanish by Europeans. See Tolbert, "Ambiguity and Conversion." On Peiresc's collecting of manuscripts and information from across the Mediterranean, see the work of Peter Miller, including *Peiresc's Mediterranean World.*

129. Monroe, *Islam and the Arabs*, 15–16 and passim.

130. García-Arenal and Rodríguez Mediano, *Orient in Spain*, 304–5.

131. García-Arenal and Rodríguez Mediano, *Orient in Spain*, 300–303.

132. As for example the later French translation, *Histoire de la conqueste d'Espagne par les mores . . . Avec une Dissertation de celuy qui l'a mise en François sur la verité de cette Histoire, conferee avec celles d'Espagne, & quelques Manuscrits Arabes, Turcs, & Persans pour y server de Preface & de prevue*, Paris: Claude Banbin, 1680. Also discussed in García-Arenal and Rodríguez Mediano, *Orient in Spain*, 159.

133. Luna, *History of the conquest of Spain*, f. a3r.

134. Luna, *History of the conquest of Spain*, f. a3r.

135. García-Arenal and Rodríguez Mediano, *Orient in Spain*, 159.

136. Luna, *History of the conquest of Spain*, f. a3r.

137. García-Arenal and Rodríguez Mediano, *Orient in Spain,* 162.

138. Garcia Pedraza, *Actitudes ante la muerte*, 2: 1010.

139. Recent research shows how Arabic knowledge through translation was far from being absent or marginal to Cervantes's own literary creativity and sociopolitical thinking. Montcher, "Cervantes anticuario"; and Byrne, *Law and History.*

EPILOGUE

1. Stewart, "Cidi Hamete Benengeli," 111–27.

2. García-Arenal, "Miguel de Luna," 262.

3. Rawlings, *Debate on the Decline of Spain*, 50–53. Also note that in his own work of fictive translation, the *Lettres persanes*, which first appeared in 1721 (the same year as the last premodern French edition of Luna's work), Montesquieu reported the highly negative impression of the fictional Persian ambassadors who were his protagonists, using their "translated" epistolary dialogue as an anti-Spanish polemic.

4. Pérez, *Dissertationes ecclesiasticae*, in Borbón, *Cartas para ilustrar la historia*, 8.

5. There was also some doubt about the credibility of this ambassador as official emissary. See Conde Pazos, "La embajada turca."

6. That Brattuti was from Ragusa meant that he likely had some exposure to the role of translators in shaping multinormative legal interactions between Ragusans and Ottomans, in analogy to al-Ḥajarī's work between Spain and Morocco, which was discussed in Chapter 4. On the Ragusan context, see Zecevic, "Translating Ottoman Justice."

7. *Chronica dell'origine, e progressi della Casa Ottomana* (Vienna 1649); *Chronica dell'origine e progressi della casa Otomana, composta da Saidino Turco eccellentissimo Historico in lingua turca; parte seconda* (Madrid, 1652); *Anales de Egipto* (Madrid 1678). See also Rothman, "Dragomans and Turkish Literature," 402.

8. Reiter, "In Habsburgs sprachlichem Hofdienst," 197–200 and passim. On the intensive diplomacy between Ottomans and Austrian Habsburgs, through official embassies and local borderlands diplomacy, see Radway, *Vernacular Diplomacy*.

9. On the sources pertaining to Urrea and Colville (and earlier bibliography), see Floristán, "Intérpretes de lenguas orientales"; and on Dobelio, see García-Arenal and Rodríguez Mediano, *Orient in Spain*, 245–94.

10. Henin, *Descripción de los reinos*.

11. Malcolm, "*Behemoth Latinus*," 90.

12. García-Arenal and Rodríguez Mediano, *Orient in Spain*, 403.

13. On this figure and later criticism, see Monroe, *Islam and the Arabs*, 30–32. See also González Castrillo, "Un filoarabista de mediados," 121–45.

14. On the comparative history of these institutions and the late foundation of the program for the *jóvenes de lengua*, see Cáceres Würsig, "*Jeunes de langues*," 127–44.

15. Casiri received his appointment as head Arabic librarian in the royal collections (succeeding Andrés de San Juan and winning out over Andres's nephew Juan Amon de San Juan) in 1754 and published the two volumes of the *Bibliotheca Arabico-Hispana Escurialensis* in 1760 and 1770. García Ejarque, *La Real Biblioteca*, 463–65.

16. The San Juan family in particular left their mark on this project. See the provenances in Guillen Robles, *Catálogo de los manuscritos árabes*, 8–16, 50–51, passim.

17. See discussion of the *Libros de rendención* in the BNE in Chapter 4. Also see Hershenzon, *Captive Sea*, 171–74.

18. On this episode, see especially Feria García, "El tratado hispano-marroquï de amistad (I), (II)."

19. Noradounghian, *Recueil d'actes internationaux*, 77, 334. On Ottoman treaties with Europeans in the eighteenth century, see Boogert, *Capitulations*, 19–24.

20. Torrecilla, *Guerras literarias*, 128. On Spain's North African treaties in the 1780s, see Feria García, "El tratado hispano-marroquï de amistad (I)," 11–12.

21. Cole, *Napoleon's Egypt*, 30 and passim.

22. See the recent study and critical edition from 2016, which includes indications to a copious bibliography, see Cadalso, *Cartas Marruecas*.

23. Cadalso opened his novel situating the *Cartas* in line as direct heirs to Cervantes. The first sentence reads, "Since Miguel de Cervantes composed the immortal novel in which he criticized so intelligently some of the customs and vices of our grandfathers—which their grandsons have replaced with others—criticism of the most civilized nations of Europe have multiplied from the pens of authors who are more or less impartial; however, those that have had the most success among men of the world and of letters are those called "Letters" (*Cartas*), which are supposed to have been written in one country or another by travelers who are native to kingdoms that are not only far away but opposite in religion, climate, and government." Cadalso, *Cartas Marruecas*, 109.

24. Cadalso was also strongly influenced by other Enlightenment literature, including Montesquieu's *Persian Letters*, which he took not only as a partial model but also as a platform from which to debate the relative merits of French and Spanish society in an early publication, "Defense of the Spanish Nation against the Persian Letter 78 of Montesquieu." Cañas Murillo, "Introducción" in Cadalso, *Cartas Marruecas*, 46–47.

25. *Natījat al-Ijtihād fī Muhādana wa-l-Jihād*. See Matar, *In the Lands of the Christians*, 116.

26. Cañas Murillo, "Introducción," in Cadalso, *Cartas Marruecas*, 52–54.

27. "Some of the letters maintain all of the style and even the genius (*genio*), shall we say, of the Arabic language, which was their original; their phrases would seem ridiculous to a European, sublime and "Pindarcic" [when set] against the common epistolary style; however, our elocutions would also seem unending to an African. Who would be correct? I don't know. I don't dare to say, nor do I think anyone could say it unless they were neither African nor European. Nature is the only one who could judge, but where would we hear her voice? I don't know either. There is too much confusion among all the voices to hear that of the common mother [tongue?] in the issues which present themselves in the daily life of men." Cadalso, *Cartas Marruecas*, 111.

28. Cadalso, *Cartas Marruecas*, 335. García-Arenal and Rodríguez Mediano, Orient in Spain, 423–24.

29. García Ejarque, *La Real Biblioteca*, 519–20.

30. García Ejarque, *La Real Biblioteca*, 449.

31. Lourido Díaz, "El estudio del árabe; and Lourido Díaz, "El estudio de la lengua árabe."

32. Paz Torres, "Pablo Hodar."

33. Monroe, *Islam and the Arabs*, 44.

34. On the Quranic symbolism of this image of Cidi Hamete's pen in Cervantes, and the symbolism of both authors (fictitious and real) rendering the final volume of the knight's story *maktūb* (divinely inscribed), see López-Baralt, "El calamo supremo."

Bibliography

PRINTED PRIMARY SOURCES AND DOCUMENT COLLECTIONS

An Account of South-West Barbary: Containing what is most remarkable in the territories of the King of Fez and Morocco. Written by a person who had been a slave there. London: Printed for J. Boyer, 1713.

Alarcón y Santón, Maximiliano, and Ramón García de Linares. *Los documentos árabes diplomáticos del Archivo de la corona de Aragón.* Madrid: CSIC, 1940.

Alcalá, Pedro de. *Arte para ligeramente saber la lengua arauiga emendada y añadida y segundaente imprimida.* Granada: Juan Varela de Salamanca, 1505.

Alcalá, Pedro de. *Vocabulista aráuigo en letra castellana.* Granada: Juan Varela de Salamanca, 1505.

Aldrete, Bernardo de. *Vocablos arábigos que ai en el Romance.* In *Origenes de la lengua Española,* coll. Gregorio Mayans i Siscar, 225–34. Madrid: J. de Zuñiga, 1737.

Almosnino, Moses. *Extremos y grandezas de Constantinopla.* Madrid: Francisco Martínez, 1638.

Amador de los Ríos, José. *Memoria histórico-crítica sobre las tréguas celebradas en 1439 entre los reyes de Castilla y de Granada.* Madrid: Real Academia de la Historia, 1879.

Arroyal Espigares, Pedro. *Diplomatario del reino de Granada: Documentos procedentes de la sección Registro General del Sello del Archivo General de Simancas año de 1501.* Monumenta Regni Granatensis Historica, Diplomata 1. Granada: Universidad de Granada, 2005.

Aviso verdadero y lamentable relacion, que haze el capitan don Francisco de Sandoval y Roxas, Cautivo en Fez, al Excelentisimo señor Don Pedro de Aragón, dandole quenta de las sacrilegas acciones que han obrado los perfidos Mahometanos con las Santas Imagenes, y cosas Sagradas que hallaron en la Mamora: Entrega de dicha Plaça: Trato que hizo el Governador della con los Moros; y lo demas que verá el Curioso. Madrid, 1681. In Bauer Landauer, *Papeles de mi archivo,* 2:93–97.

Baeza, Hernando de. *Relaciones de algunos sucesos de los últimos tiempos del reino de Granada.* Edited by Emilio Lafuente y Alcantará. Madrid: Rivadeneyra, 1888.

Bauer Landauer, Ignacio. *Papeles de mi archivo: Relaciones de África.* 6 vols. Madrid: Editorial Ibero-Africano-Americana, 1922–23.

Bejarano, Francisco. *Documentos del reinado de los reyes católicos: Catálogo de los documentos existentes en el Archivo Municipal de Málaga.* Biblioteca Reyes Católicos 8. Madrid: CSIC, 1961.

Bodin, Jean. *Six livres de la République.* Paris: Jacques du Puys, 1576.

Borbón, Faustino de. *Cartas para ilustrar la historia de España árabe.* Madrid: Imprenta de don Blas Román, 1796.

Botero, Giovanni. *The Reason of State.* Translated by P. J. and D. P. Waley. New Haven, CT: Yale University Press, 1954.

Cadalso, José. *Cartas Marruecas*. Edited with "Introducción" and notes by Jesús Cañas Murillo. Vigo: Editorial Academia del Hispanismo, 2016.

The Canons and Decrees of the Council of Trent. Translated by Rev. H. J. Schroeder. Charlotte, NC: TAN Books, 2011.

Cansino, Jacob. "Relación de los servicios del traductor." In *Extremos y grandezas de Constantinopla*, ed. Mosé ben Baruj Almosnino, 20–35. Madrid: Imprenta de Francisco Martinez, 1638.

Castillo, Alonso del. *Sumario é recopilación de todo lo romançado por el liçenciado Alonso del Castillo, romançador del Santo Oficio, desde antes de la guerra del reyno de Granada, y en ella y después que se acabó hasta oy día de la conclusión desta recopilación, ocho días del mes de henero deste presente año de mill e quinientos e setenta e cinco, fecha e recopilada por horden e mandado del Illustrísimo e Reverendísimo Señor don Pedro de Deça, Presidente de la Real Audiencia desta ciudad de Granada e General deste reino, etc., 1575*. Memorial Histórico Español 3 (1852): 1–164.

Catálogo de de los documentos de la Fundación Sergio Fernández (España y Europa). Santiago de Chile: Biblioteca Nacional de Chile, Editorial Andres Bello, 1983.

Cervantes Saavedra, Miguel de. *El ingenioso don Quixote de la Mancha*. Madrid: Juan de la Cuesta, 1605.

Colección de documentos para la historia del reino de Murcia. Nogués: Academia Alfonso X el Sabio, 1969.

Colección de privilegios, franquezas, exenciones y fueros concedidos a varios pueblos y corporaciones de la Corona de Castilla, copiados de orden de S. M., vol. 6. Madrid: Imprenta Real, 1883.

Covarrubias Orozco, Sebastian de. *Tesoro de la lengua castellana o española* [1611]. 2nd corrected ed. Nueva Biblioteca de Erudición y Crítica 7. Madrid: Editorial Castalia, 1995.

Cruces Blanco, Esther, and José María Ruiz Povedano. *Inventario de acuerdos de las actas capitulares del concejo de Málaga (1489–1516)*. Monumenta Regni Granatensis Historica. Granada: Universidad de Granada, 2004.

Documentos das chancelarias reais anteriores a 1531 relativos a Marrocos. Lisbon: Academia das Sciências de Lisboa, 1915.

Documentos de corpo chronologico relativos a Marrocos (1488–1514). Coimbra: Universidade, 1925.

al-Fishtālī, 'Abd al-Azīz. *Manāhil al-Safā'*. Rabat: Maṭbū'āt Wizārat al-Awqāf, 1984.

García-Arenal, Mercedes, Fernando Rodríguez Mediano, and Rachid El Hour, eds. *Cartas marruecas: Documentos de Marruecos en archivos españoles (siglos XVI–XVII)*. Madrid: Consejo Superior de Investigaciones Científicas, 2002.

García Fuentes, José María, ed. *Visitas de la Inquisición al reino de Granada*. Monumenta Regni Granatensis Histórica Actas 3. Granada: University of Granada, 2006.

García Luján, José Antonio. *Documentos de la Casa de Granada: Linaje Granada Venegas, Marqueses de Campotejar*. Huescar: Asociación Cultural Raigadas, 2010.

Garrido Atienza, Miguel. *Las capitulaciones para la entrega de Granada*. Granada, 1910.

Gaspar Remiro, Mariano. *Los últimos pactos y correspondencia íntima entre los Reyes Católicos y Boabdil, sobre la entrega de Granada*. Granada: Universidad de Granada, 1910.

al-Ghassānī, Abū 'Abd Allah Muḥammad bin 'Abd al-Wahab. *Riḥla al-Wazīr fi-l-Iftikāk al-Asīr*. Edited by Abderrahim Banhadda. Tokyo: Research Institute for Languages and Cultures of Asia and Africa, 2005.

González de Santalla, Tirso. *Manuductio ad conuersionem Mahumetanorum in duas partes diuisa*. Tomus Secundus. Madrid: Bernardo de Villa-Diego, 1687.

Gracián de Aldrete, Diego. *Historia de Thucydides que trata de las guerras entre Peleponeses y Athenienses.* Salamanca, Juan de Canova, 1564.

Gracián de la Madre de Dios, Jerónimo. *Tratado de la rendención de cuativos.* Madrid: Biblioteca de la Historia, 2006.

Guadix, Diego de. *Recopilación de algunos nombres arábigos que los árabes pusieron a algunas ciudades y otras muchas cosas.* Madrid: Trea, 2005.

Guerra de Lorca, Pedro. *Catecheses mystagogicae pro advenis ex sexta Mahometana.* Madrid: Pedro Madrigal, 1586.

Guerrero Lafuente, María Dolores. *La memoria de la ciudad: El segundo libro de actas del cabildo de Granada (1512–1516).* Monumenta Regni Granatensis Histórica, Acta 4. Granada: University of Granada, 2007.

Gurmendi, Francisco de. *Doctrina phísica y moral de príncipes.* Madrid: Andrés de Parra, 1615.

Gurmendi, Francisco de. *Libro de los cualidades del rey.* 1621. Eusko Legebiltzarra—Parlamento Vasco, http://www.liburuklik.euskadi.eus/handle/10771/8887.

al-Ḥajarī, Aḥmad ibn Qāsim ibn. *Kitāb Nāṣir al-Dīn ʿalā ʾl-Qawm al-Kāfirīn.* 2nd ed. Ed. and trans. P. S. Van Koningsveld, Q. al-Samarrai, and G. A. Wiegers. Madrid: Consejo Superior de Investigaciones Científicas, 2015.

Henin, Jorge. *Descripción de los reinos de Marruecos: (1603–1613), Memorial de Jorge de Henin.* Edited by Torcuato Perez de Cuzmán. Rabat: Universidad Mohamed V, 1997.

Hurtado de Mendoza, Diego. *Guerra de Granada, que hizo el rey don Felipe II contra los moriscos de aquel reyno, sus rebeldes.* Lisbon: Luis Tribaldos de Toledo, 1627.

Islamic Law Materialized. https://www.ilm-project.net/en/front

Koningsveld, P. S. van, and Gerard Wiegers. "Five Documents Illustrating the Early Activities of Miguel de Luna and Alonso del Castillo in Deciphering and Translating the Arabic Passages of the Parchment found in the Torre Turpiana in Granada." In *Nuevas aportaciones*, ed. García-Ferrer, García Valverde, and López Carmona, 217–58.

Londaiz, Pedro. *Informe juridico militar en defensa del Maestro de Campo Don Juan de Peñalosa y Estrada, Governador que fué de la Plaça de San Miguel ultramar, conocida vulgarmente con el Nombre de Maamora-Y en que se defienden tambien D. Bartolomé de Larrea, Veedor de aquella Plaça, y el Capitan Juan Rodriguez, en la Causa Criminal, que se sigue contra ellos por el señor Fiscal del Consejo Supremo de la Guerra, que los supone culpados en la pérdida de aquella Fuerça.* N.p., 1681.

López Tamarid, Francisco. "Compendio de algunos vocablos arabigos." In *Origenes de la lengua española*, coll. Gregorio Mayans i Siscar, 233–67. Madrid: J. de Zuñiga 1737.

Luna, Miguel de. *The history of the conquest of Spain by the Moors together with the life of the most illustrious monarch Almanzor: And of the several revolutions of the mighty empire of the Caliphs, and of the African kingdoms / composed in Arabick by Abulcacim Tariff Abentariq, one of the generals in that Spanish expedition; and translated into Spanish by Michael de Luna, interpreter to Philip the Second; now made English.* Translated by Michael Taubmann. London: F. Leach, 1687.

Luna, Miguel de. *Segunda parte de la historia de la Perdida de España, y vida del Rey Jacob Almançor; en la qual el Autor Tarif Abentarique prosigue la primera parte, dando particular cuenta de todos los sucessos de España, y Africa, y las Arabias, hasta el Rey Don Fruela.* Granada: Sebastián de Mena, 1600.

Luna, Miguel de. *La verdadera historia del rey don Rodrigo en la cual se trata la cavsa principal de la pèrdida de España, y la conquista que de ella hizo Miramolin Almançor, Rey que fuè de Africa, y de als Arabias; y vida del Rey Jacob Almançor. Compuesta por el Sabio Alcayde*

Abulcacim Tarif, de Nacion Arabe. Nuevamente Traducida de Lengua Arabiga por Miguel de Luna, vezino de Granada, Intreprete[sic] de el Rey, nuestro señor. Granada: Rene Rabut, 1592; Granada: Sebastián de Mena, 1599.

al-Maqqarī, Aḥmad ibn Muḥammad. *Rawdat al-'As.* Rabat: al-Maktabah al-Malikiyyah, 1983.

Mariño Gómez, Primitivo. *Carlos V: Norte de África.* Tratados internacionales de España. Madrid: CSIC, 1980.

Mármol Carvajal, Luis del. *Descripcion general de Africa, Parte I.* Granada: Rene Rabut, 1573. Facsimile ed. Madrid: CSIC, 1953.

Mármol Carvajal, Luis del. *Historia del rebelion y castigo de los moriscos del reyno de Granada.* Málaga: Juan Rene, 1600.

Meneses García, Emilio. *Correspondencia Del Conde de Tendilla (1510–1513),* vol. 2. Archivo Documental Español 31. Madrid: Real Academia de la Historia, 1974.

Molina López, Emilio, and María Carmen Jiménez Mata. *Documentos árabes del Archivo Municipal de Granada.* Granada: Ayuntamiento de Granada, 2004.

Morales, Baltasar de. *Diálogo de las Guerras de Orán (1543), Guerras de los españoles en África, 1542, 1543, y 1632, Colección de libros españoles raros o curiosos,* vol. 15:239–379. Madrid: Imprenta de Miguel Ginsesta, 1881.

Moreno Trujillo, María Amparo. *La memoria de la ciudad: El primer libro de actas del cabildo de Granada (1497–1502).* Monumenta Regni Granatensis Histórica, Acta 2. Granada: Universidad de Granada, 2005.

Moreno Trujillo, María Amparo, Juan M. Obra Sierra, and María José Osorio Pérez. *Escribir y gobernar: El último registro de correspondencia del Conde de Tendilla (1513–1515).* Monumenta Regni Granatensis Historica, 2. Granada: Universidad de Granada, 2007.

Nebrija, Antonio de. *Vocabulario español-latino.* Salamanca, 1495.

Noradounghian, Gabriel Effendi. *Recueil d'actes internationaux de l'empire ottoman.* Paris: Pichon, 1902.

Núñez Muley, Francisco. *A Memorandum for the President of the Royal Audiencia and Chancery Court of the City and Kingdom of Granada.* Edited and translated by Vincent Barletta, Chicago: University of Chicago Press, 2007.

Obra Sierra, Juan. *Catálogo de protocolos granadinos: 1505–1515.* Granada: Archivo Histórico de Protocolos de Granada, 1989.

Ordenanzas de Granada de 1552. Facsimile ed. Granada: Ayuntamiento de Granada, 2000.

Orozco, Alonso de. *Catecismo provechoso* in *Obras Completas de Alonoso de Orozco,* 1: 607–724. Madrid: Biblioteca de Autores Christianos, 2001.

Osorio Pérez, María José, and Emilio de Santiago Simón. *Documentos arábigo-granadinos romanceados.* Granada: Centro de Estudios Históricos de Granada y su Reino, 1986.

Pérez, Joesph. *Dissertationes ecclesiasticae: In quibus pleraque ad historiam Ecclesiasticam et politicam Hispanie, remque diplomaticam spectantia accurate discutiuntur.* Salamanca: Lucas Perez, 1688.

Pérez de Ayala, Martín. *Doctrina cristiana en lengua arábiga y castellana para la instrucción de los moriscos del Ilustrísimo Sr. Dn. Martín Pérez de Ayala* [1566]. Valencia: Imprenta Hijos de F. Vives Mora, 1911.

Pérez de Ayala, Martín. *Sínodo de la Diócesis de Guadix y Baza.* Granada: Universidad de Granada, 1994.

Pérez de Ayala, Martín, and Juan de Ribera. *Catechismo para la instrucción de los nuevos convertidos de moros.* Valencia: Pedro Patricio Mey, 1599.

Pérez de Chinchón, Bernardo. *Libro llamado Antialcoran, que quiere dezir contra el Alcoran de Mahoma, repartido en veynteyseys sermons.* Salamanca: Juan y Andres Renaut, 1595. Modern edition: *Antialcorano. Diálogos cristianos: Conversion y evangelización de moriscos.* Edited by Francisco Pons Fuster. Alicante: Universidad de Alicante, 2000.

Pérez de Hita, Ginés. *Historia de los vandos de los Zegríes y Abencerrages Caualleros Moros de Granada, de las Guerras Ciuiles que huuo en ella, y batallas paraticulares que huuo en la Vega entre Moros y Cristianos, hasta que el Rey Don Fernando Quinto la ganó. Agora nuevamente sacado de un libro Aráuigo, cuyo autor de vista fue un Moro llamado Aben Hamen, natural de Granada. Tratando desde su fundación. Traduzido en castellano por Gines Perez de Hita, vezino de la ciudad de Murcia.* Zaragoza: Impreso en casa de Miguel Ximeno Sanchez, 1595.

Pérez de Hita, Ginés. *Segunda parte de las Guerras civiles de Granada, y de los crueles vandos entre los convertidos moros y vezinos cristianos, con el levantamiento de todo el reyno y última reuelion, sucedida en el año 1568, y assí mismo se pone su total ruina y destierro de los moros por toda Castilla, con el fin de las Granadinas Guerras por el rey nuestro Señor Don Felipe Segundo deste nombre.* Barcelona: Estevan, 1619.

El perfume de la amistad: Correspondencia diplomática árabe en archivos españoles (siglos XIII–XVII). Barcelona: Archivo de la Corona de Aragón, 2009.

Primaudaie, F. Élie de la. *Documents inédits sur l'histoire de l'occupation espagnole en Afrique (1506-1574).* Alger: A. Jourdan, 1875.

Rasā'il al-Sa'adiyyah. Edited by Abdallah Gannun. Tetouan: Ma'had Mawlay al-Hassan, 1954.

Respuesta que da la verdad a vna carta que con nombre del Capitan Don Francisco de Sandobal y Rojas, fu[e] fecha en Fez â catorze de Mayo deste año de ochenta y vno, parece averse escrito—segun la imprenta—al Excelentissimo señor Don Pedro Antonio de Aragon, y se ha impresso en Madrid, y Sevilla, dando cuenta â Su Excelencia de la perdida de la Mamora. Dirigida a el mismo excelentissimo señor, en defensa del Maestre de campo Don Juan de Peñalosa y Estrada, Governador que fue de la dicha plaza, etc. Cádiz, 1681.

Ribadeneira, Pedro de. *Tratado de la religion y virtudes que debe tener el príncipe cristiano para gobernar y conservar sus estados, contra lo que Nicolas Maquiavelo y los politicos deste tiempo enseñan.* Madrid: Pedro de Madrigal, 1595.

Ripa, Cesare. *Iconología.* Siena: Florimi, 1613.

Rojas, Juan Luis de. *Relaciones de algunos svcesos prostreros de Berbería. Salida de los Moriscos de España, y entrega de Alarache.* Lisbon: Printed by Iorge Rodriguez, 1613.

Saldanha, Antonio de. *Crónica de Almançor, Sultão de Marrocos (1578-1603) de António de Saldanha.* Edited by Antonio Dias Farinha, trans. Léon Bourdon. Lisboa: Instituto de Investigação Científica Tropical, 1997.

al-Shādhalī, 'Abd al-Ṭarīf. *Nuṣūṣ al-Itifāqiyyāt Dawliyya Mubrama bayna al-Mamlakah al-Maghribiyyah wa Duwal Ajnabiyyah,* vol. 1. Rabat: al-Maṭba'ah al-Malikiyyah, 2006.

Siete Partidas. Madrid: Imprenta Real, 1807.

Sigüenza, José de. *Historia de la orden de San Jerónimo* [1605], 2 vols. Valladolid: Junta de Castilla y Leon, 2000.

Sotomayor y Valenzuela, Luis Joseph. *Breve relación y compendioso epítome de la general expulsión de los Hebreos de la Iuderia de Orán.* [Oran]: 1670. Modern edition: *Brève relation de l'expulsion des Juifs d'Oran en 1669.* Translated by Jean-Frédéric Schaub. Paris: Éditions Bouchène, 1998.

Les sources inédites de l'histoire du Maroc: Archives et bibliothèques d'Angleterre, series 1, 2 vols. Paris: Geuther, 1918–1925.

Les sources inédites de l'histoire du Maroc: Archives et bibliothèques de France, series 1, 3 vols. Paris: Geuther, 1905–1911.

Les sources inédites de l'histoire du Maroc: Archives et bibliothèques de Portugal, series 1, 5 vols. Paris: Geuther, 1934–1953.

Les sources inédites de l'histoire du Maroc: Archives et bibliothèques d'Espagne, series 1, 3 vols. Paris: Geuther 1921–1961.

Les sources inédites de l'histoire du Maroc: Archives et bibliothèques des Pays-Bas, series 1, 6 vols. Paris: Geuther, 1906–1928.

Suárez Montañés, Diego. *Historia del maestre último que fue de Montesa y de su hermano don Felipe de Borja: La manera como gobernaron las memorables plazas de Orán y Mazalquivir, reinos de Tremecén y Ténez, en África, siendo allí capitanes generales, uno en pos del otro, como aquí se narra.* Edited by Beatriz Alonso Acero and Miguel Angel de Bunes Ibarra. Valencia: Institució Alfons el Magnànim, 2005.

Synodicon Hispanum, 11 vols. Madrid: Biblioteca de Autores Cristianos, 1981.

Synodus dioecesana Valentiae celebrata praeside Martino Ayala Archiepiscopo Valentino. Valencia: Ioannis Mey, 1566.

Talavera, Hernando de. *Breue y muy prouechosa doctrina de lo que deue saber todo christiano.* Granada: Meinardo Ungut and Juan Pegnitzer, 1496.

Torre, Antonio de la. *Documentos sobre relaciones internacionales de los reyes católicos*, 6 vols. Madrid: CSIC, 1949–1951.

SECONDARY SOURCES

Abad Merino, Mercedes. "'Aquí hay necesidad de persona capaz en muchas lenguas': El oficio de intéprete en las últimas fronteras de castilla." *Tonos: Revista Electrónica de Estudios Filológicos* 10 (2005), https://www.um.es/tonosdigital/znum10/estudios/A-Abad.htm.

Abad Merino, Mercedes. "Exeas y alfaqueques: Aproximación a la figura del intérprete de árabe en el período fronterizo (s. XIII–XV)." In *Homenaje al profesor Estanislao Ramón Trives*, vol. 1, ed. Agustín Vera Luján, Ramón Almela Pérez, José María Jiménez Cano, and Dolores Anunciación Igualada Belchí, 35–50. Murcia: Universidad de Murcia, 2003.

Abad Merino, Mercedes. "La traducción de cartas árabes en un pleito granadino del siglo XVI: El fenómeno del romanceado como acto judicial; Juan Rodríguez y Alonso del Castillo ante un mismo documento." *Al-Qantara* 32, no. 2 (2011): 481–518.

Aguilar Piñal, Francisco. *Bibliografía de autores españoles del siglo XVIII*, vol. 9. Madrid: CSIC, 1999.

Alaoui, Youssef el. "Ignacio de las Casas, jesuita y morisco." *Sharq al-Andalus* 14–15 (1997): 317–39.

Alaoui, Youssef el. "El jesuita Ignacio de las Casas y la defensa de la lengua árabe: Memorial al padre Cristobal de los Cobos, provincial de Castilla (1607)." *AREAS: Revista Internacional de Ciencias Sociales* 30 (2011): 11–28.

Alaoui, Youssef el. *Jésuites, morisques et indiens: Étude comparative des méthodes d'évangélisation de la Compagnie de Jésus d'après les traités de José de Acosta (1588) et d'Ignacio de las Casas.* Paris: Honoré Champion, 2006.

Alarcón y Santón, Maximiliano, trans. *Siráj: Lámpara de los príncipes por Abubéquer de Tortosa*, 2 vols. Madrid: Institutio de Valencia de don Juan, 1930–31.

Albarracín Navarro, Joaquín. *El marquesado de Cenete: Historia, toponomia, y onomástica*, 2 vols. Granada: Universidad de Granada, 1986.

Alijo Hidalgo, Francisco. "Privilegios a las plazas frontizeras con el reino de Granada." In *Estudios sobre Málaga y el Reino de Granada en el V Centenario de la Conquista*, ed. José Enrique López de Coca Castañer, 19–35. Málaga: Servicio de Publicaciones Diputación Provincal de Málaga, 1987.

Alonso Acero, Beatriz. *Orán-Mazalquivir, 1589–1639: Una sociedad española en la frontera de Berbería*. Madrid: Consejo Superior de Investigaciones Científicas, 2000.

Alonso Acero, Beatriz. *Sultanes de Berbería en tierras de la cristiandad: exilio musulmán, conversión y asimilación en la monarquía hispánica, siglos XVI-XVII*. Barcelona: Ediciones Bellaterra, 2006.

Alonso Acero, Beatriz, and José Luis Gonzálo Sánchez-Molero. "Alá en el corte de un príncipe cristiano: El horizonte musulmán en la formación de Felipe II." *Torre de los Lujanes: Boletín de la Real Sociedad Económica Matritense de Amigos del País* 35 (1998): 109–40.

Alonso García, David. "La financiación de las Guardas de Castilla a principios de la Edad Moderna." In *La financiación de las Guardas de Castilla a principios de la Edad Moderna*, ed. Enrique García Hernán and Davide Maffi, 787–804. Madrid: CSIC, 2006.

Alvira Cabrer, Martín. "La imagen del *Miramolin* al-Nasir (1199–1213) en las fuentes cristianas del siglo XIII." *Anuario de Estudios Medievales* 26 (1996): 1003–28.

Amelang, James S. *Historas paralelas: Judeoconversos y moriscos en la España moderna*. Madrid: Akal, 2011.

Andrés, Gregorio de. *Catálogo de los codices griegos de la Biblioteca Nacional*. Madrid: Ministerio de la Cultura, 1987.

Arias Torres, Juan Pablo. "Bibliografía sobre las traducciones del Alcorán en el ámbito hispáno." *TRANS 11* (2007): 261–72.

Arias Torres, Juan Pablo, and Manuel C. Feria García. "Escrituras árabes granadinas romanceadas: Una mina a cielo abierto para la historia de la traducción y la traductologia." *Trans 8* (2004): 179–182.

Arias Torres, Juan Pablo, and Manuel C. Feria García. *Los traductores de árabe del Estado español: Del Protectorado a nuestros días*. Barcelona: Ediciones Bellaterra, 2013.

Arié, Rachel. *L'Espagne musulmane au temps des Nasrides*. Paris: Boccard, 1990.

Arribas Palau, Mariano. "A propósito de una carta de Carlos II a Mawlāy Ismā'īl." *Al-Qantara* 10, no. 2 (1989): 565–69.

Arribas Palau, Mariano. "De nuevo sobre la embajada de al-Gassani (1690–1691)." *Al-Qantara* 6, no.1 (1986): 199–289.

Asenjo Sedano, Carlos. "Estudio preliminar." In *Martín de Ayala, Sínodo de la Diócesis de Guadix y Baza*, vii–xlviii. Facsimile ed. Granada: Archivum, 1994.

Azcona, Tarcicio de. *Isabel la Católica: Estudio crítico de su vida y su reinado*. Madrid: Editoral Católica, 1964.

Balagna Cousou, Josée. *L'imprimerie arabe en occident (XVIe, XVIIe, et XVIIIe siècles)*. Paris: Maisonneuve et Larose, 1984.

Barceló, Carmen, and Ana Labarta, *Archivos moriscos: Textos árabes de la minoria islámica valenciana 1401–1608*. Valencia: Universitat de València, 2009.

Barceló, Carmen, and Ana Labarta. "La toponimía en el vocabulista de Pedro de Alcalá." In *Homenaje al profesor José María Fórneas Besteiro*, Concepción Castillo Castillo and Amador Díaz García, ed. 1: 337–56. Granada: Universidad de Granada, 1995.

Barkey, Karen. "Aspects of Legal Pluralism in the Ottoman Empire." In *Legal Pluralism and Empires*, ed. Benton and Ross, 83–108.

Barletta, Vincent. *Covert Gestures: Crypto-Islamic Literature as Cultural Practice in Early Modern Spain*. Minneapolis: University of Minnesota Press, 2005.

Barrios Aguilera, Manuel, and Mercedes García-Arenal, eds. *Los plomos del Sacromonte: Invención y Tesoro*. València: Universitat de València; Granada: Universidad de Granada; Zaragoza: Universidad de Zaragoza, 2006.

Bataillon, Marcel. "L'arabe a Salamanque au temps de la Renaissance." *Hespéris* 21 (1935): 1–17.

Bauman, Richard, and Charles L. Briggs. *Voices of Modernity: Language Ideologies and the Politics of Inequality*. Cambridge: Cambridge University Press, 2003.

Benítez Sánchez-Blanco, Rafael. *Heróicas decisiones: La monarquía católica y los moriscos valencianos*. Valencia: Institució Alfons el Magnanim, 2001.

Benítez Sánchez-Blanco, Rafael. "De Pablo a Saulo: Traducción, crítica, y denuncia de los libros plúmbeos por el Padre Ignacio de las Casas, S. J." *Al-Qantara* 23, no. 2 (2002): 403–36.

Benítez Sánchez-Blanco, Rafael. "The Religious Debate in Spain." In *Expulsion of the Moriscos*, ed. García-Arenal and Wiegers, 101–30.

Bennassar, Bartolomé. *Les chrétiens d'Allah: L'histoire extraordinaire des renégats. XVIe et XVIIe siècles*. Paris: Perrin, 1989.

Benton, Lauren, and Richard J. Ross. "Empires and Legal Pluralism: Jurisdiction, Sovereignty, and Political Imagination in the Early Modern World." In *Legal Pluralism and Empires*, ed. Benton and Ross, 1–17.

Benton, Lauren, and Richard Ross, eds. *Legal Pluralism and Empires: 1500–1900*. New York: New York University Press, 2013.

Bergman, Ted L. L. *The Art of Humour in the* Teatro Breve *and* Comedias *of Calderón de la Barca*. London: Tamesis, 2003.

Bernabé Pons, Luís. "The lead books of Sacromonte." In *Christian-Muslim Relations: A Bibliographical History*, 6: 273–81. Leiden: Brill, 2014.

Bernabé Pons, Luís. "Aspectos lingüísticos árabes y religiosos islámicos en los estudios sobre mudéjares y moriscos (1975–2005)." In *Actas del X Simposio Internacional de Mudejarismo: 30 años de mudejarismo, memoria y futuro*, 297–330. Teruel: Centro de Estudios Mudéjares, 2007.

Bernabé Pons, Luis. "Introducción." In Luna, *La verdadera historia del rey don Rodrigo*, vii–lxx. Facsimile ed. Granada: Archivum, 2001.

Bevilacqua, Alexander. *The Arabic Republic of Letters: Islam and the European Enlightenment*. Cambridge, MA: Harvard University Press, 2018.

Biasiori, Lucio, and Giuseppe Marcocci, eds. *Machiavelli and Islam: Reorienting the Foundations of Modern Political Thought*. Cham, Switzerland: Palgrave, 2016.

Bireley, Robert. *The Counter-Reformation Prince*. Chapel Hill: University of North Carolina Press, 1990.

Bisaha, Nancy. *Creating East and West: Renaissance Humanists and the Ottoman Turks*. Philadelphia: University of Pennsylvania Press, 2010.

Black, Antony. *The History of Islamic Political Thought*. London: Routledge, 2001.

Blázquez Miguel, Juan. "Catálogo de los procesos inquisitoriales del Tribunal del Santo Oficio de Murcia." *Murgetana* 74 (1987): 5–109.

Bleznick, Donald. "Spanish Reaction to Machiavelli in the Sixteenth and Seventeenth Centuries." *Journal of the History of Ideas* 19, no. 4 (1958): 542–50.

Boogert, Maurits H. van den. *Capitulations and the Ottoman Legal System*. Leiden: Brill, 2005.

Boronat y Barrachina, Pascual. *Los moriscos españoles y su expulsión.* Valencia: Servicio de Reproducción de Libros, Librerías Paris-Valencia, 1901.

Borovaya, Olga. *The Beginnings of Ladino Literature: Moses Almosnino and His Readers.* Bloomington: Indiana University Press, 2017.

Boubaker, Sadok. "L'empereur Charles Quint et le sultan hafside Mawlāy al-Ḥasān (1525–1550)." In *Empreintes espagnoles dans l'histoire Tunisienne,* ed. Sadok Boubakker and Clara Ilham Álvarez Dopico, 13–82. Gijón: Trea, 2011.

Bourdieu, Pierre. *Langauge and Symbolic Power.* Cambridge, MA: Harvard University Press, 1991.

Bouza, Fernando. "Necesidad, negocio y don: Usos de la traducción en la cultura del siglo de oro." In *La traducción cultural en la europa moderna,* ed. Peter Burke and R. Po-Hsia Chia, 269–312. Madrid: Akal, 2007.

Boyano Guerra, Isabel. "Al-Ḥaŷarī y su traducción del pergamino de la Torre Turpiana." In *¿La historia inventada? Los libros plúmbeos y el legado sacromontano,* ed. Manuel Barrios Aguilera and Mercedes García-Arenal Rodríguez, 137–57. Granada, Universidad de Granada, 2008.

Braudel, Fernand. *The Mediterranean and the Mediterranean World in the Age of Philip II,* 2 vols. New York: Harper & Row, 1972.

Braun, Harald. "Making the Canon? The Early Reception of the *République* in Castilian Political Thought." In *The Reception of Bodin,* ed. Howell Lloyd, 257–92. Leiden: Brill, 2013.

Bravo, Paloma. "La présence de Tacite dans *Guerra de Granada* de Diego Hurtado de Mendoza." In *Tacite et le tacitisme en Europe à l'époque modern,* ed. Alexandra Merle and Alicia Oïffer-Bomsel, 399–414. Paris: Honoré Champion, 2017.

Brendecke, Arndt. *The Empirical Empire: Spanish Colonial Rule and the Politics of Knowledge.* Berlin: De Gruyter, 2016.

Brendecke, Arndt, and María Ángeles Martín Romera. "El *Habitus* del oficial real: Ideal, percepción, y ejercicio del cargo en la monarquía hispánica (siglos XV–XVII)." *Studia historica: Historia moderna* 39, no. 1 (2017): 23–51.

Brockey, Liam. *Journey to the East: The Jesuit Mission to China, 1579–1724.* Cambridge, MA: Harvard University Press, 2007.

Bullman, William J. *Anglican Enlightenment: Orientalism, Religion and Politics in England and its Empire, 1648–1715.* Cambridge: Cambridge University Press, 2015.

Bunes Ibarra, Miguel Ángel de. "El enfrentamiento con el Islam en el Siglo de Oro: Los Antialcoranes." *Edad de Oro* 8 (1989): 41–58.

Bunes Ibarra, Miguel Ángel de. "Entre la paz y la guerra: Tratados de amistad y treguas entre los Austrias españoles y el mundo musulmán en los siglos XVI y XVII." In *El perfume de la Amistad,* 68–91.

Bunes Ibarra, Miguel Ángel de. "Felipe II y el Mediterráneo: La frontera olvidada y la frontera presente de la monarquía católica." In *Felipe II (1527–1598): Europa y la monarquía católica,* ed. José Martínez Millán, 1:97–110. Madrid: Parteluz, 1998.

Bunes Ibarra, Miguel Ángel de. *La imagen de los musulmanes y del norte de África en la españa de los siglos XVI y XVII: Los caracteres de una hostilidad.* Madrid: CSIC, 1989.

Burbank, Jane, and Frederick Cooper. "Rules of Law, Politics of Empire." In *Legal Pluralism and Empires,* ed. Benton and Ross, 279–93.

Burke, Peter. "Cultures of Translation in Early Modern Europe." In *Cultural Translation in Early Modern Europe,* ed. Peter Burke and R. Po-chia Hsia, 7–38. Cambridge: Cambridge University Press, 2007.

Burke, Peter. "Introduction." In *The Social History of Language*, ed. Peter Burke and Roy Porter, 1–20. Cambridge: Cambridge University Press, 1987.

Burke, Peter. *Languages and Communities in Early Modern Europe*. Cambridge: Cambridge University Press, 2004.

Burman, Thomas. *Reading the Qur'ān in Latin Christendom, 1140–1560*. Philadelphia: University of Pennsylvania Press, 2007.

Burns, Robert I. *Islam Under the Crusaders: Colonial Survival in the Thirteenth-Century Kingdom of Valencia*. Princeton, NJ: Princeton University Press, 1973.

Burns, Robert I. *Jews in the Notarial Culture: Latinate Wills in Mediterranean Spain, 1250–1350*. Berkeley: University of California Press, 1996.

Burns, Robert I. *Medieval Colonialism: Postcrusade Exploitation of Medieval Valencia*. Princeton, NJ: Princeton University Press, 1975.

Burns, Robert I. *Muslims, Christians, and Jews in the Crusader Kingdom of Valencia*. New York: Cambridge University Press, 1984.

Burns, Robert I. "The Significance of the Frontier in the Middle Ages." In *Medieval Frontier Societies*, ed. Robert Bartlett and Angus MacKay, 307–31. Oxford: Clarendon Press, 1989.

Burns, Robert I., and Paul Chevedden. *Negotiating Cultures: Bilingual Surrender Treaties in Muslim-Crusader Spain Under James the Conqueror*. Leiden: Brill, 1999.

Burns, Robert I., and Paul Chevedden. "Los tratados bilingües de rendición en la conquista de Valencia." In *Sevilla 1248: Congreso Internacional Conmemorativo del 750 Aniversario de la Conquista de la Ciudad de Sevilla por Fernando III, Rey de Castilla y León, Sevilla, Real Alcázar, 23–27 de noviembre de 1998*, 259–64. Seville: Centro de Estudios Ramón Arces, 2000.

Busic, Jason David. "Saving the Lost Sheep: Mission and Culture in Pedro Guerra de Lorca's *Catecheses mystagogicae pro aduenis ex secta Mahometana: Ad Parochos, et Potestates* (1586)." PhD diss., Ohio State University, 2009.

Byrne, Susan. *Law and History in Cervantes' "Don Quixote."* University of Toronto Press, 2012.

Cabanelas, Dario. "Cartas del sultán de Marruecos Ahmad al-Mansur a Felipe II." *Al-Andalus* 23, no. 1 (1958): 19–47.

Cabanelas, Dario. "Diego Marín, Agente de Felipe II en Marruecos." *MEAH* 31, no.1 (1972): 7–35.

Cabanelas, Dario. *El morisco granadino Alonso del Castillo*. Granada: Universidad de Granada, 1965.

Cabanelas, Dario. "Otras cartas del sultán de Marruecos Ahmad al-Mansur a Felipe II." *MEAH* 7, no. 1 (1958): 7–17.

Cabanelas, Dario. "Pedro Venegas de Córdoba, Embajador de Felipe II en Marruecos." *MEAH* 32, no. 1 (1973): 129–44.

Cabrillana, Nicolas. *Almería morisca*. Granada: Universidad de Granada, 1982.

Cáceres Würsig, Ingrid. "Breve historia de la Secretaria de Lenguas." *Meta* 49, no. 3 (2004): 609–28.

Cáceres Würsig, Ingrid. *Historia de la traducción en la administración y en las relaciones internacionales en España (s. xvi–xix)*. Soria: Vertere, 2004.

Cáceres Würsig, Ingrid. "The *jeunes de langues* in the Eighteenth Century: Spain's First Diplomatic Interpreters on the European Model." *Interpreting* 14, no. 2 (2012): 127–44.

Calafat, Guillaume. "Les interprètes de la diplomatie en Méditeranée. Traiter à Alger (1680–1690)." In *Les musulmanes dans l'histoire de l'Europe*. ed. Dakhlia and Kaiser, 2:371–410.

Calafat, Guillaume, and Cesare Santus. "Les avatars du 'Turc': Esclaves et commerçants musulmans à Livourne (1600–1750)." In *Les musulmans dans l'histoire de l'Europe: I. Une intégration invisible*, ed. Jocelyn Dakhlia and Bernard Vincent, 471–522. Paris: Albin Michel, 2011.

Carande, Ramón. *Carlos V y sus banqueros: La hacienda de Castilla*, vol. 2. Madrid: Sociedad de Estudios y Publicaciones, 1949.

Cardaillac, Louis, ed. *Les morisques et l'Inquisition*. Paris: Publisud, 1990.

Carlos Morales, Carlos Javier de. *Carlos V y el crédito de Castilla: El tesorero general Francisco de Vargas y la Hacienda Real entre 1516 y 1524*. Madrid: Sociedad Estatal para la Conmemoración de los Centenarios de Felipe II y Carlos V, 2000.

Caro Baroja, Julio. *Los judíos en la España moderna y contemporánea*, 3 vols. Madrid: Ediciones Arion, 1962.

Caro Baroja, Julio. *Los moriscos del Reino de Granada: Ensayo de historia social*. Madrid: ISTMO, 1991.

Caro Baroja, Julio. *Una visión de Marruecos a mediados del siglo XVI, la del primer historiador de los "Xarifes", Diego de Torres*. Madrid: Instituto de Estudios Africanos, 1956.

Carrasco Machado, Ana Isabel. "Antonio García de Villepando." In *Christian-Muslim Relations: A Bibliographical History*, ed. David Thomas and John Chesworth, 6:49–53. Leiden: Brill, 2015.

Carrasco Urgoiti, Maria Soledad. *El moro de Granada en la literatura*. Reprint, Madrid: University of Granada 1989.

Castries, Henri de. "Les signes de validation des chérifs saadiens." *Hespéris* (1921): 231–52.

Catlos, Brian. *Kingdoms of Faith: A New History of Islamic Spain*. New York: Basic Books, 2018.

Catlos, Brian. *Muslims of Medieval Latin Christendom, c. 1050–1614*. Cambridge: Cambridge University Press, 2014.

Catlos, Brian. "Ethno-Religious Minorities." *A Comanion to Mediterranean History*, ed. Peregrine Horden and Sharon Kinoshita, 361–77. West Sussex: Wiley Blackwell, 2014.

Catlos, Brian. *The Victors and the Vanquished: Christians and Muslims of Catalonia and Aragon, 1050–1300*. Cambridge: Cambridge University Press, 2004.

Certeau, Michel de. *The Practice of Everyday Life*. Berkeley: University of California Press, 2008.

Christian, William. *Local Religion in Sixteenth-Century Spain*. Princeton, NJ: Princeton University Press, 1989.

Ciscar Pallarés, Eugenio. "'Algarabía' y 'algemía': Precisiones sobre la lengua de los moriscos en el Reino de Valencia." *Al-Qantara* 15, no 1 (1994): 131–62.

Ciscar Pallarés, Eugenio. *La justicia del abad: Justicia señorial y sociedad en el reino de Valencia*. Valencia: Institució Alfons el Magnànim, 2009.

Colás Latorre, Gregorio. "Treinte años de historiografía morisca." In *Actas del X Simposio Internacional del Mudejarismo, Teruel, 14–16 septiembre 2005*, 643–84. Teruel: Centro de Estudios Mudéjares, 2007.

Cole, Juan. *Napoleon's Egypt: Invading the Middle East*. New York: Palgrave 2007.

Coleman, David. *Creating Christian Granada: Society and Religious Culture in an Old-World Frontier City, 1492–1600*. Ithaca, NY: Cornell University Press, 2003.

Colombo, Emanuele. "'Even Among the Turks,' Tirso González de Santalla (1624–1705) and Islam." *Studies in the Spirituality of Jesuits* 44, no. 3 (2012): 1–41.

Colombo, Emanuele. "'Infidels' at Home: Jesuits and Muslim Slaves in Seventeenth-Century Naples and Spain." *Journal of Jesuit Studies* 1 (2014): 192–211.

Colombo, Emanuele. "Jesuits and Islam in Seventeenth-Century Europe: War, Preaching, and Conversions." In *Cultura e religione del Seicento europeo di fronte all'Islam*, ed. Bernard

Heyberger, Mercedes García-Arenal, Emanuele Colombo, and Paola Vismara, 315–40. Milan-Genova: Marietti, 2009.

Colombo, Emanuele. "Juan de Almarza," In *Christian-Muslim Relations: A Bibliographical History*, 9:339–42. Leiden: Brill, 2017.

Colombo, Emanuele. "A Muslim Turned Jesuit: Baldassare Loyola Mandes (1631–1677)." *Journal of Early Modern History* 17, nos. 5–6 (2013): 479–504.

Colominas Aparicio, Mònica. *The Religious Polemics of the Muslims of Late Medieval Christian Iberia.* Leiden: Brill, 2018.

Conde Pazos, Miguel. "La embajada turca en Madrid y el envío de Alegreto de Allegretti a Constantinopla (1649–1650)." *Libros de las Cortes* (2011): 10–17.

Constable, Olivia Remie. *To Live Like a Moor: Christian Perceptions of Muslim Identity in Medieval and Early Modern Spain.* Edited by Robin Vose. Philadelphia: University of Pennsylvania Press, 2018.

Corriente, Federico. *A Dictionary of Andalusi Arabic,* Leiden: Brill, 1997.

Corriente, Federico, Christophe Pereira, and Ángeles Vicente. *Aperçu grammatical du faisceau dialectal arabe andalou.* Berlin: De Gruyter, 2015.

Cory, Stephen. *Reviving the Islamic Caliphate in Early Modern Morocco.* Surrey: Ashgate, 2013.

Couto, Dejanirah. "The Role of Interpreters, or Linguas, in the Portuguese Empire During the 16th Century." *e-Journal of Portuguese History* 1, no. 2 (2003): 1–10.

Crespo Muñoz, Francisco. "Acercamiento al estudio de una figura significativa de la sociedad granadina del siglo XVI: 'Yntérpetres,' 'trujamanes,' 'romançeadores.'" *Revista del Centro de Estudios Históricos de Granada y su Reino* 17 (2005): 217–37.

Dakhlia, Jocelyne. *Le divan des rois: Le politique et le religieux dans l'Islam.* Paris: Aubier, 1998.

Dakhlia, Jocelyne. *Lingua Franca.* Arles: Actes Sud, 2008.

Dakhlia, Jocelyne, and Wolfgang Kaiser, eds. *Les musulmans dans l'histoire de l'Europe.* vol. 2, *Passages et contacts en Méditerranée.* Paris: Albin Michel, 2013.

Dakhlia, Jocelyne, and Bernard Vincent, eds. *Les musulmans dans l'histoire de l'Europe.* vol. 1, *Une intégration invisible.* Paris: Albin Michel, 2011.

Dannenfeldt, Karl H. "The Renaissance Humanists and the Knowledge of Arabic." *Studies in the Renaissance* 2 (1955): 96–117.

Davis, Natalie Zemon. *Trickster Travels: A Sixteenth-Century Muslim Between Worlds.* New York: Hill and Wang, 2006.

Dew, Nicholas. *Orientalism in Louis XIV's France.* Oxford: Oxford University Press, 2009.

Díaz Esteban, Fernando. "Una vacante de intérprete de lengua arábiga en Orán y dos versiones de los sucesos a que dio lugar en 1669." *Anaquel de Estudios Árabes* 11 (2000): 261–62.

Ditchfield, Simon. *Liturgy, Sanctity, and History in Tridentine Italy.* Cambridge: Cambridge University Press, 2002.

Ditchfield, Simon. "Translating Christianity in an Age of Reformations." In "Translating Christianity in an Age of Reformations," ed. Simon Ditchfield, Charlotte Meuthen, and Andrew Spicer, special issue, *Studies in Church History* 53 (2017): 164–95.

Domínguez Ortíz, Antonio, and Bernard Vincent. *Historia de los moriscos: Vida y tragedia de una minoría.* Madrid: Alianza Editorial, 1985.

Dozy, Reinhard. *Supplément aux dictionnaires arabes,* 2 vols. Leiden: Brill, 1881.

Drayson, Elizabeth. *The Lead Books of Granada.* Basingstoke: Palgrave, 2000.

Dursteler, Eric. "Speaking in Tongues: Language and Communication in the Early Modern Mediterrannean." *Past & Present* 217 (2012): 47–77.

Durston, Alan. *Pastoral Quechua: The History of Christian Translation in Colonial Peru*. South Bend, IN: University of Notre Dame Press, 2007.

Duve, Thomas. "Was ist Multinormativität?" *Rechtsgeschichte* 25 (2017): 88–101.

Echevarría Arsuaga, Ana. "Las aljamas mudéjares castellanas en el siglo XV: Redes de poder y conflictos internos." *Espacio, tiempo y forma. Serie III, Historia medieval* 14 (2001): 93–112.

Echevarría Arsuaga, Ana. *Almanzor*. Madrid: Silex, 2011.

Echevarría Arsuaga, Ana. "De cadí a alcalde mayor: La élite judicial mudéjar en el siglo XV (I–II)." *Al-Qantara* 24, nos. 1–2 (2003): 139–68, 273–89.

Echevarría Arsuaga, Ana. *Knights on the Frontier: The Moorish Guard of the Kings of Castile (1410–1467)*. Leiden: Brill, 2009.

Echevarría Arsuaga, Ana. "Los mudéjares de los reinos de Castilla y Portugal." *Revista d'Història Medieval* 12 (2001): 31–46.

Ecker, Heather. "'Arab Stones': Rodrigo Caro's Translations of Arabic Inscriptions in Seville (1634), Revisited." *Al-Qantara* 23, no. 2 (2002): 347–402.

Ehlers, Benjamin. *Between Christians and Moriscos: Juan de Ribera and Religious Reform in Valencia 1568–1614*. Baltimore: Johns Hopkins University Press, 2004.

Elliot, John. "A Europe of Composite Monarchies." *Past and Present* 137 (1992): 48–71.

Epalza, Mikel de. *Los Moriscos antes y despues de la expulsión*. Madrid: MAPFRE, 1992.

Ergene, Boğaç. "Evidence in Ottoman Courts: Oral and Written Documentation in Early Modern Courts of Islamic Law." *Journal of the American Oriental Society* 124, no. 3 (2004): 471–91.

Escribano Páez, José Miguel. "Negotiating with the 'Infidel': Imperial Expansion and Cross-Confessional Diplomacy in the Early Modern Maghreb (1492–1516)." *Itinerario* 40, no. 2 (2016): 189–214.

Españoles trasterados: Los moriscos. Madrid: Archivo General de España, Ministerio de la Cultura 2009.

Espinar Moreno, Manuel, María Angustias Álvarez del Castillo, and María Dolores Guerrero Lafuente. *La ciudad de Guadix en los siglos XV–XVI, 1490–1515*. Granada: Universidad de Granada and Ayuntamiento de Guadix, 1992.

Espinar Moreno, Manuel, and María Dolores Quesada Gómez. "Documentos árabigo-granadinos traducidos por Alonso del Castillo en 1565–1566." *Revista del Centro de Esutdios Históricos de Granada y su Reino*, 2nd ser., 10–11 (1996–1997): 229–55.

Extremera Extremera, Miguel Ángel. *El notariado en la España moderna: Los Escribanos públicos de Córdoba*. Cordoba: Calambur, 2009.

Fancy, Hussein. *The Mercenary Mediterranean: Sovereignty, Religion, and Violence in the Medieval Crown of Aragon*. Chicago: University of Chicago Press, 2016.

Ferguson, Heather. *The Proper Order of Things: Language, Power, and Law in Ottoman Administrative Discourses*. Stanford, CA: Stanford University Press, 2018.

Feria García, Manuel C. "La traducción fehaciente del árabe: Fundamentos históricos, jurídicos, y metodológicos." PhD diss., Departamento de Traducción e Interpretación, Universidad de Málaga, 2001.

Feria García, Manuel C. "El tratado hispano-marroquí de amistad y comercio de 1767 en el punto de mira del traductor (I): Contextualización histórica: encuentroy desencuentros." *Sendebar* 16 (2005): 3–26.

Feria García, Manuel C. "El tratado hispano-marroquí de amistad y comercio de 1767 en el punto de mira del traductor (II): Intervención de traductores e intérpretes; Daguerrotipo de la trujamanería dieciochesca." *Sendebar* 18 (2007): 5–44.

Feria García, Manuel C., and Juan Pablo Arias Torres. "Un nuevo enfoque en la investigación de la documentación árabe granadina romanceada." *Al-Qantara* 26, no. 1 (2005): 191–247.

Fernández Albaladejo, Pablo. "Entre godos y montañeses: Avatares de una primera identidad Española." *Cuadernos del Alzate* 33 (2005): 19–53.

Feros, Antonio. *Kingship and Favoritism in the Spain of Philip III: 1598–1621.* Cambridge: Cambridge University Press, 2006.

Feros, Antonio. "Rhetorics of the Expulsion." In *Expulsion of the Moriscos,* ed. García-Arenal and Wiegers, 60–101.

Flood, Barry. *Objects of Translation: Material Culture and Medieval "Hindu-Muslim" Encounter.* Princeton, NJ: Princeton University Press, 2009.

Floor, Willem, and Farhad Hakimzadeh. *The Hispano-Portuguese Empire and Its Contacts with Safavid Persia, the Kingdom of Hormuz and Yarubid Oman from 1489–1720.* Acta Iranica 45. Leuven: Peeters, 2007.

Floristán, José M. "Diego de Urrea (c. 1559–octubre de 1616), traductor de árabe, turco y persa en la corte de España: Nuevas noticias biográficas." *Boletín de la Real Academia de la Historia* 210, no. 2 (2013): 227–74.

Floristán, José M. "Francisco de Gurmendi: Intérprete de árabe, turco, y persa en la corte de Felipe II." *Boletín de la Real Academia de la Historia* 211, no. 2 (2014): 357–74.

Floristán, José M. "Intérpretes de lenguas orientales en la corte de los austrias: Tres notas prosopográficas." *Silva* 2 (2003): 41–59.

Folger, Robert. *Writing as Poaching: Interpellation and Self-Fashioning in Colonial* "Relaciones de méritos y servicios." Leiden: Brill, 2011.

Forrest, Ian. *Trustworthy Men: How Inequality and Faith Made the Medieval Church.* Princeton, NJ: Princeton University Press, 2018.

Fournel-Guérin, Jacqueline. "Le livre et la civilisation ecrite dans la communaute morisque aragonaise (1540–1620)." *Mélanges de la Casa Velázquez* 15 (1979): 241–60.

Fuchs, Barbara. *Exotic Nation: Maurophilia and the Construction of Early Modern Spain.* Philadelphia: University of Pennsylvania Press, 2009.

Galán Sánchez, Ángel. "*Fuqahā'* y musulmanes vencidos en el reino de Granada (1485–1520)." In *Biografías mudéjares, o, La experiencia de ser minoría: Biografías musulmanas en la españa cristiana,* ed. Ana Echevarría, 329–82. Madrid: CSIC, 2008.

Galán Sánchez, Ángel. "Hacienda y fiscalidad en el reino de Granada: Razones para su estudio." *Chronica Nova* 31 (2005): 11–22.

Galán Sánchez, Ángel. *Los mudéjares del reino de Granada.* Granada: Universidad de Granada, 1991.

Galán Sánchez, Ángel. "Poder cristiano y 'colaboracionismo' mudéjar en el reino de Granada (1485–1501)." In *Estudios sobre Málaga y el reino de Granada en el V Centenario de la Conquista,* ed. José López de Coca Castañer, 271–89. Málaga: Diputación Provincial de Málaga, 1987.

Galán Sánchez, Ángel. "Poder y fiscalidad en el reino de Granada tras la conquista: Algunas reflexiones." *Studia Historica: Historia Medieval* 20 (2012): 67–98.

Gallego, María Angeles. "The Languages of Medieval Iberia and Their Religious Dimension." *Medieval Encounters* 9 (2003): 107–39.

Gallego Burín, Antonio, and Alfonso Gámir Sandoval. *Los moriscos del Reino de Granada: según el Sínodo de Guadix de 1554.* Granada: Universidad de Granada, 1968.

García-Arenal, Mercedes. *Ahmad al-Mansur and the Beginnings of Modern Morocco.* Oxford: Oneworld, 2009.

García-Arenal, Mercedes. "El entorno de los plomos: historiografía y linaje." *Al-Qantara* 24, no. 2 (2003): 294–326.

García-Arenal, Mercedes. "La Inquisición y los libros de los moriscos." In *Memoria de los moriscos: Escritos y relatos de una diáspora cultural*, ed. Alfredo Mateos Paramio and Juan Carlos Villaverde Amieva, 57–71. Madrid: Biblioteca Nacional de España, 2010.

García-Arenal, Mercedes. *Is Arabic a Spanish Language? The Uses of Arabic in Early Modern Spain*. La Jolla: UCSD Department of Literature, 2015.

García-Arenal, Mercedes. "Miguel de Luna y los moriscos de Toledo: 'No hay en España mejor moro.'" *Chronica Nova* 36 (2010): 253–62.

García-Arenal, Mercedes. "Moriscos e indios: Para un estudio comparado de métodos de conquista y evangelización." *Chronica Nova* 20 (1992): 153–72.

García-Arenal, Mercedes. "Religious Dissent and Minorities: The Morisco Age." *Journal of Modern History* 81 (2009): 888–920.

García-Arenal, Mercedes. "The Religious Identity of the Arabic Language and the Affair of the Lead Books of the Sacromonte of Granada." *Arabica* 56, no. 6 (2009): 495–528.

García-Arenal, Mercedes. "Textos españoles sobre Marruecos en el Siglo XVI: Fr. Juan Bautista y su *Chronica de Muley Abdelmelech*." *Al-Qantara* 2, no. 1 (1981): 167–92.

García-Arenal, Mercedes, and Fernando Rodríguez Mediano, "Arabic Manuscripts in Motion and Converted Muslims: Between Spain and Rome." *Erudition and the Republic of Letters* 3 (2018): 367–89.

García-Arenal, Mercedes, and Fernando Rodríguez Mediano. "Los libros de los moriscos y los eruditos orientales." *Al-Qantara* 31, no. 2 (2010): 611–46.

García-Arenal, Mercedes, and Fernando Rodríguez Mediano. "Médico, traductor, inventor: Miguel de Luna, cristiano arábigo de Granada." *Chronica Nova* 32 (2006): 192–231.

García-Arenal, Mercedes, and Fernando Rodríguez Mediano. *Un oriente español: Los moriscos y el Sacromonte en tiempos de contrarreforma*. Madrid: Marcial Pons, 2010.

García-Arenal, Mercedes, and Fernando Rodríguez Mediano. *The Orient in Spain: Converted Muslims, the Forged Lead Books of Granada, and the Rise of Orientalism*. Translated by Consuelo López-Morillas. Leiden: Brill, 2013.

García-Arenal, Mercedes, and Fernando Rodríguez Mediano. "Sacred History, Sacred Languages: The Question of Arabic in Early Modern Spain." In *The Teaching and Learning of Arabic in Early Modern Europe*, ed. Jan Loop, Alistair Hamilton, and Charles Burnett, 133–62. Leiden: Brill, 2017.

García-Arenal, Mercedes, Katarzyna Krystyna Starczewska, and Ryan Szpiech. "The Perennial Importance of Mary's Virginity and Jesus's Divinity: Qur'anic Quotations in Iberian Polemics After the Conquest of Granada (1492)." *Journal of Qur'anic Studies* 20, no. 3 (2018): 51–80.

Garciá-Arenal, Mercedes, and Gerard Wiegers. *The Expulsion of the Moriscos from Spain: A Mediterranean Diaspora*. Leiden: Brill, 2014.

García-Arenal, Mercedes, and Gerard Wiegers, eds. *Un hombre de tres mundos: Samuel Pallache, un judío marroquí en la Europa protestante y en la católica*. 2nd ed. Madrid: Siglo XXI, 2007.

García Ballester, Luis. "The Circulation and Use of Medical Manuscripts in Arabic in 16th Century Spain." *Journal for the History of Arabic Science* 3, no. 2 (1979): 183–99.

García Ballester, Luis. *Los moriscos y la medicina: Un capitulo de la medicina y la ciencia marginadas en la España del siglo XVI*. Barcelona: Labor Universitaria, 1984.

García Carcel, Ricardo. *Orígenes de la Inquisición española: El tribunal de Valencia, 1478–1530*. Barcelona: Ediciones Península, 1976.

García Carraffa, Alberto, and Arturo García Carraffa. *Diccionario heráldico y geneológico de apellidos españoles y americanos*, vol. 59. Salamanca: Imprenta Comercial Salmantina, 1947.

García Ejarque, Luis. *La Real Biblioteca de S. M. y su personal (1712–1836)*. Madrid: Asociación de Amigos de la Biblioteca de Alejandría, 1997.

García-Ferrer, María Julieta Vega, María Luisa García Valverde, and Antonio López Carmona, eds. *Nuevas aportaciones al conocimiento y estudio del Sacro Monte: IV Centenario fundacional (1610–2010)*. Granada: Fundación Euroárabe, 2010.

García Figueras, Tomás and Carlos Rodríguez Joulia Saint-Cyr. *Larache. Datos para su historia en el siglo XVII*. Madrid: Consejo de Investigaciones Científicas, 1973.

García Hernán, Enrique, José Francisco Cutillas Ferrer, and Rudi Mathee, eds. *The Spanish Monarchy and Safavid Persia in the Early Modern Period*. Valencia: Albatros Ediciones, 2016.

García Luján, José Antonio. "Geneología del linaje de los Granada Venegas desde Yusuf IV, rey de Granada (1432), hasta la extincción de la varonía del linaje (1660)." In *Simposio nobleza y monarquía*, ed. García Luján, 14–43.

García Luján, José Antonio, ed. *Simposio nobleza y monarquía: Los linajes nobiliarios en el Reino de Granada, siglos XV–XIX; El linaje Granada Venegas, marqueses de Campotéjar*. Huescar: Asociación Cultural Raigadas, 2010.

García Marín, José María. *El oficio público en Castilla durante la baja edad media*. Alcalá de Henares: Instituto Nacional de Administración Pública, 1987.

García Pedraza, Amalia. *Actitudes ante la muerte: Los moriscos que quisieron salvarse*, 2 vols. Granada: Universidad de Granada, 2002.

García Valenzuela, Hortensia. *Índices de los libros de cabildo del Archivo Municipal de Granada: 1497–1518*. Granada: Universidad de Granada, 1988.

Garrad, Keith. "La inquisición y los moriscos granadinos, 1526–1580." *Bulletin Hispanique* 67 (1965): 63–77.

Garrad, Keith. "The Original Memorial of Don Francisco Núñez Muley."*Atlante* 4 (1954): 199–226.

Garrido Aranda, Antonio. *Organización de la iglesia en el reino de Granada y su proyección en Indias, Siglo XVI*. Sevilla: Escuela de Estudios Hispano-Americanos, 1979.

Garrido Atienza, Miguel. *Los alquezares de Santa Fe*. Archivum Reprints. Granada: University of Granada, 1990.

Garrido García, Carlos Javier. "El uso de la lengua árabe como medio de evangelización-represión de los moriscos del reino de Granada: Nuevos datos sobre Bartolomé Dorador, intérprete y traductor de Martín de Ayala, obispo de Guadix." *MEAH: Sección Árabe-Islam* 57 (2008): 123–37.

Ghobrial, John-Paul. "Migrations from Within and Without: In the Footsteps of Eastern Christians in the Early Modern World." *Transactions of the Royal Historical Society* 27 (2017): 153–73.

Ghobrial, John Paul. "The Secret Life of Elias of Babylon and the Uses of Global Microhistory." *Past & Present* 222 (2014): 51–93.

Ghobrial, John Paul. *The Whispers of Cities: Information Flows in Istanbul, London, and Paris in the Age of William Trumbull*. Oxford: Oxford University Press, 2013.

Gilbert, Claire. "A Mediterranean Family Business: Translator Dynasties in Habsburg Spain." In *Iberian Babel: Multilingualism and Translation in the Medieval and the Early Modern Mediterranean*, ed. Nuria Silleras-Fernández and Michelle Hamilton. Boston and Leiden: Brill, Forthcoming.

Gilbert, Claire. "A Grammar of Conquest: Arabic and the Reorganization of Granada After 1492." *Past & Present* 239 (2018): 3–40.

Gilbert, Claire. "Juegos de reputación: Honra, servicio y traducción en la Monarchía Hispánica." In *Homenaje a Araceli Guillaume-Alonso: La reputation; Quête individuelle et aspiration collective dans l'Espagne des Habsbourg,* ed. Beatrice Pérez, 475–98. Paris: Presses de l'Université Paris-Sorbonne, 2018.

Gilbert, Claire. "Social Context, Ideology, and Translation." In *The Routledge Handbook of Translation and Culture,* ed. Sue-Ann Harding and Ovidi Carbonell Cortes, 225–42. London and New York: Routledge, 2018.

Gilbert, Claire. "The King, the Coin, and the Word: Imagining and Enacting Castilian Frontiers in Late Medieval Iberia." In *Authority and Spectacle in Medieval and Early Modern Iberia,* ed. Gen Liang and Jarbel Rodríguez, 33–45. New York: Routledge, 2017.

Gilbert, Claire. "Transmission, Translation, Legitimacy and Control: The Activities of a Multilingual Scribe in *Morisco* Granada." In *Multilingual and Multigraphic Manuscripts and Documents of East and West,* ed. Giuseppe Mandala and Inmaculada Pérez Marin, 425–62. Piscataway, NJ: Gorgias Press, 2018.

Gilbert, Claire. "The Circulation of Foreign News and the Construction of Imperial Ideas: The Spanish Translators of Aḥmad al-Manṣūr." *Memoria y Civilización* 18 (2015): 37–70.

Gil Fernandez, Luis. *El imperio Luso-Español y la Persa safávida: Tomo II (1606–1622).* Madrid: Fundación Universitaria Española, 2009.

Gil Fernandez, Luis. *El imperio Luso-Español y la Persa safávida: Tomo I (1582–1605).* Madrid: Fundación Universitaria Española, 2006.

Gil Pujol, Xavier. "Concepto y práctica de república en la España moderna: Las tradiciones castellana y catalano-aragonesas." *Estudis* 34 (2008): 111–48.

Gil Pujol, Xavier. "Spain and Portugal." In *European Political Thought 1450–1700: Religion, Law, and Philosophy,* ed. Howell Lloyd, Glen Burgess, and Simon Hodson, 416–57. New Haven, CT: Yale University Press, 2007.

Giménez-Eguibar, Patricia, and Daniel I. Wasserman Soler. "La mala algarabía: Church, Monarchy, and the Arabic Language in 16th-Century Spain." *Medieval History Journal* 14 (2011): 229–58.

Girard, Aurélien. "Le christianisme oriental (XVIIe–XVIIIe siècles): Essor de l'orientalisme catholique en Europe et construction des identités confessionnelles au Proche-Orient." PhD diss., École Française de Rome, 2011.

Goldberg, Jessica. *Trade and Institutions in the Medieval Mediterranean: The Geniza Merchants and Their Business World.* Cambridge: Cambridge University Press, 2012.

González Castrillo, Ricardo. "Un filoarabista de mediados del siglo XVIII: Faustino de Muscat y Guzmán." *Anaquel de Estudios Árabes* 26 (2015): 121–45.

González Vázquez, José. "La academia Granada-Venegas en la Granada del siglo XVI y comienzos del XVII." In *Simposio nobleza y monarquía,* ed. García Luján, 413–28.

Grafton, Anthony. *What Was History? The Art of History in Early Modern Europe.* Cambridge: Cambridge University Press, 2007.

Greene, Molly. "Beyond the Northern Invasion: The Mediterranean in the Seventeenth Century." *Past & Present* 174, no. 1 (2002): 42–71.

Grévin, Benoît. *Le parchemin des cieux: Essai sur le moyen âge du langage.* Paris: Séuil, 2012.

Guilarte Zapatero, Jose María. "Un proyecto para la recopilación de las leyes castellanas en el siglo XVI." *Anuario de la historia del derecho español* 23 (1953): 445–66.

Guillén Robles, Francisco. *Catálogo de los manuscritos árabes existentes en la Biblioteca Nacional de Madrid.* Imprenta y Fundación de M. Tello, 1889.

Guillén Robles, Francisco. "Una embajada española en Marruecos en 1579." *Mauritania: Revista Ilustrada* 17, no. 195 (1944): 54–84.

Gutas, Dmitri. *Greek Thought, Arabic Culture: The Graeco-Arabic Translation Movement in Baghdad and Early 'Abbasid Society.* London: Routledge, 1998.

Gutierrez, Constancio. *Españoles en Trento.* Valladolid: CSIC, 1951.

Gutierrez Cruz, Rafael. *Los presidios españoles del norte de áfrica en tiempo de los reyes católicos.* Melilla: Ciudad Autónoma de Melilla, 1997.

Hagerty, Miguel José. "Transcripción, traducción, y observaciones de dos de los 'Libros Plumbeos del Sacromonte.'" PhD diss., Universidad de Granada, 1988.

Haliczer, Stephen. *Inquisition and Society in the Kingdom of Valencia, 1478–1834.* Berkeley: University of California Press, 1990.

Hallaq, Wael B. "Ifta' and Ijtihad in Sunni Legal Theory: A Developmental Account." In *Islamic Legal Interpretation: Muftis and their Fatwas*, ed. Muhammad Khalid Masud, Brinkley Messick, and David S. Powers, 33–43. Oxford: Oxford University Press, 1996

Hamilton, Alistair. *William Bedwell the Arabist, 1563–1632.* Leiden: Brill, 1985.

Hamilton, Bernice. *Political Thought in Sixteenth-Century Spain: A Study of the Political Ideas of Vitoria, De Soto, Suárez, and Molina.* Oxford: Clarendon Press, 1963.

Hanks, William F. *Converting Words: Maya in the Age of the Cross.* Berkeley: University of California Press, 2010.

Harris, A. Katie. "Forging History: The *Plomos* of the Sacromonte of Granada in Francisco Bermúdez de Pedraza's *História ecclesiástica*." *Sixteenth-Century Journal* 30, no. 4 (1999): 945–66.

Harris, A. Katie. *From Muslim to Christian Granada: Inventing a City's Past in Early Modern Spain.* Baltimore: Johns Hopkins University Press, 2007.

Harvey, L. P. "The Arabic Dialect of Valencia in 1595." *Al-Andalus* 36, no. 1 (1971): 81–115.

Harvey, L. P. *Islamic Spain: 1250 to 1500.* Chicago: University of Chicago Press, 1990.

Harvey, L. P. *Muslims in Spain: 1500 to 1614.* Chicago: University of Chicago, 2006.

Headley, John M. *The Emperor and His Chancellor: A Study of the Imperial Chancellery Under Gattinara.* Cambridge: Cambridge University Press, 1983.

Henkel, Willy. "The Polyglot Printing-Office of the Congregation." In *Sacrae Congregationis de Propaganda Fide Memoria Rerum: 350 Anni (1622–1972)*, vol. 1: *1622–1700*, ed. Josef Metzler, 335–50. Rome: Herder, 1971.

Herrero Sánchez, Manuel. *El acercamiento hispano-neerlandes.* Madrid: CSIC, 2000.

Herrero Sánchez, Manuel. "La Monarquía Hispánica y las repúblicas europeas: El modelo republicano en una monarquía de ciudades." In *Repúblicas y republicanismo en la Europa moderna (siglos XVI–XVIII)*, 273–327. Madrid: Fondo de Cultura Económica, 2017.

Hershenzon, Daniel. *The Captive Sea: Slavery, Communication, and Commerce in Early Modern Spain and the Mediterranean.* Philadelphia: University of Pennsylvania Press, 2018.

Hershenzon, Daniel. "Doing Things with Arabic in the 17th-Century Escorial." *Philological Encounters* 4 (2019): 151–89.

Hershenzon, Daniel. "'Para que me saque cabesea por cabesa . . .': Exchanging Muslim and Christian Slaves Across the Western Mediterranean." *African Economic History* 42 (2014): 11–36.

Hershenzon, Daniel. "The Political Economy of Ransom in the Early Modern Mediterranean." *Past & Present* 231 (2016): 61–95.

Hershenzon, Daniel. "Traveling Libraries: The Arabic Manuscripts of Muley Zidan and the Escorial Library." *Journal of Early Modern History* 18 (2014): 535–58.

Hess, Andrew C. *The Forgotten Frontier: A History of the Sixteenth-Century Ibero-African Frontier*. Chicago: University of Chicago Press, 1978.

Hess, Andrew C. "The Moriscos: An Ottoman Fifth Column in Sixteenth-Century Spain." *American Historical Review* 74, no. 1 (1968): 1–25.

Heyberger, Bernard. *Les chrétiens du Proche-Orient au temps de la Réforme catholique*. Athens and Rome: Ecoles Françaises d'Athènes et de Rome, 1994.

Heyberger, Bernard. "Polemic Dialogues Between Christians and Muslims in the Seventeenth Century." *Journal of the Economic and Social History of the Orient* 55 (2012): 495–516.

Hoenerbach, Wilhelm. "El notariado islámico y el cristiano: Estudio comparativo." *Cuadernos de Historia del Islam* 11 (1984): 103–36.

Hoenerbach, Wilhelm. "Some Notes on the Legal Language of Christian and Islamic Deeds." *Journal of the American Oriental Society* 81 no. 1 (1961): 34–38.

Hoenerbach, Wilhelm. *Spanisch-islamische Urkunden aus der Zeit der Nasriden und Moriscos*. Berkeley: University of California Press, 1965.

Irvine, Judith T. and Susan Gal, "Language Ideology and Linguistic Differentiation." In *Regimes of Language: Ideologies, Polities, and Identities*, ed. Paul V. Kroskrity, 35–83. Santa Fe, NM: School of American Research Press and Oxford: James Curry.

Israel, Jonathan I. *Diasporas Within a Diaspora: Jews, Crypto-Jews, and the World of Maritime Empires (1540–1740)*. Brill Series in Jewish Studies 30. Leiden: Brill, 2002.

Israel, Jonathan I. "The Jews of Spanish North Africa." *Transactions of the Jewish Historical Society of England* 26 (1979): 71–86.

Israel, Jonathan I. "The Jews of Spanish Oran and Their Expulsion in 1669." *Mediterranean Historical Review* 9, no. 2 (1994): 235–55.

Iverson, Reem. "El discurso de la higene: Miguel de Luna y la medicina del siglo XVI." In *Morada de la palabra: Homenaje a Luce y Mercedes López Baralt*, ed. William Mejías López, 1:892–907. San Juan: Editorial de la Universidad de Puerto Rico, 2002.

Jiménez Alcázar, Juan Francisco. "La frontera de *allende*: Documentos para su estudio; El privilegio de los homicianos de Mazalquivir (1507)." *Chronica Nova* 20 (1992): 343–60.

Jiménez de Gregorio, Fernando. "'Relación de Orán' por el vicario don Pedro Cantero Vaca (1631–1636)." *Hispania: Revista Española de Historia* 22, no. 85 (1962): 81–117.

Jiménez Vela, Rosario. *Índices de los libros de cabildo: 1518–1566*. Granada: Universidad de Granada, 1985.

Jones, John Robert. "Learning Arabic in Renaissance Europe: 1502–1626." PhD diss., London University School of Oriental and African Studies, 1988.

Jones, John Robert. "The Medici Oriental Press (Rome, 1584–1614) and the Impact of Its Arabic Publications on Northern Europe." In *The 'Arabick' Interest of the Natural Philosophers in Seventeenth-Century England*, ed. G. A. Russell, 88–108. Leiden: Brill, 1994.

Julien, Charles-André. *History of North Africa*. London: Routledge, 1970.

Kagan, Richard. *Clio and the Crown: The Politics of History in Medieval and Early Modern Spain*. Baltimore: Johns Hopkins University Press, 2009.

Kagan, Richard. *Lawsuits and Litigants in Castile, 1500–1700*. Chapel Hill: University of North Carolina Press, 1981.

Kaiser, Wolfgang, and Guillaume Calafat. "The Economy of Ransoming and the Early Modern Mediterranean: A Form of Cross-Cultural Trade Between Southern Europe and the Maghreb (Sixteenth to Eighteenth Centuries)." In *Religion and Trade: Cross-Cultural*

Exchanges in World History, 1000–1900, ed. Francesca Trivellato, Leor Halevi, and Catia Atunes, 108–30. Oxford: Oxford University Press, 2014.

Kennedy, Hugh. *Muslim Spain and Portugal*. London: Longman, 1996.

Kerlin, Gioia. "A True Mirror for Princes: Defining the Good Governor." *Hispanófila* 156 (2009): 13–28.

Khalid Masud, Muhammad, Brinkley Messick, and David S. Powers. "Muftis, Fatwas, and Islamic Legal Interpretation." In *Islamic Legal Interpretation: Muftis and Their Fatwas*, ed. Muhammad Khalid Masud, Brinkley Messick, and David S. Powers, 3–32. Oxford: Oxford University Press, 1996.

Kimmel, Seth. *Parables of Coercion: Conversion and Knowledge at the End of Islamic Spain*. Chicago: University of Chicago Press, 2015.

Koningsveld, P. S. van. "Le Parchemin et les Livres de Plomb de Grenade: Ecriture, Langue, et Origine d'une Falsification." In *Nuevas aportaciones*, ed. García-Ferrer, García Valverde, and López Carmona, 173–96.

Krstic, Tijana. *Contested Conversions to Islam: Narratives of Religious Change in the Early Modern Ottoman Empire*. Stanford, CA: Stanford University Press, 2011.

Krstic, Tijana. "Of Translation and Empire: Sixteenth-Century Ottoman Imperial Interpreters as Renaissance Go-Betweens." In *The Ottoman World*, ed. Christine Woodhead, 130–42. London: Routledge, 2012.

Labarta, Ana. "Inventario de los documentos árabes contenidos en procesos inquisitoriales contra moriscos valencianos conservados en el Archivo Histórico Nacional de Madrid (Legajos 548–556)." *Al-Qantara* 1, no. 2 (1980): 115–64.

Labarta, Ana. "Los libros de los moriscos valencianos." *Awraq* 2 (1979): 72–90.

Labarta, Ana. "Notas sobre algunos traductores de árabe en la Inquisición valenciana (1565–1609)." *Revista del Instituto Egipcio de Estudios Islámicos de Madrid* 21 (1981–1982): 101–33.

Ladero Quesada, Miguel Ángel. *Granada después de la conquista: Repobladores y mudéjares*. Granada: Diputación Provincial de Granada, 1993.

Ladero Quesada, Miguel Ángel. "Los mudéjares de Castilla en la baja edad media." *Historia, Instituciones, Documentos* 5 (1978): 257–304.

Lapeyre, Henri. *Geografía morisca*. Reprint, Valencia: Universitat de Valencia, 2009.

La Véronne, Chantal de. "Les frères Gasparo Corso et le Chérif Moulay 'Abd El-Malek (1569–1574)." In *SIHM: Archives et bibliotheques d'Espagne*, 3: 157–65. Paris: Paul Geuthner, 1956.

La Véronne, Chantal de. "Gonzalo Hernández." In *SIHM: Archives et bibliotheques d'Espagne*, 2: 364–67. Paris: Paul Geuthner, 1956.

La Véronne, Chantal de. "Interprètes d'arabe à Oran au XVIIe siècle." *Revue d'Histoire Maghrebine* 17, nos. 59–60 (1990): 117–20.

La Véronne, Chantal de. "Nouvelle note sur Gonzalo Hernández (1566)." In *SIHM: Archives et bibliotheques d'Espagne*, 3: 146–47. Paris: Paul Geuthner, 1961.

La Véronne, Chantal de. *Rélations entre Orán et Tlemcen dans la première partie du XVIe siècle*. Paris: Paul Geuthner, 1981.

La Véronne, Chantal de. *Vie de Moulay Ismā'īl, roi de Fès et de Maroc d'après Jospeh de León (1708–1728)*. Paris: Librarie Orientaliste Paul Geuthner, 1974.

La Véronne, Chantal de. "Les villes d'Andalousie et le commerce avec la Berbérie (1490–1560)." In *SIHM : Archives et bibliotheques d'Espagne*, 2: 14–18. Paris: Paul Geuthner, 1956.

Lea, Henry Charles. *The Moriscos in Spain: Their Conversion and Expulsion*. Philadelphia: Lea Brothers, 1901.

Le Thiec, G. "L'Empire ottoman, modèle de monarchie seigneuriale dans l'œuvre de Bodin." In *L'œuvre de Jean Bodin*, ed. G.-A. Pérouse, Nicole Dockès-Lallement, and Jean-Michel Servet, 55–77. Paris: H. Champion, 2004.

Lewis, B. "Djumhūriyya." In *Encyclopedia of Islam*, 2nd edition, ed. P. Bearman, Th. Bianquis, C. E. Bosworth, E. van Donzel, W. P. Heinrichs. Accessed December 13, 2019, http://dx.doi.org/10.1163/1573-3912_islam_SIM_2112.

Liang, Gen. *Family and Empire: The Fernández de Córdoba*. Philadelphia: University of Pennsylvania Press, 2011.

Llopis Mena, María Isabel. "Teoría política árabe y persa en la corte de Felipe III." PhD. diss., University of Alicante, 2016.

Lockhart, James. *The Nahua After the Conquest: A Social and Cultural History of the Indians of Central Mexico, Sixteenth Through Eighteenth Centuries*. Stanford, CA: Stanford University Press, 1992.

Loop, Jan. *Johann Heinrich Hottinger: Arabic and Islamic Studies in the Seventeenth Century*. Oxford: Oxford University Press, 2013

López-Baralt, Luce. *"A zaga de tu huella": La enseñanza de las lenguas semíticas en Salamanca en tiempos de San Juan de la Cruz*. Madrid: Editorial Trotta, 2006.

López Baralt, Luce. "El calamo supremo (al-qalam al-'alā) de Cide Hamete Benengeli." *Sharq al-Andalus* 16–17 (1999–2002): 175–86.

López-Baralt, Luce. *Islam in Spanish Literature: From the Middle Ages to the Present*. Leiden: Brill, 1992.

López-Baralt, Luce. "The Legacy of Islam in Spanish Literature." In *The Legacy of Muslim Spain*, ed. Salma Khadra Jayyusi, 1:505–50. Leiden: Brill, 1994.

López Baralt, Luce. "The Moriscos." In *The Literature of al-Andalus*, ed. Maria Rosa Menocal, Raymond P. Scheindlin, and Michael Sells, 472–90. Cambridge: Cambridge University Press, 2000.

López de Coca Castañer, José Enrique. "Granada en el siglo XV: Los postrimerias nazaries a la luz de la probanza de los infantes don Fernando y don Juan." In *Andalucía entre oriente y occidente*, ed. Emilio Cabrera Muñoz, 599–641. Cordoba: Diputación Provincial de Córdoba, 1988.

López-Morillas, Consuelo. "Language and Identity in Late Spanish Islam." *Hispanic Review* 63, no. 2 (Spring 1995): 193–210.

López Nevot, José Antonio. "Los Granada Venegas: Regidores, alguaciles mayores de Granada y procuradores de la ciudad en las cortes de Castilla (siglos XVI–XVII)." In *Simposio nobleza y monarquía*, ed. García Luján, 325–60.

López Nevot, José Antonio. *La organización institucional del municipio de Granada durante el siglo XVI (1492–1598)*. Granada: Universidad de Granada, 1994.

Lourido Díaz, Ramón. "El estudio de la lengua árabe entre los Franciscanos de Marruecos (siglos XIII–XVIII)." *Archivo Ibero-Americano* 60 (2000): 3–34.

Lourido Díaz, Ramón. "El estudio del árabe entre los franciscanos españoles: Colegio trilingüe de Sevilla-Colegio árabe de Damasco." *Archivo Ibero-Americano* 66, nos. 253–254 (2006): 9–240.

Magnier, Grace. *Pedro de Valencia and the Catholic Apologists of the Expulsion of the Moriscos: Visions of Christianity and Kingship*. Leiden: Brill, 2010.

Malagón Pareja, Jesús. "Larache en el sistema migratorio del oeste mediterráneo." In *Actas del 1er Congreso Internacional sobre Migraciones en Andalucía*, ed. Fracisco Javier García Castaño and Nina Kressova, 531–41. Granada: Instituto de Migraciones, 2011.

Malcolm, Noel. "*Behemoth Latinus*: Adam Ebert, Tacitism, and Hobbes." *Filozofski vestnik* 24, no. 2 (2003): 85–120.

Mallette, Karla. *European Modernity and the Arab Mediterranean: Toward a New Philology and a Counter-Orientalism*. Philadelphia: University of Pennsylvania Press, 2010.

Mallette, Karla. "Lingua Franca." In *A Companion to Mediterranean History*, ed. Peregrine Horden and Sharon Kinoshita, 331–44. Malden, MA: Wiley Blackwell, 2014.

Malpica Cuello, Antonio, and Carmen Trillo San José. "Los infantes de Granada: Documentos árabes romanceados." *Revista del Centro de Esutdios Históricos de Granada y su Reino*, 2nd ser., 6 (1992): 361–421.

Maravall, José Antonio. *Teoría del Estado en España en el siglo XVII*. Madrid: Centro de Estudios Constitucionales, 1997.

Marín Pina, María Carmen. "El tópico de la falsa traducción en los libros de caballerías." *Actas del III Congreso de la Asociación Hispánica de Literatura Medieval*, ed. María Isabel Toro Pascua, 1:541–48. Salamanca: Universidad de Salamanca, 1994.

Márquez Villanueva, Francisco. "On the Concept of Mudejarism." In *The Conversos and Moriscos in Late Medieval Spain and Beyond, Volume 1: Departures and Change*, ed. Kevin Inghram, 23–50. Leiden: Brill, 2009.

Márquez Villanueva, Francisco. *El problema morisco: Desde otras laderas*. Barcelona: Libertarias, 1991.

Martínez, Miguel. *Front Lines: Soldiers' Writing in the Early Modern Hispanic World*. Philadelphia: University of Pennsylvania Press, 2016.

Martínez Bermejo, Saul. *Translating Tacitus: The Reception of Tacitus's Works in the Vernacular Languages of Europe, 16th–17th Centuries*. Pisa: University of Pisa Press, 2010.

Martínez de Castilla Muñoz, Nuria. "The Teaching and Learning of Arabic in Salamanca in the Early Modern Period." In *The Teaching and Learning of Arabic in Early Modern Europe*, ed. Jan Loop, Alistair Hamilton, and Charles Burnett, 163–88. Leiden: Brill, 2017.

Martínez de Castilla Muñoz, Nuria. 2017. "The Qur'anic Manuscripts of Charles V." Paper presented at the Annual Meeting of the Renaissance Society of America, Chicago.

Martínez Góngora, Mar. *Los espacios coloniales en las crónicas de Berbería*. Madrid: Iberoamericana-Vervuet, 2015.

Martínez Ruiz, Juan. "Escritura bilingüe en el reino de Granada (siglo XVI), según documentos inéditos del archivo de la Alhambra." In *Actas del primer congreso internacional de hispanistas*, ed. Cyril A. Jones and Frank Pierce, 371–75. Oxford: Dolphin, 1964.

Martín Postigo, María de la Solerraña. "Aportación al studio de la cancillería real castellana en la segunda mitad del siglo XVI." *Hispania* 106 (1967): 381–404.

Martín Postigo, María de la Solerraña. *La cancillería castellana de los reyes católicos*. Valladolid: Universidad de Valladolid, 1959.

Martín Postigo, María de la Solerraña. "La cancillería castellana en la primera mitad del siglo XVI." *Hispania* 95–96 (1964): 348–67, 509–51.

Mata Carriazo, Juan de. "Alcalde entre los cristianos y los moros en la frontera de Granada." *Al-Andalus* 13, no. 1 (1948): 35–96.

Matar, Nabil. *In the Lands of the Christians*. London: Routledge, 2003.

Matar, Nabil. "Muḥammad ibn 'Abd al-Wahhāb al-Wazīr al-Ghassānī." In the *Encyclopedia of Literature of Travel and Exploration*, ed. Jennifer Speake, 2:485–87. London: Taylor and Francis, 2003.

Matar, Nabil. "Queen Elizabeth I Through Moroccan Eyes." *Journal of Early Modern History* 12 (2008): 55–76.

Mateos Paramio, Alfredo, ed. *Memoria de los Moriscos: Escritos y relatos de una diáspora cultural.* Madrid: Biblioteca Nacional de España, 2009.

Mayoral Asensio, Roberto. *Translating Official Documents.* London: Routledge, 2003.

Maziane, Leïla. *Salé et ses corsaires (1666–1727): Un port de course marocain au XVIIe siècle.* Caen: Presses Universitaires de Caen, 2007.

McLean, Gerald, and Nabil Matar, *Britain and the Islamic World, 1558–1713.* Oxford: Oxford University Press, 2011.

Medina, Francisco de Borja. "La compañía de jesús y la minoría morisca (1545–1614)." *Archivum Historicum Societatis Iesu* 57 (1988): 3–137.

Medina, Francisco de Borja. "Jerónimo Mur." In *Diccionario Histórico de La Compañía de Jesús: Biográfico-Temático,* 4 vols., ed. Charles E. O'Neill and Joaquín M.a Domínguez, 3:2769–70. Rome: Institutum Historicum and Universidad Pontificia Comillas, 2001.

Merle, Alexandra, and Alicia Oïffer-Bomsel, eds. *Tacite et le Tacitisme en Europe à l'Époque Moderne.* Paris: Honoré Champion, 2017.

Meserve, Margaret. *Empires of Islam in Renaissance Historical Thought.* Cambridge, MA: Harvard University Press, 2008.

Messick, Brinkley. *The Calligraphic State: Textual Domination and History in a Muslim Society.* Berkeley: University of California Press, 1996.

Metcalfe, Alida. *Go-Betweens and the Colonization of Brazil: 1500–1600.* Austin: University of Texas Press, 2005.

Meyerson, Mark. *The Muslims of Valencia in the Age of Fernando and Isabel Between Coexistence and Crusade.* Berkeley: University of California Press, 1991.

Miller, Kathryn. *Guardians of Islam: Religious Authority and Muslim Communities of Late Medieval Spain.* New York: Columbia University Press, 2008.

Miller, Kathryn. "Muslim Minorities and the Obligation to Emigrate to Islamic Territory." *Islamic Law and Society* 7, no. 2 (2000): 256–77.

Miller, Peter. *Peiresc's Mediterranean World.* Cambridge, MA: Harvard University Press, 2015.

Molénat, Jean-Pierre. "Alcaldes y alcaldes mayores de moros de Castille au XVe siècle." In *Regards sur al-Andalus (VIIIe–XVe siècle),* ed. François Géal, 147–68. Madrid: Casa de Vélazquez, 2007.

Monroe, James T. *Islam and the Arabs in Spanish Scholarship (Sixteenth Century to the Present).* Leiden: Brill, 1970.

Montcher, Fabien. "Cervantes anticuario: Letras y política en torno al Quijote de 1615." In *El Quijote de 1615,* 297–323. Guanajuato: Museo Iconográfico del Quijote and Universidad de Guanajuato, 2015.

Montcher, Fabien. "La historiografía real en el contexto de la interacción hispano-francesa (c. 1598–1635)." PhD diss., Universidad Complutense Madrid, 2013.

Mouline, Nabil. *Le califat imaginaire d'Ahmad al-Mansur: Pouvoir et diplomaties au Maroc au XVIe siècle,* Paris: Presses Universitaires de France, 2009.

Munday, Jeremey. *Introducing Translation Studies: Theories and Applications,* 2nd edition. London: Routledge, 2009.

Nalle, Sara. *God in La Mancha: Religious Reform and the People of Cuenca, 1500–1650.* Baltimore: Johns Hopkins University Press, 2008.

Newman, Karen, and Jane Tylus, eds. *Early Modern Cultures of Translation.* Philadelphia: University of Pennsylvania Press, 2015.

Nirenberg, David. "Bibliographical Essay: The Current State of Mudéjar Studies." *Journal of Medieval History* 24, no. 4 (1998): 381–89.

Nussdorfer, Laurie. *Brokers of Public Trust: Notaries in Early Modern Rome*. Baltimore: Johns Hopkins University Press, 2009.

O'Banion, Patrick. "'They Will Know Our Hearts': Practicing the Art of Dissimulation on the Islamic Periphery." *Journal of Early Modern History* 20, no. 2 (2016): 193–217.

Olds, Katrina. *Forging the Past: Invented Histories in Counter-Reformation Spain*. New Haven, CT: Yale University Press, 2015.

Oliver Asín, Jaime. *La hija de Agi Morato en la Obra de Cervantes*. Madrid: CSIC, 1958.

O'Malley, John. *Trent: What Happened at the Council*. Cambridge, MA: Harvard University Press, 2013.

Osorio Pérez, María José, and Rafael Gerardo Peinado Santaella. "Escrituras árabes romanceadas del convento de Santa Cruz la Real (1430–1496): Pinceladas documentales para una imagen de la Granada nazarí." *MEAH* 51 (2002): 91–217.

Pardo Molero, Juan Francisco. "Mercaderes, Frailes, Corsarios, y Cautivos: Intercambios entre el reino de Valencia y el Norte de África en la primera mitad del siglo XVI." In *Le commerce des captifs: Les intermédiaires dans l'échange et le rachat des prisonniers en Méditerranée, XVe–XVIIIe siècles*, ed. Wolfgang Kaiser, 165–92. Rome: École Française de Rome, 2008.

Pascual Cabrero, José Luis. "Pleito por la herencia de Abdallá de Santo Tomé, según 'La ley e açunna de moros.'" *Espacio, Tiempo, y Forma, Serie III, Historia Medieval* 26 (2013): 275–302.

Paz Torres, Maria. "Pablo Hodar, escribiente de árabe en la Biblioteca Real, y su relación con dos falsificaciones del XVIII." *Al-Andalus Magreb* 6 (1998): 209–35.

Peinado Santaella, Rafael. "Los orígenes del marquesado de Campotejar (1514–1632): Una contribución al estudio de los señoríos del reino de Granada." *Chronica Nova* 17 (1989): 261–79.

Pereda, Felipe. *Los imágenes de la discordia: Política y poética de la imagen sagrada en la España de los cuatrocientos*. Madrid: Marcial Pons, 2007.

Perry, Micha. "*Hatpasha*–Jewish *translata* Documents from Medieval Catalonia." *Journal of Medieval Iberian Studies* 10, no. 2 (2018): 167–94.

Planas, Natividad. "L'usage des langues en Méditerranée occidentale à l'époque moderne." In *Trames de langues: Usages et métissages linguistiques dans l'histoire du Maghreb*, ed. Jocelyne Dakhlia, 241–57. Tunis: Institut de recherche sur le Maghreb contemporain, 2004.

Planas, Natividad. "Une culture en partage: La communication politique entre Europe et l'Islam aux XVIe et XVIIe siècles." In *Les musulmans dans l'histoire de l'Europe*, vol. 2, 273–309. Paris: Albin Michel, 2013.

Popper, Nicholas. *Walter Ralegh's "History of the World" and the Historical Culture of the Late Renaissance*. Chicago: University of Chicago Press, 2012.

Powers, David. "The Islamic Inheritance System: A Socio-historical Approach." In *The Development of Islamic Law and Society in the Maghrib: Qadis, Muftis and Family Law*, 11–29. Farnham: Ashgate Variorum, 2011.

Powers, David. "Legal Consultations (*Futyā*) in Medieval Islam and North Africa." In *The Development of Islamic Law and Society in the Maghrib: Qadis, Muftis and Family Law*, 85–106. Farnham: Ashgate Variorum, 2011.

Puente, José Carlos de la. "The Many Tongues of the King: Indigenous Language Interpreters and the Making of the Spanish Empire." *Colonial Latin American Review* 23, no. 2 (2014): 143–70.

Puigdomènech, Helena. *Maquiavelo en España*. Madrid: Fundación Universitaria Española, 1988.

Pratt, Mary Louise. "Arts of the Contact Zone." *Profession* (1991): 33–40.

Radway, Robyn. "Vernacular Diplomacy in Central Europe: Statesmen and Soldiers Between the Habsburg and Ottoman Empires, 1543–1593." PhD diss., Princeton University, 2017.

Rafael, Vicente. *Contracting Colonialism: Translation and Christian Conversion in Tagalog Society Under Early Spanish Rule*. Durham, NC: Duke University Press, 1993.

Rawlings, Helen. *The Debate on the Decline of Spain*. Manchester: Manchester University Press, 2012.

Reiter, Clara. "In Habsburgs sprachlichem Hofdienst: Translation in den diplomatischen Beziehungen zwischn den habsburgischen Höfen von Madrid und Wien in der Frühen Neuzeit." Ph.D. diss., Karl-Franzens-Üniversität Graz, 2015.

Resines, Luis. *Catecismo del Sacromonte y Doctrina Christiana de Fr. Pedro de Feria: Conversión y evangelización de moriscos e indios*. Madrid: CSIC, 2002.

Resines, Luis. *El catecismo de Pedro Ramiro de Alba*. Granada: University of Granada, 2016.

Richter, Daniel. "Cultural Brokers and International Politics: New York–Iroquois Relations, 1664–1701." *Journal of American History* 75, no. 1 (1988): 40–67.

Rizzi, Andrea, and Cynthia Troup. "Introduction." In *Trust and Proof: Translators in Renaissance Print Culture*, ed. Andrea Rizzi, 1–9. Leiden: Brill, 2017.

Rodríguez Joulia Saint-Cyr, Carlos. *Felipe III y el Rey de Cuco*. Madrid: Instituto de Estudios Africanos, 1954.

Rodríguez Mediano, Fernando. "Al-Andalus, ¿es España? El Oriente y la identidad española en la Edad Moderna." *eHumanista* 37 (2017): 232–48.

Rodríguez Mediano, Fernando. "Diego de Urrea en Italia." *Al-Qantara* 25, no. 1 (2004): 183–202.

Rodríguez Mediano, Fernando. "Fragmentos de orientalismo del siglo XVII." *Hispania* (2006): 243–76.

Rodríguez Mediano, Fernando. "Luis de Mármol lecteur de León: Une appréhension espagnole de l'Afrique." In *León l'Africain*, ed. François Pouillon, 239–67. Paris: Karthala, 2009.

Rodríguez Mediano, Fernando. "Sacred Calendars: Calculation of the Hegira as a Historiographical Problem in Early Modern Spain." *Journal of Early Modern History* 20, no. 3 (2016): 229–65.

Rodríguez-Salgado, María José. *The Changing Face of Empire: Charles V, Philip II and Habsburg Authority, 1551–1559*. Cambridge: Cambridge University Press, 2008.

Rodriguez-Salgado, María José. *El paladín de la cristiandad*. Valladolid: Universidad de Valladolid, 2004.

Ron de la Bastida, C. "Manuscritos árabes en la Inquisición granadina (1582)." *Al-Andalus* 23, no. 1 (1958): 210–15.

Rothman, E. Natalie. "Afterword: Intermediaries, Mediation, and Cross-Confessional Diplomacy in the Early Modern Mediterranean." *Journal of Early Modern History* 19 (2015): 245–59.

Rothman, E. Natalie. *Brokering Empire: Trans-Imperial Subjects Between Venice and Istanbul*. Ithaca, NY: Cornell University Press, 2012.

Rothman, E. Nathalie. "Dragomans and Turkish Literature: The Making of a Field of Inquiry." *Oriente Moderno* 93 (2013): 390–421.

Rowe, Erin. *Saint and Nation: Santiago, Teresa of Avila, and Plural Identities in Early Modern Spain*. University Park: Pennsylvania State University Press, 2011.

Russell, Peter. *Traducciones y traductores en la península ibérica (1400–1550)*. Barcelona: Bellaterra, 1985.

Said, Edward. *Orientalism*. London: Vintage, 2002.

Salicrú i Lluch, Roser. "Crossing Boundaries in Late Medieval Mediterranean Iberia: Historical Glimpses of Christian-Islamic Intercultural Dialogue." *International Journal of Euro-Mediterranean Studies* 1, no. 1 (2008): 34–51.

Salicrú i Lluch, Roser. "Intérpretes y diplomáticos: Mudéjares mediadores y representantes de los poderes cristianos en la Corona de Aragón." In *Biografías mudéjares o la experiencia de ser minoría: Biografías islámicas en la España cristiana*, ed. Ana Echevarría, 471–96. Madrid: CSIC, 2008.

Salicrú i Lluch, Roser. "Más allá de la mediación de la palabra: Negociación con los infieles y mediación cultural en la baja edad media." In *Negociar en la edad media*, ed. Maria Teresa Ferrer i Mallol et al., 409–39. Barcelona: CSIC, 2005.

Sánchez Belén, Juan. "La éxpulsion de los judíos de Orán en 1669." *Espacio, Tiempo, y Forma* 6 (1993): 155–198.

Sánchez García, Encarnación, Pablo Martín Asuero, and Michele Bernardini, eds. *España y el Oriente islámico entre los siglos XV y XVI*. Istanbul: Editorial Isis, 2007.

Sánchez Quintanar y Sánchez-Nieto, León José. *Biblioteca Médica Hispano-Lusitana*. Valencia: Instituto de Historia de la Ciencia y Documentación López Piñero, 2008.

Santiago Simón, Emilio. "Algunos documentos arábigo-granadinos romanceados del Archivo Municipal de Granada." *RCEHGR* 1 (1987): 261–69.

Santoyo Mediavilla, Julio-César. *Teoría y crítica de la traducción: Antología*. Barcelona: Bellaterra, 1987.

Sarmiento Pérez, Marcos. *Cautivos que fueron intérpretes: La comunicación entre europeos, aborígenes canarios y berberiscos durante la conquista de Canarias y los conatos en el Norte de África (1341–1569)*. Madrid: Encasa, 2012.

Sarmiento Pérez, Marcos. "Interpreting for the Inquisition." In *New Insights in the History of Interpreting*, ed. Kayoko Takeda and Jesús Baigorri-Jalón, 47–74. Amsterdam: John Benjamins, 2016.

Schaub, Jean-Frédéric. *Les juifs du roi d'Espagne: Oran 1509–1669*. Paris: Hachette Littératures, 1999.

Schaub, Jean-Frédéric. "El lado oscura de la epopeya: la visita al conde de Alcaudete." In *Carlos V europeísmo y universalidad*, ed. Francisco Sánchez-Montes González and Juan Luis Castellanos, 443–58. Granada: Sociedad Estatal para la Conmemoración de los Centenarios de Felipe II y Carlos V, 2001.

Schaub, Jean-Frédéric. "Présentation." Critical introduction to his edition and translation of Luis Joseph de Sotomayor y Valenzuela, *Brève relation de l'expulsion des juifs d'Oran en 1669*, 7–26. Paris: Éditions Bouchène, 1998.

Seco de Lucena Paredes, Luis. "Alamines y Venegas, cortesanos de los nasries." *MEAH* 10 (1961): 127–42.

Seco de Lucena Paredes, Luis. "Cortesanos nasríes del siglo XV: Las familias de Ibn 'Abd al-Barr e Ibn Kumāša." *MEAH* 7 (1958): 19–28.

Seco de Lucena Paredes, Luis. "La escuela de juristas granadinos en el siglo XV." *MEAH* 8 (1959): 7–28.

Sénéchal, Antoine. "El cambio dinástico, la Guerra de Sucesión y la defensa del presidio de Orán y Mazalquivir (1700–1708)." *Vegueta* 16 (2016): 335–58.

"Shāhid." In *Shorter Encyclopedia of Islam*, ed. H. A. R. Gibb and J. H. Kramers, 516–18. Ithaca, NY: Cornell University Press, 1965.

Skemer, Don. "An Arabic Book Before the Inquisition." *Princeton University Library Chronicle* 1 (2002): 107–20.

Sola, Emilio. "Los avisos de Levante: El nacimiento de una narración sobre Turquía." In *España y el oriente islámico entre los siglos XV y XVI (Imperio Otomano, Persia, y Asia Central)*, ed. Encarnación Sánchez García, Pablo Martín Asuero, and Michele Bernardini, 207–30. Istanbul: Editorial Isis, 2007.

Sola, Emilio. "Carlos V y la Berbería: El context de la frontera mediterránea en la época de Carlos V." In *Carlos V. Los moriscos y el Islam*, ed. María Jesús Rubiera Mata, 321–35. Alicante: Universidad de Alicante, 2001.

Soll, Jacob. "Healing the Body Politic: French Royal Doctors, History, and the Birth of a Nation 1560-1634." *Renaissance Quarterly* 55, no. 4 (2002): 1259–86.

Soria Mesa, Enrique. *La biblioteca genealógica de don Luis de Salazar y Castro*. Cordoba: Universidad de Córdoba, 1997.

Spivakovsky, Erika. "Some Notes on the Relations between D. Diego Hurtado de Mendoza and D. Alonso de Granada Venegas." *Archivum* 14 (1964): 212–32.

Stahuljak, Zrinka. "Medieval Fixers: Politics of Interpreting in Western Historiography." In *Rethinking Medieval Translation: Ethics, Politics, Theory*, ed. Bob Mills and Emma Campbell, 147–63. Cambridge, MA: D. S. Brewer, 2012.

Starczewska, Katarzyna Krystyna, and Mercedes García-Arenal. "'The Law of Abraham the Catholic': Juan Gabriel as Qur'ān Translator for Martín de Figuerola and Egidio de Viterbo." *Al-Qantara* 35, no. 2 (2014): 409–59.

Steiner, George. *After Babel: Aspects of Language and Translation*. New York: Galaxy/Oxford University Press, 1977.

Stewart, Devin J. "Cide Hamete Benengeli, Narrator of Don Quijote." *Medieval Encounters* 3 (1997): 111–27.

Subrahmanyam, Sanjay. *Courtly Encounters: Translating Courtliness and Violence in Early Modern Eurasia*. Cambridge, MA: Harvard University Press, 2012.

Subrahmanyam, Sanjay. *Three Ways to Be Alien: Travails and Encounters in the Early Modern World*. Lebanon, NH: University Press of New England, 2011.

Szpiech, Ryan. *Conversion and Narrative: Reading and Religious Authority in Medieval Polemic*. Philadelphia: University of Pennsylvania Press, 2013.

Szpiech, Ryan. "Preaching Paul to the *Moriscos*: The *Confusión o confutación de la secta mahometica y del Alcorán* (1515) of Juan Andres." *La Corónica* 41, no. 1 (2012): 317–43.

Tarruell, Cecilia. "Circulations entre Chrétienté et Islam: Quelques réflexions à propos des 'méritos y servicios' au service de la Monarchie hispanique (XVIe–XVIIe siècle)." *Diasporas* 25 (2015): 45–57.

al-Tāzī, 'Abd al-Hādī. *Al-Mūjaz fī Tārīkh al-'Alāqāt al-Duwwalīya li-l-Mamlaka al-Maghribīya*. Rabat: Maṭba'at al-Mu'ārif al-Hadītha, 1984.

Tobío, Luis. *Gondomar y los católicos ingleses*. A Coruña: Ediciós do Castro, 1987.

Tolbert, Jane. "Ambiguity and Conversion in the Correspondence of Nicolas-Claude Fabri de Peiresc and Thomas D'Arcos." *Journal of Early Modern History* 13 (2009): 1–24.

Tommasino, Pier Mattia. *The Venetian Qur'ān: A Renaissance Companion to Islam*. Philadelphia: University of Pennsylvania Press, 2018.

Toomer, G. J. *Eastern Wisedome and Learning: The Study of Arabic in Seventeenth-Century England*. Oxford: Clarendon Press, 1996.

Torrecilla, Jesus. *Guerras literarias del XVIII español: La modernidad como invasion*. Salamanca: University of Salamanca Press, 2008.

Torres Palomo, María Paz. "Bartolomé Dorador y el árabe dialectal andaluz." PhD. diss., Granada: Universidad de Granada, 1971.

Torres Palomo, María Paz. "Don Martín de Ayala y la catequesis de los niños moriscos." In *Homenaje a Dario Cabanelas*, 509–18. Granada: Universidad de Granada, 1987.

Torres Palomo, María Paz. "Sobre la carta de Abenaboo en árabe granadino." *Miscelánea de estudios árabes y hebraicos. Sección Árabe-Islam* 18 (1969): 125–28.

Torre y Franco-Romero, Lucas de. "Don Diego Hurtado de Mendoza no fue el autor de 'La Guerra de Granada': Apuntes para un libro (V)." *Boletín de la Real Academia de la Historia* 65 (1914): 369–415.

Trivellato, Francesca. *The Familiarity of Strangers: The Sephardic diaspora, Livorno, and Cross-Cultural Trade in the Early Modern Period*. New Haven, CT: Yale University Press, 2009.

Trivellato, Francesca. *The Promise and Peril of Credit: What a Forgotton Legend About Jews and Finance Tells Us About the Making of European Commercial Society*. Princeton, NJ: Princeton University Press, 2019.

Truman, Ronald. *Spanish Treatises on Government, Society, and Religion in the Time of Philip II: The "De regimine principum" and Associated Traditions*. Leiden: Brill, 1994.

Tutino, Stefania. *Shadows of Doubt: Language and Truth in Post-Reformation Catholic Culture*. Oxford: Oxford University Press, 2013.

Tyan, Emile. "'Adl," in *The Encyclopedia of Islam*, 2nd edition. Ed. P. Bearman, Th. Bianquis, C.E. Bosworth, E. van Donzel, W.P. Heinrichs. Accessed December 13, 2019 http://dx.doi.org/10.1163/1573-3912_islam_COM_0019.

Valensi, Lucette. *Ces étrangers familiers: Musulmans en Europe (XVIe–XVIIIe siècles)*. Paris: Payot, 2012.

Valledares, Rafael. "Juristas por el rey: Felipe IV y la reivindicación de sus dominios, 1640–1665." In *Hacer historia desde Simancas*, ed. Alberto Marcos Martín, 787–814. Valladolid: Junta de Castilla y León, 2011.

Van Gelder, Maartje, and Tijana Krstic. "Introduction: Cross-Confessional Diplomacy and Diplomatic Intermediaries in the Early Modern Mediterranean." *Journal of Early Modern History* 19, nos. 2–3 (2015): 93–105.

Venuti, Lawrence. *The Translator's Invisibility: A History of Translation*. London: Routledge, 2008.

Vernet, Juan. "La embajada de al-Gassani." *Al-Andalus* 18, no. 1 (1953): 109–31.

Viguera Molins, María José. "Partición de una herencia entre una familia mudéjar de Medinaceli." *Al-Qantara* 3, nos. 1–2 (1982): 73–134.

Vincent, Bernard. *Minorías y marginados en la España del siglo XVI*. Granada: Diputación Provincial, 1987.

Vincent, Bernard. "Reflexión documentada sobre el uso del árabe y de las lenguas románicas en la España de los moriscos (ss. XVI–XVII)." *Sharq al-Andalus* 10–11 (1993): 731–48.

Vincent, Bernard. *El río morisco*. Valencia: Universidad de Valencia, 2006.

Vincent, Bernard. "Le tribunal de Grenade." In *Les morisques et l'Inquisition*, ed. Louis Cardaillac, 199–220. Paris: Publisud, 1990.

Vivar, Francisco. "Tucídides y *La Guera de Granada* de Hurtado de Mendoza." In *Memoria de la palabra: actas del VI Congreso de la Asociación Internacional Siglo de Oro. Burgos-La Rioja 15–19 de julio 2002*, vol. 2, ed. Francisco Domínguez Matito and María Luisa Lobato López, 1819–1826. Madrid: Iberoameriaca-Vervuert, 2004.

Wansbrough, John. *Lingua Franca in the Mediterranean*. Richmond, UK: Curzon Press, 1996.

White, Joshua. "Fetva Diplomacy: The Ottoman Şeyhülislam as Trans-Imperial Intermediary." *Journal of Early Modern History* 19 (2015): 199–221.

White, Joshua. *Piracy and Law in the Ottoman Mediterranean*. Stanford, CA: Stanford University Press, 2017.

Wiegers, Gerard. *Islamic Literature in Spanish and Aljamiado: Yça of Segovia (fl. 1450), His Antecedents and Successors*. Leiden: Brill, 1994.

Wiejers, O. "Some Notes on 'Fides' and Related Words in Medieval Latin." *Archivum Latinitatis Media Aevi* 40, no. 2 (1975–1976): 77–102.

Windler, Christian. "De l'idée de croisade à l'acceptation d'un droit spécifique." *Revue Historique* 301, no. 4 (1999): 747–88.

Witkam, Jan Just. *The Arabic Type Specimen of Franciscus Raphelengius's Plantinian Printing Office*. Exhibition catalogue. Leiden: University Library, 1997.

Woolard, Kathryn. "Bernardo de Aldrete and the Morisco Problem: A Study in Early Modern Spanish Language Ideology." *Comparative Studies in Society and History* 44, no. 3 (2002): 446–80.

Woolard, Kathryn. "Introduction" In *Language Ideologies: Practice and Theory*, ed. Bambi B. Schieffelin, Kathryn A. Woolard, and Paul V. Kroskrity, 3–47. New York: Oxford University Press, 1998.

Woolard, Kathryn. "Is the Past a Foreign Country? Time, Language Origins, and the Nation in Early Modern Spain." *Journal of Linguistic Anthropology* 14, no. 1 (2004): 57–80.

Yahya, Dahiru. *Morocco in the Sixteenth Century: Problems and Patterns in African Foreign Policy*. London: Longman, 1981.

Yannakakis, Yanna. *The Art of Being In-Between: Native Intermediaries, Indian Identity, and Local Rule in Colonial Oaxaca*. Durham, NC: Duke University Press, 2008.

Zecevic, Selma. "Translating Ottoman Justice: Ragusan Dragomans as Interpreters of Ottoman Law." *Islamic Law and Society* 21 (2014): 388–418.

Zhiri, Nina. "A Captive Library Between Morocco and Spain." In *Dialectics of Orientalism in Early Modern Europe*, ed. Marcus Keller and Javier Irigoyen-García, 17–32. London: Palgrave, 2018.

Zhiri, Nina. "Mapping the Frontier Between Islam and Christendom in a Diplomatic Age." *Renaissance Quarterly* 69 (2016): 966–99.

Zhiri, Nina. "The Task of the Morisco Translator in the Early Modern Maghreb." *Expressions Maghrébines* 15, no. 1 (2016): 11–27.

Zomeño, Amalia. "From Private Collections to Archives: How Christians Kept Arabic Legal Documents in Granada." *Al-Qantara* 32, no. 2 (2011): 461–79.

Zomeño, Amalia. "Los notarios musulmanes de Granada después de 1492." *Cuadernos del CEMYR* 22 (2014): 195–209.

Index

Acknowledgments

Making this book has been an opportunity to rely on the good faith of many friends, colleagues, and institutions. Research was supported by grants from the University of California, Los Angeles, the Fulbright Commission, the Spain-US Program for Cultural Cooperation, the Social Science Research Council, the Huntington Library, the American Historical Association, the American Philosophical Association, and Saint Louis University's College of Arts and Sciences and Office of the Vice President for Research. Invaluable time for writing was supported by a fellowship from the National Endowment for the Humanities during the 2017–2018 academic year. The generosity of these institutions has made possible a sustained engagement with primary-source repositories without which conceiving of and writing this book would have been impossible. The personnel of many archives and research libraries across Europe, the US, and Morocco, as well as those at UCLA, Saint Louis University, the Consejo Superior de Investigaciones Científicas in Madrid, and the Institute for Advanced Study in Princeton, have ensured ready access to essential sources and bibliography over many years. I am endlessly grateful for the skill, organization, graciousness, and good cheer of these institutions and their staffs.

The intellectual and professional journey that produced this book has been fostered and facilitated by many mentors, colleagues, and friends. Teo Ruiz has been my principal guide and model for teaching and scholarship about Mediterranean, Iberian, and European history since we first met in 2007, and through innumerable conversations in Los Angeles, Paris, New York, and now St. Louis. Teo and his wife, Scarlett, bring great humanity to our profession, and both have taught me the sustaining power of friendship in all intellectual pursuits. David Sabean's insights into the anthropological and sociological dimensions of history have been foundations upon which much of my own questions about language are built, and continue to inspire new directions in teaching and research. Mercedes García-Arenal has given endlessly of her expertise and encouragement since we first met in 2008, as have Jim Amelang, Isabel Aguirre Rodríguez, Alfredo Alvar, Aracelie Guillaume-Alonso, Rachid El Hour, Amalia García Pedraza, Xavier Gil Pujol, Fernando Rodríguez Mediano, Roser Salicrú i Lluch, and Amalia Zomeño. The marks of the generous advice, erudition, and scholarship of these colleagues is strongly evident across this book. In Morocco, Leila Mazïane, Abdelmajid Kaddouri, and Ahmad Chouqui Binebine helped facilitate access and orient me in the royal and national collections, and it was Nina Zhiri at the University of California, San Diego who graciously made the necessary introductions. I am honored to have a profound intellectual and professional debt to Maribel Fierro. She, along with Kathryn Miller, first encouraged my interests in translation and intellectual exchange across linguistic and religious boundaries in Spain when I was still an undergraduate at Stanford. Maribel helped initiate my first forays into archival research in Spain and has remained a constant source of encouragement and intellectual inspiration ever since.

Since those early research visits, I have been lucky to connect with outstanding scholars throughout a modern-day Republic of Letters, one which articulates around archives and conferences related to medieval and early modern Iberian and Mediterranean history. Brian Catlos and Sharon Kinoshita have been mentors and cheerleaders at regular meetings of the Mediterranean Seminar across the US. The 2015 NEH Summer Institute in Barcelona, which they led on the theme "Negotiating Identities," proved to be a formative intellectual and personal experience. The conversations and presentations of that month helped forge new directions for the present book. Over the past decade, myriad conversations around archival coffee machines or other sites of scholarly commensality in Spain, France, Italy, Belgium, Morocco, Portugal, and the UK, along with animated discussions during conferences and presentations, have proven endlessly productive and inspiring thanks to Sabahat Adil, Rosemary Admiral, Marta Albalá Pelegrin, Abby Balbale, Mohamad Ballan, Adam Beaver, Jody Blanco, Étienne and Aurélie Bourdeu, Harald Braun, Travis Bruce, Thomas Burman, Guillaume Calafat, Carlos Cañete, Pedro Cardim, Hilario Casado Alonso, Cédric Cohen-Skalli, Emmanuele Colombo, Fabrizio d'Avenia, Max Deardorff, Rachel Deblinger, Andrew Devereux, Benjamin Ehlers, Hussein Fancy, Heather Ferguson, Barbara Fuchs, Aurelién Girard, William Goldman, Camilo Gómez-Riveras, Mayte Green Mercado, Daniel Gullo, Katie Harris, Josh Herr, Josie Hendrickson, Daniel Hershenzon, Martin Jacobs, Richard Kagan,

Seth Kimmel, Tijana Krstic, Guy Lazure, Gen Liang, Valeria López Fadul, Ruth MacKay, Davide Maffi, Saul Martínez Bermejo, Núria Martínez del Castillo, Anat Mooreville, Katrina Olds, Aaron Olivas, Javier Patiño Loira, Sarah Pearce, Beatriz Pérez, Marissa Petrou, Juan Pimentel, Natividad Planas, Roberto Quirós Rosado, Kathryn Renton, Erin Rowe, Carrie Sanders, Carolyn Salomons, Nir Shafir, Zur Shalev, Nuria Silleras-Fernández, Jake Soll, Zrinka Stahuljak, Aaron Stamper, Ryan Szpiech, Cecilia Tarruell, Pier Mattia Tommasino, Francesca Trivellato, Stefania Tutino, Lucette Valensi, Bernard Vincent, Daniel Wasserman-Soler, Elizabeth Wright, Antonio Zaldivar, and Nina Zhiri. Meanwhile, sustained engagement with scholars working toward a social history of language has allowed me to develop a more sensitive and comparative perspective to the history of translation and its social aspects. These scholars include Gadi Algazi, Sonja Brentjes, Larissa Brewer-García, Liam Brockey, Paul Cohen, José Carlos de la Puente, Simon Ditchfield, Natalie Rothman, and Yanna Yannakakis.

Thanks to a generous leave from teaching at Saint Louis University in Spring 2017, a good portion of this book was first drafted while a "family member" at the Institute for Advanced Study in Princeton, where my husband and most important intellectual interlocutor, Fabien Montcher, was the inaugural Sir John H. Elliott Member. The occasion to meet and correspond with Sir John that followed was a wonderful boost at a key moment in my writing process. The intellectual and personal connections made during that time continue to be a great gift, particularly the ongoing exchanges with Francesca Bellino, Celine Bessière, Antoine Borrut, Muriel Debié, Nicola di Cosmo, Thomas Dodman, Maya Gabily, Andrea Guidi, Yu-Chi Lai, Pascal Marichalar, Giuliano Mori, Ohad Nachtomy, Patrick O'Banion, Katrin Pietzner, Frank Rexroth, and Roberto Tottoli.

Saint Louis University has been the ideal environment in which to thrive as a faculty member. Without the guidance and encouragement of Hal Parker, this book would simply not exist. Filippo Marsili, Doug Boin, and Luke and Aubrey Yarbrough helped make St. Louis a home and an intellectual haven from the get go. Chris Pudlowski and Kelly Goersch in the Department of History and Teresa Harvey in the Center for Medieval and Renaissance Studies have taught me about the endless possibilities that come from being a great team, while making my work possible and enjoyable. Damian Smith, Lorri Glover, Mark Ruff, Jen Popiel, Silvana Siddali, Phil Gavitt, and Torrie Hester read chapter drafts and grant applications with sharp eyes and good cheer while offering advice and support as I learned to combine teaching and writing with our collective work as faculty. Flannery Burke, Katrina Thompson-Moore, Cathleen Fleck, Tom Madden, Nate Millett, George Ndege, and Steve Schoenig have been constant sources of encouragement. Michal Rozbicki and the Center for Intercultural Studies supported—intellectually and financially—the 2017 conference "The Tasks of the Translator: Developing a Sociocultural Framework for the Study of Translation across the Early Modern World (15th–18th Centuries)," which gave me and colleagues from varied fields and disciplines an important opportunity to work through the connections between social history and translation studies. Tom Finan and the Walter J. Ong, S. J. Center for Digital Humanities responded to an urgent and belated call for a map, which was produced with great skill and efficiency by Domhnall Hegarty. Edward Holt, Beth Petitjean, Mikhail Faulconer, Meg Smith, and Dru Swadener provided essential research assistance at different stages of the project. I am extremely grateful to Jerry Singerman and the team at Penn Press for their graciousness and professionalism throughout the publication process.

Many colleagues have read or heard portions of this project as it developed—some many times—and their feedback and suggestions along the way have been invaluable. Any missteps in the previous pages are wholly my own.